Shadows on the Mountain

Shadows on the Mountain

The Allies, the Resistance, and the Rivalries That Doomed WWII Yugoslavia

Marcia Christoff Kurapovna

WILEY

John Wiley & Sons, Inc.

Copyright © 2010 by Marcia Christoff Kurapovna. All rights reserved

Published by John Wiley & Sons, Inc., Hoboken, New Jersey
Published simultaneously in Canada

Map on p. xvi, UN Cartographic Section, map of Former Yugoslavia, no. 3689 Rev. 12 June 2007

Photo credits: pp. 153, 154, 155, 156, 157, 158 (top and bottom left), National Archives, College Park, Maryland, OSS Still Pictures, File 226; pp. 158 (bottom right), 159, 160, the Bildarchiv, World War II, Austrian National Library, Vienna.

For general information about our other products and services, please contact our Customer Care Department within the United States at (800) 762–2974, outside the United States at (317) 572–3993 or fax (317) 572–4002.

Wiley also publishes its books in a variety of electronic formats. Some content that appears in print may not be available in electronic books. For more information about Wiley products, visit our web site at www.wiley.com.

Library of Congress Cataloging-in-Publication Data:

Kurapovna, Marcia.
    Shadows on the mountain : the Allies, the resistance, and the rivalries that doomed WWII Yugoslavia / Marcia Kurapovna.
        p.   cm.
    Includes index.
    ISBN 978-0-470-08456-4 (cloth: alk. paper)
    1. World War, 1939–1945—Yugoslavia.   2. World War, 1939–1945—Underground movements—Yugoslavia.   3. Yugoslavia—History—Axis occupation, 1941–1945.
4. Yugoslavia—Foreign relations 1918–1945.   5. Great Britain—Foreign relations—Yugoslavia.   6. Yugoslavia—Foreign relations—Great Britain.   7. World War, 1939–1945—Diplomatic history.   8. Mihailovic, Draža, 1893–1946.   9. Tito, Josip Broz, 1892–1980.   I. Title.
    D802.Y8K85 2009
    940.54'2197—dc22

                                                                    2009009772

Printed in the United States of America
10 9 8 7 6 5 4 3 2 1

*In memory of my forever loved and
so much missed brother, Douglas*

You shall read that we are commanded to forgive our enemies; but you never read that we are commanded to forgive our friends.

—Cosimo I de' Medici, d. 1574 (attributed)

Belgrade, which glistened in his nostalgia like human laughter through tears.

—On the homecoming of Serbian writer and war veteran Miloš Crnjanski

Serbia is a great mystery.
The day doesn't know what the night contrives
Nor the night, what the dawn gives birth to;
The bush doesn't know what the next bush dreams
Nor the bird what goes on
Among the boughs. . . .
In that land the enemy
May not trust in the hare's track
Nor in the print of the oxen's hooves
There are perhaps secret resolutions
In the Reapers' songs
And the strokes of the woodcutter's axe
And the hidden lullaby from the cradle

—Desanka Maksimović,
A Reminiscence of the Uprising
(Spomen na Ustanak), 1946

Contents

Photo gallery begins on page 153.

Preface

Since the 1990s international focus has shifted from the Balkans to the Middle East and other troubled regions of the world, but it is always a good time to write about Serbia—an extraordinary, young/old country whose modern history may be read as an indictment of the West's own troubled twentieth-century identity. To write about Serbia, and the former Yugoslavia, is to undertake a fascinating journey into the heart of contemporary European history. Yet anyone writing about Serbia must remain constantly on the defensive—to respond to usually knee-jerk, ill-informed hostility toward the country and to the questionable tallying of its various abuses and atrocities as recorded by less than scrupulous international media. Rarely, if ever, can one discuss Serbia from an objective, respectful distance. Should one be motivated by the desire to treat this highly complicated country with fairness and an appreciation for its courageous contributions to the military victories of the West in World Wars I and II, one inevitably runs the risk of being labeled "pro-this" or "pro-that." A writer and historian, whose interest in the country may be purely academic, and who has no political, personal, or financial relationship with Serbia or anyone or anything representing it, will still be viewed, by and large, as a kind of agent for Europe's favorite rogue state.

And yet mysterious Serbia continues to attract interest from those able
to see past the country's isolated relationship to the modern West. These
are the readers who come to understand the story of a country that heeded
the call of Western values in two world wars, took up arms for those values
unlike most of the country's past and current regional neighbors—and
all of it at catastrophic expense to Serbia's own future as a state and the
well-being of its people. Certainly, the aim of this book is not to present
Serbia as a "victim"—the country's deep historical, political, and strategic
flaws are well documented in the narrative that follows. But the chronicle
of this country teaches us a larger, more abstract lesson, one that shows a
different dimension to a country so often misrepresented in newspapers
and historical accounts.

The idea behind this book is to highlight how the story of modern
Serbia raises questions about how one defines the meaning of loyalty and
commitment to the ideals one is fighting for in wartime, and what it is that
leads actors in a common cause to undermine one another through perverse political shortsightedness and outright treachery. Most World War II
books concentrate on the battles and strategies of ally against enemy. This
book is about the behind-the-scenes battles of ally against ally. It is a story
about that simple, sordid, singular reason that outward "friends" maneuver
in wartime in such a way as to ensure one another's ultimate destruction:
a complete and utter lack of trust.

As far as plot is concerned, this narrative describes, in a complicated nutshell, how a Royal government (Great Britain) betrayed a
Royalist government (the Kingdom of Yugoslavia) to exclusively support a Communist government (that of Tito) against the wishes of an
ally and a Democratic government (the United States) in order to keep
another Communist government (that of Stalin) from gaining control, while that Communist government (of Stalin) betrayed its own
Communist partners (the Yugoslav Partisans) to support the Royalist
government (the Kingdom of Yugoslavia), which was then supported
by this nominal Soviet ally, but later cut off, and all the while those
Royalists officially remained an ally of the Communist government,
though actively despising it. There was a Serbian resistance group called
the Chetniks, which resisted German forces, Italians, Croatian-Ustaše,
Albanian Muslims, and the Partisans, and collaborated with them all.
There was a Communist-led Yugoslav group called the Partisans, who

resisted the Serbian Chetniks, the Germans, the Italians, the Albanian Muslims, and the Croatian-Ustaše, and collaborated with them all. The Muslims longed for the rule of the old Catholic Austrian monarchy in Bosnia-Herzegovina, joined the Germans in the fight, and sought to slaughter the Chetniks, who sought to return the favor—later on, the two cooperated on occasion. Add to that American intelligence and British intelligence, which were ostensibly working together, yet all the while each spent more time guarding against the possibility that the other was going to slip a knife in its back.

In particular, this story is about a soldier who was executed by his fellow countrymen a year and some months after the close of the war. The soldier was accused of many things, some of them true, most of them not. In this story he is the personification of the theme of complete and utter mistrust among friends and allies. He is a casualty of all the mindless distortions; easy-come, easy-go commitments; and the tedious ruthlessness of powers compounded with his fight for freedom. His name is often, and wrongly, associated with the word *collaboration*, one of the more egregious examples of unfair propaganda against Serbia's reputation, not to mention one of the most damaging.

The World War II saga of Serbia, and of Yugoslavia in general, becomes particularly poignant in light of contemporary events. Serbia today is increasingly isolated from the world and constantly backed into a diplomatic and geopolitical corner. As of this writing, it is a few weeks after the ten-year anniversary of the 1999 NATO bombing of Serbia—a country with the dubious distinction of having seen its capital bombed by both Axis and now "Allied" forces; Croatia and Albania, meanwhile, have been admitted into the Atlantic alliance. The political and social situation in the self-proclaimed and widely recognized new state of Kosovo is depressing and violent. Relations between Croats, Muslims, and Serbs in Bosnia, fourteen years after the November 1995 Dayton Accords designed to bring to an end the Yugoslav wars of secession, have not improved: outwardly, there may be no more war; from within, the levels of mistrust and demoralization appear insurmountable.

Furthermore, it is apt, and perhaps relevant, to draw some parallels between the story of Yugoslavia, past and present, and the U.S. experience in Iraq. One could say, for example, that the Dayton Accords did for the warring factions of Yugoslavia what President George W. Bush's "most successful" general (David Petraeus) accomplished for Iraq (up through President Barack Obama's election): that is, to offer each of three main sides the same military, economic, and local-territorial incentives. However, just as that deal seems to be crumbling in Iraq (the Sunni-Shiite-Kurd quagmire not improving substantially, and the Kurds becoming particularly ambitious), a similar attempt to unify the Croats, the Bosnian Muslims, and the Serbs in Bosnia back in the 1990s has just not been able to hold up. Keep in mind that there are (still) two thousand peacekeepers from the European Union in Bosnia—a large number considering the country's small size. The Serbs, who want out of the loose confederation that Dayton established, are pressing for their own independent state, arguing every complex reason imaginable, from unfair representation and blocked trade to the need for compensation for the loss of Kosovo. As always with the Balkans, every point of view has validity, but there is no one vision that is thought valid for all.

Writing on the Balkans has often failed to command a large general audience for the simple reason that it does not bring out the larger lessons in the stories of a group of unhappy countries in southeastern Europe. But a country like Serbia must be seen not merely as a product of its own environment, but understood in the abstract—that is, as a country that has demonstrated the very best and very worst in humanity itself and the fight for ideals. No book that merely recounts a record of gruesome civil wars, ethnic violence, and trials and tribulations will command a large audience. But any book that investigates what it means for a country to have once upon a time taken the side of the winning team at the expense of its own existence deserves a wide readership. That is the story of Serbia, and it is a lesson confined to no region and no border or periphery, but one that is universal and eternal.

Acknowledgments

I would like to thank my agent, Jack Scovil, and my editor, Hana Lane, for their advice, attention, patience, and, most of all, their belief in the importance of this complicated subject matter. I would like to thank my parents, Sylvia and Gilbert, for their unflagging moral and material support. And special thanks to the magnificent Austrian National Library in Vienna for its incredible collections and beautiful setting, a privileged haven for any writer.

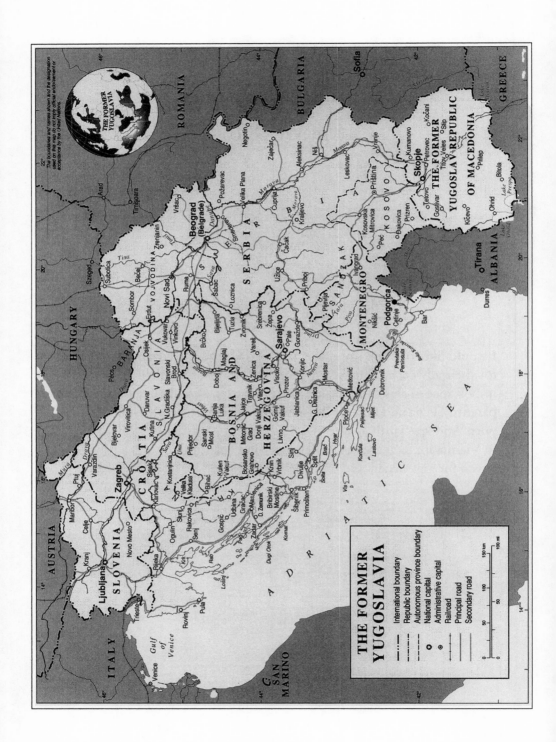

THE FORMER YUGOSLAVIA

PROLOGUE

The Blue Graveyard

> It is useless to attempt a description of what they suffered, as the story of that march toward the sea and the ships is told and understood in a few words. Fifteen thousand died on the way and those who saw the sea and the ships had nothing human left of them but their eyes, and *such eyes!*
>
> ——THE *NEW YORK EVENING SUN*, 1915

In early November 1915 a young American relief volunteer stationed in Mitrovica, Kosovo, watched as a column of 30,000 Serbian boys between the ages of twelve and eighteen marched past. In the dead of the Balkan winter, they were on a ten-week journey from Serbia across the Albanian mountains to a sea grave just beyond the coast of the Greek islands of Corfu and Vido, once the sun-blessed retreats of ancient gods, but now known as the Islands of Death. Starting out from as far north as Belgrade, most of the boys would die in the Prokletije Planina—the mountains of "the Damned," or "the Cursed"—bordering Kosovo, Montenegro, and Albania, and so named for their horrific impenetrability and their eerie-looking rounded peaks that jutted into the sky like long black tombstones. With faces still bleeding from the whips cracked at them by the officers who had organized their march, the boys were forced to cross the eight-thousand-foot terrain in this dark corner of the Dinaric Alps with neither horse nor guide, as incessant rain and snowy gales obliterated their tracks.

The boys who survived made their way across this daunting frontier of Kosovo on through to Albania, to the coastal cities of Scutari (now

Shköder), and Durazzo (now Durrës) then down to Valona (now Vlorë), in search of the sea and ships they were told they would see "within a couple of days." Those who did not fall to the ground out of fatigue and starvation had maintained themselves on a diet of tree roots and bark; many were abducted by Albanian snipers or mauled by wolves. They slept in the snow while fewer and fewer woke again each morning.

It was the time of Serbia's "Great Retreat," and the American was Fortier Jones, a Red Cross volunteer in Serbia during the early months of World War I who also took part in that country's tragic and magnificent exodus to the Adriatic coast. For the soldiers on that journey who arrived at Corfu, it was an odyssey that would ultimately end in Salonika, Greece, where six months later, in the summer of 1916, this emaciated corps of warriors would reemerge, phoenix-like, to take up arms once more and drive the Allied triumph in the Balkan theater of World War I.[1] By the late fall of 1915, however, the situation in Serbia seemed anything but destined for victory.

World War I had broken out a little more than a year earlier, on June 28, 1914, with Vienna's declaration of war against Serbia. This "war to end all wars," as it was grandiosely dubbed at the time, pitted the Central Powers of Germany, Austria-Hungary, Bulgaria and, unofficially, the Ottoman Empire against the Entente Powers of France (and her colonies), Great Britain (including Canada, Australia, and South Africa), Russia, Belgium (and colonies), Japan, and the Kingdom of Serbia. Later, Italy, Greece, Romania, and, as of April 1917 the United States, entered the Entente side. That first year, a series of swift victories reinforced the Serbian belief that the war was theirs to win. The Serbian First, Second, and Third Armies, with their legendary Šumadija, Moravska, Dunavska, and Drinska Divisions, "who endured submission with set teeth" in the words of one Serbian writer, were the heroes of a string of well-executed successes beginning with the first Allied victory of the entire war, the Battle of Čer (Jadar) in August 1914 under the command of Field Marshal Stepa Stepanović.[2] This was followed by the Battle of the Drina at Mackov Kamen and Novi Sad, which took place during the better part of that autumn, when the Serbians destroyed the Austrian Fifth Army of Field Marshal Oskar Potiorek's Austrian Balkan Army Group.[3] Then came the spectacular Battle of Kolubara in November and December 1914—the "Miracle of Kolubara," named after a major transport river in western Serbia, which brought the Serbian military to the attention of the Entente powers.[4]

At Kolubara, the formidable Serbian field marshal Živojin Mišić pushed back the Austrian Fifth and Sixth Armies led by the Austro-Croat general Stefan Sarkotić with his Thirteenth Territorial Army of Croatia and Slavonia and the powerful Second Bosnian Regiment, the most decorated regiment of any Austrian military brigade in the war.[5] These armies were routed out of their stronghold by the Serbs at Mount Subovor, near the Kolubara, and forced back over the country border at the Sava and Drina Rivers. It was a decisive victory for the Serbs. But now, nearly a year later, in the autumn of 1915, the Serbs found themselves exhausted, poorly armed, with around 170,000 casualties—about half that army's prewar strength—and newly surrounded by freshly organized German, Bulgarian, and Austro-Hungarian troops.[6]

As the blinding gales of a Balkan snowstorm bound the heavens to this war-torn hell, the Serbs were fighting a losing battle at Kosovo. It would be a bitterly demoralizing experience, as only three years before, at the Battle of Metohija in late October 1912, Serbian and Montenegrin troops had liberated once and for all the *vilayet* (that is, an imperial Ottoman province in the Balkan territories) of Kosovo from Ottoman Turkish rule.[7] Now, as German troops from the north, Austro-Hungarian forces from the west, and Bulgarian forces from the south and east advanced in one giant circle of gleaming bayonets, the northern and southeastern routes along which the Serbs might have escaped were blocked off, with four of five roads already held by the enemy. The last remaining "road" led up the mountains of Montenegro and Albania—and through two equally explosive political situations: King Nikola of Montenegro had declared war on Austria and Germany in August 1914, and Albania, an "independent" country only since the summer of 1913 but now under Viennese control, was mostly occupied by Austro-Hungarian armies.[8]

Serbia had refused to sign a separate peace with the Central Powers, and the logistical circumstances in which the country now found itself, coupled with the tragic delay of military assistance from the Entente powers, forced the country's final effort at preserving honor.[9] Field Marshal Radomir Putnik, whose highly motivated forces garnered worldwide attention in the 1912–1913 Balkan Wars, decided to declare a retreat of his troops on November 23, 1915, with a few divisions stay-ing behind as rear-guard defenders attempting to delay the advance of the enemy armies.[10] Assembling mainly in Kosovo, Serbian troops from as far north as Belgrade and as far southeast as the Bulgarian/Macedonian border were joined by an estimated 2,000 French, British, and Italian troops, then in retreat from encroaching Bulgarian armies in western Macedonia, to undertake the journey to the Adriatic.

The renowned orientalist Auguste Boppe, who served as the French minister at Belgrade and the wartime capital of Niš, and his Italian coun-terpart, Baron Tommaso Squitti, led the evacuation of the Entente dip-lomatic corps from Niš to Kosovo on a dilapidated mountain train and, once at Priština, joined the march.[11] Symbolic funeral pyres were lit in the Kosovo cities of Peć and Prizren, the latter a picturesque city crowned by the stunning Monastery of Holy Archangels and the elegiac ruins of the fourteenth-century castle of Serbian czar Stefan Dušan, whose name and legendary exploits Field Marshal Putnik, a swashbuckling national idol in his own right, had invoked to inspire his troops in battle.

The Serbian army split into four groups, following three main routes through the mountains: from Elbassan to Tirana in Albania and on to Durazzo (Dürres); from Peć and Podgorica to Scutari (Shköder); and finally, through the valley of the White Drin River between Kosovo and Montenegro to Scutari.[12] Each of the army groups journeyed with a large contingent of septuagenarians—the *čiče*, or "uncles," as they were known—who had rallied to the colors in the wake of the enormous losses of men between 1912 and 1914; all were without any provisions to sustain their starving ranks. The November 13, 1915, *Times* of London reported:

> The Serbian soldier, then, has become inured to a life of extreme privation; and in the fighting of last winter it was his toughness and ability to stand hardship which more than anything else gave him the advantage over the Austrians. Again and again, I have heard from Serbian officers the same story of how their men, having had nothing to eat for, perhaps, two days, in a country stripped of all eatables and mostly knee deep in the mud, pushed on, utterly careless of whether there was any commissariat or not, and simply

hunted the Austrians day and night without giving them a moment's rest. Only men of iron, to whom semi starvation had become almost the normal condition of their existence, could have done what the Serbians did then.

"What had been the most stoical fighting body in a war of valiant armies," recounted the head of the British Field Hospital in Serbia during the war, "became for the time being no more an army, no more the expression of all the hope and valor of a nation, but a ghost, a thing without direction, a freezing, starving, hunted remnant."[13]

Meanwhile, the majority of the Serbian population, from the Belgrade upper classes to the country peasantry, also joined the Retreat, preferring the fate of a courageous shadow humanity on a hostile mountain to staying behind as an oppressed people in a hostile land. Such a national mass exodus was nothing new: in 1690 almost the entire Serbian population had poured out of Kosovo northward into the province of Vojvodina following a failed Austrian-Serbian offensive against the Ottoman armies of Sultan Mustafa II. Now, more than two centuries later, as enemy troops reached the frontiers of central and southern Serbia, around 750,000 civilian and military refugees out of a prewar population of about three million gathered on the Kosovo plain for another deadly flight to freedom, while an estimated 12,000 civilians from southeastern Serbia, headed in the direction of Greece, ended up in refugee camps set up outside Salonika by British aid workers.[14]

From all directions, enemy planes circled menacingly overhead while suspected spies or those who had tried to escape were forced to walk with iron chains fastened to their legs. Starving Austrian or German prisoners of war—estimated at some 20,000—dropped dead alongside the retreating population.[15] This road of death—"this Golgotha so bitter, this army of the living dead," as described by Colonel Borislavjević, then head of the Serbian Red Cross stationed in Kosovo—was littered with dead animals—oxen and horses in various stages of decomposition, with both dogs and humans wresting off parts of those animals' limbs for consumption. Roads were "charged at all hours with thronging humanity," while rivers were choked "with the carcasses of dead things."[16] Knee-deep in mud and snow, many went barefoot, having sold their boots to peasants or village men along the way for a piece of bread. Life had been reduced to a level of bare subsistence. Out of that estimated 750,000 who undertook the Retreat, around 245,000 Serbs—soldiers and civilians—were estimated to have died, been killed, or taken prisoner on the march.[17] Prince Alexander, commander in chief of the royal Serbian army in the stead of his ill father, King Peter I, estimated that a total of 150,000 soldiers got through to Corfu.[18] Approximately 150,000 civilians and soldiers would eventually die on that island and the neighboring island of Vido. The historian C. E. J. Fryer would compare the Retreat to the exodus of Napoleon from Russia in 1812.[19]

The autumn of 1915 had witnessed the assembly of an estimated 300,000 Austro-Hungarian and German troops on Serbia's northern border and, on her eastern flank, a 400,000-strong Bulgarian army—this last a formidable force known as the "Prussians of the Balkans."[20] Nearly all of these troops were commanded by the brilliant Prussian field marshal August von Mackensen and his seasoned lieutenant general Max von Gallwitz, who together opened the Second Serbian Campaign with an attack on Belgrade on October 7, 1915. ("We fought against an army we heard about only in fairy tales," Mackensen would say after the war, at the dedication of a monument in Belgrade honoring Serbian soldiers who died defending that city.)[21] This imperial triptych—the Heeresgruppe Mackensen, based in Romania and Bulgaria and made up of ten divisions taken from the Eleventh German Army on the Russian front; the Austrian Third Army; and the Bulgarian First Army—together created one of the most devastating war machines to ever overrun southeastern Europe.[22]

After the severe casualties of 1914, by around August 1915 Serbian forces had increased to around 250,000 troops.[23] They were poorly equipped with obsolete Debange guns and some howitzer batteries. Moreover, while the Serbs had one machine-gun section per battalion, the Germans had one per company.[24] Most tragic, however, was that for the better part of 1915 Belgrade had waited for substantial Allied military assistance, but none would be forthcoming until it was too late: the first British and French divisions began to disembark at Salonika only on October 5, while four hundred miles of mountains, malaria, and one single, dilapidated railway lay between Salonika and the Serbian capital.

The tangled origins of the Balkan theater of World War I are too complex to introduce into this narrative. But by way of summary, these origins were, above all, a matter of the geopolitics of the sea—in this case, three seas: the Adriatic, the Aegean, and access to the East Mediterranean through the Bosporus Strait and the Dardanelles. As decaying empires and newborn, nationalistic states were pitted against one another for control of such strategic prizes, the result was a raft of land-grabbing treaties between 1878 and 1916 that gave rise to the deadly "questions" of the twentieth-century Balkans: the "question" of Bosnia-Herzegovina in 1908; the notorious Macedonian Question of 1912–1914; and the Italian-Croatian "question," which would remain an issue into World War II.[25]

Thus, when the question of a deployment to Salonika in the summer of 1915 had first come up for discussion, London and Paris were divided into so-called Westerners and Easterners, who were torn between acknowledging the strategic importance of the Balkans and being wary of that region's complexity and ultimate remoteness. The Westerners included British prime minister Harold H. Asquith, the British secretary of war Lord Kitchener, and General Joseph Joffe, the commander in chief of the armies of France. This group held that the Western front of the war was the only real concern and that the main theater of war comprised France and Flanders. The Balkans simply could not compare to the eighty-five German divisions pointing machine guns at the Allies from behind the thickets of blood-stained barbed wire demarcating Belgium and France—the perverse cartography of a new world order. To weaken the Western front for a major deployment in Salonika, thought these Westerners, would be a time-consuming, troop-wasting, demoralizing death blow to the Allies. Russia, for its part, had also been cool to the idea and proposed a short-lived deal to send only a thousand Cossacks, most of whom would be brought from the Gulf of Archangel, thus requiring several months to reach Salonika.

On the Easterners' side was the French general Louis Felix Franchet d'Espérey, who had traveled extensively in the Balkans for years and developed a certain emotional attachment to the region. There was also General Maurice Sarrail, who had hoped to be sent to the Gallipoli campaign in the Dardanelles-Bosporus region. Sir John French, the commanding officer of the British Expeditionary Force, saw Salonika as a pragmatic strategic possibility, as did Andrew Bonar Law, a member of the British War Cabinet, and the British chancellor of the exchequer David Lloyd George, himself good friends with the pro-Entente Greek premier Eleftherios Venizelos.

These Easterners maintained that Europe was a single battleground and that an attack on any portion of the Allies' front should not be neglected, no matter how inconsequential the particular region. They, too, had hoped that the irritating on-again, off-again battle between the beleaguered Greek prime minister Venizelos and King Constantine of Greece would result in a decision to side with the Allies. Lloyd George, though not too popular with his country's army and navy chiefs, in early 1915 penned a four-thousand-word memo on the necessity of sending troops to the Balkans. The British secretary of imperial defense, Colonel Sir Maurice Hankey, proceeded to draw up plans for a Balkan front. Both papers spoke of "the possibility of some co-operation with the Serbian Army against Austria" and that "it might be advisable to send an advance force through Salonika, to assist Serbia."[26]

For the Serbs, meanwhile, this was all too much talk, too little action, and all of it, anyway, much too late. "It was a tragic puzzle for Serbia," reported the *New York Times*. "Every day the question was asked, 'Where are the Allies?'"[27] For as this back-and-forth debate between London and Paris was going on, Bulgaria had already begun to mobilize against Serbia in September 1915. Field Marshal Putnik, the army chief of staff, telegraphed London, Paris, and Petrograd (changed from its former German name at the start of the war) asking for 150,000 extra troops and for permission to march the Serbian army across the southeastern frontier and attack the Bulgarians before they had consolidated their control. He asserted that the Serbian army would be in Sofia, the capital of Bulgaria, in five days. If Bulgaria could be dealt with, Serbia could then direct her full strength against Austria and Germany.

Serbia assumed that the Allies would respond immediately with troops, and the dissolution of hope, as reality dawned upon the Serbs, was a wrenching spectacle: "The greatest enthusiasm prevailed when at last the arrival of French troops was officially announced," wrote British historian Gordon Gordon-Smith, who accompanied the Serbs for part of the way on the Retreat. "The municipality [in Belgrade] voted twenty thousand francs, which it could ill spare, for the decoration of the Allied troops. In a few hours, the town burst out in a mass of bunting, French tricolours and British Union Jacks were everywhere in evidence."[28] Still there was no word, while 100,000 Bulgarian troops began to assemble on the eastern border of Serbia by late September. Days passed, until finally town officials went around in the darkness, gathering up the flags and packing them in carts.

What was about to take place in Entente relations with Serbia was one of the more absurd diplomatic failures of World War I. Not only was Field Marshal Putnik's request for troops initially refused, but the Allies (the Entente powers) were convinced that the Bulgarian mobilization was *not* directed against Serbia and—most bizarre—that the Allies would fulfill Putnik's appeal for 150,000 troops by obtaining them from the Sofia government they curiously believed was about to join the Entente side any minute—this while Bulgarian troops were amassing at Serbia's border. In addition, "Belgrade was warned that if she broke the Balkan peace she would do so at her own risk and peril," according to one detailed study of Allied military attitudes toward Serbia during the war.[29] Having thus backed Serbia into a corner, "the Allies looked on helplessly while the Central Powers and their Bulgarian allies proceeded to cut her throat," as Gordon-Smith described the scene.[30]

To be sure, the Allied forces had not completely forsaken their commitments. Rear Admiral Ernest Troubridge, head of the British Naval Mission to Serbia, led efforts, with a French naval mission attached to him and a Russian naval mission cooperating independently, to counter Austria's formidable mininavy, the Danube Flotilla.[31] The Danube River, measuring almost a mile wide at its confluence with the Sava, was, with the rail link between Berlin and Constantinople, the major route through which the Germans and the Austrians sent munitions transports to the Turks. However, armed with only eight British, three French, and one 15-cm Russian gun—this last the single largest of their weapons overall—"just forty seamen gunners, torpedo men, armourers, shipwrights and some 30 marines," wrote one British soldier serving under Admiral Troubridge in Danube naval actions at the time, faced 470 enemy guns and howitzers, and 42-cm mortars, while 9 Austrian naval monitors each outfitted with a 12-cm gun patrolled the waters, shelling all the mines that had been laid in the Danube by the Allies.[32]

Meanwhile, in southeastern Serbia, 45,000 troops from the Armée d'Orient of French general Maurice Sarrail had joined forces with 13,000 British troops that October 1915 under General Sir Bryan Mahon, a Boer War veteran and commander of the Tenth Irish Division at Gallipoli, as an Anglo-French Expeditionary Force in Greek

Macedonia. The Anglo-French armies were caught severely ill-prepared, however, limited as they were by the inadequacy of the harbor facilities at Salonika and the lone track of the Vardar Valley railway, while enemy troops were advancing rapidly into central Serbia from the north and the east.

During this time, the Central Powers successfully won Bulgaria over to their side, and the government of Czar Ferdinand I declared war on Serbia on October 12, 1915. General Sarrail's forces pushed up the wild terrain and broken bridges of the mud-choked Vardar River valley, separating eastern Serbia from Bulgaria, to position troops at Gjevgjeli—the very southeast of Macedonia on the Vardar River—and at Monastir (Bitola) in the western part of that territory. Yet his troops were almost immediately overwhelmed by 80,000 Bulgarian soldiers from Czar Ferdinand's First and Second Armies. The Second Army, independent of the command of General Mackensen, moved in from the southeast from its base at Sofia toward Skopje to cut the railway to Salonika. On November 2, 1915, the Battle of Niš began with a Bulgarian advance on the main Serbian arsenal at Kraguevac, and the takeover of Niš, then the wartime capital.

The British Tenth Division under General Mahon, for its part, having arrived at Salonika in October as reluctant and disoriented veterans from the ill-fated Gallipoli campaign, had not been authorized to cross the Greek frontier until seventeen days after disembarkation at that port city in late October. Once positioned west of Lake Doiran, they were unable to take over any section of the Serbian front until November 10, just as the whole of the old kingdom was being overrun.[33] In the early morning of November 11, 1915, the Austrian flag was hoisted over the arsenal and barracks of Kraguevac and, shortly thereafter, the German flag. Just south of Skopje, the town of Veleš, the main stronghold of the Serbian army in Macedonia, had already fallen to the Bulgarians. The British Tenth Division clung to its positions until it was forced into a general withdrawal back to the port of Salonika in December. Seven hundred French were killed or wounded in the ensuing exodus, and the British, more directly in the path of the Bulgarians, lost around 1,000 men; another 1,500 had collapsed from typhus and malaria.

General Sarrail, meanwhile, was forced to withdraw his troops, delaying for two days to allow the Serbs to get away. It was a painful retreat, during which it took twenty-four hours to cover one mile.[34]

By December 12, 1915, all French and British troops had left Serbian territory, many of them joining the westward retreat of the Serbs. Of the British and French soldiers on that march, the *Times* of London commented, "Machine guns were repaired at night time with old pieces of cloth and wires, and using their petrol 'to the last liter', without saying a word to the Serbian General Staff. They suffered hunger without complaining."[35] One in ten of that British and French allied force would be listed as killed, wounded, or missing, yet "not a single German nor an Austrian nor a Turk had come under the fire of Sarrail's or Mahon's men," reported the same article.

• • •

The twenty-six-year-old Fortier Jones, in Kosovo as a U.S. relief volunteer as the collapse of the Serbian army and the roundup of Serbian boys was taking place, joined the Retreat with a caravan of two hundred Serbian men out of a sheer sense of duty and a young American's sense of adventure. He recounted his journey in bitter and beautiful detail in his 1916 book *With Serbia into Exile*, one of several unusually poignant Anglo-American works on Serbia and the Balkans to come out during and just after World War I.[36] "To me the name of Kosovo calls up one of the most terrible spectacles I shall ever see," he wrote. "Until that day I did not know the burden of the tiny little word 'war' but never shall we who traversed the Field of Blackbirds think of this war without living again the snow-filled horrors of our march."[37]

The crossing of Albania itself—the "Albanian Cavalry," as it came to be known, proved particularly harsh. The prime minister of Albania, Essad Pasha Toptani, once exiled during a civil revolt in 1912 to the wartime Serbian capital of Niš, was indeed hospitable to the grim procession of soldiers and civilians passing through his territory. Irregular Albanian guerrillas and mountain clans, however, were merciless, ambushing and killing Serbs as the refugees wandered onto the country's neglected roads and across its wild pastures.[38]

Jones walked with his contingent through a small chain of Kosovo towns left with little but the memories of a distant, bruised heroism—from Mitrovitza to Priština, then to Prizren and Peć—crossing the fault lines of the Dinaric and Albanian Alps en route to Scutari. In those mountains he encountered a dozen or so British and American aid workers also on the march, who included some nurses from the Scottish Women's Suffrage Federation and the American wife of a Serbian doctor who, as a couple, founded the highly respected Serbian Relief Committee in England. The participation of these workers in the Retreat, and of those who stayed behind at makeshift hospitals to deal with the ghastliness of the wounded, the diseased, and the dying, was one of many examples of the unsung heroism of foreign aid workers in the Balkans during this war.[39] Their mission in Serbia to stem an overwhelming outbreak of typhus in the population had, however, proved futile. The spread of the "spotted" form of this disease, turning once healthy men, women, and children into gray, then black, corpses within hours, was symbolized by the hundreds of black flags hanging from nearly every other Serbian house in towns and villages.

Often, it was the Serbian soldiers who had to boost morale for these foreign volunteers: "Voyagez, voyagez et continuez de voyager!" ("Go on, go on, and continue to go on") one Serbian major implored a pair of demoralized British aid workers.[40] Austrian soldiers, then occupying Belgrade, brought bread in daily to the hospitals and to the civilian population, then about 6,000 inhabitants. The toll of the victims was enormous: more than 70,000 had succumbed to the typhus epidemic.[41] It was the swiftest form of death during the war if the battlefield or the unforgiving terrain of the mountains did not kill a person first.[42]

The government had ordered all boys between the ages of twelve and eighteen, the raw material of future armies, to leave the country to save them from being taken by the enemy into Austria, Germany, or Bulgaria as prisoners of war. With German and Serbian cannons "heard incessantly, like rumbling thunder," Jones saw thousands of these children line up on the railway line from Belgrade, the youngest ones on top of railway cars, "crying together, longing for homes which no longer existed."[43] One evening the order came for them to evacuate at midnight, and each boy was given a rifle, a canteen, and all the ammunition their young bodies could hold. Then they were told to march and to never look back.

By the time the children reached the Adriatic coast in early February, their numbers were down to 15,000. With the Austro-Hungarian Third Army following in pursuit from the north, neither the children nor the soldiers could camp and recuperate at the Italian-held Albanian port cities of Scutari or Durazzo, where dozens of hollow-eyed Serbian corpses littered the streets, dead from starvation. They were forced to continue on to Valona (Vlorë), although Italian forces at that port city did not have adequate hospital accommodations, nor would the Italians allow so many disease-ridden men into those coastal cities or the cities on the Italian coast for fear of the infections picked up by the Serbs, who had been forced to drink from corpse-infested waters during their journey.

The children's numbers were down to 9,000 by the time they reached Valona. Italian ships with food and medical aid leaving Brindisi to cross the Adriatic were attacked by enemy destroyers and torpedoes sent from the Austro-Hungarian naval base at Cattaro (Kotor); bombs from Austrian planes meanwhile rained down on the small craft that were randomly darting to the coast to pick up the soldiers and civilians. The Allies decided to evacuate the children and those near death to the small island of Vido, while the remaining Serbs would be transported to the island of Corfu, occupied by the French since early January 1916. An estimated 152,000 Serbian soldiers would find refuge on this hospital island of Italianate houses and Victorian villas.[44] The tombstones one finds in the shadow of the olive groves of Corfu are of those who died during their first week on the island.[45]

Meanwhile, en route from Valona to Vido, the latter a patch of green and stone located just next to Corfu and windswept by the sighs of the dying on those incoming boats, another 2,000 children died of disease and hunger. The remaining 7,000 who had made it to that island were encamped in an orange grove. There they were tended to by French and Serbian doctors who sought in vain to save the remaining boys, working "without beds, medicine or milk," as Jones recounts. Hundreds of men and boys died each day. The ordeal of the burial of the dead by sea via the routine delivery of a steamship going back and forth, as if picking up and unloading cargo, was an event that would become known in Serbian history as the "Blue Graveyard."

Every morning the *St. Francis Assisi*, a great French vessel that had been based in Bari, Italy, for the war, made regular trips to Vido and Corfu to take the corpses of soldiers and the children to sea for burial. Allied war vessels at Corfu lowered their flags to half mast. "[T]he survivors lying on the straw waiting for their turn to die, 'with nothing human left of them but their eyes,'" reported an account of the entire march in the *New York*

Evening Sun, "must wonder as they look at the sea and the ship with the bodies of their dead comrades on board whether this is the sea and the ship that the only leader they had, the Serbian gendarme that saw them safely to the frontier, alluded to when he raised his arm and pointed to the west and told them to march in that direction."[46] Half of Serbia's army had perished between the battlefield and the Retreat. And so, too, the mountains and the southeastern coastlines of the Adriatic "bore on their gleaming passes and their rocky shores the lifeless bodies of twenty-thousand boys," as the *Sun* solemnly ended its report.

Later, a simple stone cross was erected anonymously on Vido, with inscriptions in Serbian and in English. The modest requiem that had been intended to commemorate the Serbian victims of the Retreat turned into a great ceremony. Claude Askew, of the British Field Hospital for Serbia, wrote of the memorial beautifully:

> Imagine the scene: the sun was shining brightly that morning, the sea was of the deepest blue, the waves lapped the shore gently . . . as if they would make harmonious echo to the solemn chanting of the Mass, and the island that Death had marked for its own became crowded with Serbian, English, French and Greek officers: but a few hours later silence reigned once more on Vido—the island had been left to its quiet repose.[47]

And so by the beginning of 1916, victory for the Central Powers seemed entirely within view. The Italians were immobile on the Adriatic, and the Serbs were dying on remote Adriatic islands and were otherwise left helpless on the Danube. Russia was being pushed back from Poland; the Dardanelles campaign was failing. France had lost around 100,000 men in ten days fighting at Artois, Belgium. The British had lost about 50,000 men in one month at Ypres.

The only miscalculation inherent in the optimism that prevailed in Berlin, Vienna, and Sofia was the failure to foresee the possibility of a sweeping change of fortune in the fate of the Serbian army. For at Corfu, the miraculous rehabilitation of those skeletal Serbian soldiers and their uncanny reemergence as a formidable fighting force took place within six months of their arrival on that Greek island. This disease-scarred, emaciated remnant of an army was ready to do battle once again as the Serbian army of legend, this time in the no-man's-land of the Salonika Front. And this time, they would make World War I history on an epic scale.

• • •

A king, a statesman, a soldier, and a poet had also been on that brutal march. The king was the seventy-two-year-old Peter I of the Karadjordjević dynasty, the grandson of the first successful rebellion leader against the Ottoman Turks in 1804 and himself a translator of John Stuart Mill's *On Liberty* into Serbo-Croatian ("O Slobodi") in 1868. Although weakened with age and the vicissitudes of a difficult life, the king marched on foot with his men in ten-hour stretches, never mounting his horse, which was led by his royal staff behind him, and carrying with him Serbia's oldest manuscript, the twelfth-century *Miroslav Gospel,* an illuminated history of Christianity. King Peter was with his twenty-seven-year-old son and Serbia's commander in chief, Prince Regent Alexander, who had waited until every soldier had been evacuated from the Albanian ports until he went on to Corfu himself. The prince, too, was a highly skilled soldier, who had led victories against the Ottoman Turks at the decisive Battle of Kumanovo, located on the border between (modern-day) Macedonia and Serbia, in late October 1912 and against the Bulgarians at Bregalnica, a river near the Vardar tributary in Macedonia, in June 1913.

The statesman was Nikola Pašić, then seventy years old (and making the crossing with his wife), a tenacious visionary whose political life would span fifty years of Europe's military and ideological glory and self-destruction. The soldier was the twenty-two-year-old Dragoljub "Draža" Mihailović, distinguished for his military bravery in both Balkan Wars and who had fought in the battles of Čer and Kolubara at the outset of World War I, with the powerful Drina Division of the Serbian royal army. Within a decade he would receive the country's highest military honors—the Order of the White Eagle and the Star of Karadjordjević—for bravery in battle, and become one of the most highly decorated soldiers in the history of the Serbian army.[48]

The poet was the twenty-three-year-old Milutin Bojić, a military mail censor during the war and one of the promising stars of Serbia's turn-of-the-century literary culture, although with the war eating away the nation's young, "Serbian literature, like the Serbian nation, was bled almost to death," as one scholar described that generation.[49] Bojić survived the exodus from Serbia and the desperation of Corfu, and yet in the end succumbed to tuberculosis in Salonika. "Our church bells toll dead instead of hours," he wrote of seeing his countrymen dying around him.[50] At the time of the Retreat he had been working on an epic poem, "Cain," in which he compared Bulgaria's attack on Serbia to the biblical Cain's attack on his brother, Abel. The poem was one of the few things he carried with him in his knapsack as he made the journey. Upon arriving at the Adriatic only to see his fellow Serbs being thrown out to the sea for burial, he penned one of the most moving poems of his generation: "Plava Grobnica" ("The Sea Grave"), which asked the world:

> Don't you feel how gently the sea swells
> Not to disturb their eternal rest?
> From the deep a sense of peace prevails
> While an exhausted moon gazes at the sea.
> I say a requiem like the heavens have yet to hear
> Over these holy waters.[51]

These four men represented an accomplished pre–World War I generation of Serbian political, cultural, and military personalities just on the cusp of ushering the country onto the international stage of European modernity. But too many bloody regional conflicts and Great Power geopolitical rivalries following the dissolution of Ottoman power would soon overwhelm this struggling new birth, which kept the fate of Serbia in a state of frustrated limbo. The kind of one-step-forward, two-steps-back striving of Serbia's turn-of-the-century generation to usher the country into a European future was reflected in the very personality of post-Ottoman, prewar Belgrade itself. "There is much room for improvement in this town of many contrasts where East meets West in striking fashion," wrote one Serbian observer of the turn-of-the-century changes going on. "Extremes are the dominant feature which may be observed both in the temperament of the Serbian people and in the architecture of Belgrade."[52]

Despite being surrounded by the looming winds of war, a sense of optimism for the country's future had been spreading: the University of Belgrade was founded at this time, as well as the national newspaper

Politika. The automobile, the cinema, and the first long-distance phone call were all introduced by 1910. A newly wealthy merchant class started to pour money into the arts, and the country's Francophile writers and poets, whose works were inspired by Lamartine's early-nineteenth-century visits to the Balkans and by France's Parnassian movement of the early twentieth century, were catapulted to international acclaim.[53]

The politicians who steered Serbia's national rebirth in the years between the Treaty of Berlin of 1878, which was marked by intrigue, and Austria-Hungary's annexation of Bosnia-Herzegovina in 1908 tended to be true European statesmen.[54] There was Pašić, the founder of the powerful People's Radical Party in 1881, whose cool refusal to buy Austrian agriculture or arms, more than anything else, directly provoked the outrage of Vienna—years before the assassination of Archduke Franz Ferdinand.[55] Milan Milovanović, at the age of twenty-five, wrote Serbia's liberal 1888 Constitution and later as an intrepid foreign minister astutely, if unsuccessfully, steered the Serbian position on the powderkeg issue of Bosnia-Herzegovina. Stojan Protić was an intellectual-turned minister of the interior who wrote widely read political articles under the pen name "Balkanicus," while Lazar Paču effected an intelligent fiscal stewardship as the minister of finance who led to Serbia's budgetary surpluses every year between 1906 and 1914.

Paču, Protić, and Pašić—and Serbia's reputation—came to be known as "Paču the mouth, Protić the pen, and Pašić the brain."[56] They followed in the footsteps of such earlier Serbian personalities as the mid-nineteenth-century Serbian foreign minister Ilija Garašanin, the decidedly unradical author of the revolutionary 1838 Constitution and of what became the defining political work of a new generation, *The Outlook* (Nacertanije), a statement of the national and territorial ambitions of the country.[57]

A parliament, the Skupština, had been founded and developed between 1805 and 1813. It was in those challenging years of the first half of the nineteenth century, when the philosophical idea of tradition and monarchy competed with the idea of parliamentary supremacy, that the first political parties were born in Serbia. These included the Liberal Party founded by Jovan Ristić, a writer and philosopher who studied under the German historian Leopold von Ranke at Heidelberg and served four times as Serbia's prime minister; and Vladimir Jovanović, one of the founders of the United Serbian Movement.[58] The Progressive Party, despite its name, emerged as the conservative, intellectual vanguard of the autocratic Obrenović royal family, the rival dynasty of the Karadjordjevićs.[59]

The country's top military leaders—the Voivode—were subjects of awe-struck European newspaper profiles, including Field Marshal and General Chief of Staff Putnik, who, though suffering from a severely debilitating asthma, accompanied his troops across the Albanian mountains in a covered sedan chair held by four men. Field Marshal Mišić commanded the valiant Serbian Second Army while Field Marshal Stepanović led the victory at the Battle of Ćer. The forces of Field Marshal Peter Bojović triumphed against the Bulgarian army at the decisive battles of Bitola and Breglanica in the Second Balkan War.

Politically, it seemed at the time that monarchy was destined for a long-term future in Serbia. The first European coronation of the twentieth century took place on September19, 1904, after the Serbian Parliament, the Skupština, proclaimed the sixty-year-old prince Peter I Karadjordjević the new king of Serbia. The French-educated Peter I was probably the most popular king in Serbian history, and during the time of his rule, from 1903 until his death in August 1921, there were few public buildings or private houses, hotels, or cafés without his portrait decorating the walls.[60] He had enrolled as a volunteer in the French army in the Franco-Prussian War in 1870, and in the 1875 insurrection against the Ottoman occupation of Bosnia-Herzegovina he fought alongside the very rebels—the *hajduks*—from whose romantic-bandit culture his forebear, Kara Djordje, rose to lead the first uprising against the Turks in 1804.[61]

King Peter was himself often on the battlefields of World War I, his own frailty offset by an overwhelming anxiety for his "children," as he called his troops. He knew how to revel in glory as well, however, and he reentered Belgrade in February 1915 after the successful battles of the previous autumn with his sons, Crown Prince Alexander and Prince George, on either side of him, "their three swords uplifted, the glittering sun on their naked blades, all the while the roar of the cannon fire was still going on in the streets," as Gordon-Smith recounted.[62] Now half-crippled but traveling on foot nonetheless, King Peter left the bed to which his doctors had restricted him, to accompany his soldiers that tragic November.

• • •

The soldier on the Retreat who had arrived on the melancholy shorelines of Corfu in January 1916 was no doubt as exhausted as the other soldiers, but he still had a lot of fight left. Unlike many of his comrades who had dumped their heavy arms along the way or sold them to Albanian villagers for food, Draža Mihailović and his men had held on to captured machine guns the entire journey through to the island. Yet no amount of armed strength or desire to continue the battle could overcome the emotional devastation of seeing some 10,000 of his fellow soldiers being taken out to sea for burial. Still, the surviving soldiers received medical care and attention from the British commissioner at Corfu, Sir Henry Bozle; from a relief committee presided over by Princess Helene Demidoff, wife of the Russian ambassador to Greece and a beauty once immortalized by the painter John Singer Sargent; and by the American Sanitary Commission in Serbia. Within a few weeks' time, the skeletal soldiers whom local nurses once had to lift like babies from their beds were now being retrained to use many of the weapons that Mihailović and other soldiers had picked up along the way, supplemented by shipments of arms carefully smuggled in by the French and British from Italy.

Little by little, ships arrived to take the Serbs over to Salonika, despite the risk of such a deadly passage. Their journey to Salonika was organized by the French, using fifteen transport and two auxiliary cruisers while escorted by British trawlers. Each of the transport ships made three and a half voyages a month. Enemy planes patrolled the coastal skies, attacking the vessels, while a proliferation of Austrian destroyers and torpedoes prowled the waters. Yet not a single ship, or a single man, on the Entente side was lost during these trips. Part of that good fortune was due to clever navigation techniques on the part of the Entente: vessels would depart from Corfu traveling as if going to Marseille, then zigzag the rest of the way to Greece, confusing enemy naval operations. A special pier in Salonika, Micra Pier, was made for the incoming ships, the first of which reached Salonika on April 15, 1916, and the last arriving in late May 1916.

No sooner had the Serbs, already physically rehabilitated and spiritually energized, disembarked from the ships dressed in English khaki or French blue uniforms than they were already busy organizing one or another *slava*—a sort of daylong religious festival-feast, with spontaneous banquets and dramatic orations filled with the many heroes of the

Serbian epic oral tradition. An ebullient *kolo* would usually follow, with the occasional French or English officer unable to resist taking part in the rhythmic camaraderie of that warmhearted dance. These new arrivals carried photos of wives and children left behind in Serbia, and took out ads in Swiss newspapers—the only foreign press the Germans allowed into occupied areas—on the heartbreaking off chance that a relative might see them and respond. "During their stay not a single violent act has been committed by them, not an egg eaten nor a glass of beer drunk that they have not paid—and paid well—for," wrote the Greek newspaper the *Athenai* of the newly arrived soldiers. "No woman has been insulted by them, nowhere have they provoked quarrels, which are almost inherent to armies. Corfu has not seen a Serbian drunk or causing a disturbance in the streets. Few armies can boast of such qualities."[63]

King Peter I, meanwhile, had arrived a few months before, taking up residence in Salonika with his sons Prince Regent Alexander and Prince George, these last two adapting to their new government in exile quite differently: Prince Regent Alexander remained withdrawn and studious, poring over military maps and growing a beard to disguise his identity. Prince George, more impetuous, enjoyed going about town in a trench coat to survey the nest of spies that was the Salonika world in wartime.[64]

While at Corfu, Nikola Pašić made the island the temporary seat of the Serbian government. In March 1916 he left with Prince Regent Alexander for Rome, Paris, and London to persuade the Allied governments that Serbia could still make important contributions to the Allied war effort. Part of the Serbian army elements that reached Corfu, they argued, could be reorganized into a fighting corps and placed under Allied command at Salonika. Given the expansion of the war to the southeast, and with Montenegro now on the Entente side of the war as of January 1916, the liberation of Serbia was in the Allies' interest, mainly because of their vital interest in Salonika and access from there to sea routes through the Dardanelles and the Bosporus Strait, as mentioned earlier.[65] Meanwhile, the French, the British, and the Italians had delivered new military necessities and re-equipped the now reorganized but decimated army. Under the command of General Peter Bojović, a former hero of the Second Balkan War, the remnants of the Serbian army—around six divisions, or about 147,000 men—were ready to be transported to Salonika.

Not too many months later, the Serbs and the French would break the Bulgarian front at Monastir in southern Macedonia, with the monks of Mount Athos raising the green silk banner of Stefan Dušan and singing a "Te Deum" in celebration. The Serbian army had returned to life full force and on to victory. Mihailović himself would participate in one of the great counteroffensives against the Germans in September 1916, one that military historians would later call the first stage in the ultimate downfall of the Central Powers in the Balkans: the assault on Dobropolje.[66] The 1915 Retreat was thus not in vain, nor was Mihailović's decision to hold on to their weapons to finish the fight they were once told had been irretrievably lost.

If Mihailović and his brothers in arms were now about to make World War I history, it seemed fated considering the already distinguished military career of this tall, sandy-haired young man who was fast becoming one of the most highly decorated soldiers in the Royal Serbian (and later Royal Yugoslav) army. In 1912, at the age of nineteen, Mihailović had served in the Drina Division at the famous Battle of Kumanovo against the Turks in the First Balkan War, and in 1913 he had fought with the Morava Division against the Bulgarians in the Second Balkan War. In both wars he was honored for bravery in battle. As written earlier, he had participated in the Entente's first victory at the 1914 Battle of Ćer and at the Battle of Kolubara, where he was again recognized for bravery on the battlefield. Now about to join the Allied victory on the Salonika Front, Mihailović would receive the highest military honors in the Serbian Army.

Whether Mihailović had imagined, while waiting on Corfu for his deployment to the backwoods of Macedonia, that the fate of his country would be inextricably connected to his own, is impossible to say. A portent of his worst battles to come, however, was evident as early as his young military days on the battlefields of Ćer: the Drina and the Kolubara rivers. Then fighting in the Austrian armies of Austro-Croatian field marshal Stepanović in the autumn of 1914, Mihailović witnessed the crossing of the Thirteenth Territorial Army of Croatia and Slavonia as it came over the Drina into Serbia. Among the soldiers of the Croatian regiment was a certain reserve sergeant known, like Mihailović, for his bravery and commitment: the Croatian-born Josip Broz, later known simply by his nom de guerre "Tito."

• • •

For all the renewed force of their Serbian allies in southeastern Europe, the Entente powers were in no mood that summer of 1916 to take on a front in Salonika yet again. Greece was still uncommitted in the war, as was Romania, and as the majority thinking went, if anyone was going to do the fighting for Serbia, it would be these two neighbors of Serbia, not the overextended armies of the Entente. With the first round of defeats in the Balkans in 1915 and the depressing losses of that year for the Entente in general, another shift of men and matériel to Salonika to fight in the mud of Macedonia had no great appeal for the Western powers. Furthermore, there was mutual contempt between the Entente and the Serbian sides. If the British base at Mudros (in the northern Aegean) was still not enough, and if Greece was to join the war on the side of the Central Powers, the unspoken thought on everyone's mind was this: shipping in the Danube, the future of Constantinople, access to the Aegean—all worth fighting for, but was Serbia itself worth the commitment?

At a meeting of Entente leaders at Calais on December 4, 1915, as British and French troops were retreating in Salonika, Serbia, and southeastern Europe from the overwhelming force of the Central Powers, British prime minister Harold Asquith soberly announced: "In the opinion of the military advisers of the British Government, the retention of the present force of 150,000 at Salonika is from a military point of view dangerous and likely to lead to a great disaster . . . preparations should be made without delay for evacuation."[67] The French first said yes, then at a subsequent meeting two weeks later at Chantilly said no; the Italians, the Russians, and the Serbs supported the French policy of keeping open the Balkan front. Eventually the British begrudgingly agreed. The cynical interpretation of their change of heart was that in the event of victory, London did not want the French to have the territorial upper hand in the postwar Near East. The official reason was, of course, that the Alliance must be held at all costs.

By the spring of 1916, General Sarrail was already at work establishing an immense fortification for his troops, consisting of a seventy-mile defensive line, eight miles north of Salonika, extending from the lake district at Laganza in southern Macedonia and running eastward to the Gulf of Orfano and the marshes of the Vardar Valley, approaching Bulgaria, and finally ending in the eastern Greek Kavala region. The men who constructed this entrenched camp, a mass of birdcage-like barbed wire meant to keep the Allies from being "pushed into the sea" by the Bulgarians, later earned its tireless architects the title of "the Gardeners of Salonika" from the skeptical Georges Clemenceau, who was soon to begin his second term in office as French premier and was wary of any French commitments abroad.[68]

Still, the fortification was as effective as it was impressive to behold: the nearest Bulgarian posts were twenty-five miles from the fortified line, manned in the center and east by five British divisions and in the west by three French divisions. In May 1916 Draža Mihailović joined the Gardeners as platoon leader in the Twenty-third Infantry Regiment of the Royal Serbian Army's Vardar Division, after being transferred to the Salonika Front and assigned to positions in the area of the Ostrovo Lakes in northern Greece.

Many months of watching and waiting lay ahead. The Germans and the Austrians were no more enthusiastic about the Salonika Front than were their Entente counterparts in London and Paris, and they had for the most part pulled out of the area after the autumn 1915 successes against Serbia. Now thirty-six thousand French, Serbian, and, soon, Italian infantrymen waited in the Vardar Valley. The French, under General Sarrail, and the Serbs, commanded by Field Marshal Živojin Mišić, were encamped along the Vardar River in eastern Macedonia, while the four divisions under General George Milne, a veteran of the Second Boer War, who replaced General Mahon in May 1916, positioned themselves along the Struma River, which extends into northern Greece from its mouth at the Aegean and continues through western Bulgaria.

The news that Romania had joined the war on the Entente side in July 1916 would be a short-lived consolation. As part of the deal, the Entente had offered the whole of the Banat territory bordering Hungary and Serbia, one-half of it part of the Vojvodina province.[69] Yet the Allies were desperate. In addition to the failures of 1915, two horrific battles that ushered in the nihilism of the twentieth century as did few other events were taking place on the Western Front that summer and autumn of 1916: Verdun and the Somme, with their million and a half casualties. The inclusion of Romania now appeared masterly, but it was only a temporary solution: the Central Powers struck back furiously against Romania and by December 1916 occupied Bucharest. The Allies' newest partner was literally knocked out of the war. The Allies on the Salonika

Front, it seemed, would have to make do as the reduced force that they now were.

A strong sense of military insecurity on top of being relegated to southern Macedonia might have been enough to break a man's spirit were it not for the sudden arrival of an odd gaggle of storybook brigades—the kinds of adventurers who would have found their way to whichever front in any war touted the best prospects for battle honor. The Second and Fourth Brigades of the Russian Expeditionary Force arrived in Salonika between August and November 1916 after having traveled from Archangel to Brest, then to Marseille and on to Salonika. The brigades were made up mostly of Russian peasant soldiers and some Cossack troops. They came streaming through the Greek frontier as one broad, bright barrier of steel, eight men abreast and carrying gleaming bayonets. They cheered and sang, infused with the highest of war-ready spirits, and running to embrace the first (and somewhat disconcerted) French soldiers who came into view. Later to arrive were six squadrons of the magnificent Spahis, a Moroccan brigade of blue-turbaned, long-haired warriors led by General Juinot-Gambetta, a nephew of the radical politician Leon Gambetta, who in 1870 had sailed out of Paris in a hot-air balloon to organize a resistance movement in provincial France.[70]

This dissident atmosphere was further enhanced by the arrival in Salonika of Essad Pasha Toptani, the exiled prime minister of Albania, who set up a resistance movement in the port city and brought along one thousand Albanian soldiers for the fight in Macedonia. Last but not least to join this spirited assembly was the forty-year-old daughter of an Irish clergyman, Flora Sandes, the beloved *naša Engleskinja* ("our English lady") to the Serbs. Sandes was a British nurse who had arrived in Serbia in 1915 as part of an ambulance unit, followed the country on its Retreat to the Adriatic, and now resurfaced in Macedonia with only her wit, charm, and rolled-up sleeves to outdo the men pushing cannons through the mud of the Vardar Valley.[71]

Facing them was the army of the Heeresgruppe von Scholtz, consisting of the 101st and 107th divisions of the drastically reduced German Eleventh Army commanded by General Friedrich Wilhelm von Scholtz, who had led the German Eighth Army in its victory against the Russians at the August 1914 Battle of Tannenberg, in Poland. Replacing Erich von Falkenhayn in 1917 as the German supreme commander, General Paul

Beneckendorff von Hindenburg and his chief of staff General Erich von Ludendorff wanted their exhausted German armies to have as little as possible to do with the operations in Macedonia. They sought to shift the bulk of the fighting to the Bulgarian First Army and its seven additional divisions under General Nezerov, and to the newly formed Turkish 177th Rumelia Division, a part of the Bulgarian Army as of September 1915. To be sure, the Central Powers were still an intimidating collection of soldiers confronting the Serbs and their odd, colorful allies on the Salonika Front. But certainly they were not nearly so entertaining.[72]

The combined force of these diverse brigades led to the first major success of the Allies in Macedonia at the nine-week Battle of Monastir (modern-day Bitola), a town of some 60,000 inhabitants eighty miles from Salonika, fought between August and November 1916. Somewhat suddenly, 18,000 Bulgarian troops started to advance south and west across Macedonia, boasting to local peasants that they would be in Salonika in a week. General Sarrail met with General Milne and General Count Alfonso Petitti di Roreto, commander of five thousand freshly arrived Italian troops, to strategize an enveloping tactic whereby French and Serbian artillery would be positioned on the western bank of beech forest–rich Lake Ostrovo, just a few miles south of Lake Ohrid near the Albanian-Macedonian border. Draža Mihailović, though terribly wounded during the brief but decisive Serb victory against the Ottomans at Monastir in November 1912, had arrived at the Ostrovo region with the Vardar Division on August 20 as part of a machine-gun company that would reinforce the French and Serbian armies. Just behind the lake, perched on the stony two-thousand-foot mountains of Kajmakcalan and Moglena, British, Greek, and Italian troops were to act as reserves.[73]

As the battle dragged on, an influx of twenty-two German battalions, including the Thirteenth Saxon Jägers—a traditional German reconnaissance team made of huntsmen and foresters—and seventy-two artillery batteries, came in to boost the Heeresgruppe von Scholtz while Bulgarian troops found their way through a gap in Allied defenses between Monastir and Florina, another major town just to the south in the Greek territory of Macedonia. Column upon column of Bulgarian troops descended on the Allies; five times they stormed the area, and five times they were pushed back.

The capture of Monastir was celebrated as a major triumph; General Sarrail claimed it was the first victory of French arms since the Marne (where in the first weeks of the war French forces reversed an Allied retreat toward Paris to beat back the German forces on the Western Front). Despite the victory for Sarrail, the stubborn general's openly Socialist politics were not welcome among the conservative French elite military structure dominated by Generals Ferdinand Foch and Henri Philippe Pétain. Nor were they too embraced by President Clemenceau himself. In a restructuring of French forces in 1917, Sarrail was replaced by the masterful general Marie Louis Adolphe Guillaumat, commander of the French Second Army at Verdun.

Despite the success at Monastir that autumn of 1916, the morale of the Allied forces would drop considerably the next year. A fire swept through Salonika in August 1917, leveling a good 50 percent of the city. British soldiers around Lake Doiran and in the Vardar Valley were being ravaged by malaria and influenza, with 20 percent of that force being diagnosed with malarial cases that autumn, while the last stores of quinine were destroyed in the Salonika fire. Greece had entered the war on June 29, 1917, on the Allied side, and Prime Minister Eleftherios Venizelos, Greece's hard-pressed champion of the Entente, promptly resigned. In other places, too, the world seemed about to go up in flames. The last battle of attrition, the Battle of Passchendale (or the Third Battle of Ypres), was fought in Belgium, a country awash in mud and mustard gas, leaving half a million Entente and a quarter million Central Powers troops dead. The United States entered the war in early April 1917, just around the time that Vladimir Lenin, disguised as a railway worker, arrived at Finland Station in St. Petersburg.

Serbian military morale, plunging from the exuberant highs of those first heady months on the front, was at an all-time low. The famous Salonika Trial of Captain Dragutin Dimitriević had begun in the spring of that year. As a twenty-six-year-old army captain, he had been part of the plot to murder the last Obrenović king in 1903, and in 1911 he founded the Black Hand organization, which later carried out the assassination of Archduke Franz Ferdinand. In 1916 he had been posted to the Salonika Front after his journey to Corfu as chief of military intelligence of the Serbian Third Army. Dimitriević and three accomplices were executed by firing squad on June 26, 1917. Then there were so many rumors of Serbian terrorist cells and dissident elements in the Third Army—with many of its Serb troops having deserted to the Bulgarians—that Field Marshal Peter Bojović was forced to break it up, the rest of the soldiers being merged with the Serbian First and Second Armies.[74]

Despite the inflammatory political situation around the Salonika Trial and the breakup of the Serbian army, the year became a watershed for the rise of the Yugoslav cause. The Yugoslav Committee, like the newly formed Polish and Czechoslovak National Councils, enlisted the support of influential friends, such as the prominent archaeologist Sir Arthur Evans and the journalists Wickham Steed and Robert Seton-Watson. The Committee had pursued a vigorous campaign for the dismemberment of Austria-Hungary and the union of South Slavs, using as effective propaganda Bulgaria's aggression against Serbia to generate sympathy in the press.

A meeting between Ante Trumbić, the leading Croat parliamentarian, and Prince Regent Alexander in Paris in April 1916 failed to resolve the conflicting points of view between the Serbian and Croatian positions on how power would be shared in a unified state. Pašić, though still immensely dissatisfied with the loss of Bosnian territories and now of the Banat in the north, nonetheless knew that unless he started to align his views with the conflict-weary West, Serbia would be isolated. On May 30, 1917, the Southern Slav members of the Parliament in Vienna, organized into a "Yugoslav Club," issued a dramatic public declaration that called for the unification of the Serbs, Croats, and Slovenes living in the monarchy into an independent entity under the Habsburg aegis. Led by Serbian prime minister Nikola Pašić and Croatian statesman and exile Trumbić, a full sovereign state was created that summer with the "Corfu Declaration" of July 20, 1917. The following year, on December 1, 1918, the Kingdom of the Serbs, Croats, and Slovenes—the first Yugoslavia—was born.[75]

• • •

Back on the warfront, the gloomy mood among the Allied troops was about to be lifted again in 1918. A Serbian military mission had gone to Petrograd in 1916 to organize Serbian detachments from among the prisoners of war captured by the Russians in their early offensives against the Austro-Hungarian army. In time, Croats, Bosnian Christians, and

Slovenes (though far fewer of them) came to join the Serbian Volunteer Division, made possible by the hopeful spirit of Yugoslav unity. Yet once Russia started to retreat inward owing to the revolutionary convulsions taking place in that country in 1917, these "Yugoslavs" asked to be transferred to the Macedonian Front to aid Russia's nominal allies—a journey from Archangel to France as the Russian Cossacks had made before them, but this time hampered by the Bolsheviks now in power who tried everything to stop them.

Bolshevik commissars, who interviewed each man in the first group of 10,000, denied them the route to the West, forcing the men to go via the trans-Siberian railroad and the Chinese Eastern Railway to Japanese-held ports. From there, ships took them to Hong Kong, across the Indian Ocean to Egypt, and on to Salonika. The first company of this division, mostly men from Bosnia-Herzegovina, arrived on March 29, 1918, having traveled fourteen thousand miles in eleven weeks.[76]

They were the object of fascination in Salonika that spring. They joined the front in groups of fifteen to fifty. Many were attached to the existing six divisions, while the preexisting Vardar Division, to which Mihailović now belonged, was transformed into a South Slav Force—in effect, the first Yugoslav army. Mihailović, fighting alongside these extraordinary men who braved revolution and an odyssey halfway around the world, collaborated closely with these groups. It was from their stories that he first learned about the nature of Communism in Russia. The creation of the Serbian Volunteer Division was one instance of the word *Chetnik*, used to describe some of these volunteer soldiers, the word itself stemming from the word *ćeta*, meaning "group" or "squadron." The term, like that of *comitadjis*, had first come into use in association with Macedonian independence movements against Ottoman control between 1904 and 1912, and Chetniks made up powerful, irregular forces during the Balkan wars of 1912 and 1913 as well as in World War I. The guerrilla-style tactics of these early Chetniks would profoundly influence Mihailović in the years to come.[77]

Also in 1918, Field Marshal Louis Felix Marie Franchet d'Espérey arrived on the scene as the chief of the Allied armies on the Salonika Front, replacing General Guillaumat. Naturally, d'Espérey's last name could not be spared the laconic wit of his Anglo-Saxon comrades: he came to be known, or taunted, as "Desperate Frankie"—and the nickname wasn't entirely just wordplay. He had been removed as commander of the French army of the north after being knocked back by a German advance on the Marne, and General Foch, then commander of the Allied armies, had to hurriedly summon up British, French, and American troops to check the offensive. General Guillaumat was brought back to lead the northern armies. Somewhat perturbed, but still seeing Macedonia as an opportunity to use his talents more independently, d'Espérey prepared for Salonika, and not entirely without a sense of residual affection for his old Balkan stomping ground. With a major military debacle behind him and a skeptical set of bosses back home, enormous pressure was put on the fifty-eight-year-old general and the expanded Allied armies in Macedonia. Yet "desperate" is hardly what would describe the turn of events to take place on the Salonika Front under his command.

Those Allied forces in Macedonia, once a poorly equipped, strategic afterthought, had grown into a dedicated mass of some 700,000 troops. There were nine divisions of Greeks, six divisions of French, six divisions of Serbs, four British divisions, and one Italian division. Even the Czechs contributed 600 men. They were still outsized by the Central Powers but somehow were more inspired.

The two battles of the Salonika Front that would bring the Balkan theater of war to a close—the Battle of Doiran and the Battle of Dobropolje—were about to unfold. The British and the Greeks, led by Field Marshal Milne and the Greek general Emmanuel Zymbrakakis and his Seres Division, headed in the direction of the Vardar Valley near Lake Doiran, which the British had twice failed to capture in 1917. Now, on September 14, 1918, the French and the Serbs, under Field Marshal d'Espérey and Field Marshal Mišić, headed north to attack Bulgarian positions against the lake, where they also met Austro-Hungarian armies led by Field Marshal von Mackensen. The Bulgarians were led by General Vladimir Vazov, brother of the "Dostoevsky of Bulgaria," the writer Ivan Vazov.[78]

A storm of Allied bombardments fell upon Bulgarian trenches, which lined the Vardar Valley around the hills of the so-called Petit Couronné (the "small crowned" hill), the Grand Couronné, and the "Devils Eye," which together framed the Vardar Valley at three points north, south, and east. Although the bunkers of the Bulgarians were exceedingly well constructed and at first successfully held back the Allies, the French and the Serbs would eventually defeat that army. Von Mackensen ordered his Austro-Hungarian and Bulgarian forces out of the Vardar Valley. On the Allied side, 14,000 men died, were incapacitated, or were taken prisoner—in other words, more troops than British general Bernard Montgomery was to lose in Britain's twelve-day campaign at El Alamein in World War II. Though Bulgaria had retreated, she counted only 2,000 casualties.

Immediately following these horrific losses, however, the next two weeks would prove to be the final act in a victory once wholly unexpected by the Entente powers. Ever since fighting had broken out in mid-September, the Serbian First Army had sought a bridgehead on the Crna River, running through southern and western Macedonia, while French and Greek troops began to enlarge the western flank of the Allied troops by storming and settling in on the slopes of a seven-thousand-foot mountain, the Dzena, an assault lasting some forty-eight hours. With extremely poor communication channels, the armies were obliged at times to use carrier pigeons to send messages back and forth to one another.[79]

On September 23 the Serbians crossed the Vardar River, and on the twenty-fourth the French cavalry entered the strategic city of Prilep, while the British opened up the road to Strumitza in northern Macedonia. Both actions created a domino effect of Allied conquests of Bulgarian fortifications. When the British entered the town of Strumitza on the twenty-sixth, the Serbians reached Veles, in southeastern Macedonia, while the Italian, French, and Greek troops together marched near the Serbian and Bulgarian borders. By the evening of the twenty-sixth, the Bulgarians asked for a suspension of hostilities.

On September 29 the Allies broke through the Bulgarian lines at Dobropolje, a region between Monastir and the Vardar Valley, an action in which Mihailović participated with the Vardar Division. The Bulgarian armies were starting to dissolve and were increasingly on bad terms with the Germans of von Scholtz's troops, although Prince Boris—to become king of Bulgaria within a couple of weeks—went desperately around to his men on the battlefield hoping to inspire them to fight. The Serbs, "the hardiest troops in Europe," as one British correspondent at the scene described them, "were tough and frugal, traveling for days without regular rations, living off the countryside."[80] They now began to liberate the area held by enemy troops, led by the Šumadija Division and a cavalry division attached to the Serbian Second Army, further supported by the Seventeenth French Colonial Division (with its colorful Senegalese Saphi troops). Allied air squadrons, meanwhile, also participated through the bombarding and ceaseless machine-gunning of the enemy troops and convoys.

On September 30 the Bulgarians surrendered to the Allies in Salonika, and Czar Ferdinand of Bulgaria, one of the great statesmen of the Balkans, whose Bulgarian armies fought valiantly and very effectively, went gracefully into a productive exile. From there he watched as his world was lost for good: a son who disappeared after a visit to Adolf Hitler in 1943, the end of the Bulgarian monarchy in 1946, and his last surviving son, Prince Kyrill, killed by Communists. The Serbian army liberated Belgrade on November 1, 1918, and only two days later the whole territory of the Kingdom of Serbia was again free. A somber editorial about the Salonika Front in the *London Times* published that November, just before the Armistice, sought to remind the world of the contribution of this much-maligned and forgotten army: "These men in our Eastern armies have had the dust and toil without the laurel, of the race to victory."[81]

Draža Mihailović, meanwhile, after more than five years of war and maintaining positions at Lake Ostrovo and at Dobropolje with the Vardar Division, was promoted to the rank of first lieutenant and awarded one of the highest honors in the Serbian military, the Order of the White Eagle, for outstanding service in battle. He was the only one in his division (the Vardar) to receive the Victoria Cross, the highest honor of the British military. Yet "the race to victory and the lost laurel," as the British press dubbed the Balkan triumph, would return with a catastrophic force in the life of Mihailović less than three decades later.[82]

The Allied victory in Europe was announced on November 11, 1918. The Allied tragedy of the Balkans, however, was only about to begin.

1

Lawrence of Yugoslavia: An Allied Awakening inside a Civil War

Together we were close to each other in body and soul
But did the mountains divide us
Or the rivers?
As David saith, ye mountains of Gilboa
Let there be no dew, neither let there be rain,
For Saul you did not save, nor Jonathon,
O the mercifulness of David
O ye kings, O hear
Is it Saul you are bewailing, O Founder?
For I found, saith the Lord,
A man after my own heart.

—*HOMAGE TO LOVE*, SERBIAN SACRED POETRY,
PRINCE STEFAN LAZAREVIĆ TO HIS BROTHER
PRINCE VUK LAZAREVIĆ, THIRTEENTH CENTURY

In the autumn of 1943, a tall, gallant officer from the American wartime intelligence agency, the Office of Strategic Services (OSS), crisscrossed the mountains of Partisan-held Serbia and Bosnia on horseback and on foot in search of lost and wounded American airmen who, en route from Allied air bases in Italy to the Axis-coveted oil fields at

Ploesti, in Romania, had been shot down by German air patrols. The thirty-two-year-old, Minnesota-born-and-bred major Linn M. "Slim" Farish was a multitalented engineer who specialized in the building of aerodromes and had previously worked all over the world as an oil geologist, but he was known in the OSS as "Lawrence of Yugoslavia," for his epic-worthy stoic heroism in that broken land and his passionate concern for its political and democratic future.

Farish would hardly have described himself in such romantic terms, but others did. His "ability, integrity, loyalty, unselfish devotion to duty and great love for his fellow men caused him to be held in the highest respect, admiration, and affection by Americans, British and Yugoslavs," one OSS report commented on the charismatic leader of the rescue mission.[1] He was so impatient for action that he enlisted in the Canadian army before America's entry into the war in order to get onto the battle-fields of World War II as quickly as possible. Farish's daring alarmed even his future boss, OSS director William J. Donovan, who was also known for his enthusiastic pursuit of heroic missions. Donovan warned Farish that if he did not stop his search for the downed airmen, the young adventurer would collapse from exhaustion. "Major Farish refused to listen to our protests," wrote one OSS officer in a memo summarizing Donovan's plea, "because he knew that American airmen (some of them wounded) were in hourly peril and he was confident he could bring them out safely."[2] The stubborn Farish ignored the appeals of the will-ful Donovan, and into the summer of 1944 he continued to comb the mountains of Serbia in hopes of finding his missing comrades.

For over two and a half years before Farish's arrival, Yugoslavia had been embroiled in a violent civil war within the larger World War II southeast-Balkan theater. This civil war pitted the Partisan-Communist forces of that country and the royalist-nationalist Chetniks against each other; both of these groups fought against the Axis-controlled terror of the Croatian Ustaše, whose main target, in turn, was the Serbian pop-ulation in general. Farish, Stanford University–educated and a former Olympic star, had been named the OSS's senior American officer in the Anglo-American Mission to Tito's Yugoslav National Liberation Army, made up that autumn of around 300,000 men organized across eleven corps and numerous divisions, brigades, and squadrons. Farish arrived on that mission by parachute on September 16, 1943, with British brigadier

Fitzroy Maclean, serving under the aristocratic Scotsman's command, while himself serving as commanding officer of a sub-mission to locate downed airmen and organize their evacuation from Yugoslavia. Traveling thousands of miles over mountainous terrain through enemy territory, Farish located and developed the first evacuation landing strips in Yugoslavia within remote, hard-won pockets of anti-Axis resistance. His intelligence gathering would serve as the basis for the Anglo-American supply program to the Partisans. He was "a large rugged man like a bear, with an amiable grin," wrote Maclean of his American mission partner in his memoir *Eastern Approaches*. "Call me 'Slim,'" said Farish to his equally passionate British counterpart, and thus began what Maclean described as an excellent friendship and working partnership between the two men—although one, it will be seen, quietly rife with Anglo-American rivalry.[3]

The extraordinary distances Farish crossed in the Balkans resulted in his aiding in the rescue of around a hundred American and Allied airmen with the help of fellow mission members and the Partisans themselves. Farish would undertake three missions to Yugoslavia, including additional briefing missions to OSS headquarters in Cairo and to OSS chief Donovan in Washington, D.C., between September 1943 and the early summer of 1944, with one final visit in August 1944. The missions included Farish's arrival at Tito's then headquarters at Jajce, in western Bosnia, during September and October 1943 to locate landing grounds for the future evacuation of downed airmen, and again in January and March 1944, when Farish and fellow officer Lieutenant Eli Popovich met with Tito personally to ask for the Partisan leader's aid in helping the organization of those rescues. Farish would return once again in April through June 1944, this time to Macedonia as part of the OSS's Columbia mission with Popovich and wireless transmission operator Arthur Jibilian. Despite the constant menace of Axis forces, Farish's operations in Yugoslavia were successful across the board, owing, as he saw it, to the well-organized Partisans, whom he admired greatly and whom he found, as a resistance movement, to be "comparable with the American revolutionary war."[4]

The first American flyer to be evacuated from Yugoslavia was a P-47 pilot, Lieutenant Gerald Johnson, who, in January 1944, had been rescued from the Yugoslav mainland by the Partisans and later evacuated from the

Adriatic island of Vis, Tito's Partisan headquarters as of November 1943, under Farish's direction. When Lieutenant Johnson mentioned that he had not been adequately briefed prior to his mission regarding the free areas in Yugoslavia, Farish obtained some maps and outlined those areas of Yugoslavia where Axis forces had no immediate presence. These became the first accurate escape maps developed for the use of the U.S. Army Air Corps in Yugoslavia.

Farish's success in evacuating the airmen was largely the result of the OSS decision to enhance its mission presence and its military aid to the Partisans in early 1944, following the general exploration of Partisan territory that Farish undertook in the autumn of 1943 under Brigadier Maclean's command. Farish was still attached to Maclean's mission when he returned to Yugoslavia for the third time, on a mission to Macedonia formally under the command of British major John Henniker-Major, on April 16, 1944. Accompanied once again by the American lieutenant Eli Popovich and Arthur Jibilian, Farish parachuted into German-held territory in Macedonia in Vranje, near the border of Bulgaria. Their immediate assignment was to locate areas in enemy territory suitable for use as landing fields that would make it possible to rescue downed American and Allied airmen, whose numbers were starting to reach into the hundreds.

The first four airmen the three encountered were the survivors of an attempted air raid on the Ploesti fields, who had landed near Skopje and were brought to Major Farish by the Macedonian Partisan leader General Mihailo Apostolski, who would accompany Farish, Jibilian, and Popovich during the time they were in Macedonia. When the Partisans around Vranje suddenly came under attack by Bulgarian and Chetnik forces, the party ended up marching six days and five nights "almost entirely without sleep" and under fire for most of that time. After crossing the main Skopje-Nis (Serbia) railway line on April 23, 1944, they passed again through enemy lines at Leskovac, located in southern Serbia on the direct route to Salonika, "in the full light" of Axis searchlights used to protect the entrance to the city, once one of Serbia's most flourishing.[5]

Confronted with what would become an ongoing threat from Axis forces, the men left Leskovac, crossing enemy lines near the area of Toplica, in the southeastern corner of Serbia, near the Macedonian border and surrounded by the wild Kopaonik Mountains. At Toplica, Farish's party established a makeshift headquarters in the Radan Mountains, one of the largest mountain ranges in southern Serbia. Ever on the move from hostile Bulgarian troops, the men later passed under a rain of rifle fire through the enemy lines to the Macedonian mountain chain known as the Bela Kamen, where the Serbians and their French and British allies had fought decisive battles at the Salonika Front in 1917 and 1918. Over the course of several miserable weeks in this Macedonian outback, and directing themselves toward the Serbia-Kosovo border, Farish finally found a site he considered suitable for use as a landing field for evacuations: Lipovica, a prominent village with a nearby airfield, located near where the borders of Kosovo, Montenegro, and Serbia meet.

Farish's first rescue was of two American airmen who had been wounded in a parachute descent and trapped near a Bulgarian garrison. Farish rounded up horses from the Macedonian Partisans, and he and his small party entered a village near Lipovica where the men were thought to have fallen. Only the sight of modest, beautiful Serbian monasteries typical of Serbia's "old South" softened the grim poverty of the area. Yet such beauty was obscured by the unexpected and unsightly presence of a large Bulgarian garrison only a few miles away. In an effort to avoid enemy detection, Farish and his team hid themselves in the obscurity of the Bela Kamen Mountains to set up radio contact with OSS headquarters in Bari, Italy, where the U.S. Fifteenth Air Force was stationed, to arrange for Allied transport planes to be sent over. On the way back to their base, Farish and his men found five more airmen who had bailed out of an aircraft in the Toplica valley and who had been escorted by Partisans to Farish's headquarters. Though Farish and his party were successful in finding downed airmen and reassured by Partisan cooperation, they hardly ever felt a moment's worth of calm. For the next ten days the area around their mountain base would be bombed and strafed every afternoon by twenty to thirty German ME-109s.

In spite of the hardships that Farish and his team endured, they were not insensitive to the beauty of the terrain around them or to the spirit of camaraderie that tended to pervade these missions, whether assigned to Partisans or, elsewhere, to their monarchist rivals, the Chetniks. Dobrica Ćosić, in his beautifully written memoir of Partisan life, *Far Away Is the Sun*, wrote of the mountains of the Morava valley in the evening as seen by his otherwise emotionally detached protagonist, describing "the beauty of the night . . . a beauty made purer and sterner by the sharp frost . . . as though the moonlight was drinking up all his anxieties and fears, all his ceaseless, prolonged and tormenting pre-occupation with the company and the struggle."[6] Farish, like his OSS and SOE colleagues in Yugoslavia and the American airmen awaiting rescue, lived such Balkan nights with a sense of relief, sleeping under the stars with hay as a blanket, silently enjoying, if only for a few hours, this eerie and mysterious land that also knew how to pause on occasion from the devastation of war.

But those pauses were indeed brief. The Germans and the Bulgarians had learned about Farish, and Axis forces kept a constant lookout for him through patrols and police; seldom could he move about freely. In addition to being under almost constant attack from small-arms fire, he was subjected to heavy machine-gun fire as well as artillery shelling. He also faced the burning of villages and underbrush near where he hid at times. On at least seven occasions Farish passed through heavy concentrations of German and Bulgarian forces, and yet "[t]he high morale of Major Farish and his party was contagious especially among the natives who joined him in the face of knowledge that they would be tortured to death if discovered by the enemy," reported one OSS memo on Farish's exploits.[7]

About a month before the men were able to organize any rescues, they had made their way from Macedonia to Serbian Partisan headquarters, where they met the Partisan commander, Petar Stambolić (who would become prime minister of Yugoslavia in the 1960s), to ask for Partisan cooperation in saving downed Allied airmen. Stambolić "gave every possible aid," placing at Farish's disposal the Yugoslav Air Force personnel who knew the territory.[8] With the aid of these officers, three airfields were located (two of which were subsequently lost to the Axis). Yet still more attacks were to come. On May 18, 1944, an American heavy bomber was shot down. Axis gunfire prevented Farish and his men from reaching the three wounded American airmen left stranded where the bomber crashed, and ten days passed before Farish received word that the three were still alive.

On May 31 Farish's group tried to get through enemy lines once more. Taking a circuitous route, they spent three nights and four days on the move under constant Bulgarian attack until crossing enemy lines on June 3. They located the three men around the village of Lipovica, all of them wounded, one very seriously. The next morning, Farish and his party managed to escape with the wounded men on an ox-drawn cart, while

Bulgarian forces heavily attacked the village. A day or so later, Farish and Jibilian set out to return to Partisan headquarters in order to make contact with Allied forces in Bari, Italy, to let them know that planes would be needed for evacuation—once the men could remain in place at a landing strip for at least one day, that is.

This would be their most arduous trip yet. Traveling for nearly forty-eight hours without rest or sleep, they arrived at the base of the Radan Mountains, where they were once again involved in an attack on another village, "barely escaping by running their horses under fire from mortar and machine guns," according to one OSS report on the mission.[9] In the meantime, Popovich stayed behind to take care of the wounded, and he managed to do the impossible by leading them through enemy lines. He, Farish, and Jibilian all ended up at Partisan headquarters in Serbia at the same time around June 7, only to find that the wounded airmen had wandered off in the direction of Lipovica, where three of the men had been picked up and where there was an airstrip; the men were somehow under the impression that an evacuation plane was to arrive that night.

However exhausted Farish and Jibilian were, they set out once more to find the men who were headed to Lipovica. As it happened, Axis bombing of villages in the area started up almost immediately, with the Germans eventually occupying the airfield. Farish, Jibilian, and one of the airmen in good condition withdrew to the Bela Kamen Mountains—where, it will be recalled, Farish's team had picked up two wounded American airmen earlier—to figure out another evacuation alternative. Farish decided on one of the other landing strips he had discovered at the beginning of his mission, in the Jastrebac Mountains, in south-central Serbia. Popovich, meanwhile, was dispatched to round up the wounded airmen. Farish thus went to work on the landing strip's preparation. Jibilian, who had sent out a total of 259 wire messages to Bari over the course of his journeys and ordeals, made arrangements for evacuation planes to retrieve the thirteen men, whom Popovich, "with innumerable hardships and difficulties," would eventually find and bring back to Avidlovac on June 14.[10] The planes arrived on June 16 in poor weather conditions, until a last-minute, sudden clearing of the weather allowed a successful rescue effort of the thirteen men, while a large enemy garrison loomed some five miles away.

Farish and Popovich then continued to scout out advanced landing fields in Croatia, while Jibilian was recalled to Bari. Farish came into contact with other American officers, notably Captain Conrad G. Selvig and later Lieutenant Nels J. Benson, who were working with the Partisans in Croatia, both attached to Farish's general mission to the Partisans. Selvig had first dropped into Bosnia on April 6, 1944, and proceeded by foot to Partisan Croatian headquarters at Lika. At this time, the landing ground at Bunic, a village near Lika, was open and available for landing operations, with an airstrip equipped with an Italian electric flare path and a generator pulled by a tractor. With many airmen bailing out over the area and encountering no Axis interference at first, Selvig's optimism was frustrated when, for the rest of April and into early May, despite the many signals sent out from downed airmen, no rescue planes landed at the strip. A German offensive on May 10 in the surrounding area of Krbovsko Polje, an area resonant with the memory of one of Croatia's bloodiest historical battles, forced the mission to move north, and there Selvig discovered an old auxiliary landing field of the Yugoslav Air Force at Gajevi, directly south of Zagreb, right on the south-central border with Bosnia. Here members of the Partisan Fourth Corps, some 23,000 men strong, were scattered throughout the area to patrol the airstrip.

During Selvig's mission, he collected twenty-four airmen and four British prisoners of war who had escaped their captors. The first aircraft arrived on the night of June 8 without prior notice, while Selvig had been "eight hours" away from the landing ground. The American airmen dug the aircraft out of the mud in which it was stuck, and the plane had to be pulled out by fifty oxen. On the night of June 9 the plane left with the twenty-four American airmen, the four British POWs, and five Partisans. Such was the first Allied air contact with Croatia.[11]

The British and the Americans allowed wounded Partisans to be transported back and forth, and the Partisans took good advantage of such generosity. In early July 1944, sixty-two American- and British-operated DC-3s landed at the Gajevi airstrip, which Farish, Popovich, and Lieutenant Benson (taking over from Captain Selvig) had constructed with Partisan help. Twelve Russian-operated American planes landed as well, with fifty tons of supplies brought for the Partisans, who in turn presented to Farish a diverse group of evacuees to be taken to Bari. These included, in addition to 164 American airmen, a total of 957 Partisan wounded; 177 Partisan couriers, officials, and students; 38 Jewish refugees; and 680 more civilians. Several wounded Italian soldiers, veterans of the Garibaldi Division then fighting with Tito, were also present, as well as 821 Partisan orphans among whom were 69 babies in one plane who had been "collected under the very noses of the Germans and . . . taken to a hidden airport."[12] ("The best passengers I have ever had," reported the pilot to the *Los Angeles Times* correspondent at the OSS base in Bari.)[13] Later that month, another hundred Jewish Yugoslavs appeared on the Gajevi strip with Partisan papers stating that they were to be evacuated. After an exchange of hurried signals with Bari, Lieutenant Benson finally received his okay, and the evacuation of those Yugoslav Jews began.[14]

Some Partisans had set up a makeshift evacuation hospital near the airstrip to alleviate the problem of transporting the wounded back and forth. When air force rescue planes did not come through one evening because of bad weather, Farish had over eighty ox-drawn wagons loaded up with wounded on the airstrip to take them to the Partisans' makeshift hospital. "Those poor armless and legless guys made a five hour trip in a cruelly bouncing wagon with rain steaming down all for nothing," wrote Farish in his report back to the OSS that autumn. "Three cases died that night. Despite my urgent appeals for stretchers and blankets, by far the greatest majority of the wounded were sent out almost naked and lying on the bare floor of the planes."[15]

Just before being summoned to help coordinate this diverse group of evacuees, Benson had parachuted into Croatia on the night of June 10, 1944, as part of the Altmark mission, to take over the landing-strip operations at Gajevi from Captain Selvig. His own exploits would have qualified him for the "Lawrence of Yugoslavia" title as well. Over the course of this mission, the twenty-four-year-old Benson would help to rescue 164 American airmen in the process, and not without a good dose of drama, to boot. Though well assisted by members of the Partisan Fourth Corps, Benson had given no thought to the possibility of enemy action against his activities. But, sure enough, in late June, the first Dornier 17 flew overhead, making one strafing run on some laborers on the field and then flying away. From that point on, Benson had a reconnaissance plane circling overhead almost every day. The attacks continued until early July. Then on July 4 another Dornier 17 came whizzing overhead, dropping 1,100 kite bombs onto the airfield. There were no direct hits to the strip itself, but the attacks left two bomb craters twelve feet across and ten feet deep just fifty yards apart on either edge of the approach end of the airstrip's flare path. Even so, that evening eight rescue aircraft managed to land between the two bomb craters without mishap.

But only then did the enemy air strikes begin in earnest. Lieutenant Benson and his men had learned to expect enemy air attacks early in the morning, and so on July 26 they were not surprised to suddenly find three CR-42s attacking them at dawn; for the first time their own quarters were damaged. For forty-five minutes the planes made low strafing runs on the three small buildings Benson and his men occupied, dropping three bombs on them. The men moved to a local house, yet the attacks began again in the late afternoon with four planes this time, catching Farish taking a short rest inside. Benson managed to get only twenty yards from the house when the first strafing run pinned him down. He hid in a one-foot-high cornfield that felt "as big as the Empire State Building" with the gunfire missing him by half an inch. The angle of one of the bullets was such that when it exploded, its force went away from Benson, stinging him sharply in the leg, but giving a Partisan soldier who was hiding in the field with him severe face wounds and resulting in the loss of his left eye.[16] The raid lasted for an hour and forty-five minutes and resulted in five casualties. The damage to the buildings made them uninhabitable. On the evening of June 26, Benson, Farish, and the men moved to a house in the hills south of the air base, as the daily strafing of all buildings near the airstrip continued.

As the Germans began to close in, the evacuation team abandoned Gajevi, and it became necessary to start looking for yet another landing strip. Soon they found one: a long, well-drained plain about a mile and a quarter west of the village of Glina, in a remote corner of northwestern Croatia. In early August the first landing operation took place at Glina, and soon the landing ground operations fell into a well-organized pattern, with supplies coming regularly to help clean up the wounded.

It was at Glina that Benson first encountered the unreliability of Russian aircraft (alternating with Anglo-American or American-operated landings), coming in at staggered intervals. Several planned rescue missions of wounded airmen were missed owing to the pilots of these planes either misunderstanding the prearranged landing times or misreading the flares shot up by Benson.

Meanwhile, a constant stream of Allied visitors, including everyone from Major Randolph Churchill, Winston's personal emissary to Tito, to weeklong inspection tours by Farish, passed through Glina. This reassuring spirit of comradeship, however, did little to make matters less complicated. When one Lieutenant Egone Bessiggio arrived at Glina on July 22, with thirteen Americans, nine British, sixteen French, and "five other escapees" in tow, the Partisans, immediately suspecting an Italian spy, arrested Bessiggio and refused to let the others leave. Despite the insistence of two of the newly arrived Americans, who vouched for him as an SI (Special Intelligence) man from Bari—of Italian origin, perhaps, but a man fully in the Allied camp, they argued—the Partisans would hear none of it. Bessiggio and the men languished in prison as Benson undertook a quasi-diplomatic mission to persuade the Fourth Corps to release them. The Partisans refused, insisting on obtaining a clearance from Tito, which came a month later, all the while Benson was unable to visit them "or bring them tobacco."[17]

Not too long after that, Benson was with the Partisan Fourth Corps when a clash with Croatian Ustaše forces broke out on September 13 at Cazin, in northwestern Bosnia on the border with Croatia. The Partisans killed 130 Ustaše members and took 180 as prisoners. The violence and death became etched in the memory of the lieutenant, as he recalled in his later report the "white bodies gleaming in the sun" of Ustaše dead stripped of their clothing, which "were still there when the Partisans were forced to retreat five days later."[18]

Despite the extraordinary events unfolding before his eyes, Benson helped to oversee sixty-two Anglo-American landings at Gajevi, thirty-nine American-operated landings at Glina, and twelve Russian-operated landings at Glina during his four-month stay in Croatia. On September 24 Benson was summoned back to Bari, but poor weather delayed his trip until October 10. After releasing his radio to Randolph Churchill ("to help him with his mission"), Benson left Partisan territory for good, with perhaps the most diverse record, shared with Farish, of rescues behind him: over 150 Allied airmen, nearly 1,000 wounded Partisans, nearly 1,000 orphaned children, and over three dozen Jews were flown to safety at Bari.

Such stories highlighted Farish's favorable reports on the Partisans, both after his first mission to those forces in September 1943 and in subsequent reports in March and July 1944. Farish's affection for the Partisans was boundless, seeing few of them as Communist ideologues but as enthusiastic, modest, dedicated civilians wanting to liberate their country from foreign occupation. The first report had been provided to President Franklin Roosevelt before the Tehran Conference in November 1943, thus encouraging the president to adopt the British pro-Tito stance for which, among other things, that conference became most known. (Ironically, at that conference, Soviet foreign minister Vyacheslav Molotov had suggested to his British counterpart, Anthony Eden, that the Soviets might provide a liaison to General Draža Mihailović's Chetniks, "in order to get better information," an idea that never materialized.)[19]

While Farish was critical of the Chetniks overall, he believed Mihailović's Chetniks to be an exception, and that the field reports on them from his liaison officers "should be taken into consideration."[20] But his heart was first and foremost with the Partisan cause, and in his March 1944 report he urged the United States to get more involved. "As matters stand we are running a poor third in our relations with the Partisans," he wrote, "which I feel is out of proportion to our interest in them and the actual aid we are giving them. The Russian mission is completely staffed and commanded by high-ranking officers. Brigadier Maclean is a direct link between the prime minister and Marshal Tito."[21]

In a later report submitted to the OSS, Farish expressed disappointment that the Partisans and the Chetniks could not be reconciled. He feared the escalating violence and brutality that would stem from a full-scale civil war in Yugoslavia—a war that would be fought with weapons Farish had helped to provide. In September 1944 Farish was killed in an airplane crash in Greece, en route to a rescue mission in that country when the motors of his transport plane failed for an undetermined reason. A posthumous OSS award of the Distinguished Service Cross to Farish in 1945 cited his "extraordinary heroism" and "his resolute conduct in the face of great peril."[22] It was Farish's basic love for the Yugoslavs, however, that perhaps made his character most memorable: "A normal, peasant type group of people, unwilling to submit passively to oppression, have brought this atmosphere of freedom into being," he wrote in a March 9, 1944, report for the OSS on his activities. "It is these common people who have served so well and suffered so gravely, that we must consider. Nothing that we can do for them will be out of proportion to their contribution to the common cause."[23]

• • •

Around the time that Farish's mission had regrouped to look for Allied soldiers stranded in Partisan-held territory, another group of Americans had made emergency parachute landings in Serbia, only this time falling into the Chetnik-controlled areas of central Serbia. Late one afternoon in January 1944, the airmen had parachuted into the deep snows of the Zlatibor Mountains of southwestern Serbia, which provided a soft, if bracing, cushion for the ten of them, who now found themselves stranded in the dark Balkan wilderness. The three engines of their B-17, en route from Bari, Italy, to survey oil fields in Ploesti, Romania, had been hit by German fighter planes, separating them from what had been the team's one-hundred-plane mission to Romania. In addition to facing Germany's dominance of Yugoslav airspace, flying conditions in the Balkans were among the most challenging in Europe, and it was not long before hundreds of American pilots, once coasting the heavens just above Yugoslavia's intimidating mountain peaks, came suddenly tumbling down from the skies like modern-day sons of Icarus, aspiring heroes shot down by greater forces.

The uninjured men moved blindly in the forest-dense darkness of the mountains as the winter evening closed down upon them, knowing German patrols could spring upon them at any moment. The leader of the crew, the twenty-year-old Texan Gus Brown, after orienting himself, decided to walk with his men across the mountain range through to Montenegro and on to the Adriatic Sea in hopes of reaching Allied transport there, perhaps unaware that such a plan was eerily similar to an epic chapter of Serbian history just thirty years prior. Except Brown and his men would not make history by undertaking a journey by foot to the Adriatic, but, as fate would have it, by simply staying where they were. For theirs would be a year of outstanding joint Chetnik Serbian–American heroism, and they were to be among the first in a series of rescue missions of Allied airmen by the Chetniks against what would become nearly impossible political and logistical odds. Brown and his airmen became the first American crew to be rescued by Serbian Chetniks, and Brown himself was the first American airman to meet General Mihailović.

The airmen had been moving silently through the mountain woods when a sudden explosion of gunshot tore through the still night air. A violent chorus of dogs barking aggressively followed the explosions, while a tense murmur of human voices echoed from all directions. A trail of lanterns appeared, heading down the mountain in the direction of the airmen, casting lambent shadows on the dense blocks of trees. The young Americans hid under their parachutes, camouflaging themselves in the snow as the light from the lanterns came within thirty feet of where the airmen sought cover. Then the lanterns abruptly turned and began to trail off in another direction. As the wind-bitten, subzero temperatures of the Balkan winter continued to wear down the motionless young airmen, they began, in their panic, to holler, fearing more the possibility of being left to freeze to death in the ice and snow than the risk of being discovered and taken prisoner or shot by Germans.[24]

Someone answered from afar, and the Americans waited a good half hour until they saw a figure standing right at the back of their parachutes. "American," said one of the airmen cautiously, and he and his comrades stood and threw up their hands. Suddenly, a group of Serbian Chetniks came pouring down the mountainside, greeting the men warmly and kissing them in the traditional manner on both cheeks. Cigarettes were offered—that most appreciated of soldier-to-soldier peace gestures—and the Chetniks accompanied the men off the mountain and out of the forest, on what would become a six-week journey by foot to the headquarters of the Serbian Chetnik leader Mihailović.

What Brown and his men did not realize then is that they were the first American crew to land in territory controlled by Mihailović and his men. About six months later the Halyard Mission, a rescue described by the OSS as "one of the most glamorous events of the war," would take place in the same territory.[25] Brown and his American men were, however, extremely cautious: like all American crews en route through Yugoslavia from the Allied bases at Bari, Lecce, or Foggia, Italy, where they were originally stationed, they had been warned to avoid the Serbian Chetniks at all costs and to trust only Tito's Partisans, whom they would recognize by their caps with red stars. Yet the unexpectedly warm reception offered to the young men almost at once alleviated any anxieties they had about the Chetniks, and without a moment's hesitation they proceeded to follow their Serbian guides to a small house in the mountain woods.

En route, shooting started anew in the distance as another group of Chetniks began to fight off an encroaching German patrol unit. Once at the Chetnik village house, the Chetnik guards took out Serbian plum brandy—the legendary slivovitz—and the American airmen started drinking toasts to the Allied cause. The next day thirty Chetniks and some horses for the men were organized to accompany the men to a village near the ever-shifting headquarters of Mihailović, which was at the time fifteen miles from the southwestern town of Pranjani.

Their month-and-a-half-long journey involved a series of deft hide-and-seek maneuvers through valleys, mountain paths, rivers, highways, railroads, and railroad stations that often boasted the formidable presence of a massive, armored German train resting imperially on the tracks, a symbol of Germany's universal sense of supremacy reaching deep into the Balkan backwoods. The thirty or so Chetniks leading the American crew members stayed with the men the entire way, sharing everything with them, even giving the Americans half of their own rations.[26] Six of the Americans made the journey without shoes; the Chetniks themselves were mostly without shoes, walking in snow two feet deep with rags wrapped around their feet for the journey. The group traveled carefully around the heavily monitored Serbian cities of Užice and Požega, at one point forced to camp out at a schoolhouse for a few days while German patrols lurked nearby. As soon as their courage could spur them to action, the men would be on the run again, traversing streams, stones, mountain clearings, and mud-choked highways, frequently pursued by the lone German patrol car or two, but ever energized by the rush of escaping from one danger to embrace another.

By the end of February, the airmen finally arrived at Mihailović's headquarters. There, they were told, was an American officer who had been in Serbia since mid-October 1943. This was Captain George Musulin. The twenty-five-year-old former Pittsburgh Panthers (of the University of Pittsburgh) football star—and quarterback for the Pittsburgh Steelers in 1938—was now an OSS officer. Of Serbian parentage, he had first landed near the city of Čačak on October 16, 1943, in one of the first American liaison missions to General Mihailović. Musulin was responsible for the Repartee mission, assigned to gather intelligence on German operations in the Chetnik leader's territories and to report on any German-Chetnik acts of collaboration.

Over the course of this mission, Musulin's first to Serbia, he and the Chetniks rescued thirteen airmen who had been shot down over Chetnik territory (not one of whom, testifying after the war to an American commission at the trial of Mihailović, said that they had witnessed any acts of collaboration with the Germans on the part of Mihailović or his Chetniks). In February 1944, Musulin was the last of the initial group of American OSS men who had served as liaison officers to Mihailović to depart from Serbia. Their departure had been on order (and insistence) of the British, who by that time had halted all supplies to Mihailović and the Chetniks. Nonetheless, thanks to the maverick stubbornness of these OSS airmen, and with the support of their staunch ally, OSS chief William Donovan, on August 2, 1944, Musulin, with three other OSS liaison officers as well as Colonel Robert McDowell in a small, separate SI detachment, would return again to lead the Halyard mission, the fabled rescue of hundreds of stranded airmen in those Chetnik-dominated territories.

But if that mission was indeed the stuff of fairy tales, the reality it would leave behind in the host country where it took place would prove anything but a happy ending. A somewhat heartbreaking omen of this fate greeted Lieutenant Brown, the leader of the ten downed airmen in the Zlatibor Mountains, as he arrived solemnly at Pranjani on horseback with Chetnik escorts in late February 1944 to meet Mihailović. The young airman saluted the now fifty-one-year-old Serbian general upon being introduced. But Mihailović deplored any such formalities. "All I want out of the war," he told Brown upon their meeting, "is a little bit of America in Yugoslavia." He sought no personal gain, he explained (nor did he receive any financial compensation). "I want a scrap of the Atlantic Charter and a bit of America."[27] He was unaware that only a few months earlier, London and Washington had officially decided to abandon him for good.

2

The Mountain at Dawn

The mountain draws a man to itself, to the sky, to man. There
the struggle that reigns within everything and among all things
is even more marked, but purer, unsullied by daily cares and
wants. It is the struggle between light and darkness. Only there
on the mountain are the nights so vast, so dark, and the morn-
ings so gleaming. There is a struggle within everything, and
among things. . . . Men on the mountain are an even greater
mystery.

—MILOVAN DJILAS, *LAND WITHOUT JUSTICE*

The history of Serbia is the history of its mountains, "the desolate
mountains," as the nineteenth-century Serbian writer Peter Kocić
described them, which "are as much heroes as the people who struggle
against them."[1] It is here "the whole landscape is seamed with paths as an
old man's face is seamed with wrinkles, but where they lead to is a mystery," wrote Anne Kindersley, a British traveler in postwar Yugoslavia.[2]
"The eagle makes his nest in the mountains because there is no freedom in
the valleys," goes the Serbian proverb. The mythological Vilas of Serbian
poetry were born in the mountains: beautiful, supernatural goddesses
who were mostly hostile to humans but who loved great heroes. They
are "strange and solemn beings," as the Victorian writer Edward Bulwer-
Lytton described them in his epic translation of the Kosovo ballad cycle,
"rarely seen but often making [themselves] heard from the mountain
and the wild, their voice of prophecy and of warning—menacing and

sometimes deadly to man when he invades their 'mighty solitudes,' yet gifted with beneficent powers and healing arts."[3] It was the Vilas who instructed the great Serbian hero Prince Marko Kraljević, a rebel against Ottoman rule, to go to Mount Urvina, where he would die a peaceful death. He accepted this fate and went to the mountain, where his battle wounds were immediately healed. As legend has it, the immortal prince remains there, but asleep, and he will return one day to his land below to lead and inspire the destiny of Serbia.

On the southern border of Kosovo lie the pine and sycamore-rich Šar Mountains, which the medieval Serbian king Stephan II Nemanja established as the territorial border of his realm in the early thirteenth century. The nearby Sandžak, stretching along the border of Bosnia-Herzegovina and marking the border between Montenegro and Serbia, was the center of ancient Rascia, where one of the country's most important monasteries, Mileševa, was built on a mountain to avoid the pillage of invading Ottoman Turks. It was there that Prince Lazar was betrayed to the Turks, as some legends maintain and others dispute, by his noble kinsman Vuk Branković, before the battle on Kosovo Polje in 1389.[4] Branković "fled to the mountain greenery" to protect himself and became Serbia's only soldier-leader to survive the slaughter, as recounted in one of the first Western histories of that battle by the Italian Dalmatian writer Mavro Orbini, in 1601.[5]

The Štara Planina and Carpathian mountains on the eastern part of the country and the chain of the Dinaric mountains on the western side encircle the central part of Serbia—the Šumadija or "wooded land," known as the wild heartland of Serbia.[6] Here, the country's famous oaks spread as a natural barrier to the enemy; it was under the oak of Takovo where a kiss to the Cross swore loyalty to Serbian kings. In the fourteenth century, Šumadija was settled by people driven north after the Battle of Kosovo, and the Belgian-French diplomat Ogier Ghislain de Busbecq, the ambassador of the Holy Roman Emperor to the Sublime Porte, traveling through the region, wrote about the beautiful song-laments practiced by the Serbs. The First and Second Uprisings against the Turks under Peter Karadjordjević took place in 1804 at Takovo and again in 1815 under the wary leadership of the rival dynasty of Milos Obrenović, at Topčider, just outside of Belgrade. The organization of the first guerrilla bands of World War II took place in the Šumadija, as did the worst massacre of the Serbs to occur in a single day in that war, in the mountain town of Kragujevac. Nearby is Avala, an extinct volcano, topped by the Memorial to the Unknown Soldier, by the renowned Croatian sculptor Ivan Meštrović.

In the rugged, limestone-rich Dinaric range of the southwestern part of the country one finds the historical border region between Serbia and Bosnia, Štari Vlach. This beautiful "Old Shepherd" country of meadows covered with wildflowers—silene, black vanilla orchid, lychnis—is a land where civilizations clashed and entire nationalities were uprooted, yet where families also stayed behind to dig roots even deeper into land cherished over generations. "The people are Orthodox, of mixed blood, the descendants of ancient Illyrians fleeing the Celts," writes Kindersley, "medieval shepherds from Albania seeking their fortune in prosperous Serbia; and nineteenth-century *Kutzovlachs* from Northern Greece escaping the notorious Ali Pasha of Jannina."[7] On a hill near the predominant mountain of Zlatibor—named after its special "golden pines"—one finds the borderline markings of the Kingdom of Serbia, Austro-Hungary, and the Ottoman Empire. Here, the mountain of Cer hosted one of the great Serbian victories of World War I and the nearby mountain town of Užice became the short-lived but noteworthy military state of Tito's Partisans.

Just southeast is the Golija Planina, ringed by some of the most exquisite monasteries in the country—Studenica, Sopočani, Štari Ras—where around one hundred bird species are found among sixty-foot waterfalls and where fighting against the Ottoman Turks was once at its most intense. Just at the foot of the Golija Planina and a short distance away is Ivanjica, with its fields of wild globe flowers and spruce-dominated meadows, "a town that is half apple orchard" and "whose own struggles represent Serbian history in a nutshell," as Kindersley recounts. Ivanjica, burned and rebuilt repeatedly through wars and rebellions, was the birthplace of Draža Mihailović, on April 27, 1893.[8] Some fifty years later, at the square fortress rock of the Mučanj mountains nearby, he would hold out during one of his longest struggles against his archrival, the Partisan-Communist leader Josip Broz Tito.

And it is here, slightly to the east of Ivanjica, that one reaches the most important area of all these mountains, itself but a hilly grazing area: the Ravna Gora, on the western slopes of Mount Suvobor in the northeast corner of Gorni Milanovac, in western Serbia. At Ravna Gora, the southern side of which offers a resplendent view of Serbia and eastern Bosnia, the core of what is usually acknowledged as the first resistance force of World War II was formed in mid-May 1941 out of a core thirty or so officers and privates from the Royal Yugoslav Army, led by World War I hero Draža Mihailović.[9]

Following the invasion of Yugoslavia on April 6, 1941, by Germany, Italy, and Bulgaria, Mihailović's group of Serbian officers fled to the mountains in small bands, moving into the dark, mountainous interior of Bosnia, where there was little German presence. Mihailović, stationed in Bosnia as chief of staff of the Royal Yugoslav Army, received permission from his new commander in chief, the eighteen-year-old King Peter II Karadjordjević, to stay behind and form a resistance. The king had established a government in exile from several officers from the High Command of the Royal Yugoslav Army, led by Air Force General Dušan Simović and General Bora Mirković, the plotters of the March 27, 1941, coup d'état against the Cvetković-Maček government of the king's uncle, Prince Paul, who had reluctantly sent his prime minister, Dragiša Cvetković, to sign on to Adolf Hitler's Tripartite Pact at Belvedere Palace in Vienna just days before.

The coup leaders, consisting of a nucleus of political figures and the young king, had left the country following the invasion, an escape that drew sharp criticism at home and abroad.[10] Those leaders eventually departed for Athens, the first stop in a series of moves as the Royal Yugoslav government in exile, continuing on to Alexandria, Jerusalem, Cairo, and ultimately London in June 1941, then back to Cairo in late 1943, and once again to London in March 1944. (Over the course of the war there were about a dozen so-called governments in exile that eventually settled in London: the Czechoslovak, the Polish, the "Free French" of General Charles de Gaulle, and the Swedish, to name a few.) At the time the coup was hailed as "a lightning flash illuminating a dark landscape," in the words of the *New York Times*.[11]

But the embarrassingly swift collapse of the Yugoslav army as well as the never-ending, conspiratorial infighting of the many political parties of the government in exile, was an uneasy foundation for Mihailović politically. Staunchly behind him, however, were King Peter II himself, Slobodan Jovanović, the first prime minister of the exiled government, and Božidar Purić, a later prime minister. With enough faith in the capabilities of such support, Mihailović hoped to get his resistance off the ground. Some 300,000 Serbia-based officers and soldiers from the Yugoslav High Command were now on the run through the mountains and forests of the country, approximately 180,000 would be taken prisoner by the Germans, and somewhere among such chaos were hundreds of weapons depots scattered across the Yugoslav terrain.[12]

Of course, Mihailović had not then counted on the swift organization of the Partisan movement, that it would attract not only a larger number of former High Command officers and soldiers (who were by no means necessarily Communist), but also that the reprisal policies of the Germans, aimed at demoralizing the "nationalist" sentiment among Serbs, would attract local populations to the cause of the Partisans, for which the latter established aggressive propaganda campaigns. It was those men who were suspicious of Tito's political ambitions, and did not join (or were captured by) the pro-German regime of General Milan Nedić, who were to form the foundation for this controversial and historically underrated resistance force, the Ravnogorski Pokret—the "Ravna Gora Movement."

• • •

Mihailović was an obvious choice as the leader of this initial group of men as they made the April retreat to the mountains. The handsome, fair-haired maverick had, to begin with, enormous personal appeal and sensible political views in a time of of ideological extremism. "Mihailovich had, when he cared to use it, extraordinary personal charm," recounted Jasper Rootham, a British liaison officer to Mihailović. "Whether or not in reality he was really puffed up, he always had the air of a modest and indeed sometimes of a diffident man."[13] In 1920 he married Jelica Lazarević and had four children, one of whom died in infancy and another of whom, Vojislav, would serve with his father in World War II. A devout monarchist and Christian, his politics appeared to be moderate but liberal. He protested the 1919 assassination of Stepha Radić, the leader of the Croatian Peasant Party, and was a critic of King Alexander Karadjordjević. He was opposed to the establishment of the king's decree of January 6, 1929, which gave the monarch nearly absolute rule. He was also unhappy with the new prime minister of that centralized government, General Peter Zivković of the White Hand, a radical offspring of the Black Hand of World War I.

Already intimately familiar with the terrain, which he learned as a young lieutenant during World War I, Mihailović sought long before the outbreak of war to convince the Yugoslav government of the necessity of light, fast, guerrilla-style mobile units. But his independent, rebellious tendencies had often been too much for the army hierarchy. During the interwar period he attended the graduate school of the Belgrade military academy, where he became convinced of the effectiveness of guerrillalike tactics for the military. In 1934 and 1936 he served in Sofia and Prague as a military attaché. During subsequent military posts in Slovenia from May 1937 to April 1940, he angered General Milan Nedić, then minister of the army and navy, by writing a long letter criticizing the level of preparedness of the Yugoslav Armed Forces and suggesting that they be reorganized on a territorial basis in which there would be separate Serbian, Croatian, and Slovenian armies under a joint General Staff. He urged that instead of costly fortifications as had been established along the Italian and Austrian borders following Hitler's Anschluss with Austria on March 12, 1938, properly trained guerrilla battalions should be formed. He emphasized the importance of an underground army, an intelligence network, and the ability to stage a well-timed general uprising, if necessary. Anything else, he argued, would result in the German army's forcing the Yugoslavs into a repeat of the Retreat to the Adriatic of World War I. His maverick style extended into the political sphere when he provided Czechoslovakian officers with Yugoslav passports after the collapse of Czechoslovakia in September 1938. With Germany's invasion of Poland on September 1, 1939, Mihailović helped Polish officers who fled through Romania to Belgrade, giving them passports to enter France and England.

All this proved too much for General Milan Nedić, who, although strong-willed in his own right—as a young colonel he had provided cover for the retreating soldiers and civilians during the march to the Adriatic in 1915 and 1916 and led an infantry brigade at the Salonika Front in September 1918—felt Mihailović was too independent-minded. At age forty-five Mihailović was recalled from his post as military chief of staff in Slovenia. General Nedić threatened him with court martial and expulsion from the General Staff branch. When several generals and politicians protested, he was put under thirty days' house arrest instead. He was arrested again in November 1940 for attending, in uniform, a political gathering arranged by the British military attaché in Belgrade. On yet another occasion he was arrested and sentenced to ten days in jail for refusing to withdraw a report in which he accused politicians of diverting funds intended for defense. His name was then struck from the list of promotions to the rank of brigadier general, and his military career was left on the verge of collapse.

Nonetheless, the rebel in Mihailović persisted. In spite of the arrests, threats, and demotions, he returned to the Belgrade military academy to teach a course on guerrilla warfare that was very popular among younger officers. To win support for his doctrine, he courted opposition politicians and journalists. His chief political allies were Milan Gavrilović, head of the Serbian Agrarian Party; General Dragoslav Milosavljević, chief of military intelligence; and Jovan Tanović, editor in chief of the leading Belgrade newspaper, *Politika*. Such allies were able to convince the new ruling regent, Prince Paul, the successor to King Alexander, that Mihailović's "Report" was valid and potentially very useful. Impressed by the boldness of the rebel-colonel, the General Staff issued orders to organize a Chetnik division and, in the end, to publish Mihailović's views. The division was to be made up of six full-strength battalions and one partial battalion, and to be recruited on a volunteer basis from the regular army. Mihailović and his concept of a strong guerrilla force within the Royal Army had triumphed.

Or it did at least on paper. For with the chaotic chain of events following the officers' "bloodless" coup (Mihailović was a supporter but not a participant), the Axis invasion of April 6 left Mihailović with his would-be Chetnik division as a hypothetical concept. Though he had, as mentioned earlier, the blessing of the new monarch, King Peter II, and the support of the coup leaders to stay behind and form a resistance, his struggle to gather together a consistent and loyal force from the traumatized, dispersed royal army was a daunting one. There was also the problem of money. Initially, British intelligence arranged through a courier in Istanbul to bring Mihailović's budding movement £20,000 (about $32,000).[14] Through a local system of couriers making contact with escaped military personnel, Mihailović's Chetniks received money from individual loyalists and a network of relatives.[15] According to the memoirs of the former head of German intelligence, William Höttel, writing under the pseudonym "Walter Hagen," Mihailović sent one of his lieutenants to ask for financial assistance from the ambitious, pro-German activist Dimitri Ljotić.[16] Höttel also claimed that the director of the Serbian National Bank had an agreement with General Nedić to finance "the Chetniks" (this most likely meant all "anti-Communist" groups, not just, supposedly, Mihailović's Chetniks).[17]

Sources tend to vary as to how many men Mihailović started out with and how many he came to command at any one time. At first, the Germans ignored the many Yugoslav military personnel running around loose in the capital. According to three of the standard works on the Yugoslav civil war—by the German historian Klaus Schmider, the English scholar Lucian Kuchmar, and the Croatian scholar Jozo Tomasevich—by the time Mihailović reached Ravna Gora in mid-May 1941, he had the thirty or so men with him, as mentioned previously, most from the Yugoslav Second Army.[18] Yet despite such modest beginnings, sources maintain that by late summer 1941, around a thousand men had joined Chetnik ranks—from a multilingual former Royal Army officer to a peasant-fighter patrolling the mountains. Estimates of Mihailović's new Royal Yugoslav Army of the Homeland (Kraljevska Jugoslovenska Vojska u Otadžbini or "KJVuO"), the official—and preferred—name of his growing Chetnik army numbered what sources average out to have been about 70,000 men under Mihailović's *direct* command. These numbers become somewhat confused in light of the fact that overall in Serbia, there were other "Chetnik" bands organizing themselves independently whose politics were more neutral-to-supportive of the Axis occupation. Roughly speaking, all of these "Chetnik" groups, together with Mihailović's Army of the Homeland, numbered between 115,000 and 118,000 men in total.[19]

While dominated by the Serbs, the wartime Chetniks were not exclusively monarchist-nationalist Serbs. One Croatian Chetnik commander, Matija Parać, had been a member of the Croatian *Domobrans*, or "National Home Guard," before he deserted that army to join the Chetniks. The Croatian Zvonimir Vucković was one of the top Chetnik leaders and Mihailović's trusted commander of the First Ravna Gora Corps, an experience wistfully recounted in his 2004 memoir, *A Balkan*

Tragedy, Yugoslavia 1941–1946: Memoirs of a Guerrilla Fighter.[20] Croats also participated in the formidable Dinaric Chetnik Division in Dalmatia under the powerful and controversial Vojvoda Momčilo Djurić. The Montenegrin-Serb Chetniks were the most numerous. In Slovenia, the Chetniks were originally organized in 1941 by two Slovene Yugoslav army majors: Jože Melaher, who organized the Štarjeska ("Styria") Chetnik movement, and Karel Novak, who recruited Chetniks around the Slovenian capital of Ljubljana. At first, because of their small numbers, these three or four hundred Slovene Chetniks were incorporated into an Italian anti-Communist militia, the Milizia Volontaria Anti-Communisti (MVAC), under the name Legion of Death (Legia Smrti). Later, as the MVAC took in more strongly pro-Axis Slovene forces such as the "Sokol" Legion and the Slovene Domobrans, the Chetniks, under the leadership of Novak, broke away and eventually increased their numbers to around one thousand men, unofficially named the Blue Guard.

The Slovene Chetniks were largely attracted to the promise of Mihailović that the Axis-annexed areas of Koruška on Slovenia's northern border with Austria, and Primovska, on the eastern side of Slovenia at the border with Italy, would be returned to Slovenia after the war. These Slovenes also included those who fought in Mihailović's First Ravna Gora Corps, such as the well-regarded postwar economist Aleksander Bajt; the historian Uroš Šusterić, who, like the Croatian Vucković, authored a personal account of his Chetnik experience, *From Ljubljana to Ravna Gora*; and Leon Stukelj, later a three-time gold medal Olympic gymnast.

Bosnian Muslims who served in the prewar Royal Yugoslav Army also joined the Chetniks, led by the commander Mustafa Mulačić, a commander at Bijeljina, in western Bosnia. The reasons behind this diverse following were varied. Often it a matter of ideology: The Chetnik "ideology" was monarchist and strictly anti-Communist. Hence, the presence of Croatians, Slovenians, and Bosnian Muslims who subscribed to such political sentiment among Chetnik ranks. It was also a matter of pragmatics, as in the case of Slovenian Chetniks, for example, who counted on the promises of Mihailović that he would restore to them those northern and eastern border lands annexed by the Axis after the war, as mentioned above. There was, as well, a certain aspect of social elitism: a pro-Yugoslav, pro-Serb proclivity often meant a fast-track career into the Serbian officers' elite, just as it had been socially and professionally advantageous, for example, under Austro-Hungarian rule to adopt, as a Balkan officer, a pro-Austrian stance. Despite this mixed composition of the Chetniks, the reputation of that group's guerrilla movement became almost synonymous with Serbian "nationalism"—an understandable term then but a misleading one by today's standards. Just as it is generally known that not all Partisans were necessarily Communists, one must keep in mind that most Chetniks were Yugoslav monarchists and anti-Communist, but not pro-Nazi. Serbs dominated their ranks and their political outlook.

By most accounts, Mihailović himself did not subscribe to the "Greater Serbia" ideology that some of his rival Chetnik commanders espoused, though some scholars insist his nationalism had a radical cast.[21] The controversial "right wing" element of the broad category of "Chetnik" naturally leads to the widespread belief that all or most Chetniks advocated collaboration with Axis forces. While this theme is discussed in detail in later chapters, for now it suffices to say that the issue of collaboration involves a far more complex set of wartime circumstances than one might care to untangle. The most systematic collaboration on Mihailović's official watch occurred with the Dalmatia-based Chetniks of Commander Pavle Djurisić, who, while officially under Mihailović's command, colluded independently with the Italian Second and Ninth Armies.

This collusion was directed against the Partisans and the Croatian extremist group, the Ustaše, and not intended as a betrayal of Allied strategy. Most often, in reading the anecdotal accounts of these vague friend-and-foe associations in civil war Yugoslavia, one is left with the impression of parallel agendas, "marriages of convenience," and temporary accommodations in the line of fire, rather than of intentional subversion of Allied aims. At various times certain Chetnik commanders, like the powerful and violent Dinarska Division leader Momcilo Djujic, and Pavle Djurisić, a hero of the July 1941 uprisings in Montenegro and a Chetnik respected by the Partisans, collaborated with the occupation forces of the Italian armies in Dalmatia (Croatia) and Montenegro and, in the case of Djurisić, possibly later with the Germans after being interned by them during the German Fifth Offensive (Unternehmen Schwarz) in May and June 1943.[22]

Mihailović himself met with representatives of the German commander for Serbia, General Paul Bader, in November 1941, an initiative negotiated between a German captain, Joseph Matl, and a Chetnik representative. Hoping to exploit the worsening Chetnik-Partisan rivalry, and aware of Mihailović's political vulnerability following the bloodbath of German reprisals against the Serbs in the city of Kraguevac in October of that year, the Germans sought cooperation with Mihailović against the Partisans—and Mihailović's complete surrender. Mihailović rejected the offer, and the state of hostility between the two sides continued.[23] (As will be seen later, the Partisans also met with the Germans, and at a higher level of contact, to coordinate against the Chetniks.)[24]

Certain Chetnik commanders (as well as Partisans) coordinated action with individual members of the Axis-controlled "Independent State of Croatia."[25] Yet others went off entirely on their own to cooperate with anyone for whatever gain. (These were the all-out renegades, the so-called *divlij četnici*, or "crazed Chetniks," who took orders only from themselves.) There was, no doubt, a strong pro-Axis sentiment among the so-called Serb nationalists, and in particular, the followers of the SDK, or "Serbian Volunteers Corps" of the popular leader Dimitri Ljotić, or of the Chetniks' elder statesman Kosta Pećanac; for such groups, however, these positions were more an expression of uncompromising anti-Communism than of disloyalty to the Allies. There were many traitors to the cause of Mihailović from within his own ranks, and rivals like Pećanac were ultimately an embarrassment. In fact, the hero of Ravna Gora ordered Pećanac to be shot for treason upon his capture in 1944. Nor was Mihailović terribly moved when Ljotić died in a car accident in 1945. All in all, the implication that the Chetnik movement of Draža Mihailović was somehow synonymous with Fascism is untrue.

• • •

"Frontline, hospitals, then frontline again, and love everywhere, love for bread and sugar, everything wet, everything rain and mud, fogs and dying," wrote the great Serbian poet-diplomat Miloš Crnjanski, of the brutal years he spent after he was drafted into the Austro-Hungarian army in World War I.[26] The same scene was to repeat itself nearly a quarter century later. At 5:15 A.M. on Palm Sunday, April 6, 1941, and with no declaration of war, Germany launched Unternehmen 25, the invasion of Yugoslavia, with an apocalyptic air attack on Belgrade, although the capital had been declared an open city. Under the personal direction of Hermann Göring, the second-in-command of the Third Reich, twenty-one divisions invaded Yugoslavia (with a division consisting of 30,000 to 45,000 troops on average); six were armored and four were motorized. The other Axis-aligned powers also invading Yugoslavia—Italy, Hungary, and Bulgaria—brought that number to 51 divisions, against Yugoslavia's eventual 28 divisions (and that country's 600 antiquated airplanes).[27]

Yugoslav forces were split into three groups: the first defending Croatia from Fiume to Slavonski Brod (a city in the southern part of Croatia-Slavonia, on the Sava River); the second protecting the Bulgarian frontier; and the third countering Italian attacks from Albania. But the lack of preparation and the weakness of these forces, as well as the pullout of the British expeditionary force from Greece later that month, meant a poor defense for Yugoslavia. Over the course of 500 German and Italian air-raid sorties, 5,000 Serbs or Yugoslav citizens were killed in Belgrade, and a total of 17,000 civilians were killed in Serbia, while an estimated 200,000 to 334,000 Yugoslavs were taken prisoner.[28]

The British government expressed its "outrage" at the invasion but would not commit Imperial troops to the country. The United States labeled the attacks "barbaric," and Secretary of State Cordell Hull announced that Washington was going to send military supplies to Yugoslavia as quickly as possible, but such promises turned out to be somewhat exaggerated.[29] The Lend-Lease Agreement of early March 1941, to provide aid to countries "vital" to the interests of the United States, had been suspended for Yugoslavia after Prince Paul signed the Tripartite Pact with the Axis powers on March 25. After the coup two days later, however, the program was reinstated. But only as of May 1942 did President Franklin Roosevelt authorize supplies to be sent directly to Yugoslavia—and even then he sent only food to the country, which never showed up.[30] The Soviets, for their part, remained silent, and the Soviet media did not mention the invasion until three days after the fact.

Whatever the international reaction, the first signs of a Serbian resistance emerged from the broken capital of Belgrade itself. "Belgrade, the White City, scarred and seared by the Luftwaffe's fury," in the words of historian Stephen Clissold, "still reared its proud but battered head on the hillside overlooking the confluence of the Danube and the Sava river. . . . There it lay, the martyred heart of Yugoslavia, captive, but still faintly beating."[31]

On April 22, 1941, the German military government began its operations in Belgrade. A foreign ministry plenipotentiary, Felix Benzler, was assigned to Serbia, and in January 1942 the Schutzstaffel—the SS—sent its representative, August Meissner. A provisional government was established on April 30, 1941, headed first by Milan Acimović, a former minister of the interior. Later, in August 1941, a new Vlada Nationalnog Spasa, the "Government of National Salvation," was formed with General Milan Nedić, a former royal Yugoslav minister of war who was named minister president on August 30, 1941. Nedić himself was no enthusiastic pro-Nazi, but rather believed, if feebly, that he was acting in the best interests of Serbia by cooperating with the Germans, even if his government, such as it was, was unpopular. His regime had little prestige, having little responsibility and no police power, and having given many of Serbia's highest financial offices to the Volksdeutsche in northern Serbia.

Between the autumn of 1941 and the summer of 1943, the Germans ruled Serbia through Nedić, with the support of the small Serb far-right Zbor, a pro-Fascist movement started at the University of Belgrade by Dimitri Ljotić, a Paris-educated former monarchist and lawyer who had served as justice minister under King Alexander Karadjordjević. Nonetheless, the new regime was unable to prevent the buildup of resistance forces under Mihailović, and, later, under Tito.

The twelve-day war also led to the defeat of Greece and the expulsion of the last significant contingent of British soldiers on the European continent. Nonetheless, it left Germany with its resources stretched thin: around 38 German divisions, or 600,000 troops, were needed in Yugoslavia to protect supply lines to Greece and northern Africa, thus putting the redeployment of those forces for the upcoming June 22, 1941, Unternehmen Barbarossa in peril and possibly making them unavailable for the El Alamein campaign of July to November 1942 and the Battle of Stalingrad in August 1942. Eventually the German occupation army in Yugoslavia was left with around 26 divisions—and their command largely in a state of chaos. The Italian Second Army comprised five infantry divisions whose only significant interest was the Dalmatian coast. General Vittorio Ambrosio would later play a part in the Italian renunciation of its alliance with Germany in September 1943.

Just before hostilities began, Mihailović had been promoted to chief of staff of the Yugoslav Second Army with its headquarters in Djakovica, in Kosovo. He arrived just as defections of the Croatian divisions of the Royal Yugoslav Army in favor of the incoming German presence were beginning. The General Staff major Antun Marković, a Croat and chief of staff of the Sava Division of the Royal Yugoslav Army, had prevented the planned destruction of bridges on the Drava River, part of a traffic corridor in Croatia connecting central and southeastern Europe. As a result, German troops were able to cross the rivers and the border without opposition. The German Fourteenth Panzer division triumphantly entered Zagreb on April 9, 1941, with the fitting showpiece of the Croatian Colonel Nikolić riding on the leading tank. A day later, the Croatian national leader Slavko Kvaternik proclaimed the establishment of the pro-Axis Nežavisna Država Hrvatska (NDH), "The Independent State of Croatia." (The NDH would encompass a population of six million, 30 percent of whom were Serb. The borders of this new state also occupied a good portion of Bosnia-Herzegovina.)

Throughout Yugoslavia, Croatian soldiers had rebelled, refusing to fight the Germans and Italians in Zagreb. There at first emerged an auxiliary paramilitary wing of the new NDH state, the Croatian Domobrans, or "Home Guards" of the old Austro-Hungarian Empire, which were incorporated into new German death squads. Soon Hitler's representative, SA (Sturmabteilung, or paramilitary) Gruppenführer Siegfried Kasche, took command of these Domobrans and the local police force as well, assisted by Ante Pavelić's Ustaše Hrvatska Revolutionara Organizacija, the extreme nationalist military organization known simply as the Ustaše, from the verb of the same spelling meaning "to rise," and used in the nineteenth century as a name for rebels or insurgents. Ivan Šubašić, the *ban*, or governor, of Croatia, and other leaders of the Hrvatska Šeljacka Stranka, the "Croatian Peasant Party," stood by as 8,000 Croatian rebel soldiers, led by staff Colonel Franjo Nikolić, stormed the headquarters of the Yugoslav Fourth Army. That same April, the Yugoslav vice premier and head of the Croatian Peasant Party, the highly respected (by both Croats and Serbs) Vladimir Maček, resigned from the Yugoslav government and traveled from Belgrade to his birthplace in Kupinec, just southwest of Zagreb, where he was kept under Axis house arrest. His party's militia—the Hrvatska Šeljacka Zaštita, the "Croatian

Peasant Defense," while intended to protect Croatian peasants from attacks by Communists, Ustaše, Serbs, and Germans, itself degenerated into a faction of lawlessness and violence once Maček's leadership had all but disappeared.

Now a collapsing Yugoslavia began, as the Balkan saying goes, "to use its hands to remove its own eyes." The country was about to be torn apart from the inside out: by the coup d'état conspirators who fled as the country went up in flames; by the ambitions of Josip Broz Tito, whose reckless disdain for German reprisals against the civilian population formed part of his path to power; by the terrorizing designs of Siegfried Kasche, the German minister in Zagreb; by Edmund Glaise von Horstenau, German plenipoteniary in Croatia; by Maximilian von Wiechs, commander of the Second Armee Heeresgruppe F of the Balkans; by General Paul Bader, commander for Serbia, who declared martial law in the country; by the Croatian lawyer and parliamentarian Ante Pavelić and his Ustaše; and by a nascent group of various Serb-dominated Chetnik groups whose violent rivalry was their own undoing.

On July 12, 1941, the "Independent State of Montenegro" was proclaimed by the poet, PhD, and later Nuremberg war criminal Sekula Drljević, who sought to create out of Montenegro his own Fascist-oriented state. (Mussolini first established Giuseppe Bastianni as governor of the "Protectorate" there, but refused outright annexation of Montenegro.) Drljević had organized his Montenegrin separatists, known as the "Greens" (Želenasi), against Montenegrin Chetniks as well as Partisans, later served the Croatian Ustaše, and administered the Axis-run Belgrade concentration camp at Sajmište. A day after the new state's inauguration (July 13, 1941), both Montenegrin Chetniks and Montenegrin Partisans led a massive uprising against the new state— a demonstration that would catch the attention of both London and Washington. In Slovenia, meanwhile, the overwhelming presence of various loosely allied, quasi-Chetnik detachments such as the "Legion of Death" and the Slovenian Domobrans, exploded out of that country's population of 1.5 million following its swift partitioning by Germany, Italy, and Hungary.

Yugoslav Muslims, for their part, those mainly from Bosnia and themselves once loyal to World War I Vienna, streamed into two large Nazi divisions (formally organized by the Germans in 1943), while other Muslims joined the Partisans, and counted for 80 percent of those Partisans in the major Bosnian city of Mostar.[32] These Muslims constituted a powerful force. By 1934 two SS divisions had been formed: the Thirteenth Waffen Gebirgs Division der SS "Handzar," or "Handschar," and the Twenty-third Waffen Gebrigs Division der SS "Kama" in Kosovo-Metohija. The Twenty-first Waffen Gebirgs Division der SS "Skanderbeg" was made up mostly of Kosovo-Albanians and a second Kosovar SS Division was planned. (As mentioned earlier, there was a Muslim Chetnik division, led by Mustafa Mulačić, in western Bosnia.) The Blue Division, composed of Yugoslav Muslims trained in Germany and subject to direct German command, was brought to Yugoslavia. Hitler himself had no real interest in the Muslims; Heinrich Himmler, head of the SS, was highly enthusiastic about their potential as a fighting force against the Orthodox Serbs. To other officials, the use of the Bosnian Muslims was to protect German settlements in the Srem, on the northern Croatian-Serbian border. A generally German-friendly nature existed among at least a portion of Bosnia's Islamic population, this revealed in 1941 when thousands of volunteers answered a Nazi appeal for manpower to fight against the Soviet Union.

The Nazi government also organized the Volksdeutsche of Yugoslavia into several powerful divisions, with Himmler imposing compulsory military service on that population in 1942. The Volksdeutsche population of Yugoslavia in 1940 was around one million. There was the Volunteer Mountain Division (Freiwilligen Gebirgs Division) organized on March 1, 1942, made up of those Volksdeutsche from the Banat region of Serbia. (This division was finally known as the Seventh SS-Freiwilligen Gebirgs Division "Prinz Eugen.") Approximately 21,500 of these ethnic Germans from Serbia would see military combat on behalf of the Reich.

• • •

None of these groups, however, would emerge with so deadly a force as Croatia's Ustaše. The Ustaše phenomenon marked, along with so much else, the total degeneration of Croat-Serb relations after a good two centuries' worth of spirited attempts to establish unified political, linguistic, and cultural movements. These aimed at finding common cause between the national aspirations of the two sides, most prominently exemplified by the mid-nineteenth-century movement of Croatian leader Eugen Kvaternik.[33]

It is one of the more depressing facts of modern Balkan history that genuine efforts at harmonious coexistence between these Roman Catholic and Eastern Orthodox nations should have resulted in events such as the day in the autumn of 1942 when a notice was put out on the streets of Belgrade that Serbians were to avoid contact with the waters of the Sava because the number of Serbian corpses rumored to have been killed by the Ustaše was more overwhelming than the Axis-run Yugoslav state could deal with. Such gruesome anecdotes only got worse during those bitter early years of the Yugoslav civil war. On August 3, 1941, several hundred Serbs who had gathered within the sanctuary of the Orthodox Church at Glina, where the Croatian national hero Count Josip Jelacić had maintained his nineteenth-century military frontier against the Turks, had their throats slit or were beaten to death by Croatian forces with spiked clubs. Later the same year, in the picturesque mountain city of Foča, in southeastern Bosnia, those Croatian forces selected twelve sons from prominent Serbian families and killed them, while in a nearby village they slit the throats of Serbs over a vat—"apparently to fill it with blood instead of fruit pulp," as the Partisan commander and writer Milovan Djilas described the scene.[34] The violence was directed toward Serb Orthodox and Jewish citizens as well. Women and children among 1,500 Jewish inmates at Djakovo, a Croatian concentration camp, were crammed into vans one day in the summer of 1942 with water pouring through a hose that was fitted from the exhaust pipe to the interior of the vans, which drove around until half the passengers were dead.[35] Beginning village by village, family group by family group, from June 1941 the number of Serbs killed by Ustaše leadership would grow into the hundreds of thousands.

While later chapters in this book describe occasional collaboration by the Partisans and the Chetniks with the Ustaše—another example of the utter moral and political breakdown of the times—the two latter groups were the Croatian nationals' sworn enemies, and both Partisans and Chetniks tended to be revolted at the scale of Ustaše violence. For example, a joint Ustaše-German massacre of Serbs in the Kožara mountains in the spring of 1941, when 40,000 Serb peasants in the villages surrounding it were captured and sent to Jasenovac, a concentration camp about sixty miles from Zagreb, inspired outrage from the Partisans. One of the most moving war poems in modern Yugoslav literature, "Stojanka, Mother of Knežpolje," was written by a top Partisan commander, Skender Kulenović, in memory of those deaths.[36]

The worst was yet to come. One of the more demoralizing symbols of the entire war—in the Balkans or anywhere else—was that concentration camp, Jasenovac, a complex established in a field near the Sava River and surrounded by three rows of barbed wire. The camp became notorious, with its roads strewn with the corpses of prisoners. The Serbs—Orthodox Christian and Jewish—were placed in barracks, about eight hundred people in each and, when not immediately killed, were put into forced labor building dikes on the Sava River.[37] In what might best be described as a particularly Balkan brand of irony, the Ustaše official Vjekoslav Maks Luburić, who oversaw the twenty-seven concentration camps that were part of the Jasenovac network, himself was an Orthodox Christian from Montenegro. Even the women of the Ustaše, very often married to or the girlfriends of male commanders in that organization, were themselves known to be among the most brutal of ideologues. Nada "Esperanza" Luburić, the half sister of Luburić, was herself the head of the Stara Gradiska camp for women at Jasenovac. She was married to Dinko Sakić, a commander at Jasenovac, who was extradited from Argentina to stand trial with his wife for war crimes in April 1999. He was sentenced to twenty years imprisonment, while her charges were dropped for lack of evidence.[38]

Conceived without the approval of the Axis powers, the NDH policy toward the estimated two million Orthodox Serbs within Croatia's borders had been to "convert a third, expel a third and kill a third," as the passage of a speech on July 22, 1941, by Ustaše ideologist and propaganda minister Mile Budak popularly summarized.[39] The statistics estimating the number of Serbs killed by the Ustaše between 1941 and 1944 are extreme in range and generally cited as between 250,000 and 700,000 victims. (Separate statistics for the number of Jews, Orthodox Croats, and gypsies number in the thousands and tens of thousands). While a respected Yugoslav writer-historian such as Ivo Banac set the number of Serb victims at 120,000, German generals tended to agree with statistics citing larger numbers: Generaloberst Alexander Löhr estimated 400,000 victims, while two other high-ranking German officers,

Generaloberst and commander of the Second Panzer Army in Yugoslavia, Lothar Rendulić, and the Balkan special envoy Hermann Neubacher, put the number at a half million or more.[40] In a report for the United States Holocaust Museum, one scholar maintains that 800,000 Serbs were killed.[41] Elsewhere, the Holocaust Museum puts the number of Serbs killed by the Ustaše between 330,000 and 390,000, with 45,000 to 52,000 Serbs murdered in Jasenovac.[42] The level of violence inspired Jasper Rootham, an SOE liaison to Mihailović's Chetniks in 1943, to question whether a "biological war" against the Serbs was under way, in which "the opponents of Serbia within the Jugoslav state were determined to reduce the numbers of the Serbs [such] that in any postwar election or plebiscite they were converted from a majority to a minority."[43]

What on earth had gone so terribly wrong? "Vengeance," to quote Djilas again, "the breath of life one shares from the cradle with one's fellow clansmen in both good fortune and bad, vengeance from eternity. It was centuries of manly pride and heroism, survival, a mother's milk and a sister's vow, bereaved parents and children in black, joy and songs turned into silence and wailing. It was all, all."[44] This quote from his illuminating memoir *Land without Justice* sums up the warped desire for "payback" that sent a country over the edge. Stated dramatically, one could argue that since the year 1100, with the ascension of the Hungarian crown over Croatian lands, the latter nation had been passed from one foreign power to another. While Croatian nobility rejected Hungarian-elected governors in favor of the Habsburgs in the sixteenth century, this "freedom" was more or less a pact for protection against the ever-present invading Ottomans. The first real sign of total independence—whether from Hungary, the Ottomans, Austria-Hungary, or the Serbs and royal Yugoslav government—came only in the twentieth century and in the form of a very strained collaboration between Croatian national leadership and heavy-handed Serb monarchists. The tenuous alliance between the two sides resulted in the founding of the Kingdom of the Serbs, Croats, and Slovenes, as stated in the prologue of this book, on December 1, 1918. In theory, the new state constitutionally allowed for a high degree of Croatian autonomy. In practice, however, the Serb-Croat relationship disintegrated from a tense, nominal partnership to open animosity.

For the Croatians, hopes for national freedom had quickly dissolved into disillusionment with the establishment of dictatorial powers by the

Yugoslav (Serbian) king Alexander Karadjordjević, whose grip on the new constitutional monarchy was defended as a measure against the then growing power of Communism in the early 1920s. What's more, the Serbs defended their political dominance in the new monarchy as just, in light of the Serbian sacrifices in World War I against Austria-Hungary (into which Croatia had been formally incorporated in 1868, while Slovenia was incorporated into the Empire of Austria in 1813).

Such were the beginnings of a bitter mutual contempt and lack of trust that would poison relations between Serbs and Croats up through World War II. The prewar efforts of King Alexander's successor, his nephew Prince Paul Karadjordjević, and Croatian Peasant Party leader Vladimir Maček to grant full autonomy to Croatia within the framework of the monarchy had been the last all-out effort to salvage "Yugoslavia." But with the outbreak of World War II, the memory, as the Croatians often proclaimed, of brutal dictatorial rule under King Alexander became the basis for Croatians' zeal for an Axis-sponsored vengeance. Ante Pavelić, the leader of the Ustaše, a lawyer, and onetime Croatian representative in the parliament of Royal Yugoslavia at Belgrade, became extreme in his views after Serbian authorities put a price on his head and sent him into exile in Bulgaria following his participation and leadership in Vienna-based nationalist Croatian groups. Such vengeance found fertile ground within an ongoing Partisan-Chetnik, Communist-monarchist civil war, inspiring the Ustaše to ideological excess. Now Serb-Croat tensions would become ripe for exploitation on a scale of cruelty that defies summary. Partisan and Chetnik violence was no less vile, of course, but did not encompass the systematic extermination policies of the Ustaše.

It should be noted that many Croatians protested the slaughter. It was not a pan-Croatian frenzy, as an estimated 120,000 Croats had joined the Partisans, who were themselves often the object of Ustaše violence.[45] Leading figures from the Croatian Roman Catholic Church also protested. While certain individuals, such as the Sarajevo archbishop Ivan Štarić, a sworn enemy of Orthodox Serbs and alleged secret member of the Ustaše, or Gregorij Rožman, the bishop of Ljubljana (Slovenia) and a strong Nazi supporter, helped to create an unfortunate image of the Roman Catholic Church in the Ustaše years, many forgotten names from that same Church risked their lives to take a stand against the anti-Serb (and anti-Jewish) violence. Archbishop Aloysius Mišić of Mostar circulated a letter to Roman Catholic bishops in Croatia on June 30, 1941, which was read to nearly every Catholic congregation in the country, that those who murdered and confiscated the property of others would not be granted absolution—that is, they would be effectively excommunicated from the Church. Archbishop Aksun Akamović of Djakovo was active in preventing the deportation of the Jews. Mixed views surround the reputation of Archbishop Aloysius Stepinac, once a decorated soldier awarded the Order of the Star of Karadjordje by the Kingdom of Yugoslavia during World War I. On the one hand, as Tomasevich writes, "Despite the archbishop's growing misgivings about the Ustasha regime, the Croatian Catholic hierarchy gave the Independent State of Croatia and the Ustashas a last formal expression of support in a pastoral letter issued by the Episcopal Conference on March 25, 1945."[46] In 1946, a Belgrade court found him guilty of collaborating with the Ustaše. On the other hand, others maintain that Archbishop Stepinac was one of the leading voices against Ustaše violence, and on May 14, 1941, the archbishop sent a letter to Ustaše leader Ante Pavelić condemning the massacre of Serbs at the church at Glina. His sermons against Nazism in the Cathedral of Zagreb were famous with the Croats, and he was credited with saving the lives of hundreds of Jews.[47]

The Germans themselves were disgusted by the actions of the Ustaše. An SS report on the killings noted, "The Ustasa units have carried out their atrocities not only against male Orthodox of military age, but in particular in the most bestial fashion against unarmed old men, women and children . . . because of these atrocities innumerable Orthodox have fled to [central] Serbia and their reports have roused the Serbian population of great indignation."[48]

While Italians were the original sponsors of an "independent" Croatia and of the organization of the Ustaše, several sources maintain that Italian generals grew to be appalled by the levels of violence.[49] From September 9, 1941, onward the Italians reoccupied most of Herzegovina, and the Serbs were allowed to return to their homes.[50] The Italian Second and Ninth Armies in Dalmatia protested to Foreign Minister Galeazzo Ciano that they did not wish to have a role in the deportation of the Jews. General Pirzio Birolli, governor in name of Italian-controlled Montenegro, and General Mario Roatta, commander of the Italian Second Army in Dalmatia, men by no means without their own violent reputations, neither conducted reprisal killings anywhere on the level of the Ustaše (or the Germans), nor "rounded up" Serb and Jewish populations in Yugoslavia for the purpose of methodical mass murder.[51] Where the Jewish population itself was concerned, as German demands intensified, "a number of Italian army officers and diplomats delayed the proposed transfer of Jews by painstakingly verifying the nationalities of the intended victims, and at the same time making their internment more secure."[52] None of the criticisms or obstacles introduced by their nominal Axis sponsors stopped the ferocity of the Ustaše. The eight-century Croatian dream of nationhood had dissolved into the nightmarish, new dark ages.

* * *

While Yugoslavia was committing a slow suicide, Mihailović and what remained of his initial core group, it will be recalled, had assembled in the woods of Ravna Gora with a steady stream of fleeing soldiers from the Yugoslav army pouring in to take up arms with his upstart, guerrilla-style resistance movement. As mentioned earlier, the men began referring to themselves at once as the *četnici*, from the word for squadron or group, and also a word used in the nineteenth century to describe anti-Ottoman or anti-Austrian rebel groups. As was stated earlier, Mihailović did not like the name, however, preferring to view his Chetnik organization as the legal continuation of the the "Royal Yugoslav Army of the Homeland." (In December 1941, Mihailović would be named major general of that army, and in January 1942, he would officially become "War Minister and Chief of Staff of the Supreme Command of King Peter II.")

In the first few days after Mihailović formed his Ravnogorski Pokret—his movement—the question still hung over him as to whether to surrender to the occupation authorities in light of the demoralized state of many of the fleeing officers and soldiers. Despite this wariness, Mihailović nonetheless committed himself to forming his resistance "and thus," wrote the well-regarded historian of World War II Yugoslavia, Jozo Tomasevich, "began the life of a very controversial resistance movement in Yugoslavia."[53] It would be this combination of judicious caution and ambitious defiance that defined—and sometimes blurred—Mihailović's strategic decision making. Whatever the later controversies, Mihailović's Chetniks grew to become arguably the second most powerful resistance movement in wartime Europe after the Partisans—in second place to the Warsaw Uprising, according to one historian.[54] The Ravnogorski Pokret was the centerpiece of the entire wartime Chetnik movement; about thirty-six mountain *korpus* and divisions throughout Yugoslavia were organized, nearly all loyal to Mihailović's ultimate authority and chosen from among the most capable leaders during the days of the uprising.[55]

Mihailović's Chetniks were at the outset comprised mostly of clean-cut captains, majors, and colonels who, under the war cry of *za kraljai i otadžbinu*—"For King and Fatherland"—would become, within months of taking refuge in the mountains, the wild-looking fighters normally associated with the image of that resistance group. Among the Orthodox Christian Chetniks, beards were grown long as a symbol of humility and self-sacrifice, in the sense of renouncing concern for one's looks, a kind of religious symbol of selflessness. As the Partisan leader and writer Milovan Djilas explained, "[I]t was the Chetnik custom to wear a beard as long as the country was in captivity."[56] These Serbs buried their dead with Orthodox chants and blessings and, for senior Chetnik officers, fired the three traditional volleys of gunfire. Often they used the blood and bones of those killed to mark the borders of Serbian lands, in honor of what they called the struggle for "Cross and Freedom."

The men acted swiftly, recruiting the members of gendarme and police forces in local towns and villages. Mihailović informed the Yugoslav government in exile of his movement by sending a clandestine Chetnik courier to Istanbul on June 19, 1941, to report that "a Colonel Mihailović" was organizing a resistance against the Axis. Bit by bit, his resistance took on a political and administrative structure. In August 1941, while Nedić was forming his puppet government in Belgrade, Mihailović established a civilian advisory body composed of Serbian political leaders. By September, Mihailović had established contact with the British when one of his radio operators succeeded in getting through to a British ship in the Mediterranean using equipment powered by hundreds of pocket batteries. The first radio message addressed by Mihailović to his own government was received on September 13, 1941, announcing that he had assembled the remnants of the Yugoslav Army in the mountains of Serbia to continue resistance.[57]

As other officers got word of Mihailović, Chetnik ranks at Ravna Gora grew steadily—a mix that would include the steadfastly loyal, the opportunistic, and the downright treacherous.[58] Foremost among these rivals was his fellow World War I veteran Kosta Pećanac, an organizer of Chetnik forces on the Salonika Front in 1917 and a hardened anti-Communist who saw himself as the true leader of the *ćetnici*, and not Mihailović, who was in his eyes a young upstart. By 1935, Pećanac's "Chetnik Association" was prohibited in certain *banovinas*—Yugoslav administrative units—because of the opposition among Croats and Slovenes to his Chetniks during that time. Zagreb and Ljubljana saw Pecanac's men only as auxiliary forces of King Alexander and his controversial rule. Nonetheless, by 1938 Pećanac's organization had grown so powerful that it counted around 500,000 members, composed mainly of members of the Serbian lower classes and peasantry, itself the result of the assassination of King Alexander in Marseille in 1934.

With this kind of popularity, and as there had been no official international recognition of the royal government in exile until the end of 1941, Mihailović, in asserting his position as leader, had to deal with a chaotic situation in which various officers like Pećanac became local chieftains and warlords, competing with him to project themselves as *the* strategic leader. Nonetheless, since the beginning of his Ravna Gora movement, Mihailović, well-known by the coup leaders now in London, had been counting on their political and military support to be coordinated with the British military. He was assured of that support once and for all when the Yugoslav government in exile named Slobodan Jovanović, a staunch supporter of Mihailović, as prime minister, and Mihailović himself as minister of the Yugoslav Army, Navy, and Air Force on January 11, 1942.

Unlike the many female Partizankas, to be discussed later, there were very few women fighters. Some women were used for local reconnaissance work. Yet one day in the terrible spring of 1941 the Serbian Chetniks received into their ranks one of the more unusual figures of the war, an American woman who left behind a life of wealth and privilege as a Wisconsin senator's daughter and heiress to fight with the Chetniks against the German occupation and the Partisans.

Ruth Mitchell, the strong-willed sister of the great World War I pilot Brigadier General Billy Mitchell, was a tall, thirty-four-year-old, Titian-haired beauty who was based in Belgrade as a freelance journalist and was in that city at the time of the Axis invasion of Yugoslavia. Fiercely anti-Tito, she joined the Chetniks through Pećanac, Mihailović's sworn rival, whom she later abandoned in favor of Mihailović's better reputation. Mitchell, fluent in German, had been serving as a member of the Chetnik forces as a courier and spy when the Germans captured her, and it was only the neutrality of the United States at the time of her capture that kept her from being executed as a Chetnik. She spent a year in a Gestapo prison in Belgrade, and after that was sent by the Nazis to a mental institution in Württemberg, Germany, at Leibenau, where the killing of prisoners and the spectacle of mental breakdowns formed the daily routine for its detainees. Her steel constitution and fierce sense of humor saw her through horrendous living conditions and a bout with scurvy. Being a member of the Chetnik fighters allowed her a narrow, lucky escape from death: Mitchell was the only foreign female fighter ever admitted to membership in that entire guerrilla organization.[59]

• • •

Just as the Chetniks had begun their revolt by going into the mountains, so did the Partisans. They "went to the forest," as the Yugoslav saying goes, an expression describing the taking up of arms against an invader in a wild and mountainous land. The "forest" in this case was to become the short-lived "Republic of Užice," a city some fifty miles from Serbia's main weapons arsenal at Kragujevac and a main Yugoslav railroad terminus, located in the dense, wooded regions of Bosnia where Tito would establish the headquarters for his forces in 1941. The Partisans in Yugoslavia had had a fitful climb to political power, however, and Communism did not at first seem destined for a bright future in Yugoslavia, whatever the excesses of King Alexander's rule may have been.

While Yugoslavia was one of the few countries in Europe to remain a monarchy after World War I, Communism had an unusual history in Yugoslavia and distinguished itself on two accounts in the history of Communist parties, according to Ivan Akumović, a historian of Communism in Yugoslavia.[60] The Communist Party of Yugoslavia (CPY) "was the only section of the Comintern to respond to Stalin's call to organize a Partisan movement in 1941 and the only Communist party to resist him for five years," Akumović wrote.[61] It was founded in April 1919 and was one of the first to join the Comintern, also known as the "Third International," following two attempts by European socialist parties and labor syndicates to organize an international Communist party between the late 1860s and 1916. Its electoral successes in the following year, along with its rhetorical inducements to violence and organized strikes, were cut short by government legislation, and the party was made illegal for two decades. Factional struggles within the Communist leadership, leading to the interference of the Comintern, culminated in the Moscow trials of 1937 when that body dismissed its entire central committee, except for one man, Josip Broz, known by his nom de guerre, Tito. He was instructed to carry out a thorough party purge, and five of Tito's predecessors in the post of secretary general and a large number of Communist officials disappeared in the Soviet Union. "The latter," explained Akumović, "were replaced by militants picked by Tito himself."[62]

Tito, a name he first used in 1934 during a meeting of the Central Committee of the Communist Party in Vienna, was also known by the covert names of "Valter" in Moscow, and "Engineer Tomachek" in Zagreb. He was a Croat metalworker born in Kumorevec, Croatia, in 1892, a part of Yugoslavia that was then still a part of the Austro-Hungarian Empire. He served in the Austrian Army in World War I and was wounded in Russia, where he stayed in a prisoner-of-war hospital and camp until he escaped, just before the Bolshevik Revolution. He remained there, married a Russian woman, and became a member of the Communist Party. After returning to Yugoslavia in 1920, he became active in the Communist Party and attracted the favorable attention of the Comintern, which summoned him to Moscow in 1936 to work in its Balkan secretariat. He was sent to Paris to organize the flow of volunteers to fight in Spain and then returned to Yugoslavia to reorganize the party there. At the beginning of 1939 the Comintern confirmed his appointment as secretary-general and some months later registered its formal approval of his reorganization of the CPY.

Valter-Tito seemed in every way a man in whom Moscow could have full confidence. Of unassailable working-class origins, in addition to marrying a Russian wife, he fathered a son who would serve as an officer in the Red Army. He spoke fluent Russian, and though he never attained the "life-threatening honor" of holding high office in the brutal political culture of the Comintern, he was well versed in its ways and well regarded by its leaders, particularly by its secretary general, the Bulgarian Georgi Dimitrov.

But despite Tito's dynamism, the CPY had difficult beginnings in transforming itself into an effective underground largely because small landholding predominated in Serbia. Mass support in Yugoslavia was unlikely, and there was very little support in particular in the countryside. The party's influence was felt most strongly in the trade union movement, and its greatest success was at Belgrade University. A campaign persuaded the moderate left-wing student groups to join with the Communists in the "United Student Youth," and this kind of students' popular front was dominated by Communists. Through this youth movement the CPY succeeded in almost monopolizing political life at Belgrade University until the Russo-Finnish war of 1939, and it also served as the best recruiting center for Tito's party.

Every year trained party members went down to generate agitation among the young, and the result was that party membership rose from 1,000 in 1934 to 12,000 in 1941. The membership of the United Student Youth, formally called the Studenti Kommunistija Organizatjia Yugoslavia (SKOJ), rose from 3,000 in 1935 to 30,000 on the eve of Hitler's invasion of Russia. A general trend toward totalitarian movements was also on the rise in Croatia and Romania, though in both cases the local brand of Fascism—the Croatian Ustaše and the Romanian Iron Guard—proved more fashionable among students. The CPY applied in all its rigors the Bolshevik principle of organization. The party decided everything. It laid down party propaganda; it even entered people's private lives. (In the course of the Fifth Party Conference of 1940, Tito declared: "Comrades usually think their private lives are solely their own concern. This is a mistake. The party must on the contrary pay attention to the private life of every member.")[63]

Attention to private life also extended to the vast number of women who were Partisans. These heroic, tragic women saw themselves to be like the sixteenth-century Croatian heroine Mila Gojsalić, who lit gunpowder in the camp of thousands of Ottoman Turks then occupying the (Croatian) Dalmatian Republic of Poljica and, in one devastating act of rebellion, blew up the camp and herself along with it. In the ensuing confusion the local Croatian population was able to defeat the rest of the Ottoman army.

The Partisan women considered themselves to be cut from that same cloth of self-sacrifice. One hundred thousand Yugoslav women are said to have joined the Partisans during World War II, an estimated 96 percent of that number under the age of twenty. In Macedonia, women were among the original volunteers when Partisan groups were formed there in August 1941, and one Macedonian Partisan, Dara Dragisić, was not only one of the bravest soldiers in the First Macedonian-Kosovo National Liberation Brigade formed in 1943 but also was elected a political delegate.

The first women's Partisan group was formed in Lika, in Bosnia, on August 25, 1942, and in the following months several more brigades were founded as "everyone wanted to 'go to the woods,'" in the words of one scholar of Partisan women in Yugoslavia.[64] Brigadier Fitzroy Maclean wrote of being guided through the woods by a female Partisan.[65] As one magazine, *Udarnik* ("The Shock Worker"), wrote on the Partizanka phenomenon: "We looked with suspicion on the military skill of the women comrades. But all that doubt today has disappeared like summer light in the morning fog. . . . In the fight which developed the young Partisan women, together with their Partisan comrades fearlessly attacked the enemy's horses, trucks, even the tanks. And the old experienced soldiers were amazed at the young peasant girls who only yesterday took rifle in hand."[66] The share of women who lost their lives relative to the total number of women in the corps was almost 20 percent; the total number of women Partisans who died was 25,000.[67]

As a Partisan commander, Djilas often commented that Partisan women were braver than their men. In one exploit, a group of Ustaše attacked a village, leaving two Partisan soldiers wounded from a mortar. The platoon leader Mileva Radivojević with another woman Partisan ran to the aid of the wounded, and while under a rain of bullets they dragged the wounded men for over a half mile. The Ustaše saw them and shouted that all the women must be taken alive. Under heavy fire, the two young women succeeded in bringing the wounded men to safety.[68]

Living conditions were so harsh that many of the women stopped menstruating and could bear no children after the war. Impossibly strict codes of morality were enforced, and sexual relations were frowned upon. "Love," said Šaša Bozović, a lone Partisan rebel who ended up a captain and a battalion political commissar, "showed itself in carrying a rifle for one's beloved or in giving an apple."[69]

• • •

Meanwhile, relations between Moscow and the Yugoslav Partisans were not quite so warm and enthusiastic. From the mid-thirties, the expansionism of Fascist Italy and Nazi Germany began to loom as another and perhaps more immediate danger to Yugoslavia. The Soviet Union, faced with the same threat and anxious to strengthen anti-Fascist forces, instructed the Yugoslav Communists to drop their call for the dismemberment of Yugoslavia and campaign for the defense of the Yugoslav State—that is, ironically, to support the monarchy—and the exiled Yugoslav government's outward alliance with the Soviet Union. The Soviets were obviously aware of the opportunities before them.

The counselor of the Soviet embassy in Belgrade, V. Z. Lebedev, might have accompanied King Peter and his government in their flight to Montenegro as the first stop in the Axis invasion of Yugoslavia, but long after that government fled to Allied territory, Lebedev stayed behind to make contact with local Communist leaders. Nor were the Yugoslav Communists alone in wanting to see links established between their country and Moscow. While Bolshevism was feared and despised, a nineteenth-century-type "pan-Slav" sentiment was strong among many segments of the Yugoslav population, particularly the Serbs and the Serb-Montenegrins. The government, alarmed at the prospect of the eventual "bolshevization" of the Balkans, remained extremely wary of allowing any opening for Soviet influence. Some informal contacts had nevertheless taken place at the League of Nations, and a protocol had been signed in Geneva providing for mutual abstention from hostile propaganda. In April 1940 the Yugoslav government approached the Soviets to inquire whether they would be prepared to establish economic relations. Despite being in the throes of revolution and trying to establish a Communist new world order, a wary Moscow replied that it wished to see the monarchist status quo maintained in the Balkans and was prepared to discuss economic links with Yugoslavia. On May 11, 1940, a trade and shipping agreement was signed by the two countries.

During this time, the CPY, though banned by and hostile to the Yugoslav government, had been among the most vocal advocates of formal political links between Belgrade and Moscow. In the euphoria of the CPY's Second Congress in Vukovar in 1920, it had expressed the hope that the new state would become a Soviet republic and join a Balkan-Danubian federation. Until the mid-1920s the party's course had been charted by its Serbian secretary, General Sima Marković, who held that the Yugoslav Communists should not allow themselves to be deterred by the nationalities issue and opposed Comintern directives to exploit national resentment for its own propaganda ends. After unsuccessful attempts to follow Comintern guidance by working with Stjepan Radić's Peasant Party and the Macedonian IMRO, the CPY in 1928 called openly for "self-determination," to the point of secession, of Yugoslavia's constituent people and minorities. By the spring of 1934, the Comintern was still demanding the secession of Croatia, Slovenia, and Macedonia. Hitler's rise to power, with its implicit threat to the Soviet Union, led to a revision of strategy. The demand for secession was now presented as an idea that would only play into the hands of Nazi and Fascist expansionists. The need for Yugoslav unity was stressed and the right to self-determination played down.

It was at this stage that Tito began to make his mark in the Comintern, and the CPY's strict devotion to the Soviet line was immediately noticed by Moscow. Yet at the Fifth Conference of the CPY, held secretly in Zagreb in October 1940, disagreement over the Macedonian question was the first sign that Tito was at this stage already thinking independently of the Comintern. Still, outwardly, the Yugoslav Communists maintained a united front with the Soviet Union. The war, as the CPY manifesto issued at its outbreak had been quick to point out, was being waged between the "bourgeois imperialists" of the pseudo-democracies and the Germans and Italians; the Yugoslav people, however, looked to the Soviet Union and Stalin for "salvation." The CPY would be the vanguard of that salvation.

Of course, Tito accepted help where he could, even if it meant mixing with the more classic manifestations of bourgeois capitalism. Vladislav Ribinikar, the wealthy and influential owner of the Belgrade daily, *Politika*, turned over his large villa in Belgrade as the meeting point of Tito and his fellow ideologues. A frequent guest there was the Slovenian Communist

Edvard Kardelj, later to become one of the highest-ranking members of Tito's Communist government. The beautiful villa had remarkably survived the horrific bombings of April 6, as did the Communists who took refuge there. It was the right place at the right time to hammer out an ambitious political vision for the future of Yugoslavia, for Tito remained mostly aloof from the wartime events taking place around him, as well as from the Royal Yugoslav officers' coup d'état and its popular support.

"The Communists," wrote Stephen Clissold, the Oxford historian of Yugoslav-Soviet relations, "had found themselves, as Tito would express it in his rigid Marxist phraseology, isolated from the 'aspirations of the broad popular masses.'"[70] Tito remained calm, almost unmoved, by Europe's upheaval and by the course of events unfolding in Yugoslavia in late March and April 1941. He would find willing supporters among the very wartime Western allies he privately so despised for the triumph of that program, and for the long-sought immortality he craved for his name.

Years later, that very name, by order of the CPY, was written in four big blocks of trimmed wood across the hills of the mountain-ringed Bosnian city of Drvar, where the Nazis descended on May 25, 1944, to execute a failed but significant attack on the Partisan leader's life, an operation known as Unternehmen Rösselsprung ("Operation Knight's Move"). The Tito monument remains there to this day. The truth behind Tito's postwar rule of Yugoslavia, however, would never find such bold exposure until well after his death. For Tito's power, esteemed by many, left behind another signature on the mountainous country he came to dominate, in the form of a brutal and corrupt political, economic, and moral legacy that for so many years remained hidden from the world, dark and indecipherable.

3

Lawrence of Yugoslavia II: Into the Partisan-Chetnik Quagmire

Blood is my daylight and my darkness, too.

—Ivan Goran-Kovačić, quoted in the memoirs of British SOE mission leader F. W. D. Deakin

As civil war threatened to push Yugoslavia into the bloody abyss of ethnicity, ideology, and warring factions within factions, the British and the Americans were faced with the seemingly impossible task of having to weed out which side in that broken country was not only friendly to Allied interests, but which could be trusted after the civil war's conclusion. Already at war, the British, by order of Churchill, were the first to establish their fact-finding missions to Yugoslavia, well before the Americans arrived on their own missions to investigate the complicated political landscape and to rescue their fellow Allied airmen. As reports began to trickle in to London about the anti-Axis uprisings of 1941, the task became to see who, between Tito and Mihailović, would emerge the better player in the great game of Allied interests. What resulted would become one of the saddest chapters of miscommunication, subversion, and deceit in the history of the Allied cause during World War II.

The British started off in the fullest spirit of unbiased inquiry, attracting to the cause of the Special Operations Executive (SOE), the intelligence

79

agency founded in July 1940 by Winston Churchill and Hugh Dalton, then minister of economic warfare, a throng of first-rate men who would eventually become anything but detached, dutiful functionaries assigned to routine intelligence gathering in a beaten-up backwater. The first British liaison officers and sub-mission leaders to Yugoslavia—the SOE missions of William Hudson (to Tito and Mihailović), Major Terence Atherton (also to Tito and Mihailović), Colonel William Bailey (to Mihailović), Brigadier C. D. Armstrong (to Mihailović), Jasper Rootham (to Mihailović), F. W. D. Deakin (to Tito), and the independent, Churchill-assigned mission of Brigadier Fitzroy Maclean (to Tito)—were characters of a very particular, one might say "British," variety. These were men cut from the cloth of the British soldier-scholar-adventurer-gentleman-poet tradition of nineteenth-century Richard Burtons and Wilfred Thiesigers, the adventure-addicted, spiritual godfathers of these new World War II spies and saboteurs. As SOE mission officers to Yugoslavia (or, in the case of Maclean, as a personal representative of Churchill), they became the official representatives of the British General Headquarters, Middle East, accredited, as stated earlier, either to the Partisans or Chetniks (or both). The mission directives were usually the same, regardless of the particular assignment: to coordinate efforts with the Allied offensive in the Mediterranean with regard to attacking the main Axis lines of communication; to avoid getting involved in the civil war; to keep an eye out for collaboration with the Axis forces; and to make clear to the two camps the British position on their activities.

Yet their involvement went beyond the parameters of their assignment. The men usually became as personally dedicated to their tragic, wartime homeland as they were intellectually astute in analyzing its often unfathomable local military and political dynamics. This was reflected not only in the introspective nature of their reports but in the books that a few of them wrote after the war. Such memoirs have not, sadly, received the attention they deserve: Deakin's lyrical *The Embattled Mountain*, for example, or Rootham's melancholic, frustrated, and at times humorous *Missfire: The Chronicle of a British Mission to Mihailovich*. Maclean's chapter on the Balkans, from his relatively popular work, *Eastern Approaches*, is probably the best known English language work of that Yugoslav civil war period. Such books recount not only the hardship of enduring—and making sense of—a Balkan civil war, but the sense of high hopes, disappointment, and often embittered feelings (particularly between the Chetniks and the British) regarding radio censorship, meager supplies, and worst of all, political preferences. Then, too, none of these men, no matter how war-hardened, could resist the sentimental aspect of their respective Balkan missions. As Rootham recounted:

> In the flickering light of the fires there darted to and fro the bearded, long-haired figures of the Chetniks and there passed us, creaking and groaning on the steep hillside, a wooden cart pulled by two sleepy, docile oxen. It was piled high with containers full of rifles and ammunition. The contrast between this lovely European landscape and the sandy distance I had just left, between the great Liberator roaring overhead and the poor little ox-cart, was so intense that for a moment I hardly believed it was real. I was much moved. There was it seemed to me something brave and yet poignant about it. . . . I felt sentimentally proud that it was a British aeroplane which was disappearing over the crest of the near-by hill. The ox-cart with its rifles seemed a symbol of Serb defiance to the German invader, and the aeroplane a symbol of British power, good faith and Victory.[1]

Their on-the-ground experiences were far from romantic, however, and in several instances both British (which included Canadian, Irish, Australian, South African, and New Zealand nationals) and American liaison officers died in battle or from wounds, or were killed intentionally or accidentally by the Partisans or Chetniks themselves. In some instances they were taken prisoner by Ustaše or German forces and never heard from again. Many fell to their deaths upon parachuting into the mountains of Yugoslavia, shattering their bones upon contact with the unforgiving terrain. There is a particularly chilling scene Maclean recounts in his book, about a fellow officer who was mistakenly dropped into enemy territory owing to the error of their Italian pilot, and a crewmate quickly throwing that parachutist's mess kit after him "so that he should not be unnecessarily uncomfortable in his prison camp."[2]

Five members of one British mission who parachuted into Kosovo to sabotage the Allatini chrome mines were captured and shot dead by Bulgarian forces in April 1944. A British officer, sent from Yugoslavia to organize an uprising in Slovakia in August 1944, was captured by Slovak forces and sent to the Mauthausen concentration camp in Austria, where he perished.[3] "The final light before the frightful night / The lightning swooping off the polished knife / The cry too white still in my blinded sight," wrote the poet Ivan Goran-Kovačić.[4] The lines from this poem sum up what both sets of Allies—the Anglo-American and the Yugoslav—bitterly suffered during these missions in their attempts to understand the actions of one another, when the blinding darkness of war often obscured the sacrifice that one side made for the other. The tragedies the British mission leaders endured in Yugoslavia neither deterred their absolute dedication to the fulfillment of their duty, nor diminished the profound emotional investment of these men in that broken and heart-breaking land.

• • •

The initial establishment of the British (and later the American) missions in Yugoslavia involved several steps. The British had known, mainly through the SOE offices in Belgrade, of the rivalry between the Communist and monarchist anti-Axis elements well before the outbreak of war and after the invasion of Yugoslavia. When first word of the rebellions in that country came through to London, Prime Minister Churchill and the SOE strove at the outset for fully "Yugoslav"–type missions. In late summer 1941 they had been informed of the outbreak of resistance throughout Serbia and Montenegro mainly through anti-Axis coup leader turned Yugoslav government in exile prime minister Dušan Simović. Simović, then settled in London, was himself indirectly informed by Yugoslav intelligence established in Istanbul and Cairo, which monitored what little information came out of occupied Yugoslavia.

The main task of coordinating this intelligence was given to an official of the Royal Yugoslav government, Jovan Djunović, the government in exile's representative in Cairo. Djunović, in turn, kept in contact with Tom Masterson, director of British SOE regional headquarters in Cairo and the former head of an oil business in Romania, located in the

Egyptian capital's storied Mena House hotel. (This headquarters, serving the whole of the Middle East, was also known as Special Operations Force 133. Its counterpart, Force 136, served the Far East, and Force 137, the South Pacific.) Masterson sent British authorities a steady stream of fragmentary reports about what was going on in Yugoslavia. Churchill became gradually intrigued by these first official communications regarding "patriot" forces, which had risen up across Yugoslavia. On August 28, 1941, the British prime minister sent a memo to Hugh Dalton, the director of the SOE. "I understand from General Simović that there is widespread guerrilla activity in Yugoslavia. It needs cohesion, support, and direction from the outside. Please report what contacts you have with these bands and what you can do to help them."[5]

Dalton then formulated the following policy that month:

> The Yugoslavs [the exiled Royal Yugoslav Government], the war office, and we are all agreed that the guerrilla and sabotage bands now active in Yugoslavia should show sufficient active resistance to cause constant embarrassment to the occupying forces and prevent any reduction in their numbers. But they should keep their main organization underground and avoid any attempt at large scale risings or ambitious military operations which could only result at present in severe repression and the loss of our key men. They should now do all they can to prepare a widespread underground organization ready to strike hard later on, when we give the signal.[6]

Thus, the idea that the first mission be "Yugoslav" and the instruction to Captain William T. Hudson, the first British officer to have contact with either of the two sides in wartime Yugoslavia, were based on a very vague directive: "to contact, investigate, and report on all groups offering resistance to the enemy, regardless of race, creed or political persuasion."[7] The Royal Yugoslav government in exile in London saw matters somewhat differently, however. Naturally aware of the Communist presence within Yugoslavia, but expecting British sympathy not only for the monarchy but with regard to the anti-Axis officers' coup in Belgrade on March 27, 1941, the Yugoslav government hoped to edge British sympathy toward the Mihailović side. Two Royal Yugoslav officers of Montenegrin origin who were involved in the coup (and who had subsequently fled to Greece and to Cairo), Major Zaharije Ostojić and Major Mirko Lalatović, were selected by Jovan Djonović, the Royal Yugoslav representative in Cairo, to undertake the mission to Yugoslavia. A Royal Yugoslav noncommissioned officer, Veljiko Dragičević, also of Montenegrin origin, was chosen as the W/T (wireless transmission) operator, and he would bring along two radio sets, a Mark III set, which weighed fifty-five pounds and could not run on storage batteries, and a small J set, which could not run for more than thirty minutes, with a range only of thirty miles. It was hoped by the Yugoslavs that the British would entrust them exclusively to carry out the fact-finding trip. The British, however, whatever their sympathies with the Yugoslav government in exile at that time, insisted on sending one of their own.

And so, William Hudson, with the code name Marko, came on the scene, a dashing champion boxer and mining engineer who had worked as a consultant at the Zajača antimony mines in western Serbia before the outbreak of war. Hudson set off from Malta (where the SOE had a base to field wireless communications) on September 20, 1941, with his three Montenegrins, "in great heart" in the submarine HMS *Triumph*.[8] The men, not knowing what to expect when they landed, rowed onto a deserted beach on the Montenegrin coast near Petrovac, thinking it the safest landing point (and where the Royal Yugoslav officers with Hudson might have some family contacts), where they were picked up by local Partisan guerrillas and taken to the village of Radovče, some sixty miles inland.

The party leadership had been informed of their arrival two or three days after their landing only through the Partisan network of patrols and sharp-eyed peasant informers. At Radovče the men were met by Arso Jovanović, a former Royal Yugoslav officer of Serb origin who had joined the Partisans; Mitar Bakić, the head of the CPY's secret military intelligence committee; and Milovan Djilas, the Partisan representative for Montenegro and the Sandžak, all of whom were with the Partisans of Montenegro following the general popular uprising there against the Italians in July 1941. Hudson and his men were received cordially, but with suspicion. While the brave American OSS officer "Slim" Farish had been dubbed "Lawrence of Yugoslavia" by admiring comrades and colleagues, the Partisans were not so eager to associate the name of romantic British adventurers in foreign lands with high-minded causes. "We saw in Lawrence of Arabia not an idealistic hero," wrote Djilas of this first encounter with Hudson, "but the perfidious, arrogant champion of an empire."[9] When Hudson was later about to leave the Partisans, one commander half-joked to Djilas that their suspect ally "should be shot."[10]

Hudson's first message was received by an SOE W/T station in Malta on September 26, 1941. In it he reported his observations of the "Montenegrin Freedom Force," represented by Partisan groups in Montenegro, whose organization and dedication convinced Hudson that aid should be sent to them. With that first report, the British authorities were introduced to the complexities on the ground. Ostojić and Lalatović, of course, were anxious to get to Mihailović headquarters and were urged to do so via Djonović, the Royal Serbian officer gathering intelligence out of Cairo, from Bogoljub Ilić, then the minister of war in the Yugoslav government in exile. On September 10 the SOE W/T station in Malta picked up a message revealing the presence of Mihailović, and about a month later, on October 9, SOE Cairo instructed Hudson to go to Mihailović headquarters. Once there, he was to give the Chetnik leader a British radio code for communicating with SOE Cairo, code name "Villa Resta." Through that code, all messages, even those to his own government, would be known to the British.

Hudson sent another message on October 16, once again asserting his positive impressions of Communist activity against Axis forces in Montenegro, and that the "nationalist forces" (the Chetniks) were, in the meantime, standing on the sidelines "waiting." But the problem was that Mihailović had been instructed, most likely from the Yugoslav minister of war in London, General Ilić, not to engage in any sabotage except against locomotives, trains, and so on, so that the population would not be exposed to reprisals. Hudson's mission mates Lalatović and Ostojić communicated this particular news to Malta, presumably over Hudson's set and without the latter's knowledge, on October 13, on or around the date that Hudson set off to make his journey to Mihailović headquarters in Ravna Gora per SOE Cairo instructions (on October 9). Thus the confusion, exacerbated by poor-quality, time-delayed radio communications, over whose side—British or Yugoslav—had what power over which decisions the mission was to make was mounting dangerously.

The political atmosphere of the journey was particularly tense: Hudson traveled to Ravna Gora with just Ostojić from his team. The other Serbian officer, Lalatović, and the wire operator stayed behind in Montenegro, presumably bent on securing the channels of Cairo-Malta-Montenegro lines of communication for the benefit of the Royal Yugoslav government. With a gift from the Partisans of two horses to carry their baggage and their radio transmitter, Hudson and Ostojić began the long journey across Montenegro to Serbia along with a Partisan military escort as well as the top Partisan commanders Arso Jovanović, Milovan Djilas, and Mitar Bakić, all of whom, it will be recalled, were in Montenegro at the time of Hudson's submarine landing. These events were taking place at a time— the autumn of 1941—when the Partisans and Chetniks had begun the first of a small, later failed, series of attempts at a united front against the Axis. This "allowed" that the high-level Partisan delegation could make its way on the arduous trip with Hudson and his mission to Chetnik headquarters, although in the end they remained behind. They brought the British officer first, however, to Partisan headquarters at Užice.

Behind the scenes, messages continued to be mixed: On October 20 Hudson received an urgent message from Cairo—presumably from the Royal Yugoslav (exile government) representative there, Jovan Djonović, and the British representative of the SOE, Masterson—asking if he, Hudson, had ciphers that could be worked to London and whether SOE Malta had arranged communication with Mihailović. Then Cairo also asked if another submarine operation could be arranged and if supplies would be sent in short order, presumably to Mihailović. Hudson, meanwhile, reached Tito headquarters in Užice, the two men meeting on October 24, 1941. The Partisan leader insisted that he, and not Mihailović, was doing the bulk of the fighting. Hudson, already impressed by what he had seen in the Partisan organization, allegedly offered Tito technical data, a radio transmitter code—just as Mihailović had been given the "Villa Resta" code—and contact with the SOE Cairo. But Tito declined, saying that he preferred Allied help via the Soviets. Ostojić, the Royal officer with Hudson, continued on to Ravna Gora while Hudson stayed on in Užice. Meanwhile, Ostojić, once at Ravna Gora, briefed Mihailović on Hudson's positive feeling toward the Partisans. Hudson eventually continued on to Ravna Gora, only with a Partisan escort, arriving there in early December. Obviously, "the četnik leader did not receive the first

British liaison officer as warmly as might have been expected," according to one scholar of the Yugoslav civil war.[11]

Tito and Mihailović had tried on several occasions to reach a truce between their two sides. The two met for the first time on September 19, 1941, at Tito's initiative. The talks were inconclusive because of the ideological differences, although correspondence between the two men continued. The second meeting was on October 27, 1941, at Brajici, between Užice, a city located in southwestern Serbia and a main Yugoslav railroad terminus, and Ravna Gora. Hudson went with Mihailović, and Tito wanted Hudson to participate in the meetings, though Mihailović did not. This second meeting ended with a certain degree of agreement, in which Mihailović was to obtain half of the production of the Partisan-held Užice ammunition and rifle factory and Mihailović promised Tito part of the parachute drops he received from the British. But this too was short-lived, and a series of brutal clashes broke out in Užice almost immediately, with each side accusing the other of making the initial provocations. Mihailović sent a series of radio messages pleading for British support, but when Hudson became aware of the severity of the clashes between the two sides, he advised Cairo to stop sending arms to Mihailović (by this point, only one consignment, on November 9, 1941, had been received). When Hudson told Mihailović of this, the Chetnik leader became incensed, and relations between Hudson and the Chetniks, which had begun poorly in view of Hudson's disagreements with his travel companions, Ostojić and Lalatović, went from bad to worse.[12]

Then a third meeting was proposed by Tito to Mihailović with the hope of resolving their differences, this time between November 18 and 20 at Čačak, a main industrial town some eighty-five miles south of Belgrade, with two follow-up meetings on the twenty-seventh and twenty-eighth of that month, although in this third round the two leaders did not attend. Tito was represented by Alexander Ranković, later the interior minister under the Tito government of postwar Yugoslavia, Ivo Lola-Ribar, the youngest member of Tito's Central Committee, and Peter Stambolić. Mihailović was represented by Major Lalatović and Major Radoslav Djurić—the latter playing a tragic role in Mihailović's postwar fate. An eight-point agreement was reached, only to fall apart again when the Partisans refused to consider peace unless Mihailović agreed to close cooperation, including joint headquarters, "with their identity, political commissars, propaganda, etc."[13] This too all fell apart in light of the German First Offensive, which took place in late November and forced the Partisans to retreat south into Italian-occupied territory. The Chetniks returned to Ravna Gora, although "remnants of their forces were under German attack throughout December."[14]

It had so happened that Hudson forgot his radio transmitter at Užice when he met Tito, and after arriving at Ravna Gora, he had to depend on the Chetnik transmitter. Given Hudson's less than successful first outing with Mihailović, he was eager to recover his own. As soon as Hudson returned to Užice, however, the Germans had overrun the city, and he had no choice but to retreat south with the Partisans. During that retreat he found one of the Partisans with his original radio transmitter and retrieved it, and then decided to return to Mihailović's headquarters. To Hudson's mind, in spite of the cool reception by Mihailović initially, he had been instructed to go to Mihailović headquarters, and he sought to fulfill that duty. As events around Užice began to calm down, a hundred or so Partisans were making their way north, and Hudson decided to accompany them, only to be ambushed by a wild Chetnik unit not under Mihailović control, which attacked them and took Hudson and the Partisans prisoner, confiscating the transmitter. Hudson escaped one evening from the local Chetnik camp where he was held, however, and stealthily made his way back to Ravna Gora. He did not, of course, have that radio transmitter.[15]

The story of Hudson and his transmitter takes on an interesting dimension in this chapter of wartime Yugoslavia for three reasons. First, as Deakin wrote of the Hudson episode, it showed how the competition for Allied aid between the Partisan Communists and the exile government's monarchists/Chetniks first came to the fore with Hudson's arrival. Second, it demonstrated how difficult and sensitive it was for an Allied officer to send an objective report, let alone an accurate, thoroughly considered one, without the interference of constant local military observation, suspicion, poor equipment, and the politically sensitive, perhaps ideologically biased, wartime communications labyrinth between Cairo and London through which those reports had to be sent. Third, the sudden disappearance of Hudson that would soon follow and the subsequent British-led search for him contributed further to both the Partisan and the Chetnik mistrust of the British and vice versa.

Somehow during Hudson's comings and goings between the Chetnik and the Partisan camps in search of his ever elusive transmitter, Hudson disappeared from all contact with Cairo and London, with no one hearing of him or from him for the next four months, beginning on or around October 19, 1941. A complete blackout then fell upon the sole W/T links between Hudson and Mihailović, and Cairo and London began to believe that the Germans at some point had come in and scattered the forces of both Mihailović and Tito. The British were now cut off from any information relating to events taking place within the country. At that point the SOE decided to send in three missions, in an attempt to renew contact on the ground and locate surviving resistance groups, but also to learn the fate of Hudson and Mihailović.

And thus the tragic story of Major Terence Atherton unfolded, a story of one British officer's inextricable mix-up in the rivalries not only of Partisan and Chetnik groups, but of Chetnik against Chetnik. It was a mission that, like Hudson's, inadvertently, started British-Partisan-Chetnik relations off on the wrong foot—again. On January 17, 1942, the submarine *Thorn* left from Alexandria, Egypt, carrying on board two new missions. The first was called Henna, with two Royal Yugoslav officers aboard, Lieutenant Rapotec and Sergeant Stevan Shinko, both of whom were Slovenes. The idea was to come ashore at Split, where, it was believed, a group of Mihailović supporters were encamped; there they hoped to establish wireless contact and collect information on the local situation.

The second party was commanded by the British officer Atherton. His mission was to contact the group on whom Hudson had last reported, to find Hudson's and Mihailović's whereabouts, and to establish a coastal supply base. A former freelance journalist married to a Muslim woman from Sarajevo, Atherton had escaped to Egypt from Yugoslavia in April 1941 and then moved to Jerusalem, where he became accredited as a war correspondent to the British forces in the Middle East for the *Daily Mail*. While in Jerusalem, the scoop-hungry reporter volunteered to return to Yugoslavia, where he longed to be part of the events unfolding there. The SOE took Atherton on, and he left with a Royal Yugoslav Air Force captain, Radoje Nedeljković, and an Irish radio operator, Sergeant Patrick O'Donovan, on the Hydra mission, landing by rubber boat on February 4, 1942, near Petrovac, on the Montenegrin coast, where Hudson had landed. This mission, however, never established radio contact with Malta or Cairo, nor was it announced to Tito. Worst of all, their arrival coincided with a plan for a Soviet mission to arrive in Partisan territory (which would happen only two years later), and Tito, who had had no contact with the British since meeting Hudson in December 1941, received Atherton with suspicion. Tito thought that Atherton's arrival during an anticipated Soviet landing, along with Hudson's silence, was an indication of anti-Partisan views on the part of the British.

In addition to Atherton's problems, a fourth mission, code-named Disclaim, which landed near Sarajevo, had been picked up by the Ustaše on February 7, 1942, and turned over to the Germans. In a series of anxious communications between Tito and his representative in Bosnia, Svetozar Vukmanovic-Tempo, it was learned that the men from the Disclaim mission had been picked up near where Tito was hoping to meet Soviet emissaries. Just as he questioned the timing of Atherton's arrival, Tito was quick to suspect that the timing of that British mission into Yugoslavia was part of a British-Russian joint endeavor about which he had not been informed, further intensifying his distrust. The Soviets never came, wary as they were of Tito and of appearing to stray from the Allied line, resulting in turn in strained relations between Tito and the Soviets.

While Atherton did not find Hudson, he did find himself sucked into a vortex of events that would tragically overtake him. He was, all at once, in private consultation with a Mihailović rival Chetnik, keeping daily contact with the Partisan supreme staff, and denouncing Mihailović as a collaborator—actions that resulted from a series of shortsighted judgments and ultimately cost him his life. The rival Chetnik in question was General Ljubo Novaković, who was one of Mihailović's blood enemies and who desperately wanted to assume the commanding position of the Chetniks. Atherton disappeared from Partisan headquarters at Foča, a town on the Drina River in southeastern Bosnia, on the evening of April 15, 1942, after dining with Vladimir Velebit, a member of Tito's Supreme Staff. He had left with his radio operator, O'Donovan, and Nedeljković (the Royal Serbian officer with Atherton's Hydra mission), and with Novaković, under mysterious circumstances.

Novaković, rebuffed by Mihailović for an independent leadership mission and dismissed by Kosta Pećanac, an archrival of Mihailović's after they briefly worked together in central Serbia, had formed a small band of his own—one that caught the attention of Tito, who knew of Novaković's poor relationships with the main Chetnik leaders. Making matters more interesting, Novaković was married to the sister of Major Ostojić, the Royal Serb officer who had accompanied the first British mission to Yugoslavia under William Hudson (and who was, at this point, still missing). After a brief collaboration between Chetnik and Partisan guerrilla groups, or *odreds*, against the Ustaše slaughter of the Serbs from mid-1941 through the first half of 1942, Tito saw in Novaković further possible enemy-of-my-enemy advantage. The powerless but ambitious Chetnik might be useful, thought Tito, in rallying the Bosnian Chetniks under Partisan command and weakening the expansion of Mihailović's influence in that region and in Montenegro. However, on the evening that Novaković left with Atherton and the other two men of the mission, he left behind a note to Tito threatening the Partisan leader with the organization of 5,000 Bosnian Serbs which he, Novaković, would now organize.

Tito was incensed, fearing that the British had devised an elaborate plot to build up the Chetniks. Making matters worse, in Tito's mind, another British mission had landed in Dalmatia at the end of March. Tito wrote to the Central Committee of the Communist Party in Croatia: "We now have certain proof that the British, through their agents in Yugoslavia, are working not to remove but rather to intensify the differences between ourselves and other groups such as the Chetniks. England is supporting different Chetnik bands just as the Germans are doing and egging them on."[16] Tito was cautious about expressing his anger, however: "In public, the alliance between the Soviet Union, Britain, and the United States must continue to be stressed, and the latter two Powers are to be depicted as our allies. But their agents and pawns in our country must be opposed."[17]

Meanwhile, Atherton and his radio operator, O'Donovan, were lost in the wilds of eastern Bosnia, and the first bit of information to surface about them came from Major Ostojić, now a commander with Mihailović forces in the Sandžak and Montenegro. There, he met a lone Yugoslav officer wandering around his area who turned out to be Nedeljković, the officer who had accompanied Atherton on his mission to Yugoslavia and who disappeared with Atherton and the others the night of April 15. Ostojić then wrote to Mihailović about Atherton and O'Donovan in the middle of May. In that letter, Ostojić reported that Atherton had been "set free" by Novaković and was now lost in Bosnia somewhere, trying to make contact with Mihailović. Ostojić informed Mihailović of Atherton's sympathy for the Partisans ("the Communists"), yet Mihailović was open to finding and meeting the British officer. Not too long after receiving this initial news, Mihailović received a letter from Atherton "somewhere in Bosnia" saying that he was trying to reach the Chetnik leader's head-quarters, whereupon Mihailović signaled to London that he was "taking all necessary measures to locate him."[18]

Hudson, all the while, had been at Mihailović headquarters, saying that he was "treated by Mihailović as a prisoner."[19] When Hudson learned of the developments regarding Atherton, he set off for the Sandžak and Montenegro to find Ostojić at his new Chetnik command post. There, he questioned Nedeljković, who could offer little more than to say that he had separated from the Atherton mission under orders to cover other areas of Yugoslavia while the rest went on to Serbia. On June 20 a formal inquiry followed, ordered by Mihailović under pressure from Hudson. It was concluded that Atherton and his party had left Foča, in south-eastern Bosnia, on April 15 escorted by a Chetnik leader, Spasoje Dakić, who, according to the memoir of liaison officer F. W. D. Deakin, "might have been operating in some loose association with the movement of Mihailović," and who, for unclear reasons, later killed Atherton and his radio operator, O'Donovan.[20] The rebel Chetnik Novaković, for his part, was shot to death by the Chetnik Fifth Mountain Brigade at the end of 1943. For a while, the Partisans felt the British had blamed them for the deaths of Atherton and O'Donovan, given Tito's unconcealed anger with regard to the Britain-Mihailović relationship and the long silence follow-ing the debacle of those first two missions, which would last about a year. Ultimately, a Chetnik commander, the Royal Air Force captain Franc Berginec, who went over to the Partisan side in 1943, confirmed the first version of events. A few days later, Berginec committed suicide after being critically wounded by gunfire, to avoid being captured by the enemy.

• • •

With the various attempts to locate William Hudson over the course of 1942 having met with failure, the SOE Cairo decided to parachute a senior mission to Mihailović's headquarters, in increasingly frustrated hopes of getting some idea about the true state of affairs in Yugoslavia. It was now autumn of 1942, and the only information the British had about Yugoslavia over a year into the war and about the pivotal events of the past months came from the uneven reports of William Hudson. Another mining expert with experience in Yugoslavia was thus attached to SOE Cairo for the new assignment, Colonel S. W. Bailey, a former staff member of the British-owned Trepča mines in Serbia who was fluent in the Serbo-Croat language and considered a specialist on Balkan affairs. He had headed the SOE staff in Belgrade during the summer of 1940 and knew the personalities involved in the March 27, 1941, coup d'état. He parachuted into Serbia on Christmas Day 1942, with a particularly difficult mission, however. His arrival came at a time when Mihailović had cooled to British requests for active cooperation with them, owing to the inadequacy of supplies the Chetniks were receiving and his perception of British favoritism to the Partisans. The civil war between the two sides, meanwhile, continued to worsen.

Colonel Bailey had an overall positive impression of the Chetniks, but he saw right from the start that Mihailović was "determined to eliminate all rivals before attacking the armies of occupation." Mihailović was further convinced, wrote Bailey, that all Croatian guerrillas not under his direct command "were a hundred percent Communist and must be destroyed."[21] The complicated matter of Bailey's relationship with Mihailović and his protest that his reports concerning Mihailović were not getting through to the proper channels at SOE Cairo or London are covered in a later chapter. In February 1943 Bailey proposed to his superiors a plan to organize the British missions around the Chetniks and the Partisans. Bailey was of the realistic opinion that there was no hope in trying to reconcile the two rival groups and thus suggested a geographical division based on the current areas of influence of either side as the best hope for an "incidental" united front against the Axis. There would be a "Tito Republic" in Western Croatia and a "Mihailović Republic" in Serbia, including Serb enclaves in Bosnia. The presence of Tito in Western Croatia would give the Germans new cause for anxiety, and Mihailović, in Bailey's words, would be deprived of "his principal excuse for not fighting the Axis."[22] Neither side would have to negotiate with the other, using instead Bailey or Hudson as emissaries, and as a result neither would lose face among their rivals. Mihailović generally agreed to the proposal and accepted Bailey's idea that British sub-missions be allowed into Serbia to help carry out independent sabotage against agreed-upon targets. Mihailović was still convinced that the British would not take Tito seriously. "Can a convict like Josip Broz who is listed with the Zagreb police . . . alias leader of the Communists under the name of 'Tito,' be compared with the Yugoslav army as a national fighter . . . ?" wrote Mihailović to his government in a telegram of March 8, 1943.[23] A few months later, in April 1943, nine sub-missions with independent radio links to Cairo were dropped into Serbia, sent to selected strategic points in Serbia to collect evidence of Chetnik strength, to conduct independent sabotage operations, and to keep an eye out for acts of "collaboration"—charges that would soon swell into a massive controversy, with the Chetniks accusing SOE Cairo and the BBC of deliberate censorship (and the Partisans accusing the BBC of same as well). The later defense of Mihailović against these charges by the very British officers in Yugoslavia who were often gravely critical of him became a notable example of the sense of valor and integrity that defined these missions.

Bailey's proposal was, however, rejected outright by London. Sir George Rendel, the ambassador to the Royal Yugoslav government in exile in London, was against the idea of transferring Tito to Croatia, thinking that such an action would exacerbate the rivalries there between the Serbs and the Croats. Worse, to Rendel's thinking, was the possibility that these rivalries, combined with the Axis stronghold on Croatia, and then Tito's political exploitation of both, would eventually result in a Communist regime in Croatia. This regime, in turn, might become part of a Central European Communist bloc were Hungary and Austria to move in the same direction after the war. The alternatives, on the other hand, were not ideal either. The British could not rely upon their ally, the Soviets, as that would eventually mean all-out Partisan support, and Mihailović still controlled most of Serbia. It would further mean a complete break with the king, which the British were not willing to do. All-out support for Mihailović was also impossible, as that would mean a clash with the Russians and later possibly the establishment of a "pan-Serb" Yugoslavia. And so, British policy tentatively embarked upon one of the glorious failures of its wartime policy—that of supplying the two sides of the Yugoslav civil war and thereby unintentionally heightening the scale of that rivalry to its grotesque fever pitch of 1943 to 1944. Now, early assistance to the Partisans was urged while the current scale of support to Mihailovic—a meager scale thus far, as will be seen—was to continue.

With nine sub-missions having been organized as liaison to Mihailović, the British would now organize missions specific to the Partisans. There were a couple of probing missions sent ahead, so-called blind missions, as SOE Cairo was not entirely certain where Partisan headquarters were located—there would be ten Partisan headquarters in all by mid-1944— shifting as they did, like Mihailović, to avoid German detection. The first such blind mission was led mainly by Canadian volunteers of Yugoslav descent: Hoathley I, which went into Bosnia on April 21, 1943, and the second, Fungus, which was parachuted into the Lika area of Croatia on the same day. Tito, who had not heard from the British in over a year, was not keen on these new missions appearing from nowhere. Furthermore, a top-level delegation of Partisans had met just a few weeks earlier with the Germans to negotiate a ceasefire after the violent Unternehmen Weiss ("Operation White" or "The Fourth Offensive"), one of the largest of the six Axis offensives to take place in Yugoslavia, which began January 20, 1943, against both Partisans and Chetniks; it is also referred to in Yugoslav/Partisan history as the Battle of the Nerevta. More embarrassing to Tito, those negotiations also included joint action against a British landing in return for territorial accommodation. Croatian Partisan headquarters would not allow the men of the Fungus mission to make contact with Cairo, but eventually Tito relented, and SOE Cairo determined that a formal mission to the Partisans in Croatia should be sent.

Thus the first official British mission specifically to the Partisans consisted of Major William D. Jones, Captain A. D. N. Hunter, and radio operator Ronald Jephson, who "slowly and comfortably" landed in "the moonlit turfs of Croatia," as described by one account of the missions to Yugoslavia, on May 18, 1943.[24] When it was finally established, however, that Berane, Montenegro, was the main Partisan headquarters, this short-lived mission was soon replaced by a larger one, named "Typical." In one sense, this mission to the Partisans may be said to be the "first" in terms of its scope and the length of time on the ground. What's more, the mission landed at the onset of one of the most vicious German offensives in Yugoslavia, Operation Black (or the Fifth Offensive), also known as the

Battle of Sutjeska, directed, again, at both Partisans and Chetniks. The offensive began on May 15, 1943, and would last through June. The Typical mission was the first mission of all to experience what the Yugoslav rebel forces were dealing with on the ground.

Sir Frederick William Dampier Deakin, whose memoir has often been referred to in this chapter, was considered "one of the last British heroes of World War II."[25] As a young Oxford don, he had assisted Churchill in his biography of the Duke of Marlborough, and he would later write a famous portrait of the Hitler-Mussolini relationship.[26] After the war he would help the prime minister in the writing of his wartime memoirs. But like so many of his generation, he lived as both a man of thought and a man of action. Before the war broke out, Deakin had joined the Queen's Own Oxfordshire Hussars, and in 1941 he was transferred to Cairo to work at the Yugoslavia affairs section of the SOE. His first real taste of war, however, came when the Cairo office assigned the then twenty-nine-year-old Deakin to a parachute drop over Yugoslavia as head of the Typical mission to the Partisans. Deakin and five other crew members—his fellow officer W. F. Stuart, a disciplined, strong-willed forty-two-year-old Canadian who had spent many years in the Balkans and was well-versed in its languages and the history of the region's various nationalities; Corporal William Wroughton, a radio operator; Ivan Starčević, a Canadian of Croatian origin; Sergeant John Campbell; and a Palestinian Jew named Peretz Rosenberg, who was also a radio operator—all jumped from a Halifax bomber that left from Derna, Libya, only to arrive in a violent electrical storm over the skies of Montenegro on May 28, 1943. No sooner had the men landed in the Dumitor Mountains on the northeast border between Montenegro and Bosnia than they found themselves right in the middle of Operation Black.

What followed for Deakin, as recounted in *The Embattled Mountain*, stands as one of the more moving first-person accounts of the Partisan experience through the eyes of an outsider. In what came to be known in most Partisan lore/Yugoslav histories as the Battle of the Sutjeska, the six men of the Typical mission, escorted by Partisan soldiers from the Dumitor Mountains, found themselves trapped in a very narrow area between the Sujetska and Piva rivers, near the mountain stronghold of Vučevo, by 2,000 troops of the Partisan Third Division, which was dedicated to the protection of the wounded in the central Partisan hospital. The Partisans were preparing to lead the wounded and the fighting units in an urgent sortie across the Sutjeska, while German intelligence, meanwhile, had learned of the presence of Tito and his forces around that area and sealed the whole line of that river by reinforced German units, numbering around 40,000. (The total number of Partisans fighting in Unternehmen Schwarz was around 20,000, against approximately 100,000 German troops.) Any such crossing would have been met by an overwhelming frontal assault, yet the Partisan commander, Sava Kovačević, "a Montenegrin hero in the epic tradition of centuries," in the words of Deakin, decided to break up the division and send them scattered across the river, fighting independently, taking their wounded with them.[27]

The Germans waited for the men atop a hill, the Krekovi, in a disconnected line of dugouts, and as the Partisans stormed across the river, Kovačević ran directly into a German commander. The two men, Kovačević and the German, as each swiftly drew his revolver, were instantly killed by each other's bullets. So as not to demoralize the other men, Kovačević's body was quickly covered with branches by Partisan officers as the rest of the troops swept past. They held out in isolated pockets, overrunning smaller German units in the woods, beating them with rifles or stabbing them, as ammunition had been exhausted. The Germans then set out on a "merciless annihilation," and German, Bulgarian, and Italian troops combed the region looking for the hidden Partisans and wounded. Nurses as well as wounded were ruthlessly killed. Nor did the members of the Typical mission fare so well. While crossing the Tara River into the valleys of Bosnia with Partisan troops led by Tito in an attempt to avoid the strafing of German fighters overhead, Deakin and Tito sustained serious wounds from an exploding bomb that killed Deakin's fellow SOE officer, Captain W. F. Stuart. Eventually, the Partisans and Deakin and the remaining men of his mission were able to reach relative safety in eastern Bosnia. (The Chetniks, attacked from an entirely other direction, meanwhile, had escaped to Serbia.)

It had been Deakin's impression, like William Hudson's before him, that the Partisans were doing the bulk of the fighting against the Axis in general, while the British communication intercepts, the ULTRA program, revealed a large discrepancy in the number of casualties between Partisans and Chetniks during Unternehmen Schwarz. This was based on messages decoded from the German Enigma program, which showed that Schwarz had left 5,697 Partisans killed but caused only 15 casualties among the Chetniks.[28] This information was one catalyst in the British decision to begin air drops of matériel to the Partisans on June 25, 1943. Later, in September 1943, after the Italian Armistice and the surrender of arms by Italian divisions in Yugoslavia to the Partisans, the surge in armaments to the Partisans also tipped the strategic scales immensely in the Partisans' favor, as is also described in a later chapter.

With such reports supporting an increasingly pro-Partisan position in the mind of Churchill, the prime minister ordered one of the more elegant personalities in this saga to Yugoslavia to serve as his personal representative to Tito. "What we want," wrote Churchill, "is a daring Ambassador-leader with these hardy and hunted guerrillas."[29] On September 29, 1943, the thirty-two-year-old Brigadier Fitzroy Maclean—"a man of daring character" in Churchill's words—stepped onto the Yugoslavian stage, parachuting into Tito's regional headquarters at Jajce, in western Bosnia (with his American co-officer, Linn "Slim" M. Farish), arriving one week after Italy had surrendered to the Allies on September 8, 1943. The Eton- and Cambridge-educated Scottish aristocrat and foreign service officer had already lived a life of brash daring and adventure, gathering intelligence in Moscow during the Stalinist purges and famously getting himself elected to Parliament as a conservative MP in order to quit the Foreign Service and enlist in the army when war broke out. Churchill sought out men he knew and trusted such as Maclean and Deakin, and the former was appointed a non-SOE liaison to Tito, directly reporting to Churchill.

The Maclean appointment was at the highest level of missions to the Partisans, after which the SOE no longer played so significant a role in Yugoslav affairs. (Brigadier C. D. Armstrong was, theoretically, Maclean's counterpart with the Chetniks but he had no such personal relationship with the prime minister.) The Scotsman's parachuting into Yugoslavia caused a "mild sensation" at the House of Commons, "for I had never attended the House and none of my fellow members had the faintest idea who 'the honourable Member for Lancaster' was," he recounted in *Eastern Approaches*.[30] Maclean brought with him four other officers—two brash members of the Scots Guards, a gunnery expert, and, famously, Randolph Churchill, the son of the prime minister, whom Maclean found to be "dependable, possessing both endurance and determination" and whom Maclean felt "would get on well with the Jugoslavs, for his enthusiastic and at times explosive approach to life was not unlike their own."[31] He also brought with him the legendary major "Doc" Roberts, a New Zealander who commanded a Partisan field hospital, operating by candlelight in stables and cowsheds, speaking no Serbo-Croatian but having much affection for the "Pattersons," as he called them.[32] Maclean's critics held that the aristocratic brigadier held a rather naive view of Tito, despite Maclean's own upper-class background and intense dislike of Communism, having experienced firsthand the Soviet Union at the depths of that country's darkness and despair. However controversial his admiration for Tito, Maclean's field reports focused on Partisan military strategy and less on the nagging question of Partisan political ideology.

These writings, in turn, reinforced Deakin's own influential assessments of the Partisans. Together, the views of the two men helped to bring about the dramatic shift in British policy from official support of Mihailović to support of Tito. Maclean himself thought that *all* support should go to the Partisans. "We're getting . . . little or no return militarily from the arms we dropped to the Chetniks," he observed in a report, "which had hitherto exceeded in quantity those sent to the Partisans."[33] He argued that the arms delivered to the Chetniks were more likely to be used against the Partisans than against the Germans (and those officers attached to the Chetniks would later say the same of deliveries to the Partisans). "On purely military grounds," Maclean concluded, "we should stop supplies to the Chetniks and henceforth send all available arms and equipment to the Partisans."[34]

Nonetheless, around the time that Maclean was writing this report, the original American OSS liaisons to the Chetniks landed in Serbia in late summer and early autumn of 1943, one of the most aggressive periods of activity on the part of the Chetniks against the Axis forces. These officers included, first, Captain Walter R. Mansfield, landing in Serbia in mid-August 1943, followed by Colonel Albert B. Seitz and Captain George Musulin in late September that year. The Chetniks were involved in a half-dozen major attacks on those forces, and each time the enemy death toll was around 200 to 300. At Mučanj, to the south of Užice, on July 31 the Chetniks engaged a Bulgarian force, inflicting several casualties. On August 29 they derailed two troop trains and killed 200, while at Prijepolje on September 11 they attacked a German garrison

1,000 strong, killing another 200. The next day at Priboj, a town that lay
at the strategic crossroads between Serbia and Bosnia-Herzegovina, they
forced the surrender of an Italian garrison of 1,800 men.[35]

Such victories large and small continued on through the autumn and
early winter. On October 5, the Chetniks attacked an 800-strong German
garrison, killing "several hundred" of them, according to one summary
of Chetnik activity of this period.[36] After that attack they blew up the
Belgrade-Sarajevo rail line at Višegrad. On October 14 Mihailović forces
killed several hundred Ustaše. Four major railway bridges were destroyed,
and the tracks were torn up on the Sarajevo-Užice line. "In addition
to these actions—taken on their own initiative," wrote David Martin,
a British writer and postwar activist for the Chetnik cause, "they were
instrumental in compelling the surrender of the Italian Venezia Division
at Berane [Montenegro] and of substantial Italian units at Kotor and
other points."[37] There were two large-scale attacks by German forces on
Mihailović's headquarters, one on September 5 and the other on October
10 (1943). "This record is all the more remarkable," wrote Martin, "given
the fact that Mihailović received "pathetically little support in terms of
arms and ammunition."[38]

In late November Mihailović celebrated such victories by throwing a Thanksgiving celebration by the campfire in Ravna Gora for the
American mission with him, a giant letter "A" lit in flares across
the surrounding hills, filling the nighttime air with brazen defiance and
emotion, not to mention the Chetnik leader's love for America. Yet neither the military triumphs nor the expression of loyalty would amount
to much. For in late November and early December 1943 in Tehran,
Churchill, Roosevelt, and Stalin met to decide, among other things, that
military and political support for Mihailović was to come to an immediate end and that all supply deliveries to the Chetniks would stop. As that
conference was going on, Tito and his Partisans were over in another set
of mountains five hundred miles from Mihailović and his Americans, in
Jajce, Bosnia. There the Partisans convened to draw up the future political program of the Yugoslav state, which had just, in effect, been handed
over to them. With that, Mihailović was as good as gone.

4

The Balkan Prize

And they yearn to slay each other with the gilded scimitars;
but to whom the realm belongeth, no man of them doth know.

—"Urash and the Sons of Marnyava," from *The Battle
of Marko Kralyevich* (Serbian epic poetry cycle), 15th century

What was the importance, exactly, of Yugoslavia to the Axis or to
the Allies? Where the Germans were concerned it was, just as in
World War I, a question of Salonika, the strategic linchpin of the Balkan
corridor. "There seemed to be the idea, held principally by the French,"
wrote Viscount Cunningham of Hyndhope, the British Admiral of the
Fleet in World War II, "that in the spring of 1940 the Germans would
come down through the Balkans. The French had the view that we
should forestall them by landing a strong force at Salonika."[1] Bulgaria,
which signed the Tripartite Pact with the Axis powers on March 1, 1941,
wanted northern Macedonia, the "Uncontested Zone" of the 1912 treaties, which had followed the Balkan states' victory against the Ottoman
Empire. This area included all the country from Kyustendil, in the west-
central part of Bulgaria, south of Sofia, to Lake Ohrid, in the extreme
southwestern corner of today's Macedonia. These could not be ceded to
Bulgaria if Yugoslavia were to have a corridor to Salonika. Any territory
that passed into the hands of Bulgaria, so thought the Yugoslav General
Staff, would be occupied by German troops and thus serve to complete
the strategic envelopment of Yugoslavia—a repeat of World War I, essentially. "The military situation of Yugoslavia is quite simple," said one State

Department assessment of the situation. "Even though she might have to withdraw her forces to the Danube and the Sava, she is fairly strong so long as hostile forces do not appear on her Bulgarian frontier. . . . If they do she loses 75 percent of her defensive strength. If they reach Salonika also one may put the decline at 90 percent."[2]

For Yugoslavia, surrounded by Bulgaria and the Axis powers, Salonika was the one naval base and the only port through which Yugoslavia could maintain communication with Turkey (a neutral state until near the end of the war), England, and the United States. Serbia itself covered all of the north-south and north-to-southeast communications, vital in case major operations took place anywhere in the eastern Mediterranean. Were the Axis to get Salonika, these communications would be cut. The Yugoslavs maintained that they would enter the war in the event of a German attack on Greece only if such an attack came west of the Struma valley—that is, near the southeastern Serbian-Bulgarian border—and then only when the Yugoslav government decided what constituted a threat to Salonika and when that threat was imminent.

Salonika itself was once again to enter the picture following the German invasion of Yugoslavia on April 6, 1941. There was one main sticking point between the Yugoslav government (consisting, one must keep in mind, not just of pro-monarchist Serbs but also of Royalist Croats and Slovenes) and those more nationally minded Croats and Slovenes who sought complete independence from the monarchy. In preparing for the eventuality of war, the strategic interest of the nationalist-minded Croats and Slovenes focused on their own Adriatic ports, while Salonika was entirely of no interest as a kind of Yugoslav rallying point against the Germans.[3] While officially opposed, with the royal government, to German occupation of Yugoslavia, they were not so concerned as the Serbs regarding the encroachment of the Germans.

Yugoslavia was also of great interest for its natural resources. Of these, Germany was interested primarily in Serbia's strategic minerals and in exploiting their untapped potential. The chrome mines in Macedonia, which languished before the war, had been reopened and modernized. Within the first two years of the war, approximately 73,000 tons of chrome ore were sent from these mines to Germany. Antimony mines in western Serbia were used by the Germans to facilitate the extraction of the ore. The Trepca mines, once managed by the British, produced zinc and lead and ranked with Germany as one of the two largest lead producers in the world, producing 75 percent of the total Yugoslav output. (Because of transportation difficulties, the production of bauxite, used mainly for strengthening steel, was curtailed. This led to a severe decrease in aluminum production, then based around Ljubljana, Slovenia, for the Germans.) Most of all, the Germans were interested in the extraction of copper from the Bor mines, east of Kragujevac, the traditional military arsenal of Serbia, and then one of the leading copper mines in Europe. It was the biggest such mine controlled by the Germans, producing about 60,000 to 100,000 tons of copper annually, representing between 30 and 50 percent of the total copper supplies available to Germany. The significance of these mines for Allied wartime strategy was duly noted: "The Germans have made extensive plans for developing the Mine [at Bor] and employ three times the pre-war amount of Labour," read one British intelligence analysis.[4]

Germany's Oil-Arms Pact with Romania in May 1940 led to the peak of German economic hegemony in the Balkans between mid-1940 and the autumn of 1941. In June 1940 deliveries to the Reich were up from about 20,000 tons in February to 105,000 tons, with deliveries averaging over 100,000 tons per month for the rest of that year. By July 1941 two pipelines had been constructed linking the Ploesti fields with the Danube port of Giurgiu. The Danube tanker fleet was also enlarged. In the following years Romania became, in the words of one German diplomat, a "filling station which functioned like an automaton.[5]

Also of interest to the Germans was the industrial manpower that Yugoslavia had provided to Germany. Before the outbreak of the war, Germany used to import seasonal agricultural workers from Yugoslavia; during the war, labor, obviously, was needed not only for agricultural but also for industrial endeavors. When a Nazi-loyal regime was established in Serbia and the "Independent State of Croatia" was created after the German invasion of Yugoslavia, special bureaus were organized in both states with the task of recruiting laborers for the Reich, and from Serbia alone hundreds of thousands of peasants and industrial workers were organized into special squads and then sent to Germany. These squads, moreover, received a new education necessary for the full realization of Nazi Germany's planned "New World Order."

During the campaign in Greece and Crete, Yugoslav communication lines through the Morava-Vardar Valley were used for almost the entire German troop movement, and during the Africa campaign of the summer of 1942, Yugoslav rail lines made for the easiest and quickest military transportation system. During the Italian campaign, Slovenian railroads began to operate at an unprecedented capacity, carrying troops and matériel to and from Italy. Yugoslavia also became a regrouping center for the German forces; divisions were brought there for recuperation and the formation of new detachments. Given Germany's strategic interest in Yugoslavia, the Balkan region became one of the most sensitive areas in Europe.

• • •

Around this time, the Hellenic army had beat back the Italian forces that invaded Greece on October 28, 1940, forcing the Italians to retreat by mid-December. Greece was now occupying most of Albania, tying down around 530,000 Italian troops. If Germany wanted to put an end to the Greek campaign in Albania by force, Yugoslav territory would provide the most convenient base. When Italy declared war on Greece in 1940, Yugoslavia was placed in a critical position. What happened to Mussolini's plans in Greece is a familiar story: In October 1940, without informing Berlin, Mussolini ordered nine divisions—some 100,000 men—to move from Albania into northern Greece. The Greek army proved ready for war, however, and the Italians, lured into the mountains bordering Greece and Albania, were attacked by columns of Greeks who managed, only a month later, to regain all lost territory and who then began to push into Albania. The war reached a stalemate by winter, with the Greeks controlling more than a quarter of Albania; an Italian offensive in March 1941 failed to dislodge them. While the Italians suffered substantial losses, Hitler was planning the invasion of Russia, Unternehmen Barbarossa, which would take place in the spring of 1941. Concerned about the security of his southern flank, and especially the possibility of British air attacks from Greece, Hitler intended to finish what his ally had started. But Hitler had not wanted war with Yugoslavia.

Italian and German policies in the Balkans differed. Italy had territorial claims on Yugoslavia and had long aimed at destroying the kingdom since its inception at the end of World War I. Germany, on the other hand, had no such immediate policy, and Hitler would have preferred Yugoslavia's benevolent neutrality. He had no wish to involve himself in a complicated war in the Balkans when he was secretly preparing his giant blow against Russia.

Meanwhile, Prince Paul Karadjordjević, acting as regent to the seventeen-year-old King Peter, wanted to bide his time until Yugoslavia was in a position to come out openly on the side of the Allies. At this point, Hitler had already made up his mind about the fate of Yugoslavia a year or so earlier. "He speaks with a great deal of calm and becomes excited only when he advises us to give Yugoslavia the coup de grace as soon as possible," wrote the Italian foreign minister, Count Galeazzo Ciano, of his meeting with Hitler in Salzburg on August 12, 1939.[6] The prince sought to keep Germany and Italy at bay, for any failed relations with those two would strengthen the claims of Hungary, Austria, and Bulgaria, all enemies, on Yugoslav territory.

This sense of international isolation on the part of Yugoslavia, and hence, Belgrade's caution with the Axis powers, was understandable. For one thing, the country could not expect any military aid in the event of war. It was not part of British policy to defend countries like Yugoslavia, where there were no British long-term interests, and the British government made it clear to the Yugoslavs that it did not have the means to help them militarily or equip them with arms and ammunition should war break out. Prince Paul continued to ask for military aid, yet was told by the British Legation in Belgrade that Yugoslavia was one of the countries to which Britain could in no circumstances give direct naval and military assistance.

Yugoslavia now had no friendly neighbors other than Greece, and the foremost concern in Prince Paul's mind was whether or not signing on to the Tripartite Pact with Germany would be to Yugoslavia's practical advantage. Finland, which was no Fascist state, joined up with the Germans after Hitler's attack on the Soviet Union on June 22, 1941. Sweden cooperated with the Germans during the war, refusing passage for Allied troops through her current territory to help Finland, while allowing the Germans later to send troops from Finland through Sweden to Norway. This act violated Sweden's pledge of neutrality and also put Norway at risk. Turkey, in spite of British prodding, refused to be drawn into war against Germany. During the war and afterward, the actions of Finland, Sweden, and Turkey were more or less accepted and forgotten.

Yugoslavia would be a separate case, though, and the country ended up in a kind of damned-if-she-did, damned-if-she-didn't, relationship with her allies. Prince Paul, an unabashed Anglophile, maintained excellent relations with the British. He had been on good terms with the British minister in Belgrade, Sir Nevile Henderson, and Sir Ronald Campbell, Henderson's successor, and he had a direct personal telephone line with the embassy. He rejected the idea of allowing police supervision of the embassy, which was imposed on other missions in Belgrade. This relaxed attitude regarding observation, however, might have contributed to the ease with which SOE (Special Operations Executive) agents in Belgrade were able to complete their role in the March 27, 1941, coup d'état and the ultimate removal of the prince from Yugoslavia without resistance.

But despite the prince's warm personal relations with the British, London maintained its distance from Belgrade's anxieties. First off, the British tended to view Prince Paul politically as veering from the pro-Western path that King Alexander, his predecessor, had sought to define for the Yugoslav kingdom. Prince Paul, it was said, was drawing too closely into the German camp. King Alexander himself, however, shortly before his assassination in 1934, had sought good relations with Germany as the situation in Europe was starting to veer toward ideological extremes. The British in Yugoslavia also recognized this. On December 28, 1933, Sir Henderson had reported back to London: "Instead of the Balkans continuing to be, as formerly, a constant danger to the peace of Europe, it is Europe today which is the sole danger to the peace of the Balkans."[7] That same year he wrote, "An appreciation in this country of Germany's possible value as a counterpoise to Italian policy, intrigues and interference in the Balkans is beginning to gain ground. It is therefore possible that the next few years . . . will see a marked advance toward a closer understanding between Yugoslavia and Germany. The Yugoslav nation as a whole relies on England to maintain the peace of Europe. Piqued though they are by what they regard as British public indifference to their own country."[8]

On the April 16, 1934, King Alexander told Henderson that there was no immediate danger at all of his going over to the German camp. Yugoslavia was a member of the Little Entente, an alliance formed in

1920 between Czechoslovakia, Yugoslavia, and Romania to forestall any resurgence of Hungary's loyalty to the Habsburg dynasty. But all of this was essentially meaningless in view of Yugoslavia's anxiety with regard to Italy (and the Entente was destined to break up anyway by 1938). The Treaty of Rapallo (1920) and the Treaty of Rome (1924) had given over large amounts of territory from Yugoslavia to Italy, including the "Julian March" border areas between Italy, Slovenia, and Croatia; the Dalmatian coastal cities; and the former Croatian city of Rijeka, which became the Free State of Fiume in 1920; Fiume, the city, became part of Italy in 1924. But Italy continued to want more. As a means of keeping Italy at bay, King Alexander was bound to keep the door open for Germany. In his report of the conversation, Henderson commented, "It is Italy who holds the key of the solution. . . . It is this consideration which is largely responsible for the Yugoslav receptiveness towards Germany. This is only natural."[9]

Italy had come into this renewed position of strength vis-à-vis Yugoslavia, by way of the French. Of the countries in Europe most alarmed by the rise of Hitler, it may be said that France, through its foreign minister Louis Barthou, took the most action initially, even offering territorial concessions to Germany to bring the latter back into the framework of the League of Nations. Beyond its commitments to the Little Entente, France, under Barthou's plan, also planned a grand alliance between European countries and the USSR, as well as a Mediterranean security agreement involving Italy and Yugoslavia, to thwart German ambitions. King Alexander was in favor of the French plan, but insisted that the French support Yugoslavia against the designs of Mussolini, who wanted much more of the Croatian territory of Dalmatia for his growing Nuovo Italiano Imperio than the treaties of post–World War I had granted Italy. King Alexander was further troubled over the Italian dictator's support of the separatist movement of Ustaše leader Ante Pavelić in Croatia. In early October 1934 Barthou was killed by a policeman's bullet in Marseille during the chaos that followed the assassination of King Alexander by the Bulgarian revolutionary Vlado Chernozemski, who had plotted with Ante Pavelić's Ustaše and also the Internal Macedonian Revolutionary Organization (IMRO). Relations between Italy and Yugoslavia then worsened dramatically. Pavelić, who was sentenced in absentia for plotting the murder, fled to Italy, and Mussolini refused to extradite him to Yugoslavia.

Then, one of the most serious consequences for Belgrade developed when Germany occupied Czechoslovakia in the spring of 1939 and, with that, took over the famous Skoda arms factory in Bohemia, once the main source of Yugoslavia's supply of armaments. Yugoslavia could not immediately break off these vital commercial-military links, particularly as the West was unable to provide an alternative supply. A swift series of German invasions then followed throughout 1940: On March 1, Germany invaded Norway to secure, among other things, control of the Atlantic from its icefree harbors; to reach the iron ore mines of Sweden; and to prevent a British and French invasion. The collapse of the Low Countries—Belgium, Holland, and Luxembourg—then followed in mid-May, followed by Germany's swift conquest of France that same month and Italy's declaration of war on France in June. This horrifyingly rapid chain of events in Europe cut Yugoslavia off from the possibility of help from the Western side. By 1941 it would have required a leap of faith for the Yugoslav government to place trust in Britain's ability to save the country from Hitler's aggression.

But whatever the Royal Yugoslav government's "excuses," the coup d'état that followed Prince Paul's signing of the pact was a disaster, precipitating the German attack on Yugoslavia (and Greece), as described earlier. The specifics of the coup itself were as follows: on the morning of March 27, 1941, officers, mostly Serbs, from the Royal Yugoslav Air Force, under the leadership of General Pilot Bora Mirković and the commanding officer of the air force, General Dušan Simović, overthrew the (Dragiša) Cvetković–(Vladko) Maček government—that is, the Serbian prime minister and the Croat vice premier, respectively, whose 1939 Agreement sought to guarantee more Croatian autonomy within the constitutional monarchy of the Royal Karadjordjević ruling house. It was a nonviolent, "bloodless" coup against that government's signing of the Tripartite Pact with the Axis powers at Belvedere Palace in Vienna. Now in its place was young King Peter II, the nephew of Prince Paul. He was proclaimed the reigning monarch and General Simović was appointed the head of government. Prince Paul was arrested and handed over to the British. (Anthony Eden, the British foreign secretary and no friend of the prince's since their days at Oxford, exiled Prince Paul and his consort, Princess Olga, to Kenya under charges of treason. Months later they were able to move to South Africa.)

The Serbian population was jubilant at the coup—as was much of the world. With that event, Prime Minister Winston Churchill famously declared that Yugoslavia had "found its soul" and wrote in his memoirs that the coup was "one tangible result of our desperate efforts to form an Allied front in the Balkans" and to prevent "all falling piecemeal into Hitler's power."[10] Celebrations took place all over Serbian towns, and Hitler, incensed, ordered leaders to postpone the invasion of the Soviet Union and destroy Yugoslavia immediately, with an emphasis on severe punishment of the Serbs. (It is thought that the invasion of Yugoslavia had an indirect effect on Hitler's defeat on the Russian front, as the delayed attack on the Soviet Union pushed that campaign into the harsh winter, whereupon the German army was decisively defeated by the Red Army.)

Hitler was convinced that the British were behind the coup, and those suspicions appeared to be correct. Sir Cecil Parrott, then a tutor to King Peter in the Karadjordjević royal household and later ambassador to Czechoslovakia during the Prague Spring of 1968, wrote in his memoir of his years in Serbia that Hugh Dalton, the minister in charge of the SOE, sought such a turn of events. "We sent a wire to our friends to use all means to raise a revolution [in Belgrade]," Parrott quotes Dalton as saying. "This was a unique case of the Foreign Office and the British Legation together with 'the Ministry of Ungentlemanly Warfare' [the SOE] as Dalton called it, engineering a coup against a government with which they enjoyed more than friendly relations."[11]

British intelligence, in the form of the Secret Intelligence Service (SIS), had been active in Belgrade since the 1930s. By the late 1930s, Section D of the SIS was organized specifically for clandestine activities and became the nucleus of the new Special Operations Executive, the brainchild, as mentioned earlier, of Churchill and Dalton. Belgrade became the main center of Section D activities in the Balkans. According to British scholar David A. T. Stafford, the British subsidized many Serbian political parties whose leaders would later resign after the signing of the Tripartite Pact—the Serb Peasant Party, the Independent Democratic Party, and the Narodna Odbrana ("Defense of the People") among them, while the sometime head of the Serb Peasant Party, Milos Tupanjanin, was known as "the principal agent of the British intelligence service among the Serbs."[12]

The execution of the coup is thought to have been largely the product of behind-the-scenes work of the British air attaché, Captain A. H. H. MacDonald, who worked with the rebel air force generals Simović and Mirković, both of whom were reportedly receiving money from the SOE.[13] It is also thought that the British government played more of a role than is generally acknowledged, citing the presence of a longtime operative of the British Intelligence Service, T. G. Mapplebeck (who was not SOE), who became the assistant of Captain MacDonald, as the key contact figure. Hope was invested in the air force, and with the younger army officers—in particular the General Staff. It was at this time that the military attaché at the British Embassy, Lieutenant Colonel C. S. Clarke, close friends with the head of Serbian intelligence, first met Draža Mihailović, in the summer of 1940.[14] As relations with Serbian army officers grew, so did trust. By March 1941 MacDonald reported that General Simović was "head of an organization intending to carry out a coup d'état" and that "we should not have to wait more than a few days."[15]

Yugoslavia's collapse was speedy and complete. "There followed in twelve days time the deepest humiliation a nation can suffer in its history," wrote Parrott, "the utter defeat of its army and a degrading capitulation, while leaders of the coup fled the country and left the people to suffer the consequences."[16] The coup instigators tried to present their actions as a protest against the government's capitulation to Germany. It may be argued, however, that their motives were not entirely honorable. The rash nature of the coup, and the quick retreat of its conspirators, highlighted the recklessness of the Serb officers who led it and the little regard they had for Croatian and Slovenian caution in pursuing a policy exclusively in the Serb interest.[17] It was, furthermore, convenient for the officers to portray Prince Paul's negotiations with Maček and his endeavors to bring about a Serb-Croat understanding as caving in to Croatian demands, and the signing of the Tripartite Pact as a "sellout" to the Germans. The situation was, in either case, far more complex. Maček tried to convince Prince Paul to resist the coup, but did not succeed. Maček, in turn, remained in Yugoslavia under close surveillance by both the pro-Axis NDH (Nezavisna Država Hrvatska, or the Independent State of Croatia) and the Serbian puppet regime.

Months prior to the coup, the British attitude toward Yugoslavia had swung from accepting Yugoslavia's neutrality to that of pressuring the

Yugoslavs for a more aggressive stance against Germany. The reason for this was the deteriorating Balkan situation: Romania had joined the Tripartite Pact on November 23, 1940. Early in 1941 the British sent a mechanized force to Greece. The British now wanted the promise of full Yugoslav support if Greece were to be attacked by the Germans through Bulgaria, even if the Germans promised not to attack Yugoslavia in that operation. The promise of the postwar restoration of the Italian-Yugoslav border was offered in return, but Prince Paul rejected such terms and refused to meet British foreign secretary Anthony Eden.

A genuine Anglophile, Prince Paul was educated at Oxford and, before becoming prince regent, had spent much time in England, where his two sons were born; he always spoke English at home with his wife and family. His children had English nurses and went to school in England. His wife's sister was the duchess of Kent. In the spirit of such loyalty toward Britain, he sought to find out what aid, if any, the British would extend were Belgrade to go to war. The British would not commit to any assistance, according to the report from a Yugoslav military delegate in Athens, who had been in discussion with British military representatives.[18]

The prince was upset that the British had failed to understand the real intentions of Bulgaria—again something of a replay of the Balkan theater of World War I. The prince had refused to withdraw troops from Croatian and Slovenian frontiers, fearing the resulting disunity of Yugoslavia. He emphasized in a memo to Arthur Bliss Lane, the American minister at the U.S. Legation in Belgrade, that "Yugoslavia would under no conditions sign the Tripartite Pact nor would it join 'new world order' which is same thing."[19] The Germans knew Yugoslavia would resist, hence they proceeded via Bulgaria rather than taking the easier and more logical route through Yugoslavia. The prince added that the ammunition shortage was critical, as the only factory at Kragujevac could be demolished in two days and the British could not or would not furnish bullets for new Yugoslav guns.[20]

The British were ruthless in their treatment of the Yugoslav government, and Prince Paul in particular. Churchill believed that there were no neutrals in the war—only nonbelligerents—and that they must not be allowed to stand in the way of great powers fighting for their existence. For this reason, he ordered the British minister in Belgrade, Sir Ronald Ian Campbell, to get on the case of Prince Paul. On the other hand, from the perspective of the prince, his small nation was in a struggle for survival, and any number of options—including temporary deals with the devil—had to be considered.

Prince Paul, in return, feebly attached a series of conditions to his signing the Tripartite Pact: that German military troops could not enter Yugoslavia, that the sanctity of Yugoslav borders would be respected, and, further, that there would be no expectation that Yugoslav troops would be called upon to fight for Germany. Yugoslavia would allow the transport of war material from the north to the south and the breakdown of anti-Axis influence in the country, and would become part of the economic framework of the German Reich. The pact would be signed in eight days.

Pressure was building on the prince regent. It was for him a question of whether it was better to hand over a country intact or one in ruins. Once the Germans got to Salonika, however, Yugoslavia would be completely surrounded. To which Lane replied, "If we wished to pursue the comfortable easy course we would not have passed the Aid-to-Democracies bill, and that our past and present attitude towards small nations including Yugoslavia is proof of that sympathy."[21] An annoyed Prince Paul countered that at the moment when Europe "is being sacked and Yugoslavia is faced with disaster long-winded speeches continue in [the American] Senate on a Lend-Lease Bill."[22] His pessimism surfaced darkly. "I am out of my head; I wish I were dead," he said to Lane, who wrote to Washington, "I have never seen Prince so upset and unless he is an excellent actor. He ranted about Bulgarian perfidy, British stupidity and opposition of Croats but he refused to consider possibility of not signing pact and capitulating to Germany."[23] Prince Paul maintained that the Germans had definite plans to go to Salonika and then make demands on Yugoslavia. There were two courses open to him: to resist, at the cost of two or three hundred thousand lives and devastation of the country, the establishment of totalitarian conditions, and the partition of the country between Germany, Italy, Hungary, and Bulgaria; or to keep quiet and permit the country to be occupied under oppressive conditions without the loss of life.

The prince had refused Hitler's invitation twice before. Then he visited Hitler in Berlin on March 21, and, expecting significant concessions from Germany, signed the Tripartite Pact with the Germans. "Yugoslavs seem to have sold their souls to the Devil," wrote Sir Alexander Cadogan, the permanent undersecretary at the Foreign Office, in his diary, of the event. "All these Balkan people are trash."[24]

• • •

Whether anyone—Soviet, British, American—was actually taking the Serbian view into consideration did not seem evident. Prince Paul's minister of the court, Milan Antić, explained the prince's position to Cecil Parrott, the British chargé d'affaires to the Karadjordjević royal family during the war. "The Prince's aim," declared Antic,

> was to maintain the best possible relations with the German government so that with its help Mussolini's underhand hostility towards our country could be neutralized. We knew that the Italians were supporting the Croat Ustaše; they were also trying to draw Maček into their sphere of influence with the object of tearing Croatia away from Yugoslavia and taking it under their wing. We were aware, too, that Mussolini had intended settling scores with us at the end of 1939 and the beginning of 1940 but had been checked each time by the Germans, who did not consider it to be in their interest to have a conflagration in the Balkans. Finally Mussolini attacked Greece, but without Germany's agreement, as Hitler himself told Prince Paul when they met at Berchtesgaden a few days before the signing of the Pact.[25]

Prince Paul's attitude showed the extreme difficulty in which he was placed. The prince, having to assess the chances of military victory, was told by his advisers that the country could not hold out for more than a week, and that, even with British help, the Greeks could not resist much longer. The Karadjordjević ruler had also public opinion, especially in Croatia, to consider. It was thus nearly impossible for him to come to a decision until he was sure that there was no option other than surrender to the Germans or fighting them. "When Anthony Eden was told by his Minister [Campbell] that if we needed the Yugoslav's help we must offer them military equipment and if possible make a demonstration in the Adriatic, his reply had been guarded," wrote Parrott. "We could not promise to supply more than petrol and lubricants, he said, and later, three ton lorries."[26]

Parrott further says,

> In his book *Eastern Approaches*, Brigadier Fitzroy MacLean writes that "King Alexander's assassination did not lead to any change in the character of the regime he had established. If anything it became more oppressive under the rule of his cousin." This is an astonishing statement. When I arrived in Yugoslavia before the assassination the Croat and Slovene leaders were under lock and key. After Prince Paul took over, Dr. Korosec, the Slovene leader was released and made Minister of the Interior and the Prince set Dr. Macek free and repeatedly conferred with him about a settlement of the Croat question. Prince Paul had actually done his best to try to modify the dictatorial regime of King Alexander. He had achieved an understanding with the Croats. But he had received little help from the Western democracies and with his disappearance from the scene his country reverted to totalitarian rule.[27]

The prince regent explained this to Lane. "While many Serb voices cry for the war against the Axis, the deep silence of the Croats and Slovenes marks their reluctance to take any step that would bring the armies of Germany and Italy into their land. Am I to hand over to King Peter a country which is intact or one that is in ruins?"[28]

The Americans, for their part, played the role of peripheral mediator, urging Prince Paul to stay on the side of the Allied powers, noting that, in any case, the Tripartite Pact would not be any guarantee against future German attacks. Despite the increasing German threat to Yugoslavia, however, Washington remained essentially unmoved by the whole Balkan question. When Robert D. Murphy, the political adviser at Allied Force Headquarters (AFHQ), accompanied Roosevelt to the Cairo Conference in November 1943, he attempted to explain to the president the situation between Tito and Mihailović. Franklin Roosevelt was not interested. "We should build a wall around those two fellows and let them fight it out," he said, not entirely joking. "Then we could do business with the winner."[29] Such comments echoed those of the German commander in Croatia, Edmund Glaise von Horstenau, who once remarked that it was Germany's luck that the civil war between the Chetniks and the Partisans meant that the two would fight each other to the last man.[30] Murphy added, "Neither then nor later did Roosevelt ever have any consistent policy towards Yugoslavia."[31] U.S. foreign policy took on a more or less indifferent attitude toward the Balkans and Italy after the fall of Rome in September 1943 and the abdication of King Victor Emmanuel III. The State Department came to accept Tito's leadership as a fait accompli, following the report of an OSS agent, Major Richard Weil Jr., of April 1944, which was perhaps more remarkable in its naive view of Tito's ambitions than in its powers of prophecy.[32]

• • •

Yet more vague was the reaction of the Soviets to the turn of events in Yugoslavia. "We will do nothing," was the response of a military attaché at the Soviet Legation in Belgrade when he was asked what position Soviet Russia would assume in the event of an Axis attack on Yugoslavia.[33] The March 27 coup in Belgrade garnered no word from Moscow, no "congratulations," nor even any mention of the "overthrow" of anything monarchist or "imperial," with one lone cable quietly dispatched from Moscow to Belgrade saying only that congratulations were *not* sent "perhaps because of an oversight on the part of the Soviet Government, or because the idea did not occur to anyone."[34] It was only in September 1941 that Moscow named Ambassador Aleksander Bogomolov as minister to King Peter.

The Soviet attitude toward the Royal Yugoslav government—still its official wartime ally—was maddeningly ambiguous for Belgrade. At the time of the German bombing of Yugoslavia and the collapse of the Yugoslav state, the Soviet Union had, less than a year earlier, concluded diplomatic relations with the Yugoslav government as a means of strengthening her position in the Balkans. Under the terms of the Molotov-Ribbentrop Pact, the Red Army advanced into Romania and occupied Bessarabia (the eastern part of modern Moldova) and Northern

Bukovina (in northeastern Romania). Obviously, Russia was not indifferent to events in southeastern Europe. But whether that country was going to side with Belgrade or not remained anyone's guess. One indication of Soviet ambivalence was the failure to supply any of the arms and war material promised to Yugoslavia, even though discussions for that material had been several months along before the Axis invasion of that state. In November 1940 these discussions were discontinued, and although the Yugoslavs asked the Soviet minister to Belgrade to deliver a full list of their military requirements before he left for Moscow in March 1941, no deliveries were made to the Yugoslav Royal government. What's more, five days after the March 27 coup, Momčilo Ninčić, the foreign minister in the new government, informed his envoy in Moscow, Milan Gavrilović, that the Soviets were ready to sign a military and political pact with Yugoslavia. And thus the draft of a "Pact of Mutual Assistance" was drawn up, only to have Vyacheslav Molotov, the Soviet foreign minister, reject it with the view that it would end the Soviet Union's "friendly" relations with Germany.

Moscow then produced an alternative draft of a "Friendship and Non-Aggression Pact" with the Yugoslavs, which Gavrilović was instructed to sign. On April 4, the day before the pact was signed, Molotov summoned the German ambassador, Friedrich Werner Graf von der Schulenburg, to assure him, rather futilely, that the pact was in no way directed against Germany but was meant solely as a contribution toward preserving peace. The signing of the Yugoslav-Soviet Friendship and Non-Aggression Pact on April 5, 1941, obviously did little to keep Hitler from invading the Yugoslav state the next day. Ambassador von der Schulenburg told Molotov on the morning of April 6 that Germany felt impelled to attack Yugoslavia and Greece, and Molotov was told to say nothing of the pact signed only the day before unless he, Molotov, himself raised the matter. The Soviet foreign minister thus simply declared that it was an unfortunate set of circumstances and that was that. In other words, just as the Soviet Union was declaring the strength of a new phase of Soviet-Yugoslav diplomacy in preventing the spread of war, German bombs were dropping on Belgrade and German tanks were plowing through Yugoslavia's skeletal military forces.

With the start of the German invasion of the Soviet Union on June 22, 1941, another one of these "pacts," the diplomatic farce that was the

"Non-Aggression Pact" between Moscow and Berlin, fell apart, and the Soviets found themselves in desperate need of allies. The Yugoslav government in exile was now under the political protection of the British, and Moscow sought to exert some control over that weakened Yugoslav government as well. The Yugoslav politicians, eager to envision a postwar settlement, sought out Soviet representatives in London with a somewhat naive, if hopeful, view toward Soviet aid that would later restore an independent Yugoslav state with prewar frontiers, and establish an internal structure that would be decided upon by the Yugoslav people and government. On August 28, 1941, a formal agreement to restore diplomatic relations was signed, and shortly afterward a Soviet minister was accredited to the Yugoslav government in exile. The Friendship and Non-Aggression Pact between Moscow and Belgrade, which had been concluded between the two governments a day before the German invasion of Yugoslavia, was still considered by the Soviets to be in force. Nonetheless, "friendship" is not the word to describe relations between the two countries. Later the same year, the Yugoslav government protested Moscow's sponsorship of a "Pan-Slav Congress"—its cozy appeal to ethnic independence masking a Communist agenda—in which the right of Montenegrins and Macedonians to seek self-determination was championed.

Tito, meanwhile, was waiting in the wings, albeit impatiently. The Soviet government had primarily two concerns: first, the failure of the Yugoslav Communist Party to penetrate official circles in Belgrade and, more important, Stalin's ambitions to move Russia's economic and military frontiers to the Adriatic. Moscow's attitude toward Mihailović had less to do with political or personal considerations than it did with the larger questions of Russia's postwar aims in the whole of the Balkans. The Soviets knew they had to proceed carefully with their propaganda. For although the Communist party of Yugoslavia had made powerful social and political inroads since its inception, opposition to Communism, in general, remained strong throughout the country and in particular within Serbia. The Yugoslav foreign minister Alexander Cinčar-Marković saw no threat of any "bolshevization" of the Balkans. Upon the defeat of the Yugoslav armies after the Axis attacks, the Soviet authorities were promising him armaments, munitions, and planes. Although there had been sufficient time at least to have discussed the quantities and means of shipment, no steps had been taken by the Soviet authorities to follow through on their promises. Tito begrudgingly acknowledged that the Soviet government, at the time the assurances were given to the Partisan leader, wanted to keep an eye on developments before committing to any deliveries and that had Yugoslavia been able to offer effective resistance, such deliveries probably would have been made. The Soviets were not at all fazed by the continued presence of the Yugoslav monarchy, which Moscow viewed as weak, in any case. "Well, I too should prefer to deal in Yugoslavia with a King Peter, although he is a weakling, than with an adventurer," Stalin said to Churchill on the subject of King Peter's relations with Tito.[35] It was a matter of time before the old kingdom was to collapse anyway. As Stalin told Tito in late 1944 about accepting King Peter on the throne for appearances' sake to the Allies: "You need not restore him forever," he said. "Take him back temporarily and then you can slip a knife into his back at a suitable moment."[36]

• • •

Prince Paul wrote a moving letter to his brother-in-law, the duke of Kent, from his exile in Kenya on August 18, 1941, nearly five months after the coup and the subsequent Axis invasion of Yugoslavia.

> I did my best for my country according to my lights during nearly seven years among the most eventful and difficult in the history of the world. During all that time I worked hard and walked hand in hand with your country till the last minute when I was unable to act differently owing to internal complications, when my efforts tended to prevent the splitting up of my country as Croats and Slovenes insisted on the pact being signed as well as the War Minister, and Chief of the General Staff. The short disastrous campaign that followed proved that the country was unable to resist and that a large part of it did not desire to fight. It is childish to talk of our "flirting" with Germany and of my visit to Hitler as if it had been a *partie de plaisir* and a meeting with a pretty woman! Hitler manifested for a long time the

wish to see me and I avoided doing so for ages. I sent my Minister of Foreign Affairs first; then the Prime Minister and Minister of Foreign Affairs went together later. Hitler again insisted on seeing me and for a few weeks again I turned a deaf ear. At last I was asked by my chief ministers including Dr. Maček to "sacrifice myself" (that's the way they looked at it) and try and see if I could get round him. As to what concerns Anthony [Eden] it is again linked with our attitude and fright of Germany. We were surrounded by Germans, Italians, and Hungarians; Bulgaria and Romania already had German troops and it is nonsense to pretend that we were not frightened—we were—and I defy anyone not to be under the circumstances.[37]

The sense of frustration in that letter echoed what the prince had said to the American minister Arthur Bliss Lane in the weeks leading up to the prince's government signing the Tripartite Pact on March 25. Lane was furious that Prince Paul was even considering signing and argued that Yugoslav "moral integrity" was at stake. The prince countered that it was about peace or war, and that not to sign would mean the decimation of Yugoslavia. Yet Lane would have none of it. The prince turned to him calmly. "You big nations are hard," he said wearily to the American minister. "You talk of honor but you are far away."[38]

5

Allied Rivals, Allied Destruction

Is there a choice, is there an order
In the long migration of landscape into landscape, wall
Into emptiness, emptiness into tree, into shadow,
Shadow into hope, hope into wall? Anyway,
There's no clean future: space stays infected
With the fever of signs, the germ of remembering—
And a mother's kiss
Transmits the saving disease.

—Ivan V. Lalic, MNEMOSYNE

Over the course of 1942, it wasn't just Yugoslavia that was falling apart, but the Anglo-American relationship began to crumble as well, with the newly independent assertion of American interests in that country. In late 1942, the ambassador of the Yugoslav government in exile in London, Constantine Fotić, had made several direct appeals to President Franklin Roosevelt concerning the gravity of the ideological struggle in Yugoslavia. According to Fotić's own account of the matter, Roosevelt asked him personally what could be done to allay the Partisan-Chetnik fighting.[1] The Yugoslav ambassador suggested that a set of American missions, biased neither toward the Partisan nor Chetnik side (as the British had originally conceived), be sent to the country.

Fotić was perhaps more open to Undersecretary of State Sumner Welles since he had assured the Yugoslav ambassador back in late December 1942 that the U.S. government had "complete confidence in the patriotism of General Mihailović."[2] But the State Department quickly nixed the idea, fearing both the Soviet reaction and problems inherent in involving American officers in a dispute between the Communists and monarchists by liaising with only one side. Furthermore, anti-Mihailović propaganda was starting to gain ground in London and Washington. Much of this had to do with the general observations of the British officers F. W. D. Deakin and Fitzroy Maclean regarding the fighting capabilities of the Partisans. These reports were in contrast to the more frequent, critical reports—and, some would say, less romanticized views—of Mihailović's command, from officers like S. W. Bailey or William Hudson.[3] The Middle East Defense Committee in Cairo, a joint military and political command separate from SOE (Special Operations Executive) operations in Cairo, began to report to London in June 1943, based largely on Maclean's and Deakin's reports, that the "Partisans are now the most formidable anti-Axis element in Yugoslavia."[4]

That tensions between the British and the American officers existed in the first place was to be expected to some degree, given the somewhat rival nature of the SOE-OSS relationship. The intention had been, under the SOE-OSS agreement of August 25, 1942, for a kind of joint agency on wartime field operations of equal footing. While the functions of the SOE mainly involved liaison and operational work, the OSS was also an intelligence agency. The SOE had, of course, an intelligence-gathering function in the field; these were not SOE staff, but MI (Military Intelligence) officers attached to SOE missions. The OSS staff officers, on the other hand, had dual tasks: that of SO (Special Operations) and SI (Special Intelligence). Still, this Anglo-American relationship was not a strong one. SOE tended to view its American counterpart as something of a rough-and-tumble kid-brother organization to its own more polished and professional team. Like the SOE, the OSS tended to attract its own brand of romantic warriors. William Donovan, the head of that agency, sought out brilliant mavericks for his wartime overseas missions. As Richard Harris Smith, the historian of the OSS, recounts, in early 1941 Ian Fleming, who would later create the James Bond series, was then a ranking officer in British naval intelligence and suggested to Donovan that his future intelligence officers should possess qualities of "absolute discretion, sobriety, devotion to duty, languages and wide experience." Their age, Fleming added, should be "about 40 to 50."[5] Donovan declined Fleming's counsel. Instead, he promised Franklin Delano Roosevelt an international organization with young officers who were "calculatingly reckless" with "disciplined daring" and "trained for aggressive action."[6] As Smith wrote, "In Rome, Bangkok, Paris and Algiers, those were the men of the OSS."[7]

The SOE and OSS missions, in turn, were directly affected by the wariness that stemmed from this kind of cultural gap between the two organizations. Writing in his adventurous memoir *Mihailovich: Hoax or Hero?*, a mostly admiring portrait of mission life with Mihailović, Colonel Albert B. Seitz noted that Brigadier C. D. Armstrong, to whose mission Seitz was attached, was "the rare type of Englishman who sneers at everything American and dislikes having Americans close to him."[8] Seitz further explained that when Armstrong delivered certain letters from British general Henry Maitland Wilson, Seitz was not permitted to hear or see the contents of the letters. His messages to Cairo, like those of Colonel Bailey and William Hudson, were also subject to censorship. Seitz says he was not allowed to speak French with Mihailović, as Bailey would go along and speak only in Serbo-Croatian. On British insistence, Walter Mansfield, one of the first OSS mission leaders to Serbia, according to his own testimony, was not allowed near Mihailović headquarters.[9]

Nor was such control limited to the Mihailović side of the mission. Major Linn Farish, who tended to get along very well with Brigadier Maclean, had to warn the Scotsman that they were "allied in name only," and that there was a danger that "American interests and actual participation in aid to Partisans will not be recognized in Yugoslavia due to the nearly 100% preponderance of British personnel" to whom they were attached.[10] Major Richard Weil, who for three weeks in early 1944 was the independent American liaison officer to Tito at his headquarters in Drvar, Bosnia, complained, "The whole show is run by Brigadier Maclean, who exercises a complete monopoly."[11]

The general anti-Mihailović stance on the part of the British, which was a fundamental sticking point between SOE and OSS views of the ground situation, was, sadly, the unfortunate product of a kind of reckless censorship of what were often positive reports on Mihailović on the part of Bailey, Hudson, and Armstrong, British liaison officers who were in Yugoslavia one to two years prior to the arrival of the OSS teams. It was frequently a matter of "mere" misattribution—unintended or deliberate—of successful Mihailović offenses to the Partisans. Nonetheless, these behind-the-scenes intrigues were not, at the time, made the subject of close analyses by the U.S. State Department, which had concluded that a purely Mihailović mission would expose American soldiers "to charges of complicity in Mihailoviyć's alleged traffic with the Axis."[12] Still, the indefatigable William Donovan had independently, without State Department knowledge, made his own plans. The organization had decided that it alone would send American officers to Yugoslavia on an initial, trial basis, and on May 11, 1943, Donovan informed President Roosevelt that he was sending two American officers to Yugoslavia, one to liaise with the Chetniks and one with the Partisans. Whatever the misgivings of the State Department, the decision did not appear to have an enormous effect on the course of American policy. A couple of days later, between May 12 and May 24, 1943, Roosevelt and Winston Churchill met at a conference in Washington, code-named Trident, to discuss organized resistance in North Africa and the planned invasion of Italy. The Balkans were not even mentioned.

One of these OSS missions to Yugoslavia employed Yugoslav nationals themselves. By July 1943, Donovan had assembled around forty Yugoslav nationals who had escaped to various areas in the Middle East following the occupation of Yugoslavia. They were brought to California as part of the USAAF (the U.S. Army Air Force, as it was known then) for eventual assignment to the new OSS headquarters in Cairo, an office established in April 1943. The training of these Yugoslav airmen had been the idea of the young King Peter, who had visited the United States in July 1942 to inquire about the possibility of formally training in the United States to fight against the Axis occupation. When the subject of these Yugoslav airmen came up again in the summer of 1943, the Yugoslav ambassador, Fotić, appealed to Undersecretary of State Sumner Welles that those men serve as a Yugoslav unit, "from the standpoint of morale in Yugoslavia."[13] Donovan agreed with this idea, and the men were put under the command of the USAAF, attached to the OSS as a Yugoslav air unit, assigned four B-24 Liberator bombers, and flown by their Yugoslav crews to Cairo, where they were officially accepted by King Peter. This highly successful first "mission" to Yugoslavia through the OSS office in Cairo ended up carrying out more than fifty wartime missions throughout the world over the course of the war. Later, many remaining members of that Yugoslav force were enlisted in the U.S. Army by President Harry Truman.

On the other hand, finding the right Americans to send into Yugoslavia seemed a far less straightforward process. That was followed by a series of trial-and-error attempts to organize the right kind of mission on the heels of the successful all-Yugoslav units. The challenge of deciding which officer to send to the Chetniks and which officer to the Partisans was one delaying aspect; bad weather that ruined planned missions and frayed tempers was another. It was only when Major Louis Huot, an American officer assigned to the new OSS headquarters in Cairo, traveled to London and met Walter Mansfield, a member of Donovan's law firm, that ideas and intentions finally solidified into concrete action for these preliminary OSS missions.

Mansfield joined Huot on his return to Cairo, and upon their arrival Mansfield was immediately ordered by Donovan, based on Huot's recommendation, to go on a one-man mission to the Chetniks, while attached to the British mission to Mihailović under Colonel S. W. Bailey. On August 18, 1943, Mansfield parachuted onto Čemerno Mountain near Mihailović's birthplace in Ivanjica. Captain Melvin Benson, meanwhile, was also sent on a one-man mission, this time to the Partisans, and attached to Deakin's mission with Tito. He dropped into Petrovo Polje, near Travnik, about 55 miles west of Sarajevo, in Bosnia, on August 22. Thus, the first representatives of the U.S. government to set foot in Yugoslavia since the U.S. Legation closed its doors in Belgrade in July 1941 were these two OSS officers, Mansfield and Benson.

Cairo had become the center of action, with the SOE and OSS headquarters there, the constant traffic of British officers, urgent communications pouring in from field officers in Yugoslavia and the Middle East, and now a new influx of American officers on their way to Yugoslavia. King Peter's government in exile was at this time headed by Božidar Purić, after the highly respected and erudite former prime minister Slobodan Jovanović resigned in July 1943, largely out of disgust with the inability of the exile government to reconcile the Chetniks and Partisans. King Peter and his government moved to Cairo from London on September 28, 1943, honoring the king's wish to be closer to his homeland. General Wilson, the commander in chief, British Forces, Middle East, who had responsibility for everything east of the Adriatic, also had his headquarters there. (Meanwhile, American diplomatic representation to the Cairo-based Yugoslav government in exile changed from Ambassador Anthony Drexel Biddle Jr. to Lincoln MacVeagh, who had previously been ambassador to the Greek government in exile.)

The pace of American officers being sent to Yugoslavia began to pick up. As mentioned earlier, British brigadier C. D. Armstrong led the high-level mission to Mihailović, parachuting in with Lieutenant Colonel Alfred B. Seitz, of the U.S. Army, on September 24, 1943. On October 16, 1943, Lieutenant George Musulin dropped into Chetnik-held Yugoslavia. In November of that year Captain George Vujchinich, originally slated as the first mission leader to the Partisans, joined Slovenian Partisan headquarters. Captain George Selvig went to the Partisan Supreme Headquarters at Jajce, Bosnia, that December. The arrival of the Americans was of supreme importance to both the Chetnik and Partisan sides, as for the first time since Yugoslavia's capitulation, the United States was actively involved in Yugoslav affairs.

Meanwhile, not all was well with the Yugoslav government in exile, the political body backing the Chetnik-led resistance. The breaking down of King Peter's faith in his own advisers began on February 25, 1943, when Ivo Šubašić, part of the coalition government in London, handed Bernard Yarrow, a Russian émigré who became a lawyer with Sullivan and Cromwell and later an OSS intelligence specialist on Yugoslavia, a copy of a letter that had "the effect of a bombshell," in Yarrow's words.[14] It concerned General Dusan Simović, who led the anti-Axis coup d'état in Yugoslavia on March 27, 1941, forcing Yugoslavia out of the Tripartite Pact and bringing the country over to the side of the Allies. This letter, written on April 4, 1941, by the general, was a "definite offer" on his part to collaborate with the Germans, permitting certain Italian divisions to enter Yugoslavia. "The whole letter," wrote Yarrow in a subsequent memo to the OSS, "is drafted in the most treacherous terms and is definitely anti-British and anti-American."[15] Šubašić, maintaining that he was bound by a promise not to reveal the name of the possessor of the original letter, went to King Peter the following day so that the young monarch would be aware that one of the regents whom he had appointed after the coup was a traitor.

The revelation stunned the king, who immediately removed Simović. But it was the first in a series of events designed to destroy the king's faith in his government's willingness to support him. The treachery grew even more complex. Šubašić, outwardly the king's ally, grew in power as he grew closer to Tito. Milan Grol, the government in exile's foreign minister and vice premier, then resigned, only to later be put under house arrest by the Tito regime. Jurej Sutej, the minister of finance to whom the king was particularly close and hoped to have as head of the Croatian Peasant Party, eventually joined Tito's Communist hierarchy. Well before the close of the war, the Titoist takeover of what dwindling power the exiled government still commanded would be nearly complete.

Then, too, the rifts between the British SOE and the American OSS started to grow even more substantial. An obscure but significant matter of obstructing German access to a mine first brought this SOE-OSS rivalry to the fore. Lieutenant George Musulin first met with the Serbian Chetnik leader on December 12, 1943, when Musulin went to ask the Chetnik leader for help in destroying an antimony mine used by the Germans that was producing 75 to 100 tons of antimony, a metal used in tempering steel for shells. The mine was located in Lissa, Serbia, near Ivanjica, and Musulin and a team provided by Mihailović were to undertake a complex series of operations to destroy the compressors, the smelters, and the electrical equipment used to produce the antimony. Musulin asked for one hundred well-equipped Chetniks to do the job, and Mihailović promised his fullest cooperation and sent a high-ranking Chetnik with the American officer to assist him.

The British, however, were not in favor of this move. Apparently, General Wilson was upset that Mihailović had not followed through on his order to blow up two bridges across the Ibar and Morava rivers, for which Wilson had given a deadline of December 29 (1943). British sub-mission officer Jasper Rootham was to blow up one of the bridges, and Brigadier Armstrong the other. But Mihailović never gave the command to his troops. For by that time, Musulin had already been told by British officers with the various missions that they were going to drop Mihailović completely and evacuate all liaisons to the Chetnik leader, hence the feeling that they did not want to have anything more to do with any activity in that area. When the subject of the mine came up, SOE Cairo instructed Musulin that he was not to take part in its destruction. Presumably, the British saw that operation as less important than the bridges and other projects. Yet the lack of interest in the mine operation might also have been evidence of a general distancing from Mihailović on the part of London. "I showed the cable to a British sergeant who was staying with me at the time . . . and he could not quite figure it out either," reported Musulin later.[16] And so the mine continued to turn out antimony for the German army.

Yet if the British dissuaded Mihailović from the mine attack because London no longer felt the Chetniks could be trusted, the comportment of the Partisans vis-à-vis that same mine might have made London wary as well. As recounted by Colonel Albert Seitz in a May 1944 report following his return from Serbia that February, "At Ivanjica [the area where the Lissa mine was located], the Partisans left off an attack against [an] antimony mine one hour distant in order to fight Chetniks . . . and as a result accomplished exactly nothing against the mine. To me that was the important military objective."[17] Seitz went on to report:

> On January 21st, upon approaching Jablonica, just east of Rudo [at the confluence of the Lim and Uvac rivers in Bosnia] our column [of Chetniks] encountered six or eight Germans who were pursued and killed. Heavy firing was indulged in and when the British party, of which I was a member, came to an exposed part of the road we were forced to take cover. My impression of an excellent encircling maneuver by the Partisans was ruined because I had watched a party of Partisans climb up a steep hillside at headlong speed and saw them shooting, not at either Germans or Chetniks, but at us. . . . [I]t was propaganda as to fighting technique and ability that might have been fatal to some of the British party, and had one been killed it would probably have been blamed on the Chetniks.[18]

Musulin, who would emerge as one of the pivotal players in the Chetnik-American relationship and the rescue of Allied airmen in the summer and autumn of 1944, was assigned to a second round in his mission to Mihailović territory in January 1944. That month marked the beginning of the rescues of American airmen in that country. It had been originally thought that most of the men had bailed out over Montenegro and were wandering lost in that country. Yet Musulin ended up not going to Montenegro because just at that time—and seemingly all at once—American airmen were dropping down mainly into Serbia—this largely due to the extended bombing around eastern Romanian oilfields to which so many airmen had been assigned. Upon Musulin's arrival in Serbia that January, he received a cable from Mihailović telling him that the crew of one B-17—the same crew of Lieutenant Gus Brown described in chapter 1—had parachuted into the area under Mihailović's control, in the Zlatibor Mountains. Later, Musulin received another cable from Mihailović telling him that a second crew of airmen dropped from a B-24 had parachuted into Chetnik territory. Musulin would abruptly be called back to Bari, Italy, as British insistence on the Allied abandonment of contact with Mihailović went into effect, while more and more airmen parachuted into Serbia and were collected by Mihailović's Chetniks. A little more than six months later, the problems arising from Allied political cynicism, confused communications, controversial rescue missions, and high-risk evacuations would be overcome in order to accomplish a monumental act of heroism on the part of both the American and Serbian sides.

The British evacuation plan to remove all British—and, implicit in that decision, all American—officers attached to the Chetnik leader was under way in accordance with decisions made at the November–December 1943 Tehran Conference. While Musulin began the second part of his mission (in January 1944), the other two officers attached to Mihailović, Walter Mansfield and Albert Seitz, were moved into territory held by Tito, as was Captain Hudson, before leaving the country altogether. The OSS became increasingly frustrated with the British government. Lieutenant Colonel Paul West, the chief operations officer at the OSS base in Bari, commented in one December 13, 1944, memo, "The British Foreign Office are carrying the ball, and they have left the British military well back in the field. As a consequence there is no fixed policy for Greece, and no fixed policy for Yugoslavia. It would be hard to imagine a more chaotic situation than the existing one."[19] A little while later, on January 10, 1944, the Yugoslav prime minister, Božidar Purić, met with the British and American ambassadors to ask whether the Liberator planes Roosevelt had committed to the Yugoslav government in exile in 1942 could at last be used for supplying war matériel to the Chetniks. The request could not have been more futile—nor the timing more ill-considered. For two days later, on January 12, 1944, SOE Cairo submitted a full report to London on the evidence against Mihailović as an Axis collaborator (Purić's request was ignored). In particular, the report maintained that during the Germans' Operation White (January–March 1943), Mihailović directed operations in the Neretva valley against the Partisans in cooperation with the Axis. As Yugoslav civil war historian Walter Roberts wrote, "That there was a mutually advantageous Cetnik-Italian relationship is beyond a doubt. But it was not the kind of collaboration characteristic of the relationship between the Germans and the Croatian Ustase."[20]

What counts as "censorship" or "misattribution" in a wartime situation is somewhat difficult to define. But there had been enough clear-cut cases of questionable selectivity on the part of SOE headquarters in Cairo and, later, Bari, Italy, with the information that the office had received from its field officers. One memorable case involved the visit of British liaison officer Jasper Rootham and his mission to the Bari headquarters upon their evacuation from Mihailović territory in May 1944.

Rootham and the mission were treated "almost as if we were collaborators," said the British sub-mission leader in Serbia's northeast in an interview with the writer and pro-Mihailović activist David Martin three decades later.[21] As Martin recounts, back in Bari, Italy, the men were greeted by Major General William Stawell, the officer commanding the British SOE, who said to them, "Now you must remember, you've got it all wrong. The chaps you've been with aren't really on our side at all. The only people who are, are the Partisans—and you must really snap out of it."[22] Rootham then visited the SOE Yugoslav operations room at that Allied base. A map of Yugoslavia on the wall was covered with small flags marking the positions of Partisans, Chetniks, and Germans. Covering Serbia were Partisan pins, with an occasional Chetnik pin. When Rootham approached the desk officer in charge, telling him that the map was inaccurate, saying that he had just returned from Serbia, where he had spent close to a year, the officer blandly replied that Rootham was "misinformed."[23] An angry Rootham then went to the map and wiped all the pins off with a sweep of his arm, and after that, as Rootham recounted in his interview, "no member of the British mission to Mihailović was ever permitted to enter the SOE Yugoslav operations room."[24]

• • •

But whatever the case—inaccurate field reports, false military maps—these errors, intentional or not, were largely ignored. Not too long after the Rootham incident, London told its ambassador to the Yugoslav government in exile, Ralph Stevenson, that Mihailović would no longer receive any military support, and that there was to be no publicity regarding the matter. The American OSS liaison to Mihailović, Captain Walter Mansfield, and the SOE liaison to the same, Colonel S. W. Bailey, returned to Cairo on February 20, 1944; Seitz and Hudson left for Italy and then Cairo almost a month later. On February 21, SOE Cairo informed the State Department that the thirty British officers attached to Mihailović had all been withdrawn. Pressed by British demands to American secretary of state Cordell Hull, an OSS communication of February 28, 1944, instructed Musulin, now the last Allied liaison in Mihailović territory, to depart at once. That said, Washington wanted to make clear that it was not going to automatically follow the directives of the British. "State," read the OSS memo of that date by William Donovan, "does not enjoy being met with the British fait accompli."[25] The memo continued somewhat dryly: "The [State Department] considers it advisable to meet the wishes of the British with respect to withdrawal of the OSS officer now at Mihailovic headquarters [Musulin] and that OSS instruct its representative to leave with his British colleagues. However, in conveying its decision, [the State Department] and we would reassert the American right through OSS or otherwise, to obtain intelligence in any important area independently of the British."[26] On March 2, 1944, Donovan wrote another memo, titled "British Request for Concurrent Withdrawal of British and American Officers With Mihailovich," in which he coolly analyzed the British decision, and then plainly stated, "OSS Cairo has prepared at least two intelligence teams to send into Mihailovich territory at the earliest possible date."[27]

To be sure, not all British officials were pleased with the policy change, either. British Labor Party politician Richard Crossman, writing almost a decade later in the British publication the *New Statesman*, recalled:

> I remember the awkward moment when the Government dropped Draza Mihailovich and backed Tito. In future, our directive ran, Mihailovich's forces will be described not as "patriots" but as "terrorist gangs"; in future we shall also drop the phrase "red bandits" as applied to the Partisans and substitute "freedom fighters." . . . I assumed that the men far above who made the policy-decisions, were as cynical about the distinction between bandit and Partisan as we were. Only later did it dawn on me that British Cabinet ministers, archbishops and newspaper editors actually believed our propaganda and took this moral double-talk seriously.[28]

The withdrawal of Musulin from Mihailović headquarters would mark the beginning of a six-month period during which there was no official Allied presence among the Chetniks whatsoever. Supplies to Mihailović had already come to a dead stop by the end of November 1943. But, as mentioned previously, the Americans had been gradually becoming more and more independent-minded with regard to Yugoslavia and the development of Washington's own policy decisions concerning Chetniks and Partisans alike. While Donovan was contemplating the organization of intelligence teams to Mihailović—what would later generate strong protest from London—he garnered British consternation that spring of 1944 by deciding to build up the OSS presence with the Partisans, in view of the generally positive reports from the earlier (autumn 1943) OSS missions. Colonel John C. Toumlin, the OSS chief in Cairo, suggested allowing the SI unit of the OSS—that is, the "Special Intelligence" aspect of that organization—to have such functions in Yugoslavia, and the United States began to reorganize its missions to the Partisans along such lines. Officially, the British welcomed the idea of such an American mission but still sought to keep the logistical upper hand.

Tensions had been running high for some time. In the late summer of 1943, a dispute broke out between the OSS and the SOE over the right of the SO (Special Operations) section of the OSS to use its own independent ciphers to handle communications in Yugoslavia and Greece, based at the OSS War Station in Heliopolis. The OSS wanted to conduct intelligence operations in those countries without the knowledge of the British. The British urged the use of common communications means through their own ciphers headquartered at the SOE War Station at Mena House (Cairo). Yet "equality in the field," argued one OSS memo, could be assured only if the OSS maintained the right to its own safeguarded communications.[29] "Surely, if the Americans have a better chance of succeeding than the British," continued the memo, "it is because they are American and not British: if the organizers who go in must ask the local groups to use British ciphers and communicate with their American friends through the British War Station and British HQ, our organizers will be little more than British agents in American disguise, and will be treated as such by the groups with whom they deal."[30] Nonetheless, the British insistence on common communications through Cairo, argued on the basis of the joint operations clauses of the SOE/OSS Agreement of 1942, eventually won out.

Yet not quite a year later, and around the time Donovan became convinced of the value of sending fully independent American intelligence teams to Yugoslavia, the American desire for "equality in the field" with the British grew more pronounced. When Churchill announced in a speech on May 24, 1944, that Allied objectives in Yugoslavia would concentrate on bringing "all elements" to collaborate "under the military direction of Tito," the Americans scoffed. "Since it is my understanding," wrote one OSS official, "that the United States is not seeking to bring all forces in Yugoslavia under the leadership of Tito, I am advising PWB [the OSS's Psychological Warfare Board] that we are unable to approve this line." The memo criticized the "divergent lines of propaganda" between the two Allies. "PWB will try to avoid as long as it can the Tito issue, but it stresses the pressing necessity of a line of propaganda equally acceptable to the American and British governments."[31]

• • •

Back in London, the Yugoslav king's onetime prime minister, Šubašić, had become something of a one-man government in his dealings between the Russians, the British, and the OSS (through Bernard

Yarrow, the Russian émigré turned American lawyer and OSS specialist on Yugoslavia). By July 1944 he had grown fully convinced of the power of Tito. The British-sponsored Tito-Šubašić Agreement immediately ousted General Mihailović as minister of war and commander in chief of the Yugoslav army. And on September 12, 1944, King Peter, at the urging of Churchill, renounced his position as supreme commander in chief of the Yugoslav army. The king was further politically coerced into believing that the Tito-Šubašić Agreement was the reality he must accept if his monarchy were to survive, and he appealed—entirely against his will—to his Yugoslav officers in a broadcast to put themselves under the command of Tito.

Churchill, for his part, tried to play down the agreement as a temporary deal with the devil; King Peter tried to be cautiously optimistic. On November 17, 1944, the men met, the British prime minister holding in his hand the proposed draft agreement between Tito and Šubašić. He told the king that "things could have been worse and that the agreement at least was a partial victory since it recognized for the time being the Constitutional Monarchy."[32] King Peter responded that he would sign only on the condition that he alone name the regency and not merely endorse Tito's appointees. Churchill became impatient, telling the king that he could not accept certain clauses and reject others. "I thought you would accept the agreement wholeheartedly and my advice to you is to sign it," said the prime minister.[33] King Peter still insisted on naming his own regency and would not yield on that point, even when urged by members of his royal family to sign it.[34]

In late December 1944, Šubašić warned King Peter that if he refused to sign the agreement, "he will forever forfeit his chance to be King."[35] He added that in the event of the king's refusal to sign, a new government would be formed nevertheless. King Peter was infuriated and sought to disavow Šubašić immediately for overstepping his authority, and especially for a trip he was planning to Moscow to consult with Stalin. An anxious Churchill had warned the king not to do anything until Šubašić returned. He said, "I have asked Stalin personally not to reach any decision when he sees Šubašić until the latter reports to the King and until I have an opportunity to study the agreement. Therefore you cannot violate my promise to Stalin by acting prematurely. You wait until Šubašić comes back and the three of us will sit down and thrash the whole matter out."[36] King Peter, despondent, began to prepare a memorandum explaining the unconstitutionality of the entire agreement. But it would be too late.

• • •

The OSS, though more skeptical of Tito, conceded to a certain extent to the new Tito-led power structure in Yugoslavia in the second half of 1944 and began to focus significant attention on the Partisans. There were eleven SI (Special Intelligence) teams, totaling forty-eight officers and enlisted men, while SO (Special Operations) counted eleven officers and ten enlisted men—that is, a total of sixty-nine personnel, up from seventeen at the beginning of the year. (Eventually, the SO branch of these OSS missions to Yugoslavia was canceled altogether, as intelligence gathering became Donovan's primary concern. At this point, he directed the SI to add forty new agents, thus a total of eighty-eight SI agents in Yugoslavia.) In a deal with the SOE, it was decided that the Americans would have an "active representation" in over fourteen of the planned thirty-six missions to the Partisans (to be sent to the ten headquarters maintained by the Partisans). Three of these would be under American command. In August 1944, the formation of an Independent American Military Mission to Tito, with twenty-six officers among them and thirty-three enlisted men, was put under the command of Captain Ellery C. Huntington, who would be in charge of American personnel within the missions headed by British brigadier Maclean. The British, meanwhile, kept their total presence with Partisan Yugoslavia at around two hundred or so men.

Back in Cairo, after General Wilson became Allied Supreme Commander for the Mediterranean, the SOE's base there diminished in importance. The Allies had landed in Sicily and southern Italy in July 1943, and after the Italian Armistice of September 8, the British Eighth and American Fifth Armies started to make their way north, seizing a complex of air bases at Foggia, Brindisi, and Bari in the southern and eastern part of the Apennine Peninsula. Now supply and air operations to Yugoslavia and the Balkans would be transferred from Tocra, in Libya, to these bases. General Wilson wanted the SOE and OSS to relocate their Yugoslav sections from Cairo to Italy. While the SOE concurred, the OSS decided to keep its headquarters in Cairo—at least for a while. In any case, the advance OSS base at Bari, with SO and SI functions, now fell under Wilson's jurisdiction, with SO handled by Robert P. Joyce, a foreign service officer on loan to the OSS. The SI function at Bari happened to be highly pro-Partisan and was headed by Major Frank Arnoldi, whose short-lived appointment featured a female office staff dressed in Partisan uniforms with red stars. A series of shuffling of SOE/OSS agency locations swiftly followed. Whatever American plans to keep the OSS organization in Cairo alive lasted up until April 1944, when General Wilson succeeded in having all Yugoslav matters, including American OSS operations, transferred to Algiers, the site of Allied Forces Headquarters (AFHQ). The advance headquarters of those Allied Force operations was then in Caserta, Italy, near Naples. Ultimately, the whole of AFHQ was moved from Algiers to Caserta on July 21, 1944.

The actual supplying of the Yugoslav rebel groups across the Adriatic to Yugoslavia transferred from Force 266, which had served both the SOE and the OSS in sending material to the Partisans and the Chetniks, to Force 399, the so-called Balkan Air Force, as of June 1944. This force would now send supplies only to the Partisans, from its base in Bari.

• • •

The intensification of the American presence with the Partisans was not wholly well received by the British, who were anxious that the sudden influx of American supplies to the Partisans would bring Tito and his forces more under the political and military influence of the Americans. To illustrate the difference in aid, between June 1941 and June 1943 the British had dropped 23 tons of supplies to the Chetniks, and 6 to the Partisans.[37] The amount to the Partisans increased to 125 in the second half of 1943, when the British added 32 bombers to dedicate to supply operations, and in the first quarter of 1944, an additional 300 tons was dropped.[38] In October 1943 Captain Louis Huot "begged, borrowed and contrived," according to one analysis, to get General Donovan and General Eisenhower to mount a supply operation to the Partisans involving 6,000 tons of supplies delivered over a three-month period.[39] When the OSS started to send supplies to the Partisans even more aggressively from January 1944 through April 1944, as Partisan ranks rose from 200,000 to 300,000 troops, those U.S.-supplied amounts totaled 11,000 tons. During that year (1944), the Allies gave the Partisans, for example, over 100,000 rifles, over 50,000 machine guns and submachine guns, 1,380 mortars, over 97,500,000 rounds of small-arms ammunition, 700 wireless sets, and 260,000 pairs of boots.[40] Bolstered by this largesse, Tito asked the Americans in July 1944 to send 10 speedboats, 60 transport planes and 30 planes daily to deliver supplies respectively to the forces in Yugoslavia and the civilian population, and 80 tanks, not to mention linens and medicine.[41] Milovan Djilas credited Captain Huot with providing eight times as much aid as the SOE during 1944.[42]

In contrast, Lieutenant George Musulin, in his July 1944 report for the OSS, described a Chetnik force consisting of 1,230 men, "with a potential mobilization strength of 12,000 if supplied with arms."[43] He counted 800 Mauser rifles, 250 Belgian rifles, 100 Italian carbine models of 7-mm caliber, 10 American rifles of .30 caliber, 20 British rifles of 8-mm caliber, 35 Czech light automatic weapons, all with "only ten to 100 rounds of ammunition per gun."[44] The equipment was from the old Yugoslav army, and from captured German and Italian arms. "I saw no trench mortars, light or heavy machine guns, cannon or medical supplies," Musulin continued. "Many of the men were barefooted and almost all were poorly clothed."[45] Just around the time that Musulin was summoned back to OSS base headquarters in Bari, Italy, in February 1944, American ambassador to Belgrade Lincoln MacVeagh, in a memo of February 4 "deplored" the "virtual cessation" of supplies to Mihailović, warning of the disproportionate generosity of the Allies to Tito and that "[o]ne should not shut one's eyes to the ultimate effects on Yugoslavia's future of such opportunism, since we may have to deal with these effects in due time."[46]

During the month of September 1944, large amounts of sabotage material were delivered by the Americans to the Yugoslav Partisans. However, many of the shipments were blocked by the SOE on the Adriatic island of Vis, the Partisan headquarters that was also fortified as an operational supply base for the Allies. Again, apparently, the British did not want the Americans to take the lead in cooperating with the Partisans. According to one OSS memo describing SOE objections of such shipments, "the availability of American supplies to the Partisans definitely weakens the hold" that the British maintained over all activities in Yugoslavia."[47] There was no objection to the notion that "the Partisans have the use of these supplies but rather that they should be delivered through British channels."[48] The report continued: "The only difficulty encountered in the past month has been in connection with transportation of the above supplies from Italy to Vis. The shipping across the Adriatic is completely controlled by British agencies and according to [the SOE], its policy is to delay shipments of American supplies for the Partisans."[49]

Huot complained that the British only wanted the Americans to be a "shipping company" and to have no closer involvement with Tito on the command level. Huot had particular reason to be critical of the British, as they had sought to kick him out of his OSS post after the self-described "gun-runner for Tito" was caught sneaking off one gorgeous summer afternoon too many to enjoy lunch with Tito at the latter's rose-trimmed villa on the island of Vis.

It was, however, the establishment of the Air Crew Rescue Unit (ACRU) by the OSS on July 14, 1944, that would prove to be the major disruption in Anglo-American intelligence relations in Balkans. Joint British and American efforts to supply and rescue a great many airmen in Partisan territory continued uninterrupted. It will be recalled, however, that there had been no representation in Mihailović (Chetnik)–controlled Yugoslavia by the SOE or the OSS organizations after late February 1944, when Musulin, Seitz, and Mansfield were recalled from the country. Furthermore, even within the Partisan-controlled rescue-operation territories, there were dangerously few escape alternatives and a lack of coordination as to which escape routes were available.

Somewhat ironically, it was the pro-Partisan major Linn Farish who had insisted to General Ira C. Eaker, the commander in chief of the Mediterranean Allied Air Forces and father of "precision bombing" in the USAAF, that a greater American presence was needed in the region, including the Chetnik-controlled areas, dedicated to locating and returning U.S. air crewmen (and any Allied airmen) who had been downed in the Balkans. General Eaker subsequently approached OSS headquarters to make personnel available for Yugoslavia who would have knowledge of the language and the area. After the order setting up the unit was issued on July 14, 1944, Colonel George Kraigher, of Serbian origin and fluent in Serbo-Croatian, was designated as a commanding officer of the unit.

Colonel Kraigher requested that the OSS furnish wireless transmitter operators and that all communication be handled exclusively through OSS radio stations. A week earlier, on July 7, 1944, Force 399, the Balkan Air Force Unit, had been activated at Bari, Italy, to bring air support for SOE and OSS operations in the Balkans. (This new unit was in turn managed by the British Desert Air Force, whose job it was to protect the British Eighth Army.)

If organizational changes were acceptable, however, relinquishing control over American rescue operations was not. In a memo of July 17, 1944, OSS officer Robert P. Joyce (newly in charge of the SO section in the newly reorganized OSS at Bari) wrote that "after several weeks of inconclusive negotiations at Bari and at Caeserta as to how best American airmen could be evacuated from enemy occupied territory, it developed that the British authorities were reluctant to relinquish control of such operations to the Americans."[50] At the same time, the Americans were upset that "A Force," the rescue arm of the British Desert Air Force, was not doing more in the way of evacuations in Yugoslavia.

The Americans were also starting to insist that, given the amount of aid that the Americans were sending to Partisan territory specifically and that they had been sending to Yugoslavia in general, they should have the independence to conduct such rescue missions. Eventually, General Wilson relented, as did Brigadier Fitzroy Maclean, who at least officially welcomed the idea of the American teams at the headquarters of Marshal Tito and General Mihailović to organize the evacuation of the stranded American fliers.

Churchill was wary, and expressed his concern to Roosevelt on September 1, 1944, that the proposed mission to Mihailović would only worsen the "chaos" in the country.[51] The recognition of a provisional government with Josip Broz Tito as the leader of Yugoslavia had just been confirmed that summer. "It was a difficult thing to tell Fotich [the Serbian Yugoslav ambassador to Washington, D.C.], for I am very fond of King Peter and Fotich," wrote the former ambassador to Moscow Joseph Davies in his private papers when he heard of the decision to back Tito. "[B]ut it seemed to me that the situation was hopeless; that it was tragic, but it was elementary that in the movement of great events there was inevitable tragedy affecting little countries and individual men."[52]

6

A Mission (Nearly) Impossible

Was the world really so gray? In my early memories it is almost always late fall. The soldiers are gray, and so are the people,

—CHARLES SIMIĆ

Around the time that the dust settled on London's decision to confer full political recognition to Tito and, therefore, to abandon its support for the Yugoslav monarchy, twenty-three-year-old Lieutenant Colonel Richard L. Felman, of Brooklyn, New York, had just crash-landed into a new chapter of history between Serbia and its allies. He awoke to a burning feeling tearing through his body, and only his drawn, gasping breath and drumming heartbeat were reminders of his sheer luck in surviving a crash in the mountains of Serbia. His B-24 plane, aptly named *Never a Dull Moment,* was nowhere to be seen, while smoke billowed in the distance and there was no sign of anyone from his twelve-man crew.[1]

Felman and that crew had departed at 5:13 on the morning of July 9, 1944, from the U.S. air base at Foggia, on the Adriatic coast of Italy, as part of an air armada consisting of 250 bombers, the B-24 Liberator, and the Boeing B-17 Flying Fortress. The formation crossed the Adriatic Sea into Yugoslavia, whereupon it changed course to avoid German artillery. The fighter escorts met with the bombers at the Romanian border, where their course was again changed to confuse German tracking stations. As it happened, however, the formation was attacked by a squadron of German Messerschmitt ME-109 fighter planes. The crew dropped its bombs and began leaving the target area, heading for Serbia. Felman noticed a single

139

B-17 outside the formation, which he took to be one of the two or three the Germans had captured. It was, in fact, a Messerschmitt that began firing at the bombers with 30-mm shells. Felman and the crew bailed immediately, jumping at an altitude of 18,000 feet with a temperature of 30 below zero.

Landing in a dense ravine with his parachute lines catching on a boulder some feet below him, Felman tumbled across a patch of mountain forest with a bloody face pierced by cold, sharp rock. His legs burned with the shrapnel wounds he sustained when the Messerschmitt shell hit his plane. Disoriented and yet well aware that he could have ended up where he was only by being shot down, Felman began to crawl his way carefully down the mountain toward the vague outline of a road below, tearing his uniform into blood-soaked, strips of cloth wrapped around his body. He felt an excruciating pain inside his hot, cracked, mud-soaked boots.

His attention was caught by the expanse of a magnificent chain of the green and black peaks of the Ravna Gora Mountains. The Sava River cut a muddy, treacly water route down the entire length of the mountain chain, while clusters of villages dotted its length, recognizable from a distance with their red roofs and white limestone walls. Most distinct were the rounded cupolas of small yet imposing Serbian Orthodox churches, outposts of a culture whose remoteness served to intensify the strong national character in lands cultivated by one of the poorest peasantries in Europe.

Felman came into the middle of a field, only some moments later to be greeted by two dozen Serbian civilians, men, women, and children. He instinctively put his hands to his ears: during his intelligence briefings he had been told that if shot down in Yugoslavia, he was to look for "the men with the red stars"—Tito's Partisans—and avoid the Chetniks, "who will cut off your ears" and who were rumored to be turning Allied airmen over to the Germans. Yet here he was surrounded by the very Chetniks whom he had been told to avoid, with bearded men throwing their arms around him and kissing him with the national gesture of affection and gratitude. He was given fruit, flowers, and Serbian plum brandy, *slivovitz,* and then was offered a crutch and taken to the Serbian Orthodox church in the village by a weathered but dignified-looking older man—Draža Mihailović himself, as Felman was about to learn. The two men prayed in the small church. Though separated by language, country, and religion, "the brotherhood of man," recounted Felman, "was never more in meaningful evidence."

The young airman was then introduced to Colonel Dragiša Vasić, who had been made the corps commander of the Pranjane region under Mihailović. Vasić informed Felman that a German garrison of 500 troops was stationed in the region, while a larger garrison of 10,000 was located ten miles away. German troops had located the downed bomber and had found the body of Major Thomas P. Lovett, who had died when the bomber was attacked. Local Serbian forces noted that ten parachutes had emerged from the bomber. The Serbian troops were able to retrieve Lovett's body and to bury it with a Serbian Orthodox priest officiating at the service.

While Felman was impressed with the emotional reaction of Mihailović and his troops to the Americans, his sense of Mihailović's desire for military cooperation was first demonstrated when the Chetnik leader explained to Felman his wish to have Missing in Action (MIA) notices sent to men's families in the United States. Using a shortwave transmitter to Cairo, he would wire the name, rank, and serial number of the MIAs, which would in turn be sent to Constantine Fotić, the Yugoslav ambassador to the United States. (After the war, Felman was informed by Fotić that he had received Mihailović's message and had submitted it to the U.S. War Department [now the Department of Defense]. But because Mihailović was not recognized by the United States at that time, the message was discarded and ignored. Felman's family, like hundreds of others, was sent an MIA notice unnecessarily.)

Yet darker consequences of the generosity shown to Felman, and to the other airmen, by the local Serbs came in the form of German-led reprisals. By aiding the U.S. airmen, Serbian civilians faced execution by German forces, and three days after the bailout of Felman and his crew, the Germans issued an ultimatum to turn over the ten airmen seen parachuting into the area, or Axis forces would wipe out an entire village of two hundred women and children. For Felman the choice was an easy and obvious one, and he prepared to surrender to the German forces. Being a POW in a German camp with the possibility of escape was certainly worth saving two hundred lives. Mihailović and Vasić would hear nothing of it, however, refusing to take the orders of the Germans and not wanting to sacrifice a single American—men whom they regarded as their country's salvation. The next day German troops burned the entire Serbian village. As Felman later recalled, "To this day I can smell the terrible stench of their burning flesh. One does not forget such things."[2]

Within two weeks after Felman crash-landed on July 9, 1944, the number of Americans shot down over Ravna Gora had grown to about 250. Chetniks related to the Americans how they tried to arrange for American planes to come in, but when nothing happened, the servicemen began to despair, some even falling into serious depression—these men had been down for as long as five months, and were often on the verge of surrender to the Germans, if only as a means of escaping the stark eeriness of the Balkan hinterlands. Increasing the sense of hopelessness, the American (and the other Allied) soldiers, as well as the Chetniks, gradually came to learn that Tito was receiving exclusive Allied military and political support.

Until one day, one senior officer, Lieutenant T. K. Oliver, a West Point man and son of the distinguished major general E. L. Oliver, got hold of a radio at Mihailović's headquarters. With it he began to transmit in the clear on a rare frequency, in the hope that some Allied monitoring station would pick up the message. He repeatedly broadcast these words: "We are 250 American airmen. . . . Many sick and wounded. Please notify the Fifteenth airforce to come and get us."[3] They began to get answers—but these were, in turn, all questions. Whoever was receiving the transmissions suspected that the "crew" was composed of Germans, or was a crew of Americans operating under German duress. Thus the challenge for Oliver became to find a way to get the Americans to realize that the signal was indeed for real. Lieutenant Oliver devised a clever system of encoding and decoding, using the army serial numbers of certain airmen, nicknames, insider-military slang, and describing apparel worn by his West Point roommate. Working from these vivid details, the young lieutenant managed to establish working communications, having finally convinced the monitoring station at Bari that Felman and his men were legitimate.

Reports of the downed airmen began to trickle in to the Yugoslav embassy in Washington, D.C. While in the previous chapter it was the original OSS liaison to the Partisans, "Slim" Farish, who had alerted the OSS to the need for an independent mission to Mihailović's Chetniks and of the presence of downed American airmen in that Serbian territory, broader knowledge of those airmen began, more or less, with the dissemination of reports of their plight through embassy channels. A Serbian employee at the Yugoslav embassy, Mirjana Vujnovich, began to receive reports of downed airmen in central Serbia. She wrote to her husband, George, then the operations officer at the OSS field station in Bari, Italy, about the communications she was receiving. He himself knew what it was like to be caught behind enemy lines as a medical student in Belgrade when Yugoslavia fell to the Axis powers in 1941. According to Halyard scholar Gregory A. Freeman, Vujnovich and his wife had spent months sneaking through minefields and begging for visas before they escaped from German-occupied territory. The terrain was thus familiar to the husband-and-wife team.[4]

Vujnovich at once began to organize men at the OSS base in Bari for a mission to rescue what he and his fellow officers assumed was around one hundred airmen—not knowing it was already more than double that, and growing. The OSS men knew that such transportation could be achieved only by making contact with Mihailović and airlifting the men right out of the Pranjane/Ravna Gora area where the men had landed. Such were the origins of the fabled Halyard Mission, as the OSS would dub it, a rescue and evacuation of Allied airmen with the cooperation of Mihailović, his Chetniks, and loyal local Serbs that would become "one of the most significant of the Missions" in the history of the OSS, according to one September 1944 memo of that organization. The same memo described the mission as "better than fiction."[5] Halyard was detailed to the Fifteenth Air Force and designated the First Air Force Rescue Unit; its members included George Musulin; Major Sergeant Michael Rajacich; Arthur Jibilian, a wireless transmission operator; and First Lieutenant Nick A. Lalich. (Major Vujnovich was put in charge of selecting and sending into Yugoslavia the Halyard Mission members, and Americans of Serbian-Yugoslav parentage were recruited into the OSS through the U.S. Army through one Colonel Nick Stepanovich.)

But the British were against Halyard from the outset. Scheduled to be dropped into Serbia in late July 1944, the mission was delayed as the British once more objected to the renewed attention to Mihailović. Resistance from the SOE and from the State Department forced OSS director William Donovan to appeal to President Franklin Roosevelt himself. Roosevelt agreed, and the British were ordered to cooperate. Though Halyard had been approved, Winston Churchill was very much against the idea. Evidently Vujnovich's pro-Mihailović leanings had reached Churchill. As a quick compromise Vujnovich chose Lieutenant George Musulin, a Serbian American, to lead the team instead.

Musulin and his team were anxious to get going. Assembled together at the Fifteenth USAAF at Bari, Jibilian made a successful attempt to use that air force base's radio system to secure a purported contact with Mihailović through an old British radio link in Naples, "Villa Resta," the code that William Hudson had given to Mihailović upon his arrival in Ravna Gora in 1942. Jibilian requested that a reception party be organized for the Halyard team. In response to these signals, a message purporting to come from Mihailović formed the basis for the first of several sorties to get the mission to its destination. One thing they could be sure of was that Mihailović had excellent communications, relatively speaking. "There is much to criticize in both the methods and the madness of Mihailovich's organization," the British liaison officer Jasper Rootham later wrote, "but among all its achievements, and they were many, I believe that the setting up this wireless network was the greatest triumph."[6] The sets were occasionally Yugoslav army radio equipment salvaged from the wreck of the April 1941 invasion, but usually they were homemade. "Our attention and our admiration were directed more to the fact that a wireless network existed and that, existing, it worked," wrote Rootham. "For work it did."[7] (In late 1943 Mihailović had even put into operation a shortwave radio station that was strong enough to be picked up in the United States. The station was known as "Woods and Mountains," and contact with the State and Navy Departments lasted until the middle of September 1944.) There was a desperate lack of wireless material, and during the mission's time in Serbia, entreaties for sets, spare parts, and batteries were nearly as urgent as demands for arms.

But thinking up clever radio codes would prove to be the least of their challenges. The Halyard Mission sorties were thwarted on their first several attempts to land in Yugoslavia. On July 20, 1944—the day, it should be noted, of the Count Stauffenberg–led assassination plot against Hitler—an attempt to fly out from Bari to the Pranjane area—about 350 miles—resulted in the plane flying back to Bari when no further reception and no signals from the ground came through. Because of the inevitable delay in the radio messages, the rendezvous schedules had to be set days ahead. Furthermore, the military situation in occupied Yugoslavia was highly fluid. An area that might be Chetnik-controlled when they set the meeting time and place was likely to be overrun by German soldiers the next day. Furthermore, the flights were made in unarmed C-47s without escort, which made them easy targets for German fighters based about ten minutes' flying time from the pinpoint area fifty miles south of Belgrade.

After further radio communication with Mihailović, a second sortie was flown on the night of July 25, 1944. On this night, signals were flashed from the ground, but they did not correspond to prearranged signals, and again the men from the mission were sent back to Italy. It was a 350-mile trip each way from the American airfield at Brindisi (at the foot of Italy), and as the planes crossed into Yugoslavia, the men ran into a barrage of heavy antiaircraft fire. At this point, the Halyard team prepared their parachutes, ready to bail out. The C-47s had flown safely through the barrage and began to look for the signal—and yet, there was no signal. They circled, then headed east for home and another discouraging report: "Mission unsuccessful."

The third sortie was flown out the following night, July 26, to the same spot and with the same signal plans in place. Once again, it was not to be: the ground signals had not been prearranged, and the fire of small arms was heard on the ground. The tension was almost demoralizing, yet the men held out for one more chance the next night—a rendezvous that had been organized for successive nights, lest anything should go wrong on either end. This time they met no barrage. They neared the designated pinpoint, and there saw the crimson glow of the fires. As for the signals—they were clearly the wrong ones. Musulin, with the other Halyard men increasingly frustrated by their lack of successful landings, looked down in despair. Perhaps the code had been confused—was the chance worth it? Just then, a terrific glare illuminated the plane, blinding the stressed faces of the men—German flares had begun to burst about them. From the ground came the flash of heavy small arms. This was either a trap, in which case a night fighter's attack could be expected within a few moments; or they were completely off their intended mark and had almost dropped into a nest of Germans.

In a few seconds the plane was headed back as fast as it could fly, while the Halyard team remained on lookout with an empty sense of dread for the threatening night fighters. Twice they thought they spotted the fighters, twice they eluded their detection, and then some hours later they were back at base, a weary and disheartened group. As Musulin jumped from the plane and headed for the OSS dispatching station, he had to fight back the growing fear that the Halyard Mission was going to end in failure. Meanwhile, in one of several Chetnik encampments far behind enemy lines, a group of discouraged men waited—all Americans. Many of them were sick and wounded; some wore tattered clothes and were shoeless; all of them were disheartened and embittered, assuming that they had been abandoned.

Then, finally, on the fourth attempt, the Fifteenth USAAF signals team reported a signal coming from a coded message referencing Oliver's bomber, the *Fighting Mudcat*, an obscure reference designed to throw the Germans off and to reassure Allied radio operators in Italy that the message was from a trustworthy source. A radio operator in Italy picked up the cryptic message, whose unique details helped members of the 459th Bomb Group identify Oliver. After answering a request for longitude and latitude using captured German maps of Serbia, Oliver was told to prepare for July 31 or the first clear night thereafter. And even then, tensions were prolonged another few days, throwing the assembled airmen into more despair. Yet finally, as of August 2, an incredible set of hair-raising rescue sorties would be under way.

On that day, the Halyard men—Musulin, Rajacich, and Jibilian— took off from Bari with as much determination as ever and, confident of the signals arranged by Oliver and zealous with a sense of adventure, they jumped into the right area and made contact with an ecstatic group of Chetniks and local Serbs who took them to Chetnik headquarters at Pranjane. Much to the Halyard team's surprise, there they found about 250 airmen, for whom the increasingly elusive hope of rescue was now about to become a miraculous reality. By mid-August, that number climbed to 512 Americans in addition to 137 British, Russian, French, and Canadian soldiers, all of whom had been consistently protected and aided by the Mihailović forces.

That first night was spent at the Air Crew Rescue Unit (ACRU) station, where a billet and a small hospital had been set up. The OSS medical officer assigned to the ACRU, Captain Jack Mitrani, was present with two other American doctors and a local nurse. Officially, their mission was to treat the American airmen exclusively, but Chetniks were treated as well. "They were even more lacking in supplies than the civilians," wrote Captain Walter Mansfield in his February 1944 report on his time in the Chetnik territories, describing the various makeshift field hospitals he had encountered.[8] "Paper was used for bandages and they had but little medication and this was all stolen from the Germans whenever trains or convoys were attacked," wrote Mansfield. "One could not help but admire these men, misguided as some conceive in their defense of their mission."[9]

Mihailović and his Chetniks, for their part, were in terrible physical shape and were poorly equipped. Their arms included 65 mortars, 1,200 light machine guns, 300 heavy machine guns, 90,000 rifles, and 300 machine pistols—and almost no artillery. The American officers complained sharply about the lack of arms and ammunition to the Chetniks during their time there, and what they did have tended to come from grounded planes or rescued airmen. No Red Cross aid was sent either. "For three years the Chetnik soldiers have lived in the forest, ragged and receiving no money for their services," wrote Mansfield, in the same February 1944 report.[10] "In addition, reprisals have often been visited on their families. When these factors are considered, the morale and discipline of the Chetnik army in Serbia may be considered excellent, despite the fact that it is ill-clothed. [But] in Herzegovina and Southern Dalmatia, morale is not as high. Most of the soldiers were given only two years of military training before the outbreak of hostilities."[11]

As soon as Musulin had the airmen straightened out as well as he could with their limited means, he held a news conference with his old friend Captain Zvonko Vucković of the First Chetnik Corps, who was in charge of the Mihailović troops in the two months since Musulin had left the zone (keeping in mind that Musulin had been in and out of Serbia since January 1944). He was anxious to check on German strength, realizing how precarious the situation was. What he learned from the Chetnik leader was far from reassuring: Only twelve and a half miles away, in the town of Čačak was a garrison of 4,500 Germans. Just five miles from the clearing was another garrison of 250. Their principal security lay in the mountain location, with the Chetnik troops guarding them and the support of the Serbian population.

Musulin then studied the problem of the airstrip, which was the biggest obstacle of all. With considerable work they could improve it and lengthen it by about seventy-five yards, which would give them the absolute minimum for C-47 operations. Immediately, an anxious Musulin, realizing that each hour of delay made German detection more likely, asked the Chetniks for assistance, and three hundred laborers and sixty oxcarts were assigned to work on extending the strip. Stones and dirt were hauled up from some nearby streams. With every man pitching in, the strip was gradually improved. By early August, it looked as if the men would complete the extension of the strip, so Musulin had Arthur Jibilian radio that they would start the evacuation the next night. Confirmation of the plans came through from base headquarters in Bari, Italy, and with that, August 9 became the big test.

On that night, the first evacuees, the Halyard OSS team, and the Serb villagers and Chetniks who hosted the men gathered at the airstrip to await the planes. They were surrounded by the four thousand troops of Mihailović's First Ravna Gorski Corps, who were deployed around the area to watch for any possible German interference. Lieutenant Oliver was among the first group of airmen who would be rescued. Fortune favoring the brave that day, it just so happened that the weather that night happened to be perfect. Musulin had requested six planes and gave orders for seventy-two airmen to be ready at the airstrip at 10 P.M., while numbers were assigned to everyone. The sick and the wounded received the lowest numbers, and after that the priority was established based on the length of time each man had been behind the lines. No distinction was made between officers and enlisted men, and the number per plane was kept down to twelve, given the danger of taking off from such a short runway. Before the Halyard Mission left, it had been settled that the incoming planes would be stripped down of all excess material and would carry half a gas load, little more than enough to complete the seven-hundred-mile round-trip. But even with these precautions and as anxious as they were to get back to Italy, many of the pilots doubted any of it could be done.

At about 6 P.M. that day Musulin had been riding a horse out to the strip to make a final check, when he heard plane engines. Right away he knew they were German. He dove off his horse and took cover in a ditch by the side of the road, expecting to be killed. But the Germans paid no attention—they headed instead right to the strip. There were three planes, flying in a loose formation, one Stuka, one JU-52, and the third marked with a Red Cross. Musulin watched them approach the strip; then, to his horror, the Germans touched down on the runway, creating deep craters on its freshly constructed expanse, scattering huge billows of dirt and debris everywhere. Then the planes circled around and headed back in the direction of their own airfield. Musulin swiftly mounted his horse in anger and galloped out to the field, where he met Rajacich and Jibilian, who raced over to see what damage had been done. The distraught expressions Musulin saw on their faces said enough: the construction of the airstrip had been destroyed, ruining the rescue mission right at the last minute.

To make matters worse, as Freeman recounts in his narrative of the Halyard rescues, in Italy the planes were already taking off and were due into Serbian airspace in about four hours. To try a last-minute contact to them by radio would not have made a difference, as the messages still would not have been able to reach the airfield in time. As Jibilian expressed fear that the Germans had detected his radio, which had been in frequent communication with base arranging the details of evacuation, the men now had to consider whether German night fighters would be waiting for their unarmed and helpless C-47s when they arrived within a few hours. Last and not least of these concerns was the possibility that nearby German troops were preparing for an attack that might result in the capture and death of these airmen. Musulin, effectively the man in charge of bringing these men back to safety, had the weight of the world on his shoulders. For now, he tried to take comfort in the fact that none of the airmen had been anywhere near the airstrip when the Germans buzzed it. Musulin and his men decided to wait for a miracle—and they got it.

For despite such a harrowing close call, everyone—the stranded airmen, the Halyard team, and the Serbs—assembled at 10 P.M. that night—August 9—for the now much-hoped-for (and, for the sake of morale, much-needed) first set of evacuations that had been secured between Bari and the Halyard team at Pranjane. That night the first seventy-two airmen assembled on the strip. Though six had been designated, four C-47 airplanes escorted by twenty-five P-51 fighter planes were sent from Brindisi to the pinpoint—that is, the prearranged landing coordinates—with the signals plan as agreed upon over the course of so much tense, underground communication. Mihailović, meanwhile, had organized 8,000 Chetnik guards to safeguard the areas while Musulin had a Chetnik soldier stationed at each flare ready to light them up on the signal. Jibilian waited with Musulin carrying an Aldis lamp to blink the proper identification signal. As the planes circled over for the first time Jibilian blinked "Nan," and to his relief he received the correct reply, "X-Ray."

Musulin gave the order to light up the ground fires and then shot up the green flare, his signal that the landings were to commence. All seemed to be going well, until the first plane, heading toward the strip, put its wheels down only to take off again, having overshot the field and landing, ultimately, at the end of the runway. The other three planes, meanwhile, were ordered to stay aloft until Musulin had cleared the strip, but they either disregarded or missed his green flare signals and each started to come in. Now Musulin feared a pile-up at the end of the strip, and quickly some Chetniks and airmen were sent to wheel the first plane down into a sloping depression off on the side of the runway. The men acted just in time. For the wings of the next plane just passed over the top of the first one as it was being wheeled over to the side. It missed by inches, and it became increasingly clear that the night landings were too risky. Still, the pilots of the Sixtieth Troop Carrier Command commanding the C-47s were the best of the air force. Some of them even ground-looped in landing, to slow up and stop before they reached the end of the strip.

Once confusion over signals and flares was cleared up, the landings progressed safely. The only glitch was that Lieutenant Nick A. Lalich of the OSS at Bari, who arrived in one of the planes, told Musulin that only these four planes, instead of the six that were expected, would arrive, as two of the planes had developed engine trouble and had been forced to turn back. Now with fewer planes, a growing number of men, and concerns over cargo weight for each trip, Musulin nonetheless simply promised he would get the men out the next morning.

There was a further embarrassment. The C-47 planes sent from Brindisi to Serbia, according to the pilots of the C-47s, were completely empty; they did not bring to the Chetniks any matériel, or supplies of any kind—only aid to the Halyard Mission itself, and arms and supplies that had been dropped to the Partisans beforehand. These planes would leave Bari with a payload of equipment ostensibly destined for the Chetniks as well as the Partisans, yet the entire contents would be dropped to Partisan groups. No arms arrived either. What trickle of equipment did get dropped into the Chetnik areas was designated for exclusive American use—medical supplies, clothes and shoes, and K-rations and other such material—to take care of the Americans in those Chetnik areas. Mihailović never said anything to Musulin about the empty planes arriving to pick up the Americans. "They had no arms, and no ammunition. We would see broken-down Italian rifles and German rifles and a few Enfields and no American pistols; mostly Italian pistols, P-38s and Lugers, German equipment," recounted Musulin in a report on the conditions of the Chetniks.[12]

Whatever this additional pressure, the arrival of the C-47s was for Team Halyard, to the airmen, to the Chetnik soldiers, and to the Yugoslav peasants, an immensely inspiring sight. As the C-47s began to come in at five-minute intervals, and as the Halyard team sweated out every landing, just as the planes would taxi to a stop, all fears were abandoned as a wave of screaming women and girls surrounded each plane, throwing garlands of flowers at the pilots and at the embarking airmen. As the airmen boarded in groups of twenty, they would peel off their shoes and most of their clothing and toss it to the cheering Chetniks. The pilots and crews of the evacuating planes were caught up in the excitement of the occasion. All of them wanted souvenirs: daggers, guns, Chetnik caps and opankas, the Serbian sandals made out of goatskin. While all this was happening on the ground, the escort P-51s were putting on a breathtaking exhibition overhead. They slowly formed into an awkward V formation, and with a roaring fighter escort sweeping around them, they dipped their wings in a final salute to their Chetnik friends and headed back to base and safety.

About twenty minutes after the first plane had landed, the C-47s started down the airstrip, and about forty minutes later, the motors of the planes could no longer be heard in the distance. The first part of the job had come off successfully, and there had been no incident, no German interference, somewhat surprisingly so. Musulin then sent couriers to all the rest of the airmen ordering them to be at the airstrip no later than 8 A.M. the next morning (August 10). That night Jibilian stayed at his radio trying to contact base to get confirmation for the arrival of the planes with fighter cover in the morning. Yet his efforts were unsuccessful—neither official American nor British communications would accept signals thought to be coming from the Chetnik camps. Nonetheless, the men went ahead with all the plans anyway. Early in the morning on the tenth, the men heard the explosive roar of engines in the distance—so shattering that some of the men thought a bombing mission of Balkan targets was under way. But as the planes came closer, excitement replaced uncertainty, and the men ecstatically welcomed the unexpected six C-47s, in the center of a swarm of fighter planes, that had come for them that morning.

The Serbian American Colonel George Kraigher, the commanding officer of the ACRU, had arranged with the Fifteenth USAAF to provide fighter cover for a daylight operation to evacuate the remainder of the airmen that day. Subsequently, there were two flights of six C-47 planes, one dispatched to the area that morning and again returned to the Bari airport the same day with what was by then a remaining group of 179 American airmen, and an additional 12 Russians, 6 British airmen, 4 Frenchmen, 7 Italians, and 8 Yugoslavs. The rescues continued relatively smoothly. In two hours 241 men were removed from the "Missing in Action" list. On August 11 another wave of C-47s arrived. The ground crew flashed the letters of the day. A week later there was another small evacuation, and on the nights of August 26 and 27, another 258 American airmen were evacuated.

When the last plane had disappeared behind the mountains to the east, the members of the Halyard team shook hands with one another. After five weeks of dealing with daily risk and anxiety, they relaxed for the first time, savoring the feeling of an important job well done. Through September until December more Allied airmen would be found, the very last group leaving on December 11—and Musulin, Rajacich, and Jibilian would remain in Serbia until that conclusion. But for now it was imperative that the men retreat some ten miles into the mountains, for it did not seem possible that the whole operation could have escaped the attention of the Germans on the other side of the mountain, only five miles away.

Ustaše leader Ante Pavelić talking to commander Colonel Dorčić (right) and to Pavelić's chief of staff, Colonel Birć (left).

Aleksander Cincar-Marković, Yugoslav foreign minister, 1939–1941, featured in the *Illustrierter Beobachter* (Munich), May 4, 1939.

Ustaše leader Ante Pavelić, featured in *Newsweek*, October 4, 1943.

King Peter II
Karadjordjević (left)
and Andrew Kristović
(right), member
of the secretarial
staff of the Yugoslav
government in exile.

Yugoslavia's partisan leader Marshal Josip Broz Tito (left) with Major General
Koca Popović, commander of the Partisan First Army Corps.

Wartime photo of General
Draža Mihailović.

Prewar photo of General Draža
Mihailović.

Prince Regent Paul Karadjordjević.

Partisans standing in front of a downed German plane, circa 1943 or 1944.

Lone Partisan soldier on the Dalmatian coastline of Croatia overlooking the Adriatic, circa 1943 or 1944.

Dr. Ivan Šubašić, governor of Croatia and later premier of Tito's government.

Lieutenant Colonel Vladimir Dedijer, correspondent for the Yugoslav national paper *Politika* and Tito's chief of staff, *New York Times*, April 20, 1945.

A group of Partisans, circa 1943 or 1944.

William Donovan, head of the Office of Strategic Services (OSS).

Princess Olga of Greece, consort of
Prince Regent Paul Karadjordjević,
Illustrierter Beobachter (Munich),
June 8, 1939.

Prince Regent Paul of Yugoslavia,
honoring the Italian war dead at the
memorial of the Unknown Soldier in
Italy, May 11, 1939.

Serbian Chetniks with a German
officer, circa 1943.

Prince Regent Paul of Yugoslavia
meeting a skeptical Adolf Hitler
at the opening of Wagner's
Meistersinger at the Berlin Opera,
June 3, 1939.

Croatian Ustaše soldiers, circa 1943.

German tanks in Belgrade led by General Paul Ewald von Kleist,
following the postinvasion Axis takeover of that city, April 17, 1941.

Yugoslav men running to
safety during an air-bomb
attack, 1944.

General inspection of a Bosnian regiment in the Croatian NDH army,
January 22, 1944.

160

7

Legends of Blood and Honor: The Sad, Strange End of the British-Mihailović Relationship

Here is the faithless one sitting next to you. . . . Tomorrow is Sunday, Vidovdan . . . we will see, Who is loyal, and who is disloyal.

—Ma[u]ro Orbini, *The Story of the Battle of Kosovo* (1601)

In the preceding chapters we have seen the British disenchantment with Mihailović and his Chetniks evolve. This slow, at times exasperating, turn of events that bred such severe distrust among the two former Allies, as we have seen in bits and pieces, reads more like a tragic case of gross miscommunication and irresponsible ideological biases than a case of strategy-driven military abandonment. To take a closer look at this depressing tale, we need to go back to 1942, when Mihailović was at the height of his powers, in terms of both local command and international reputation.

With the usual swell of emotion that accompanies a hero chosen for wartime propaganda purposes, Mihailović was feted in the world media, particularly in the United States, as being the greatest guerrilla fighter in Europe: "Either They Die or We Do: That Is the Cry of the Chetniks,"

161

reported the *New York Times* in March 1942. "General Draja Mihailović, Yugoslav Robin Hood, Leads Chetnik Band against Armies of Axis," read the headline of the *Washington Post* that same month. "The Balkan Eagle Fights On" announced the *Chicago Daily Tribune* in October that year.[1]

These tributes were not without foundation. Mihailović's forces had captured the attention of the Allied powers through several effective offensives against the Germans. Mihailović's military had disrupted the communication and supply lines in the Balkans at a time when German Field Marshal Erwin Rommel and the German Afrika Korps were marching on Alexandria, the Nile, and Suez that autumn. By the time Rommel launched his offensive on Tobruk, in Libya, on October 23, 1942, Mihailović, "not waiting for orders from the English command in the Near East nor from the Royal Yugoslav Government," according to one U.S. government report on these activities, "commanded Chetnik units to attack the communication lines because at that time German war material for Africa was being shipped on the Belgrade-Salonika railway."[2] On all sides of that communication line, Mihailović forces blew up railroad lines, destroyed bridges, and attacked transportation convoys and German garrisons. "Because of this action, the Germans were forced to retain 40 divisions in Yugoslavia."[3] It is likely that had they been available to Rommel before his campaign in Alexandria, "the Germans would have determined the Africa campaign to the disadvantage of the Allies," according to one OSS memo.[4] By way of recognition of the Yugoslav efforts during the time that French North Africa was being liberated, "Free French" leader General Charles de Gaulle decorated Mihailović with the Croix de Guerre with red palm.[5] Serbian efforts in the African campaign were recognized by Adolf Hitler in his New Year's speech of 1943, when he said the war in Africa was lost because communications to that theater had been disrupted in Italy and the Balkans.[6]

Recognizing the value of General Mihailović's initiative, Admiral Sir Nehry Hardwood, commander of the Mediterranean Fleet, General Claude Achinleck, commander of British troops in the Near East, and Marshal Arnold Tedder, commandant of the air forces in the Near East, together sent a telegram to General Mihailović on August 16, 1942, congratulating the Serbian leader, saying they had followed his operations "with admiration," which were "of inestimable value to our Allied cause."[7] So valued were the Chetnik operations that the chief of the

British Imperial General Staff, pursuant to Yugoslavia's Unity Day, December 1, 1942, sent the following greeting to Mihailović:

> In the name of the British Imperial General Staff, I cannot let the twenty-fourth anniversary of the unification of the Serbs, Croats, and Slovenes into one Kingdom, pass without expressing my felicitation for the wonderful undertaking of the Yugoslav. I am not thinking only of the forces which have joined the ranks of our army in the Near East in the triumphant hour, but also of your undefeatable Chetniks under your command, who are fighting night and day under the most difficult war conditions. I am convinced, your Excellency, that the day will soon come when all your forces will be able to be united in a free and victorious Yugoslavia; the day when the enemy, against whom we are jointly fighting, shoulder to shoulder will be crushed forever.[8]

On September 20, 1942, Mihailović was ordered by Slobodan Jovanović, the premier of the Royal Yugoslav government in exile, to carry out more such attacks under the command of General Harold S. Alexander, Supreme Commander for the Near East, and his Eighth Army. "The enemy communication lines are extremely overburdened and with continuous attacks you do our Allies a new favor," wrote Jovanović.[9] Despite the fact that 1942 was perhaps one of the bloodiest years in Serbian history with German reprisal policy and the Ustaše campaign against the Serbs under way, Mihailović kept the colors flying. On January 25, 1943, ebullient with expressions of appreciation from the Allies, Mihailović responded to the British via telegram:

> To Great Britain's Commanders in the Near East, Admiral Hardwood, General Alexander and Marshal Tedder: Under the forceful attacks of the three branches of the Armed Forces of Great Britain, the last action of the so-called Italian Empire has disappeared. The Yugoslav Army in the Homeland followed with admiration the course and speed of these operations. . . . The Yugoslav Army in the Homeland will

once again show the entire world who the Yugoslavs are and how they know how to fight for liberty. To Great Britain's Commanders in the Near East, pursuant to this great victory; from our mountains, the Yugoslav Army and I send greetings and sincerest congratulations for this great triumph.[10]

General Dwight D. Eisenhower, the Supreme Commander of the Allied Forces in North Africa, also gave recognition to the fighting of the Mihailović Chetniks:

The American Armed Forces in Europe and Africa greet their brothers-in-arms, the eminent and gallant military units under your resolute command. These brave men who joined your ranks in their birthplaces in order to expel the enemy from your homeland, are fighting with complete devotion and sacrifice for the mutual cause of the united nations. May this struggle bring them complete success.

Eisenhower.[11]

The Germans, for their part, bore no illusions as to the effectiveness and popularity of Mihailović's forces. On July 17, 1942, SS chief Heinrich Himmler wrote to Heinrich Müller, the head of the Gestapo: "The basis of every success in Serbia and in the entire southeast of Europe lies in the annihilation of Mihailović. Concentrate all your forces on locating Mihailović and his headquarters so that he can be annihilated."[12] In early 1943 General Reinhard Gehlen, the head of German military intelligence of Eastern Europe, reported, "Among the various resistance movements which increasingly cause trouble in the area of the former Yugoslav state, the movement of General Mihailovich remains in the first place with regard to leadership, armament, organization and activity."[13]

The anger of Premier Milan Nedić, head of the Serbian puppet regime, had also been roused, and he issued an order in the Belgrade newspaper *Novo Vreme* on January 3, 1943:

Some kind of "Command Army in the Homeland" began on September 9, 1942 to give orders throughout Serbia to the mayors of towns to leave their posts and go to the mountains, and to all others to refuse to accept the abandoned posts, recommending disobedience to our Serbian as well as to the occupational authorities. The "Command of the Yugoslav Army in the Homeland" is nothing but a small band of outlaws and desperadoes who, like blood thirsty Communist and often together with them, endeavor to defame completely the Serbian people by means of blunders and ordinary acts of sabotage unworthy of officers and honest men. To this handful of wretched non-Serbs, servants of cursed London and Moscow, I say: Keep your hands to yourselves, lunatics! And I order all government and local authorities in the country, to persecute and annihilate this band by all means, thus carrying out their duty to the Serbian people and the Homeland.

The President of the Council of Ministers [Nedić].[14]

Not to be outdone, General Paul Bader, the commander of German forces in Serbia, announced the following order, also in the same newspaper, *Novo Vreme*, on January 19, 1943:

A small group of rebels under the leadership of the former Colonel Draza Mihailović is fighting against the legal Serbian government of the Prime Minister General Nedić. These rebels consider themselves regulars of the Yugoslav army and are inspired by a criminal thirst for glory. They are trying to continue a state of war between the German and Serbian nations which ceased to exist on April 17, 1941, with the signing of the armistice. According to the articles of the International War Agreement, recognized by the Hague Conference, they are no longer considered regular soldiers and thereby fall under the war laws. The activities of these ambitious and blind fanatics, who in their criminal thoughtlessness will not take into consideration reality, constantly demand new and heavy sacrifices of the whole Serbian nation. I call upon all the Serbs to cooperate in destroying this nest of troublemakers. Whoever fails to assist in the persecution of these rebels within the limits of his power and is in the position to do so becomes thereby their accomplice and falls under the jurisdiction of the war law. Serbs, preserve peace and order!

Commandant of Serbia, General Paul Bader[15]

It was around then that General Bader issued the order proclaiming "that for every [German officer] killed, a hundred Serbs will be executed and for every mayor, ten Serbs; for every military objective destroyed, a hundred Serbs will be executed." General Bader's order had been set forth by Field Marshal Wilhelm Keitel on September 16, 1941, in two documents: one was Directive 31a to suppress "Communist Armed Resistance Movements in the Occupied Areas," issued by the German Armed Forces High Command under the signature of Keitel. In mid-September 1941 the Germans brought in a reinforced regiment, the 125th from Greece and the 2nd Infantry Division from France, and in mid-November 1941 they transferred the 113th Infantry Division from the Russian front to Serbia.

The reprisals began almost immediately after the invasion of Yugoslavia by the Axis forces and the first uprisings in Montenegro and Bosnia in the summer of 1941. Most famous were the reprisals at Kragujevac, site of the historical military arsenal of the country. On October 15, 1941, Mihailović's forces had captured a German platoon at Gorni Milanovac, near Kragujevac, and the next day, the commander of the 920th German regiment in that city sent his third battalion to free the platoon. That relief force was ambushed by both Mihailović's and Tito's forces, resulting in ten Germans killed and twenty-six wounded. The massive reprisal to follow was organized on October 19, 1941, in Kragujevac itself under the command of Franz Böhme, the German commanding general in Serbia (from September to December 1941). Around 2,300 inhabitants, according to German estimates, mostly men and high-school-age boys, were killed. The Serbian poet Desanka Maksimović immortalized the Kragujevac murders in a famous poem, "The Bloody Fairy Tale," in which she observed: "Whole rows of boys / took each other's hands / and leaving the last school class / went to the execution quietly, as if death were nothing but a smile."[16]

Kragujevac was not alone in its tragedy. The town of Rudnik was subsequently razed. In neighboring Gornji Milanovac, the town was systematically destroyed with incendiary bombs by the German forces.

Only 72 houses out of 464 were left standing. In Kraljevo, the "city of the seven kings," railway and aircraft factory workers were executed, and the Germans reportedly shot one member of each family in the town, around 1,700 civilians killed. On October 29, 1941, Felix Benzler, the German foreign ministry plenipotentiary for Serbia, reported, "In the past week there have been executions of a large number of Serbs, not only in Kraljevo, but also in Kragujevac, as reprisals for the killing of members of the Wehrmacht, in the proportion of 100 Serbs for one German. In Kraljevo, 1,700 male Serbs were executed, in Kragujevac, 2,300."[17] The killings seemed to fulfill the wish of SS Gruppenführer August Meissner, who insisted, "I like a dead Serb better than a live one." For whatever reason, the German reprisals against the Chetnik-sympathetic areas were more severe than in those areas dominated by Partisans.

· · ·

Whatever the Germans' unequivocal dislike of Mihailović, with the accompanying German violence against the Serbs, Mihailović felt compelled, nonetheless, to frequently reiterate his pro-Allied stance. Part of this was due to the inherent instability of "commanding" a large and often loose group of Chetnik forces who officially fell under Mihailović's command, but often acted independently—sometimes too independently. It was also motivated by the complication of rivals such as Kosta Pećanac, Mihailović's older, fiercely anti-Communist and Axis-sympathizer rival, and by the intrigues of the powerful Chetnik renegade Novaković, as described earlier. The "Serbian Volunteer Corps" of Dimitri Ljotić was a group that was often, and erroneously, included in the category of "Chetnik" due to the nationalist, anti-Communist (but ultimately pro-Axis) outlook of its followers. Despite this confusion, Mihailović's communications to the British from the spring of 1941 to early 1943 reveal a consistent anti-Axis disposition, and telegrams beginning in autumn 1941 demonstrate a close observation of the actions of any of his officers who were suspected of having Axis contact.

In one decree of September 26, 1941, Mihailović degraded twelve air force officers who had gone to fight for the Germans on the Russian front. On December 19, 1941, Mihailović had requested that Jovanović demote several generals for acts of collaboration with Milan Nedić, the head of the new puppet regime in German-occupied Belgrade. In another decision on the same day, several officers from Nedić's "army," made up of former Royal Yugoslav officers, were also degraded.[18] They were deprived of all their military titles, and Mihailović commanded that their names be broadcast and denounced as traitors on the exiled government's short-lived, Jerusalem-based Radio Karadjordjević, which had BBC transmission. On January 16, 1942, he demoted another 213 officers for such suspected ties and did so again in another decree on May 27, 1942, in which 286 officers from the Yugoslav Army, Navy, and Air Force were degraded in connection with their participation in a massacre of Serbs in Bosnia with the Ustaše.[19]

Mihailović's most angry invective was against other Serb rebel leaders, namely Dimitri Ljotić and Kosta Pećanac. In a telegram dated May 10, 1942, he accused Ljotić of forming armed bands whose commanders were the accomplices of the Germans "with whom they plundered Serbs for money."[20] The next telegram, also of May 10, described Kosta Pećanac as a "drunkard," with "jail birds" as guerrilla fighters.[21] On May 26, Mihailović wrote to Jovanović emphatically denying that Nedić, Pećanac, and Ljotić were working with Mihailović's forces. "I absolutely deny even the thought of working with such traitors," he wrote. "Let all Yugoslavs and particularly Serbs bear this in mind."[22]

• • •

While all this was going on, however, the British were giving only meager military support to Mihailović and his forces. The British Special Operations Executive (SOE) was then under the command of Roundell Cecil Palmer, Earl of Selborne, famously known as Lord Selborne, the minister of economic warfare, who replaced Hugh Dalton (with Winston Churchill, as previously mentioned, an original founder and organizer of the SOE). Lord Selborne was charged with encouraging resistance throughout Europe yet had only four B-24s—the popular U.S.-made bombing, naval reconnaissance, and transport "Liberator" aircraft—earmarked for supply operations in Yugoslavia and Greece. Between March 1942 and January 1943 these aircraft flew twenty-five sorties, mainly to Greece. From the start of the war in 1941 through to mid-1943, 108 Squadron aircraft, based in Tocra, Libya, had dropped only twenty-three tons of matériel to the Chetniks.[23] What's more, three tons of those supplies included 30 million occupation lire printed by the British in Ethiopia and a large supply of anti-snakebite serum from the same source. Both items, of course, were useless in Yugoslavia, and particularly insulting in light of the fact that in 1941 the British High Command had agreed to send to the Chetniks "guns, rifles, bandages, gold and other supplies," which the British Middle East Command was instructed by London on November 7, 1941, to get to the Chetniks by submarine, aircraft, or local craft.

In addition to the absurd contents of these deliveries (when there were deliveries at all) to give one an idea how little that entire 23 tons' worth of deliveries was, the Communist-backed ELAS guerrillas of Greece, with whom Churchill reluctantly threw his lot in July 1943, received 5,800 tons of ammunition and supplies between 1942 and 1944. In October 1943 alone, the Partisans received 650 tons, including 10,000 rifles, 171 light and medium machine guns, almost 3.5 million rounds of small ammunition, 4,800 mortar bombs, and much else.[24]

The insubstantial—and sometimes downright embarrassing—lack of supplies to the Chetniks only served to cultivate the early seeds of distrust in the minds of Mihailović and his men, who immediately assumed there to be an anti-Chetnik political rationale underlying the limited aid. For example, in May 1942 a B-24 dropped supplies to the Chetniks amid much celebration and anticipation. Yet those Serbs found only a crate with medical supplies, explosives, and some hand grenades—no rifles, no machine guns, and just one antitank gun. Major Jasper Rootham, part of the British mission to Mihailović (in Homolje, Eastern Serbia, under the command of one of Mihailović's subordinates), recounted in his memoir *Missfire* the uncomfortable tension that began to color the relationship between the Chetnik Serbs and the British field officers as a result. Around the time of that meager May delivery drop, Rootham told the Chetniks to whom he was assigned that five transport aircraft from the British would be sent to their forces the following month. Yet throughout all of June, ten messages came from SOE Cairo delaying the arrival of the planes for various reasons, until, in the end, not one plane came. "They [the Chetniks] were as polite as ever, and their attitude for our personal comfort and safety never flagged," wrote Rootham of this disappointment, "but their attitude became warier than before."[25]

Rootham tried to convince the Serbs that in 1942 (and 1943) there were not enough aircraft to go around, given the claims of Allied Bomber and Coastal Commands in the general war "who wanted all and more than all the four-engined aircraft they could get," he wrote. The supply of aircraft for Chetnik support did not keep pace with the growing number of missions to both Tito and Mihailović, Rootham later reflected, until early in 1944 "when the possession of air-fields in Italy had put Yugoslavia within range of two-engine transport aircraft."[26] But by the time such better opportunities for supply aircraft had come about, Mihailović had been sidelined, and it was the Partisans who benefited from the new situation. Convinced, nonetheless, of the worthiness of the Chetniks to have received more British aid, Rootham adds, tellingly:

> They came to plead for more planes. They began by explaining to us the weakness and the strength of their organization and from personal observation over the next twelve months I am convinced that on this occasion at any rate they were speaking the truth. The strength of the organization lay in its reserves of manpower and in the support which it had from the people; its weakness was its lack of material. . . . [The Chetniks] said they would be able to mobilize thirty thousand able bodied men . . . nearly all of whom were Salonika veterans. Of these they were able to arm at present less than one-tenth, of whom the great majority had only rifles, with an average of between thirty and fifty rounds per rifle. [They] had . . . only four light machine guns, and there was in Eastern Serbia at that time only mortar, a 48 mm Italian one which had arrived with [the British]. . . . I am convinced that they would have been able to fulfill their promise that they would guarantee to receive, clear and distribute in one night the loads of fifty aircraft to be dropped at ten widely separated points in Eastern Serbia.[27]

At best, Rootham had to tell them, they would probably receive about four aircraft.

Rootham's explanations were greeted with Chetnik incredulity. One Chetnik commander asked him: "Major, you tell me that the whole of the British Empire can only spare four aeroplanes for this work of supplying the Jugoslav Army in the Fatherland. I am sure that you think you are telling the truth, but you will forgive me if I say that I do not believe you."[28] (The Chetniks ended up receiving two planes—gifts from President Franklin Roosevelt, who had originally promised four.)

There was also the element of the absurd. From October 1942 until Colonel S. W. Bailey's arrival, Mihailović had received only two British air sorties. It wasn't just the Chetniks who were insulted. William Hudson, the British liaison officer, wrote a memo to SOE Cairo on September 22, 1943, angrily informing them that he had been waiting a year for a coat large enough for someone six feet tall like himself. Instead, he told them, he was sent tennis trousers, silk pajamas, and "stunted five-foot outfits." He continued, "In fact, ever since you sent me in from Cairo with bum W/T [wireless transmission] equipment your supply department has been just plain lousy."[29]

Back in Washington, things were no less absurd. Fotić reported that the president was "shocked" when he told him that the 400 tons of food sent in the autumn of 1942 as Roosevelt's gift had never been delivered and that 112 tons of it had been "appropriated for uses entirely different from those intended."[30] The president promised Fotić that he would send personal instructions that the remaining 288 tons be sent, and still, Roosevelt's personal intervention notwithstanding, no food ever arrived from the Americans for Mihailović.[31]

• • •

Meanwhile, other aspects of the British-Mihailović relationship were amiss. The years 1941–1942, it will be remembered, were excessively brutal, during which Ustaše violence against the Serbian population was at the height of its ferocity. Mihailović did not feel that the Allies recognized the peril in which they, the Serbs, found themselves, given the level of slaughter against them. In a telegram dated August 10, 1942, and addressed to Churchill, Mihailović described these horrors, reporting the (disputed) figure of 600,000 Serbs exterminated, in addition to another approximately 70,000 Serbs killed by the Germans, 30,000 by the Hungarians, and 10,000 by the Albanians. A memo from the Yugoslav government in exile of October 7, 1942, to Mihailović quoted the somewhat cool reply from the British Foreign Office to Mihailović's August 10 telegram: "Mr. [Anthony] Eden's address at the opening of [London's] Yugoslav House on September 24 significantly emphasized his and his government's admiration of Mihailović's patriotic and courageous struggle."

Yet there was a curious twist to that memo. In it, Eden, the British foreign secretary, continued on to report, "[Yugoslav Ambassador to the United States, Constantine Fotić] just wired his government that British censors in Washington had received instructions from here [London] to give as little as possible mention to Mihailović's name [in wartime radio broadcasts via the BBC]. Yugoslavs however are inclined to mark this down to British government's desire to avoid offending Russians."[32]

The Russians at that time, however, were not terribly worried about being offended one way or the other. They were maddeningly elusive in their official support of their "ally," the Royal Yugoslav government in exile. The Yugoslavs approached Andrej Vyshinsky, then deputy Soviet foreign minister, on November 17, 1941, asking that the Partisans be made to cooperate with Mihailović, arguing that the whole revolutionary movement in Yugoslavia, Chetnik or Partisan, needed to be united under the Chetnik leader, "who was the soldier best able to organize and lead the fight against the enemy."[33]

But whatever "official" support meant or not, by late August 1942 Moscow's tone began to change more openly. Mihailović, for months prior to that time, was no longer being mentioned by Moscow radio by name. Then, an indictment of Mihailović detailed in a Soviet communiqué of August 3, 1942, accused the Chetnik leader of closely collaborating with the Italians and to a lesser extent with the Germans; the indictment named other Chetnik leaders, Generals Peršić and Stanišić, as well.[34] It detailed a series of alleged acts of collaboration with the Germans occurring between March and May 1942, including the discovery of correspondence supposedly found by Partisans testifying to military contacts between Mihailović and the German-Italian occupation forces. Another allegation accused Mihailović's Chetniks of cooperating with the Ustaše against the Partisans around Mostar on May 13, 1942, and of retreating to the mountains of the Albanian frontier later that month under the leadership of General Stanišić, with whom Mihailović had been accused of collaborating with the Italians. The charges went so far as to state that the Chetniks kept a permanent "representative," the Bosnian Chetnik commander Dobroslav Jevdjević, with those Italian forces. Jevdjević did cooperate with the Italian anti-Communist militia, the MVAC, only to be later arrested by the Germans in 1943.

Mihailović's efforts to report to the Allies acts of collaboration with the Germans among his own ranks were also apparently ignored. In a memorandum of December 9, 1942, from King Peter to Churchill, the young monarch describes how the censors in London did not allow Mihailović's complete list of collaborators—those the Chetnik leader labeled with the letter "Z"—to be aired through the BBC. "The Censors no longer allow these names to be broadcast," wrote the king, "though General Mihailović continually asks that they should be."[35]

Furthermore, as the king continued in that memo, the Germans and the Bulgarians, as well as the Ustaše troops of Pavelić, had "cleaned up" various areas of Serbia, "committing atrocities" along the way, in response to Mihailović's cutting communication lines on the Zagreb-Belgrade and Belgrade-Salonika railways.[36] But, the king said, "The London radio censorship is not anxious to allow mention of these atrocities and threats."[37] The king then attacked the Partisans, who "in the midst of war" were trying "to impose social revolution on our people," and were "perpetrating great atrocities against the people," putting to death "a large number of General Mihailovich's best officers."[38] He concluded, "If the Yugoslav Government cannot counter the Communist campaign against General Mihailovich over the London wireless, the advertisement of Partisan activities from London should at least be avoided. This is all the more necessary as Soviet propaganda attributes most of the attacks carried out by General Mihailovic to the Partisans."

While these accusations of allies betraying and censoring their own allies were flying back and forth, the Germans, meanwhile, were keeping careful track of their retaliations against Mihailović supporters. The historian Walter Roberts cites two entries from the German *Kriegtagesbuch*, the German official war record, for December 1942: "December 16th: 'In Belgrade, 8 arrests, 60 Mihailovich supporters shot.' December 27: 'In Belgrade, 11 arrests, 250 Mihailovich supporters shot as retaliation.'"[39]

There was also the matter of propaganda pamphlets put out by the British and sent to Yugoslavia, in which King Peter and Mihailović were completely ignored. The British also began to publish in Cairo a newspaper, *Victory*, aimed at Serbians and urging them to take up the cause of resistance. Once again, there was no acknowledgment of Mihailović or the king or his government. Some well-placed Americans took note of this inconsistency. Martha Gellhorn, the American war correspondent, third wife of Ernest Hemingway, and no friend of monarchists, was in Italy when Yugoslav refugees began to arrive there, and she complained to the State Department that journalists were not being allowed to cover Mihailović's troops.[40] Mihailović had himself asked George Musulin to send American journalists into the area and to give them freedom to move to see if there was any evidence of collaboration (none were ever sent in). Mihailović also proposed that the British, the Russians, and the Americans send a commission composed of representatives from the three nations that would set up zones of operation from which they would receive material help and aid from the Allies and use it in the common effort against the Germans. In this way Mihailović felt that this commission would prevent a clash between the Chetniks and the Partisans. The plan, however, was rejected by the Allies.

• • •

What was going on? It has been said that the first "to go over" to the Tito side in the Yugoslav civil war was the Yugoslav section of the BBC, then headed up by Hubert Harrison, a former Reuters correspondent in Belgrade. In late 1942, on the basis of information coming from several sources, including the shortwave radio station of the Partisan High Command, "Free Yugoslavia" (then based in Tiflis, Georgia), the BBC began to talk about other "patriots" fighting the war in Yugoslavia. But such patriots were inevitably the Partisans. By January 1943, the BBC was placing greatest emphasis on the activity of those Partisans, and on January 14 the BBC censorship eliminated Lika (the mountainous area in central Croatia) and Kordun (the area just south of Lika) and several other place names from Mihailović's communications on the grounds, according to one overview of the BBC in Yugoslavia, suggesting that only the Partisans were active in those regions. On January 28, 1943, nine mentions of Mihailović were eliminated from a major broadcast (only two such mentions were allowed), and by April 1943 the BBC struck out entire sentences referring to Mihailović as a hero, despite the fact that it was still then official British policy to support the Chetnik leader.[41]

In the weeks to follow, Sir George Rendel, the British ambassador to the Yugoslav government in exile, Lord Selborne, and members of the British military mission to Mihailović complained to the BBC. Yet those broadcasts continued to pursue an increasingly pro-Tito, anti-Mihailović line. Mihailović charged that the speakers at the Yugoslav section of the BBC were almost exclusively Croats, while the remainder, if any were Serbs, were communists. Ambassador Rendel later wrote to the director of the BBC, Douglas Howard:

> It is of course nonsense to say that the speakers on the BBC are Croats though in point of fact I gather that Krnjević and Jukić, and possibly some other Croats have been making some very unfortunate speeches over the BBC. But it is perfectly true to say that many of the BBC speakers such as Zlatoper and Petrović are violently Leftist and took an active part in the anti-Mihailović meeting which was held on June 16th under the auspices of the Union of Democratic Control.[42]

Rendel went on to suggest that in light of Mihailović's communications the "whole policy of the BBC in these Yugoslav broadcasts" be carefully reconsidered.[43] Following this, Mihailović forces went on to capture Prijepolje on September 11, 1943, from a strong German garrison, yet the action was credited to the Partisans. When the Chetniks took Priboj on September 12 and forced the surrender of the Italian garrison of 1,800 men, as mentioned earlier, this was also credited to the Partisans. In late September and early October the Chetniks destroyed four bridges in the Mokra Gora area, raided Visegrad, and blew up the Visegrad bridge. Yet these actions were also credited to the Partisans.[44] About a year earlier, in November 1942, Brigadier C. D. Armstrong protested to SOE Cairo, but to no avail. "It is in your own interest to bring this home forcibly to BBC," he wrote, "otherwise when you wish to employ it to broadcast special propaganda for your own operational ends, you will discover you are using absolutely useless instruments as far as the Serbs are concerned."[45]

Such selective editing on the part of the BBC proved too much for Mihailović's patience. In a telegram dated November 13, 1942, he had complained that the London radio broadcasts were "raising anew the Partisans from the dead" and "placing them on the same level as the Yugoslav Army."[46] His exasperation swelled into outright anger. "This is diminishing the people's enthusiasm in the fight against the forces of occupation because their hatred toward Communists is unquenchable," he wrote, adding that such reports increased the chances for a resumption of violence between the Partisan and Chetnik sides, which in autumn 1942 had died down owing to a fragile (and short-lived) truce between those two sides.[47]

Mihailović minced no words, or comparisons. One of his telegrams, dated January 15, 1943, accused the BBC of "singing praises to the Partisans who have inflicted more civil war on our martyred nation than the Ustaše."[48] Mihailović further held the London radio broadcasts responsible for the breakdown of morale among his soldiers. "Some of our units," he wrote, "which heard that transmission, broke the radios in protest against our government in London and our Allies who are insulting our national pride with their senseless propaganda and thereby are placing themselves in the ranks of our grave diggers."[49] These communications continued well into the summer, endeavoring to underscore Partisan cooperation with the Germans. On March 26, 1943, Mihailović wrote in a telegram, "The Communists continue negotiations with the Germans, with the aim of exterminating us, taking advantage of our indecisions."[50] On April 13 Mihailović wrote that "the support which the Communists are receiving from abroad only sharpens the ideological conflict and it is benefiting only the forces of occupation. Had there been no Communists and their detrimental work we should have been able to offer the greatest aid in the struggle against the forces of occupation."[51]

Yet the telegrams had little effect. King Peter for his part tried once more to appeal to the British. "This campaign endeavors in all possible manners to represent General Mihailovich and the Yugoslav National Movement [the Chetniks] as traitorous anti-democratic and anti-Allied. [It] endeavors to humiliate the entire fight of a whole nation in the course of two years and a half and to pass over the more than one million victims, who have been given by the Serbian nation in Yugoslavia alone."[52] It was of little use. By the summer of 1943, the British government was almost totally on the side of the Partisans. Strangely enough, that same summer, on July 22, 1943, the Germans had published in various Yugoslav newspapers a large advertisement offering 100,000 gold marks (a parallel currency to the Reichsmark) for Tito and Mihailović each. When the BBC reported the offer in its Serbo-Croatia broadcast, it ignored the reward offered for the head of Mihailović and reported only on the reward for Tito.[53] Although the Germans themselves continued to see Mihailović as a sworn enemy to them, obviously the Allies did not.

• • •

The original image of Mihailović as an uncompromising anti-German resistance leader was now, in the eyes of the Allies, metamorphosing into that of an embittered civil war protagonist more preoccupied with his own local reputation than interested in cooperation with the Allies. Furthermore, it was around this time that the strategic differences between the Chetniks and the Partisans were coming aggressively to the fore. Tito and his Partisans stood for all-out and immediate resistance, Yugoslav-wide organization, and a firm command for the sake of long-term Communist goals.

Whatever cost this imposed upon the Yugoslav populace was a tragic but necessary aspect, all the more so since their original call to arms came in response to Comintern directives and the need to relieve pressure on behalf of the Soviets on the eastern front. Mihailović, as stated earlier, was from the outset concerned to avoid enemy retaliation and reprisals on the civilian population. He was more cautious, and his troops were disciplined but more vaguely organized. Since the beginning of the invasion of Yugoslavia by the Axis, Mihailović was careful to not exhaust his limited resources too recklessly by all-out offensives against the Axis. Revolted by the extermination campaigns of the Ustaše and by the reprisal policies of the Germans, he sought discriminate use of his forces until they could be used to assist eventual intervention by the Allies. The Yugoslav government in exile itself had a good deal of sympathy for a policy of passivity as a means of avoiding bloody reprisals against the civilian population.

It is important to keep in mind, however, when talking about the very early days of revolt in Yugoslavia and the strategy styles of the Partisans versus the Chetniks, that there were no Allied witnesses to the major role played by the Mihailović nationalists in the uprisings in Montenegro and Bosnia in the summer of 1941. Neither were there early witnesses to the Partisans. Yet the Partisan retelling of the events that summer tended to be uncritically accepted by the British officers, such as Deakin, who transmitted them, and by SOE Cairo and the BBC, which analyzed and rebroadcast them. On the other hand, the reports of those British officers observing the Chetnik side—when those reports got through at all to the proper channels—were very detailed, describing all aspects, negative and otherwise, of Chetnik comportment, and were written in the detached style of skeptical journalism. What's more, the dispatches of Colonel Hudson, the first British liaison officer to the Mihailović forces, which described numerous anti-German activities later that year (1941), were all destroyed under mysterious circumstances at the SOE headquarters in Cairo.

Such distinctions mattered little, however, as Chetnik relations with London continued to deteriorate. This time, it had to do with a series of aggressive telegrams in early 1943 between Mihailović and the British colonel Bailey, the second British liaison officer to Mihailović. Their tense exchanges carried over into a parallel series of icy correspondence between British prime minister Churchill and Yugoslav prime minister Jovanović during the first half of that year, before Jovanović's resignation. There were a couple of incidents between Mihailović and Colonel Bailey in which Mihailović vented considerable frustration, to the point of accusing the British of treachery and threatening to initiate collaborative relations between Mihailović's Chetniks and the Italian occupation army.

The most explosive of these occasions took place on February 28, 1943, when during a funeral in Lipovo, in Montenegro, not far from the onetime Partisan stronghold of Kolašin, Mihailović delivered a frustrated, impassioned speech about the Allies, in which he said, in part, that since they, the Allies, weren't helping him, he would have to, out of necessity, collaborate with the Italians, and that the Croats, the Muslims, and the Partisans were the first enemies of the Serbs (or Chetniks) and that only after they had been dealt with would he turn his forces against the Axis. His attacks against "the English" were withering. An alarmed Colonel Bailey, who traveled with Mihailović to Lipovo, was in attendance.

Mihailović's words were the acid bath in which any further Allied trust in his willingness to cooperate with them had now been drowned for good. An incensed Churchill immediately wrote to the Yugoslav government in exile. "His Majesty's Government are becoming seriously disturbed at recent developments in Yugoslav affairs and increasingly apprehensive in regard to the future unless steps are taken to effect a greater measure of unity among the various resistance groups in the country," wrote the British prime minister.[54] He continued: "[T]here is still a complete absence of unity among the different elements of resistance, that a virtual civil war continues between the forces of General Mihailovic and the Chetniks on one hand and other units of resistance on the other, and that in this struggle General Mihailovic has associated himself directly, or indirectly with the Italian army of occupation." Churchill's letter went on:

In the course of this speech General Mihailovic said that the Serbs were now completely friendless, that the English, to suit their own strategic ends were urging them to undertake operations without the slightest intention of helping them either now or in the future, and that the English were now fighting to the last Serb in Yugoslavia. He continued that the English were trying to purchase Serbian blood at the cost of an insignificant supply of arms but that he would never be a party to this "shameful commerce typical of traditional English perfidy". . . . [That] they [the Serbs] were forgotten and confined by His Majesty's Government who "shamelessly violated Yugoslav sovereignty" by negotiating directly with the Soviet Government on internal Yugoslav problems. The BBC with "revolting cynicism" had dropped its support of the "sacred Serbian cause". The Allies' "lust for fraud" was satisfied by the untimely, hypocritical and anti-Yugoslav activity of the Partisans but . . . that nothing they could do or threaten could turn the Serbs from their vowed and sacred duty of exterminating the Partisans. As long as the Italians remained his sole adequate source of benefit and assistance generally, nothing the Allies could do would make him change his attitude towards them.[55]

Churchill conceded that "words spoken in heat may not express a con-sidered judgment and that General Mihailović may feel himself temporar-ily aggrieved at the small amount of assistance which it has unfortunately for reasons beyond the control of His Majesty's Government been possible to send him recently." Nonetheless, continued Churchill, the British were not going to accept this kind of outburst. Nor were they going to accept "continued support of a movement, the leader of which does not scruple publicly to declare that their enemies are his allies—whether temporary or permanent is immaterial—and that his enemies are not the German and Italian invaders of his country but his fellow Yugoslavs and chief among them men who at this very moment are fighting and giving their lives to free his country from the foreigners yoke."[56]

The Churchill communications prompted Yugoslav prime minister Jovanović to send a stern message to Mihailović. In that message, he warned Mihailović about the consequences of his speech, "which has attracted [the British government's] special notice the passage in which you state that you consider the Partisans, Ustaše and Moslems and Croats to be your principal enemies, and that you will turn to the Germans and Italians only when you have dealt with them."[57] Jovanović warned, "Quite apart from all this, I must say that your speech of 28 February if it has been accurately reported conforms neither to the views of the British nor of the Yugoslav Government. The Germans and the Italians, who partitioned Yugoslavia and deprived our people of liberty, are our principal enemies. . . . We realize that there were occasions when you could not help join the battle with the Partisans but this cannot justify collaboration with the Italians against them." Jovanović then added a line that would bring some complication upon himself vis-à-vis the British: "We are assured by the British government that the changed military situation in the Middle East will soon make it feasible to send you all the help to which your efforts entitle you."

Sir George Rendel, the British ambassador to the Yugoslav govern-ment in exile, wrote a discreet reply to Jovanović in a subsequent memo dated April 3, 1943, tactfully warning against any misinterpretation of implied future British commitments to the Yugoslavs. Rendel wrote that the British would be "happy" to aid Mihailović in the near future, but that "although we hope shortly to be in a position to send to

General Mihailovic help on a far more considerable scale than hitherto, *provided his attitude renders this possible*, there is little prospect in the immediate future of being able to send him help on so very considerable a scale as these words [those of Jovanović's preceding communication] imply."[58] Rendel added, "The Foreign Office moreover feel that it should be made clear that this promise of further help is conditional on General Mihailovic's collaborating loyally and wholeheartedly with his British Allies."

It was now Jovanović's turn to be angry. He maintained, in a subsequent letter to Rendel, that Mihailović's speech had not been a public speech in the first place, nor one that was supposed to be given any kind of publicity. And if in his speech Mihailović complained against the Allies who abandoned him without sufficient support, it would be understandable that in speaking about it, he should lose his temper. He then added, "If there were a secret service to overhear what the Allies say about one another, much worse would be heard than that speech by General Mihailovic."[59]

Jovanović also defended his government against the implication that Mihailović's anger expressed the sentiments of the Yugoslav government. "No doubt there are disagreements in the Yugoslav government but they are in no connection whatsoever with the speech of General Mihailović," wrote Jovanović in another memo to Rendel, "and I really do not see any reason why those two separate things have been included in the same note, unless it was desired to make an attack against the Government, cramming together all which could be cited against it. In that case the speech of General Mihailovic would acquire the importance of an act for which he is not responsible alone, nor the whole Government."[60] Rendel remained unmoved. "The Partisans were killing the most Germans and Mihailović was busy killing the most Partisans," he maintained. And there seemed to be some acceptance of this, wrote Rendel later to Churchill, as "the Prime Minister [Jovanović] would not admit the accuracy of this account."[61]

There was also the matter of an alleged misinterpretation of a strongly worded speech given by Mihailović against Colonel Bailey. Bailey had submitted a written order to Mihailović on May 29, 1943, directed by General Henry Maitland Wilson, the Middle East commander in chief, that the Chetnik leader was needed to reorganize all his forces wherever they may be, consistent with the plans of the British High Command in the Middle East "in whose sphere he belongs."[62] This involved, among other things, the "recommendation" that Mihailović go to the region of Kopaonik, one of the largest mountains in Serbia, located in the eastern part of the country, and with him his "faithful officers"—about 100,000 then. ("General Mihailović does not represent a fighting force of any importance west of Kopaonik," wrote Bailey in a later memo. "His units in Montenegro, Hercegovina and Bosnia are already annihilated or else in close cooperation with the Axis; it is also difficult to say that his units exist in Croatia, Slovenia and Slavonia.")[63]

But the British colonel conceded: "The British units in Homolga (Kosovo) and in Priština affirm that the units there are strong and that their main wish is to carry out attacks on enemy communication lines according to British directions." Bailey then delivered a harsh conclusion to this memo: "The Partisans represent a good and effective fighting force in all parts where only the quislings represent General Mihailović." Such allegations enraged Mihailović. He defended the strength of his army "in all parts" of Yugoslavia and would continue to "prove its existence to the whole world." He finished, "I will not bear similar insults any longer."

But Mihailović's defense would prove futile. Bailey's more troublesome verdict regarding "quislings" stemmed from a communiqué that Bailey had intercepted in early 1943, which the Soviets picked up on and exploited aggressively. This was a message from Mihailović to Pavle Djurić, the Chetnik leader of the Dinara Division operating in the Sandžak/eastern Croatia/Montenegro region who held close contacts with the Italians. Mihailović instructed Djurić, allegedly, to prohibit his troops from any anti-Axis activity with the exception of the territory south of the Urosevac-Alexandrovo lines of communication and transport. In this message, Mihailović also told Djurić to hold back from the British vitally urgent intelligence reports, even though Mihailović remained in direct contact with the British liaison headquarters in Priština and SOE headquarters in Cairo.

The Soviets jumped in to pour oil on the fire. In an aide-mémoire of January 26, 1943, the Soviet ambassador Solomon Lozovsky informed the Yugoslav government in exile that Moscow's information pointed to Mihailović having had an "agreement" with the Italians and that Mihailović was acting according to such an agreement. Then, the Soviet Radio Broadcasting station "Free Yugoslavia" in a broadcast of July 16, 1943, accused Mihailović of "treason." The government in exile continued to support Mihailović against such charges, tolerating whatever accusations were being thrown at him in order that the country not fall to the Communists after the war.

Despite Mihailović's arguments to the contrary, the forces working against him just seemed to grow stronger. On August 5, 1943, the Soviet Foreign Office presented to the Yugoslav delegation at Kuibyshev, Russia's wartime capital in central Russia, a detailed memorandum charging that Mihailović and the Chetniks had been cooperating with the Italians against the Partisans in Yugoslavia and that "documents" had fallen into the hands of the Partisans proving the charges.

Still, the British remained vague as to their next moves with Mihailović. Foreign Secretary Eden had told Mihailović via Jovanović in a cable dated May 7, 1943, that the British would "hope shortly" to be in a position to send more material support than in the past, but only under certain terms: that the primary purpose of Chetnik resistance be directed toward the Axis; second, that there be consistent cooperation between Mihailović and Colonel Bailey ("His Majesty's Government attach particular importance to this point"); and third, that Mihailović understand the common cause that resistance movements in occupied countries can reasonably be expected to make to the prosecution of the war. With these conditions in mind, said Eden, His Majesty's Government would propose to strengthen Colonel Bailey's mission by the addition of further British military, air force, and naval officers.

Jovanović wrote to Mihailović that the British government was barely concealing their threats to abandon him completely. Yet Jovanovic's pleas for more restrained conduct and diplomatic savvy from Mihailović proved largely in vain. The angry Chetnik leader attacked the insinuation of collaboration and the failure to acknowledge the Chetniks' lack of arms. His army, he argued, was ready to assist the Allied cause, but it must have strong support, both moral and material. (Mihailović consistently maintained to his rather skeptical American and British allies that he could raise anywhere from 300,000 to 500,000 troops, if provided with arms.) And then, as if to express his exasperation for the last time, Mihailović added:

> It is not in the least necessary to continuously emphasize that my only enemy is the Axis. I avoid battle with the Communists in the country and fight only when attacked. I am ready to establish the closest and most sincere cooperation with the British Supreme Command in the Middle East, and it is through no fault of mine that this cooperation has not already been established. Colonel Bailey is with my Staff for many months now, but the British command has taken no special steps in regard to this, even though Colonel Bailey stressed a number of times that he was waiting for instruction on this matter. . . . I consider all inference that cooperation with Italians must cease and that there should be no contact nor cooperation with former General Nedić as superfluous, since I repulsed such cooperation with disgust at all attempts.[64]

• • •

During this time—now early summer 1943—Tito's movement was aggressively growing in strength. British skepticism over Mihailović's capabilities was beginning to dominate the course of British policy with regard to Yugoslavia. A communication of March 17, 1943, from Count Julian Dobrski (who became Lieutenant Colonel "J. A. Dolbey" as an SOE recruiting officer for agents in Italy), recounted that Special Operations Force 133 (as mentioned earlier, the name of the Cairo-based Middle East regional headquarters of the SOE) had made proposals for a so-called Operation Wonderland. This proposed operation would establish wireless communication between that force and a small number of Chetnik leaders opposed to Mihailović.

While Wonderland was never implemented, the operation's planning underscored what might be interpreted as the intention on the part of the SOE to further splinter Chetnik unity and to deprive Mihailović of a justification for demanding more British aid. With questionable reports of a lack of Chetnik fighting against the Germans in circulation at the time,

Churchill organized a mission to the Partisans in May 1943 in order to gather reliable information about their effectiveness, hence the mission under F. W. D. Deakin, followed by that of Fitzroy Maclean.

There was more, however. Whatever Colonel Bailey's anger against Mihailović, he, too, was frustrated by the British. His memos to SOE Cairo went largely ignored, and in a memo of September 4, 1943, he wrote that he had been in Yugoslavia for eight months and received only two telegrams from HMG ("His Majesty's Government"). Although he was the head of the nine British sub-missions in the country, he found himself without a clue as to what sub-mission locations, plans, and activities were. In November 1943 he had even tried to leave the country for a month to visit SOE Cairo to give a full accounting of his observations, upon learning that Maclean and a Partisan delegation were being brought to Egypt for negotiation. While the Foreign Office in London sent one or two memos around considering Colonel Bailey's request and the possibility of Brigadier Armstrong's going to Cairo with him to make such a briefing, the request was subsequently forgotten. It might have been no surprise to Colonel Bailey to later learn that one reason his communications were not getting through to proper channels might have had to do with the people who were actually handling his memos.

As of October 1942, the SOE Cairo desk was headed by an unabashedly pro-Partisan desk officer, Basil Davidson, who later expressed those sympathies in a book, *Partisan Picture*.[65] His deputy director was Major James Klugmann, a highly active Communist who joined the Communist Party while at Cambridge University in 1933 (where he is said to have recruited John Cairncross), was later editor of *Marxism Today*, and served on the Executive Committee of the British Communist Party. Meanwhile, many of the messages from Mihailović mission officers having to do with the chronic lack of supplies were directly addressed to Klugmann, such as one from a sub-mission that asked, "For KLUGMANN . . . from [code name] PIERRO. We are still living. You seem to have forgotten us."[66]

• • •

On August 28, 1943, the Americans reentered the discussion regarding the status of Mihailović's relationship with the Allies. Mihailović himself was desperate to appeal to the Americans directly for help. One

OSS officer had received that month an ultimatum from Colonel Bailey stating that forty supply sorties planned for September would not be flown in unless Mihailović lived up to the previous agreement to cooperate in attacks on the communication line in the Priština and Ibar Valley areas. Mihailović would concede to this, but he wanted, first off, to start sending his messages to the Allies via *American* secret code. "If secrecy is requested we must compromise ourselves with him or with the British," wrote the agent to OSS Cairo on August 28.[67] "I have told Bailey that I would help him [Mihailović] if secrecy was not requested. . . . Do not overlook the possibility that he [Mihailović] may try to play us off against the British. Please inform us which course we should follow."[68]

The OSS had to communicate to Mihailović that throughout the Balkans the Americans and the British shared "one and the same mission" and that therefore there could be no question of the Americans passing on a message without informing the British. "No matter how messages are addressed, General Henry [Maitland] Wilson, Commander-In-Chief, Middle East, sees them all," wrote the officer.[69] To underscore the point, a telegram was then sent to Mihailović: "For your private information we Americans reserve the right to transmit any message we wish, always, however, in common cipher with the British. As the sole guarantee against being played off one against the other, it is absolutely essential that you and Bailey display complete solidarity."[70]

There was, nonetheless, sympathy from the American side for Mihailović and the situation he found himself in. "It is unquestionable," the officer continued, "that Mihailovic avoided operations during the past year by every means available for the following reasons: He was faced with severe Nazi reprisals on the Serbian civilian population, driving the Serbs away from him and into collaboration, with no material from the allies. . . . The British flew in almost nothing until May [1942]. Since that time they have reached the point where it is possible to talk over operations and demand certain specific attacks."[71] Further, he continued, "there is no doubt that Mihailovic is a canny politician whose principal aim in the past has been to throw out the Partisans, subdue the Croats, preserve the strength and create one large Serbian state which he can hand over to the King upon his return. In this way he could make himself a great public hero."[72] The OSS officer noted that the collaborations with the Italians had by then dissolved. "Mihailovic's leaders in

Montenegro, and the Italian occupied areas, gave complete cooperation to the Italians this year receiving arms and food to fight the Partisans. This has all stopped now."[73]

Yet no amount of appeal to the British or to the Americans could overpower the realities on the ground, and in September 1943 the decisive appearance of surrendered Italian soldiers on the scene fundamentally changed the military balance of power in favor of the Partisans. This external shifting of the winds in favor of Tito was mainly the result of the improvised reorientation of Italian soldiers tragically abandoned in the Balkans by the government of King Victor Emmanuel III following the Italian Armistice of September 8, 1943. The Yugoslav Partisans, numbering about 50,000 to 60,000 men in the field prior to the Armistice, absorbed an estimated 150,000 of these Italian soldiers and extended their own field of action with the surrendered soldiers' armaments.

At the time of the Armistice, thirty-five divisions of the Italian Army (Regio Esercito), comprising around 600,000 men, were stationed in the Balkans (dispersed throughout Yugoslavia, Greece, and Albania)—that is, more soldiers than in Italy proper. Of that number, some fourteen Italian divisions, approximately 380,000 men, occupied areas in Slovenia, Dalmatia, and Montenegro. Thus cut off from developments on the Italian mainland, the Italian divisions were largely caught by surprise when they learned about the Armistice from radio broadcasts, just as the British officers in the Balkans themselves had not been told by their superiors in Cairo of the forthcoming Italian capitulation. Basically abandoned by the Italian Supreme Command and left on their own in hostile lands, the Italian soldiers were called upon by General Wilson in a broadcast to consider themselves as subordinate to him and not to give up their arms to the Germans.

Colonel Deakin and Colonel Bailey were given orders to negotiate an armistice with the nearest Italian commanders, which Tito scoffed at; he in turn ordered General Koća Popović to disarm the Italian Bergamo Division, which had been stationed in Split, Croatia, before the Mihailović liaison officers arrived. There was one division, the Venezia Division in Berane, Montenegro, which surrendered to the Chetnik commander Voja Lukacević, an event for which Colonel Bailey was present. In Priboj, the Italian garrison there capitulated to the Chetniks, as witnessed by the American mission leaders Captain Hudson and Captain Walter

Mansfield. Throughout the Balkans, some local commanders chose to surrender to the Germans, hoping for repatriation to Italy; a few took the Germans up on their offer to continue fighting on their side of the Axis. The Italians who were disarmed by the Germans, however, were not returned to Italy as had been promised, but were taken prisoner—an estimated 400,000 out of the 600,000 Italian soldiers stranded throughout southeastern Europe—and sent to Germany for forced labor or to be killed.[74] Some of these soldiers had the bad luck of being later "liberated" from German camps by the Red Army, only to be later transported to Soviet gulags.

Of the 200,000 or so Italian soldiers then left, a division—in this case, about 8,000 men—joined the Chetniks, as did a body of troops at Priboj; 150,000 joined the Yugoslav Partisans, formally incorporated into the Partisans' People's Liberation Army of Yugoslavia and the Partisan Detachments of Yugoslavia. The remaining 35,000 to 40,000 soldiers, one may assume, were either killed or starved to death or managed to return to Italy. These 150,000 additional fighters for the Partisans' newly formed divisions consisted of groups like the 12,000 men of the Bergamo Division, mentioned previously as an Italian garrison based at Split, on the Adriatic coast of Croatia, following the September 12 surrender of General Emilio Bercuzzi. They were disarmed by one of Tito's top commanders, and nearly all of them joined the People's Liberation Army.

The next event to follow, which would almost completely sideline the Chetniks, was the Tehran Conference, the first historic meeting of Joseph Stalin, Churchill, and Roosevelt, which took place from November 28 to December 1, 1943. The "Declaration of the Three Powers" stated that the Partisans should be supported by supplies and equipment "to the greatest possible extent," and also by commando operations.

And so in flowed a continual, massive amount of arms to the Partisans. As mentioned earlier, the sending of "50,000 light machine guns and submachine guns" in 1944, as Fitzroy Maclean described in his memoir *Eastern Approaches*, among other acts of largesse by the Allies, demonstrated the enormous amount of aid going to the Partisans.[75] In a memo of February 10, 1944, the military attaché at the U.S. embassy in Cairo, Lieutenant Colonel Sterling L. Larrabee, reported that Mihailović had received "in all only about 300 tons of supplies, mostly small arms and medical supplies," and that in the last three months, "even that trickle has stopped." Tito, on the other hand, estimated Larrabee, had received "from combined American and British sources, about 6,000 tons in the last two months alone."[76] Though the delivered weapons were intended for use against the Germans, they were also used to eliminate internal rivals. The Partisans made several attempts between October 1943 and September 1944 to penetrate Serbia, but that success would elude them until the Red Army entered Yugoslavia on September 28, 1944. Many Chetnik units, after assisting the Red Army against the retreating Germans, were disarmed and handed over to the Partisans, and some Chetnik leaders were sent to Moscow jails.

• • •

Mihailović was clearly in a no-win situation. His belief that a calculated propaganda campaign was under way against him, the rise of rival Partisan strength, the political and military attention of his Allies now turning to those Partisans, was overwhelming. Since the horrors of Kragujevac in the autumn of 1941, his fears for the Serbs' very survival as a population were another source of anxiety. The terror campaign of the Ustaše and the ruthless German reprisal policy had been nearly paralyzing, and the health and sanitation conditions in the country were very poor. For Mihailović, the memory of World War I was not so distant in his mind's eye, a time when valor and victory still brought with them the loss of 20 percent of the Serbian population as a result of typhus.

Mihailović began to question to whom he owed his first loyalties, in whose honor he owed his fighting, and whether, in the long run, the concept of one's "allies" had meaning—if it had any meaning at all. In one last attempt at gaining recognition from the Allies, Mihailović addressed a formal appeal to General Wilson, then Allied commander in the Mediterranean, to place himself and the forces of the Yugoslav army under British command, "and that I," wrote Mihailović, "may receive from you direct orders and directives for action in order to be included in the general offensive scheme of the Anglo-American Armies which shall operate in Yugoslavia," in return for ammunition, uniforms, and food. The British rejected the offer.[77]

The cause of Mihailović was not without well-placed, behind-the-scenes supporters, however ineffective they would prove to be. Carl F. Norden, head of the Division of European Affairs at the State Department, wrote in a January 1944 memo: "We have no evidence even from British sources that Mihailovitch is tacitly cooperating with the enemy or with Neditch other than the unsubstantiated assertions in the official version of the Maclean report."[78] Norden continued: "If we desire to support the British (subject to Soviet concurrence, and the Soviets are being very careful) I believe it would be preferable to act constructively rather than by supporting the British attempt to disown Mihailovitch who, whatever his recent record, was for a long time the spearhead of Yugoslav resistance to the Axis."[79] On the whole, other American diplomats agreed with this assessment.[80] Back in London, the head of the SOE, Lord Selborne, was questioning the Allied mind-set as well. The former commander was a lone voice of dissent regarding the British move to the Partisans and the abandonment of Mihailović and his Chetniks. "My sympathy is definitely with Mihailović," he wrote, "who has kept the flag flying since 1941."[81]

8

Their Brother's Keeper:
The Downfall of Soviet-Tito
Relations

For disloyalty, for any sin, brother shall not pay for brother,
father for son, kinsman for kinsman, if they dwell separately
from the culprit in their own houses; they who have not sinned
shall not pay anything; but that one who hath sinned, his
house shall pay.

—THE CODE OF TSAR STEFAN DUŠAN, 1349–1354

If the Mihailović-Chetnik relationship with the Allies—and in particular,
with the British—had begun to take on an exceptionally vindictive
tone, a similar deterioration was occurring between their ideological
counterparts, Tito with his Partisan movement, and the Soviets. It will
be remembered that the Soviet directive to resist the German occupation of Yugoslavia took place only after Germany attacked the Soviet
Union on June 22, 1941—over three months after the German invasion
of Yugoslavia. And it was only after that that the Partisans took up arms
against the Axis occupation of the country, after the Comintern ordered
the Partisans to do so on July 4, 1941. The Comintern maintained that the
defense of the USSR was at the same time the defense of the countries that
Germany had occupied. As Stephen Clissold, a former British Legation
official in Belgrade during the war and a scholar of Yugoslav-Soviet

relations, pointed out, the Yugoslav Partisans were naively convinced of the invincibility of the Red Army, believing that the war would be over in a matter of months, crowned by the Russian liberation of Yugoslavia. "Milovan Djilas, the Montenegrin Partisan leader who was in charge of its agitprop," wrote Clissold, "buoyantly proposed that the Party should issue bulletins twice a day to record each stage in the Red Army's anticipated advance."[1]

Tito himself, however, seemed to have a more realistic view of the ground situation and the likely unfolding of events. He held a meeting of the Politburo in Belgrade on June 22, and drafted a "dramatic manifesto," calling upon the Communist Party of Yugoslavia (CPY) not to "stand idly by whilst the precious blood of the heroic people of Soviet Russia is shed," but "to prepare for this grim struggle" and "organize the working masses."[2] Moscow meanwhile urged over the radio that the Yugoslav Communists should "take all measures to support and facilitate the rightful struggle of the Soviet people." Still, the Soviets tried to put the brakes on any kind of outburst of New World Order zeal. "At this present stage what you are concerned with is liberation from fascist oppression and not socialist revolution," Moscow commanded of the Yugoslav Partisans.[3]

Tito threw himself eagerly into the task. Incidents of sabotage and attacks on the Axis occupation authorities and their local collaborators were occurring throughout Serbia, and the Partisan shooting of two non-German gendarmes in the village of Bela Črvka, northeast of Belgrade, on July 7, 1941, is commonly believed to mark the beginning of the Partisan-led "general uprising." Although the first true outbreak of rebellion began in Montenegro later in the month, followed by one in Bosnia, the "official" choice of Serbia as the opening scene in the anti-Axis revolt was more or less a nod to the fact that the Supreme Staff was located there. Though mainly preoccupied with the German advance on Moscow, the Soviet High Command issued a report on August 7, 1941, acknowledging that "an open revolt" (specifying neither the Chetniks nor the Partisans) had begun against the forces of occupation in Serbia.

Tito, with then but a small staff, worked diligently from that point on to give the Partisans a sense of cohesion. His loyalists were dispatched to organize revolts in Montenegro, Bosnia, Slovenia, and other parts of the country, and on September 16, 1941, Tito himself left Belgrade to take personal command in the field. Of the various Partisan units that then formed, the units in Serbia, though not many in number, grew to be the largest after July 1941, counting 2,500 men in Valjevo and around 1,600 in Užice, and which, according to Djilas, were "a model of organization, sacrifice and self-denial."[4] The Partisans were made up mostly of Serbs, as Serbia had the largest population, but after 1943 the Croatian Communist Party was the most powerful branch of Yugoslav Communism. By late 1943, there numbered approximately 300,000 Partisan forces organized into twenty-six divisions: two located in Serbia, one in Montenegro, seven in Bosnia-Herzegovina, eleven in Croatia, and five in Slovenia.

By the late summer of 1941, the Partisan uprising was assuming full-blown proportions, and Tito kept Moscow carefully informed of his progress. He wrote in his old Russian pen name as "Valter" via clandestine wireless transmitters in Zagreb located in the home of Vladimir Velebit, a Croatian Communist and a member of Tito's Supreme Staff. There was hidden a radio transmitter through which the CPY and the Comintern (referred to in code as "Dje-Dje") had exchanged messages in 1941. The CPY had several secure lines of communication with Moscow at this time, and the party retained close contact with the Comintern. Correspondence was mainly with Georgi Dimitrov, who had a team of émigré Yugoslav Communists headed by Veljko Vlahović, the Yugoslav party representative in Moscow, to assist him, but all decisions of importance were made by Stalin and carried out by Dimitri Manuilsky, the powerful former secretary of the Comintern. After the Soviet legation was opened in Belgrade, the party was able to maintain discreet contact with its staff.

More important, however, were the two radio links that the party maintained directly with Moscow. One clandestine transmitter operated from a medical institute in Belgrade, but it was put out of action and its operator killed in the air raids of April 1941. The other transmitter was housed in a private villa in Zagreb and was operated by Velebit, a Comintern agent who had been vested by Moscow with some supervisory powers over the party as well. In addition, the Kremlin maintained its own network of intelligence agents who operated separately from the party.

Tito was reporting a rather extraordinary series of small and large victories against the Germans, in Niš (southeastern Serbia), Kragujevac (central Serbia), Zemun (a district outside of Belgrade), Belgrade proper, Pomoravlje (in south-central Serbia, near Kosovo), Valjevo (in Western Serbia), Čačak (in west-central Serbia), Sabac (in northwest Serbia), and Lazarevac (near Belgrade), destroying bridges, blowing up mines, and taking German officers hostage.[5] He also reported the rising of the Serbs in Lika and Kordun against the violence of the Ustaše, whose brutality in Sanski Most, in northwest Bosnia, was even "alarming the Germans and the Italians."[6] At the same time, the Partisan movement spread quickly throughout Yugoslavia. In Kosovo the Serbian Partisans were assisted in their operations by the Albanian Partisans, whose main headquarters were there. In Macedonia, the Yugoslav and Albanian Partisans were joined by a new Bulgarian battalion, which represented the beginning of an organized mobilization of all Bulgarians determined to fight the Axis. The Slovene Partisans penetrated deeply into Istria and German-annexed Slovenia while their southern forces merged with the Lika (Croatia) detachments.

Still, the form of uprising in which the Partisans were engaged came into question by the Soviets. As Clissold describes it, "a genuine national rising, blurred with the elements of civil war, instead of the diversionary hit-and-run tactics which characterized the activity of the Soviet Partisans, acting always as ancillary to the Red Army—was disconcerting."[7] The Balkan Secretariat of the Comintern was not yet convinced that Tito's Partisans were anything more than perhaps well-intentioned bandits, recalling Stalin's comment that he'd rather deal with the "known" figure of King Peter than the "adventurer" Tito. It was further feared that Tito and his men would fail to rouse the peasant masses to take up arms, as they were, for the most part, very conservative and highly wary of the Communists, and would attend Partisan rallies when the Partisan commanders showed up in their villages, only to return to their households filled with religious icons and pictures of King Peter. Furthermore, some of the most prominent Croat Communists, who had been arrested by the Royal Yugoslav government before the German invasion, were now being held in Ustaše prisons.

The Croatian Communists, moreover, had an independent streak. Though Tito's authority over the Central Committee of the Croat Communist Party was theoretically absolute, most Communists in Zagreb had sought independent action in the belief that Moscow's call to arms was to be heeded as soon as possible. The first attempt of the Zagreb activists was to attack and kill a Ustaše policeman; in reprisal, a group of arrested Communist leaders, writers, and intellectuals was executed. The Zagreb Municipal Committee, fearing a similar fate, organized a mass breakout from the concentration camp at Kerestinec. The Ustaše, however, heard of those plans and massacred around eighty escaping prisoners in an ambush. A round of recriminations between the Zagreb Municipal Committee and Tito's Politburo followed, and Edward Kardelj and Vladimir Popović were hastily commissioned to settle the crisis and restore the authority of the Politburo. "The dispute was patched up—but its effect may have had more than local significance," wrote Clissold. "It suggests that Moscow had, at that time, some reservations regarding Tito's leadership and was at least anxious to keep other ties in Yugoslavia. It also raises the question of whether Tito's reports of the events which were soon to develop in Serbia were given due credence."[8]

In view of Moscow's own mixed feelings about Tito, and despite the reported gains against the Germans, Tito found himself more and more frustrated with Moscow's support of Draža Mihailović, who represented the official Yugoslav government with which Moscow, all socialist idealism aside, exclusively wished to have official relations. A series of protests by Tito to Moscow then ensued, barely hiding the Partisan leader's contempt for what he saw as Moscow's propaganda in favor of the Royalist Mihailović. "Radio Moscow is broadcasting frightful nonsense about Draža Mihailović," wrote Tito, who went on to describe Chetnik violence against the Partisans led by Mihailović and his "riff raff."[9] Among other things, in a cable of November 25, 1941, he accused Mihailović and his men of killing seventeen nurses and twenty others who were on their way to Partisan headquarters in Užice; of a mangled attempt to blow up the National Bank at Užice, resulting in the deaths of "more than a hundred" workers; and the mutilation of two schoolteachers at Kosjerić, a town in western Serbia.[10] Tito warned: "It was only on account of London [the seat of the Yugoslav government in exile] that we refrained from completely liquidating Draža Mihailović. But we shall be hard put to it to hold the Partisans back from doing this."[11] With this cable, the first of Tito's charges of collaboration on the part of Mihailović were under way: "We have full proof that Draža is cooperating openly with the Germans and fighting against us. Draža's people are not firing a single shot against the Germans. All the fighting is being done by the Partisans."[12]

The Partisans sought Axis "confirmation" of Chetnik collaboration wherever they could. Accusations that the Chetniks were fighting alongside pro-Axis Croat nationalists emerged in an Axis propaganda pamphlet titled *Greueltaten und Verwustungen der Aufruhrer in Unabhänginge Staat Kroatien* (The atrocities and acts of destruction committed by the rebels in the independent state of Croatia). The work stated:

> As the Partisans, considerably influenced and led by Jews, have set forth a complete anarchy within the ranks of insurgents, a large number of Chetnik insurgents have grown cognizant of the wrong current they were following. Upon recognizing the Independent State of Croatia and its authority they [Chetniks] returned to peaceful life, whereas incorrigible elements deserted them and joined the Partisans.

Yet Moscow was still ambivalent, maintaining the line that Communist activity abroad was "outside their competence" and that it is a "purely internal question of the countries concerned."[13] In a cable of March 5, 1942, the Comintern urged Tito to broaden the basis of the united front in order to avoid a "communist character" that would alarm the West. Moscow urged him to work on uniting the anti-Axis movements and asked, hinting at cooperation with the Chetniks, if there were "no other Yugoslav patriots—apart from communists and communist sympathizers—with whom you could join a common struggle?"[14]

Tito was anxious after the Partisans were driven out of Serbia at the end of 1941 during an attack on three German motorized divisions; this forced them to lose almost all of the towns in western Serbia, as Tito tried again to elicit greater Soviet support. Fighting in the Sandžak against the Italians, he then decided to form a shock brigade, the "First Proletarian Brigade," which fought against the Italians and the Chetniks. Basing the brigade in Bosnia because of what Tito reported as Chetnik collaboration with the Italians, they encountered a tough Chetnik resistance trying to split Tito's Bosnian Partisans, and in part succeeding, as a number of Partisan detachments had gone over to the Chetniks. Tito now began an open appeal to the Soviets for arms: "We are waiting day and night for the planes. Send automatic arms, munitions, mortars. Send in some of your military experts too . . . anything you could send would be of great moral and material significance."[15] Moscow casually answered: "The technical difficulties [of sending supplies] are enormous. You should, alas, not count on our mustering them in the near future. . . . Do all you can to try to get arms from the enemy and to make the most economical use of what armament you have."[16]

Moscow itself, of course, was being given a very muddled picture of what was happening in Yugoslavia. It was after listening to a broadcast from Moscow describing Mihailović as the leader of all Yugoslav resistance and attributing the Partisans' anti-German exploits to the Chetniks that Tito ordered his forces to break off an attack on Mihailović's headquarters so as not make difficulties for Soviet foreign policy. The following day Tito sent an indignant signal to Moscow protesting such distortion of the facts. Tito's messages to the Comintern were not the only reports to reach the Soviets of the events in Serbia. Moscow also received, through information passed to them by undercover representatives in Turkey of the Yugoslav government, reports regarding the Chetnik organization headed by Mihailović and his claim to be the leader of the whole resistance movement in the country. Moscow was, at first, impressed by this claim. While divulging nothing of what they knew of Tito and the Partisans, they proposed, through their agents in Istanbul, to fly in a joint Soviet-British-Yugoslav military mission to Mihailović—an offer that was at first welcomed by the British and subsequently declined by the Yugoslav government, which sought to avoid any Soviet influence over the developing Chetnik resistance movement.

Despite the rebuff of this early offer to send in a joint mission to Mihailović, the Soviet government tried to encourage the formation of a "united anti-Fascist front," which might rally both Partisans and Chetniks in a maximum effort against the Germans. When Soviet ambassador to London Ivan Maijsky enthusiastically discussed the uprising with Anthony Eden, Mihailović and the Chetnik movement were the assumed beneficiaries. The Soviets were slow to accept Tito's allegations that Mihailović was bent on fighting the Partisans rather than the Germans, yet they maintained an ambivalent attitude toward the Chetnik leader as well. This was to persist even after the British reached the conclusion that Mihailović would contribute nothing effective to the war effort; the Soviets continued to harbor the suspicion that they might forfeit influence over a leader who in Serbia might figure as an influential political factor after the war.

The Yugoslav government in exile continued to watch closely for any signs of Soviet support for the Partisans and to discourage Partisans' attempts to start a "social revolution" in the middle of a war. In early 1942, Prime Minister Slobodan Jovanović instructed Mihailović to watch out for any early signs of help the USSR offered to the Partisans, with a view to changing by force the social and state system in Yugoslavia. By that spring, the government was reporting to Moscow that the Partisans were attacking Chetnik units, that the "Trotskyites" were attacking both Mihailović and the Partisans, and that "the Germans, Italians and Ustaše" were helping them. But Moscow would have none of it, and read such statements as a call to interfere with the activities of the Communists in Yugoslavia.

Moscow's view of the growing rivalry between Tito and Mihailović was just as detached, although it maintained a polite distance rather than overtly expressing exasperation. Individual Partisan units were Yugoslavia's "internal affair," Moscow told the Yugoslav government in exile, "in which the Soviet government did not wish to be mixed up."[17] In a feeble attempt to tone down the hostilities between the two sides, the cable added that the Soviet Union considered "everyone a Partisan" who was fighting the Germans—and consequently also General Mihailović.[18]

The attitude of Moscow really began to infuriate Tito, as he still found himself having to beg for Moscow's attention. Finally, in early 1942, he lashed out:

> I am obliged to ask you once again if it is really quite impossible to send us some sort of assistance? Hundreds of thousands of refugees are in danger of dying of starvation. Is it really impossible after twenty months of heroic, almost superhuman fighting to find some way of helping us? . . . Typhus has started to rage here . . . people dying of starvation, yet they do not complain. . . . Do your utmost to help us.[19]

Nonetheless, Moscow said only that it would not send more aid on account of "insurmountable difficulties."

Confusing the situation further was the fact that while the first accusations of collaboration were being issued by the Soviets against Mihailović, the Soviet and Yugoslav governments raised their legations to embassy status in both countries. This further frustrated Tito. "Can nothing be done to ensure that the Soviet Government are better informed concerning the treacheries and difficulties of our folk who are fighting the invaders, the Chetniks, the Ustaše and the rest of them?" he implored. "Do you really not believe our daily reports?"[20] Moscow wrote back to Tito only to ask that he make sure that the sources of his reports were authentic.

Continuing the farce on the other side, the Yugoslav government in exile was itself then trying to secure from Moscow promises that the Radio Moscow press campaign against Mihailović be stopped and that no further military cooperation could take place until the "campaign against Mihailović" was stopped. Despite Tito's protests, Moscow kept its distance from the Partisans. "How is one to explain the fact that supporters of Great Britain are succeeding in forming armed units against the Partisan detachments?" one irritated cable from the Comintern to Tito read. "Are there really no other Yugoslav patriots—apart from communists and communist-sympathizers—with whom you could join in a common struggle against the invader? We earnestly request you give serious thought to your tactics in general and to your actions, and to make sure that you on your side have really done all you can to achieve a true united front of all enemies of Hitler and Mussolini in Yugoslavia."[21] A cable that immediately followed warned Tito to tone down the Communist rhetoric as well. "Do not view the issues of your fight only from your own, national standpoint, but also from the international standpoint of the British-American coalition," read the cable tersely. "While doing all you can to consolidate positions won in the national liberation struggle, at the same time try to show political elasticity and some ability to manoeuvre." Moscow then signed off to Tito on a hopeful, perhaps even glib, note of support: "We firmly grip your plucky hands."[22]

• • •

Meanwhile, though the claims of Chetnik collaboration with Axis forces had drawn the attention of Moscow, London, and Washington, the Partisans themselves were not without their own close relationships with the enemy, and such contacts were on a far higher military and diplomatic level than those of the Chetniks. According to the wartime head of the German secret service, William Höttl, also known as "Walter Hagen," the nom de plume behind *Die Geheime Front*, a candid history of World War II German intelligence, Tito formally approached the Germans on at least two occasions with offers to cooperate. The first occurred in the summer of 1942, when the Partisans organized themselves against German occupation, and an engineer turned German-Partisan middleman who sought Croatia's then world-class wood for the manufacture of propellers appeared on the scene.[23]

The engineer's name was Hans Ott, and with him were seven other Germans in the area of Livno, in Bosnia. Ostensibly Ott was in search of superior-grade timber, but in actuality he worked for German intelligence, which was sending out feelers for possible cooperation with the Partisans. Ott was brought to Partisan headquarters to ask that he and his group be exchanged for Partisans in Zagreb jails. The Partisans accepted this proposal, and Ott was freed on word of honor, after which he informed Glaise von Horstenau of the terms of his release. Subsequently, eight Germans were traded for ten Partisans who were in Italian custody and then freed by General Mario Roatta (who had succeeded General Vittorio Ambrosio in January 1942 as head of the Italian Second Army in Yugoslavia).

While prisoner exchanges between the two sides were not new (there had been Partisan-German exchanges in the summer of 1941 in Čačak and in Montenegro the winter of 1941–1942), in this particular case there was far more at stake. During the summer of 1942 the Soviets were not sending help to the Partisans, and the latter knew that the British were supporting Mihailović. The Italians, particularly under General Roatta, commander of the Italian Second Army, were not particularly aggressive against the Chetniks, and now there were hints that the Germans might extend some kind of accommodation to the Partisans. While officially operating with the understanding that they would limit their discussions to prisoner exchanges, the Germans and Partisans met during Unternehmen Weiss ("The Fourth Offensive," January–March 1943) in March 1943 in Gornjiu Vakuf, west of Sarajevo. The commanding general of the German 717th Infantry Division, Lieutenant

General Benigus Dippold, met with three high-ranking representatives of Tito's Yugoslav Army of National Liberation: "Miloš Marković" (a pseudonym for Milovan Djilas); "Vladimir Petrović"(Vladimir Velebit), and Koca Popović (who used his real name).

Then, on 25 March Velebit and Djilas were flown in a German plane from Sarajevo to Zagreb for discussions with General Glaise von Horstenau and his staff. Tito made the offer of a *Waffenstillstand,* a truce, through Velebit, Tito's powerful thirty-five-year-old adviser (and Serbian Orthodox Christian), who approached General Glaise von Horstenau with the "astounding message" from Tito that the Partisan leader was ready to lay down arms under the condition that the Germans do not attack him in West Bosnia, and he, Tito, would refuse to arm any revolutionary acts against the Germans in Croatia. As proof of the sincerity of the offer, Tito further offered to hold off on sabotage acts for an agreed upon period of time. On March 29, German foreign minister von Ribbentrop, unnerved by the German-Partisan negotiations, prohibited all further contacts with the Partisans. Siegfried Kasche, however, replied that in all of the negotiations with the Partisans to date the "reliability of Tito's promises" had been "confirmed."[24]

The assurance to the Germans that the Partisans would attack the British if the latter were to land in Yugoslavia was as provocative a willingness to cooperate with the enemy as any statement that the Partisans held against the Chetniks as evidence of collaboration. As Djilas himself wrote:

> Neither I nor the other Central Committee members had any pangs of conscience that by negotiating with the Germans we might have betrayed the Soviets, internationalism, or our ultimate aims. Military necessity compelled us. The history of Bolshevism—even without the Brest-Litovsk Treaty and Hitler-Stalin Pact—offered us an abundance of precedents. The negotiations were held in great secrecy. There were no differences among the top leaders, except that Rankovic and I were more dubious of the outcome than Tito. As for a more permanent truce or a broader agreement no one really believed in that.[25]

"During the March discussions," wrote Walter Roberts, "the Partisan delegation stressed that the Partisans saw no reason for fighting the German Army—they added that they fought against German troops only in self-defense—but wished solely to fight the Chetniks." They also maintained that they were more oriented toward the propaganda of the Soviet Union as they dismissed any connection with the British; that they would fight the British should the latter land in Yugoslavia; that they did not intend to capitulate, but inasmuch as they wanted to concentrate on fighting the Chetniks, they sought "respective territories of interest." The three Partisan representatives signed a document confirming these conversations, and in that document they proposed not only further prisoner exchanges but also the end of hostilities between German forces and the Partisans, confirming that they "regard the Četniks as their main enemy." As Roberts then points out, on February 28, 1943, Mihailović had said the same thing (that his primary foes were the Partisans), but he said it in front of Colonel S. W. Bailey, who reported it right away to the British government (as the statements of Mihailović in general tended to be rigorously reported to SOE Cairo and London, less so in the case of the reports from the missions to the Partisans). "The written Partisan proposals," writes Roberts, "have remained generally unknown."[26] At the end of the March meetings, the Partisans left a signed document with the Germans proposing further prisoner exchanges, stating that they regarded the Chetniks as their main enemies, and proposing a cessation of hostilities between Partisans and Germans.

Another troubling aspect of the Partisans' relations with the Axis involved the number and the level of Partisan contacts with Ustaše officers, some of whom later ended up joining Partisan ranks. The secretary of the Ustaše Ministry of the Interior established informal diplomatic relations with Andrija Hebrang, secretary general of the Central Committee of the Croatian Communist Party. Hebrang went to Tito, who authorized Marko Belinić, a member of that party, to represent the Partisans in their discussions with Ustaše officials. Pavelić's war minister, General Ante Vokić, aided the Partisans with war materials, while a Ustaše lieutenant, Barisa Smoljan, who had personally admitted to killing three hundred Serbs in Mostar, joined the Partisans in 1942.

In Kordun, Croatia, the Partisans were informed of Smoljan's crimes, and rather than being punished, he was named assistant commissar of

a battalion in the Fourth Partisan Brigade. Franjo Molek, a Ustaše officer, carried out such vile crimes as rape and mutilation against Serbian
women and children in Croatia and deserted with his entire unit to
Tito. Instead of punishment for his crimes, he was awarded the rank
of major. A Major Varda, a Croatian military leader, made pacts with
Partisan forces and joined them in the civil war against Mihailović. (As
mentioned earlier, there was significant Chetnik-Ustaše collaboration as
well, by such Bosnian Chetnik leaders as Radoslav Radić of the Bosnian
"Borje" detachment, by Chetnik commander Radijov Kororić in Eastern
Bosnia, and by Urso Drenović, also in Bosnia.)[27]

In spite of these dealings, the Soviets once and for all threw their lot
in with the Partisans in January 1944. On January 3, Robert Joyce, the
OSS officer at Bari, Italy, wrote to Senator Lincoln MacVeagh,

> A source here in whom we have confidence had a conversation
> on 1 January with [Edvard] Beneš [president of Czechoslovakia,
> which also had an exile government in London] who has
> recently returned from Moscow. He quoted Beneš as making
> the following points with regard to Russian policy vis-à-vis
> Yugoslavia: That the Soviet Union was prepared to make an
> agreement with Yugoslavia but under no circumstances will
> it deal with the present government-in-exile.[28]

Moscow then added its standard diplomatic codicil regarding
Yugoslavia: "[T]he Soviet Union will not interfere in the internal affairs
in Yugoslavia and the question of the Monarchy is one to be determined
by the Yugoslav people themselves." Then the Soviets began to reveal a
bit of their postwar vision of Yugoslavia. The communication of Beneš
further revealed

> that Russia views "with sympathy" all manifestations of
> the collective will of the Yugoslav people and therefore is
> sympathetic to the Partisans' cause. The Soviet Union
> is opposed to the formation of a "Great Serbia" or an
> independent state of Croatia and in general to any splitting
> up of Yugoslavia territory. That the Soviet Union views

"sympathetically" the annexation to Yugoslavia of the "Julian March", including the city of Trieste provided there is unity amongst Serbs, Croats and Slovenes.[29]

All that said, in early 1944 it was not clear whether the Soviets really believed in what they were doing at all. Not only had Soviet foreign minister Molotov been the lone, and somewhat surprising, voice at the 1943 Tehran Conference when he suggested that the Russians send a mission to the Chetniks, as mentioned earlier, but by the time of the first Soviet mission to the Partisans on February 23, 1944, the Soviet delegation stopped first in Italy to ask the Allies, somewhat helplessly, what they should do once they got to Yugoslavia. What's more, the Soviet delegate to the Partisans was Lieutenant General N. V. Korneyev, "a poor man . . . not stupid, but an incurable drunkard," in the words of British brigadier Fitzroy Maclean.[30]

The Partisans, meanwhile, waited with exuberance and gala receptions, hoping that a significant increase in supplies would result. They would be disappointed. Other than the release of more Partisan prisoners held captive in Italy in exchange for German prisoners released by the Allies, and some communications indicating that the Soviets were increasingly indifferent to the Yugoslav government in exile, there were no significant increases in aid. "The relations between the Soviet mission and the Partisans, enthusiastic at first," wrote Roberts, "became less so as time went by. Tito soon found out that the Soviets were mainly eager to give advice. He wanted supplies, which the Soviets were unable to deliver. And so the Soviet mission began to lose its original attraction for the Partisans. For his part, the Soviet general Ivan Korneyev told Maclean that he would have preferred a post in Washington."[31]

Still, these cool relations didn't keep the Russians from taking credit for aiding the Partisans. On June 28, 1944, a communication directed Soviet aircraft operating from Bari to deliver supplies to the Russian mission at Tito headquarters and "to give all possible aid to the Partisans."[32] The original number of aircraft from the Soviets to the Partisans was eight, although they then complained that this was too little. The number was raised to twelve, with the condition set by the Soviets that no objection be made if the Soviets operated out of Allied bases. The OSS was itself amused to see that the British were excited that the Soviets were going to use American aircraft to drop British and American goods in Yugoslavia as a gift from Russia to the Partisans. This is what the British had been doing for months, flying American aircraft (frequently piloted by American airmen) to drop British and American goods as an exclusively British gift to the Yugoslavs. Later, the British decided to present a gift to Marshal Tito: an American DC-3 landed in Yugoslavia, and an American jeep and trailer were brought off the plane and presented to the Partisan marshal as gifts from the British. "America was giving substantial assistance through indirect gifts to the Partisans but all the credit is being taken by the British and the Russians," said one OSS report.[33]

Whoever was doing the delivering under what auspices or national flags, however, the Partisans were, as of 1944, receiving, according to Brigadier Maclean, a "steady flow" of supplies: "over 100,000 rifles, over 50,000 light machine guns and sub-machine guns; 1,380 mortars; 324,000 mortar bombs; 636,000 grenades, over 97,500,000 rounds of small-arms ammunition; 700 wireless sets; 175,000 suits of battle-dress, and 260,000 pairs of boots."[34] Tito appreciated the largesse that the Allies provided, but he remained wary. After the Tehran Conference in late 1943, he was invited to dine at Allied headquarters in Caserta with General Henry Maitland Wilson and Winston Churchill. Tito showed up with two dozen Partisan guards carrying tommy guns, who lined up on both sides of the dining room. "I say, Marshal," said General Wilson. "Isn't this a most unusual procedure?" To which Tito answered, "This is, General, a most unusual war."[35]

The lack of trust would only grow worse. As described in chapter 3, Tito became wildly suspicious of the ultimate objectives of the British following the chaos of the Major Arthur Terence Atherton mission to the Partisans. But the one incident that more than anything else made Partisan distrust of the British irreversible was an emotional issue: the death of Ivo Lola-Ribar, Tito's youngest Central Committee member and an aspiring star in the CPY. As he was preparing for a seminal meeting of the Central Committee, Lola-Ribar was killed by a German fighter plane during a takeoff from Glamočko Polje, in Bosnia, on November 27, 1943, which the Partisans later claimed was the result of the British failure to provide a fighter escort from Italy (according to F. W. D. Deakin, there was never such a request).[36] The occasion at hand was the second meeting of the

Antifašističko Veječe Narodnog Oslobodenja Jugoslavije (AVNOJ), or "Anti-Fascist Council of National Liberation of Yugoslavia," at Jajce, in late November 1943, a milestone gathering at which Tito would be proclaimed a "Marshal" of the new "National Committee for the People's Liberation of Yugoslavia."

Much to the outrage of the Soviets who were not told in advance of the meeting, and to the basic indifference of the British, who saw Partisan power as a done deal in Yugoslavia, the basic political platform of a postwar Titoist government was first promulgated at this meeting. This included denying King Peter the right to return to the country ("outside of a popular referendum"); revoking the authority of the Yugoslav government in exile, and organizing Yugoslavia as a federal government "based on the principle of self-determination." (The first AVNOJ meeting and the announcement of more general postwar political designs had taken place exactly a year earlier, in November 1942, at Bihać, in northwest Bosnia.)

A Dornier D-17 escorted by Croatian Domobrans had been delivered to take Lola-Ribar to Jajce, when some minutes after takeoff a German "Storch" reconnaissance plane attacked with bombs and machine-gun fire. While Lola-Ribar attempted to jump out of the plane, he was killed by an exploding bomb, as were two British officers and another Partisan. The young Partisan had been a top fighter, a Central Committee member, and a close friend of Tito's, and he represented the early romance of the antimonarchist university students' movements during the prewar years. His death was, in the words of Deakin, "a major tragedy" for the Yugoslavs.[37]

According to Djilas, the Lola-Ribar family embodied the ideal of what the Communists of Yugoslavia aspired to achieve. Lola-Ribar's brother, a Partisan fighter in Montenegro, had been killed a month earlier. The two brothers' father, Dr. Ivan Ribar, then president of AVNOJ, was once the left-leaning head of the prewar Kingdom's Constituent Assembly that had banned the CPY (the Communist Party of Yugoslavia). "Now his sons had fallen for the Communist cause and he was president of the assembly [AVNOJ] that would legalize the power of the Communists."[38] Lola-Ribar was buried in a tin coffin on November 30, lying in the chapel of the Jajce graveyard, where a broken

Moše Pijade, the Serbian-Jewish leader of the 1941 Montenegrin uprising and the oldest of Tito's entourage, eulogized that "revolutionaries are dead men on leave."[39] Meanwhile, over in Tehran, the "Big Three" meeting was preparing to recognize the Partisans as the only political power in Yugoslavia, at the urging of Churchill. And yet, the British mission officers in Yugoslavia were not invited to Lola-Ribar's funeral or to his later ceremonial tribute at Jajce.[40]

9

Night into Death into Day

Mother Earth has promised to tell her secrets to Heaven.

—Serbian proverb

Back at Ravna Gora, now early autumn September 1944, the leadership of the evacuations of the airmen had been taken over by Captain Nick A. Lalich, replacing George Musulin, who left Mihailović territory, ostensibly called back to Bari to prepare new escape route maps. As seen earlier, the British Foreign Office distrusted Musulin, Tito was suspicious of Musulin, and SOE Cairo did not think too highly of him either. Even members of his own camp voiced their dislike. "Musulin and [George] Vujnovich are not to be trusted," wrote the decidedly pro-Partisan Louis Huot in an OSS memo on the Halyard mission. "They both have strong, immature opinions."[1] Such views had further consequences. Musulin, although he was leader of the rescue mission that would oversee the evacuation of several hundred Allied airmen, never received any acknowledgment or any replies to the messages he sent out. When he went to the OSS office in Bari, Italy, in late May 1944 to check his personnel file, none of the messages he had sent out of Yugoslavia were in it. None had been forwarded by SOE.

Musulin did have a chance to strike back, offering his observations in a postmission report to the OSS on the consequences of such behind-the-scenes politics. He wrote:

> Tito's soldiers say that they have to fight Mihailovich's men to get through to attack the Germans and such key

208

targets in Serbia as enemy truck lines and mines producing copper, chrome and lead from Germany. Mihailovich says that the Partisans attack his forces in an attempt to wipe out Serb resistance to Partisans efforts to win the civil war and establish Communism. The British have made commitments to supply Balkan resistance groups and they supply only the Partisans. More than half of these supplies are made in America and are dropped mostly from DC 3s piloted by Americans operating under British control. It naturally follows that Tito's men are using these American arms against both the Germans and the Chetniks. Mihailovich and his group are not pro German but rather are most friendly to the United States and have offered assistance and cooperation in taking care of American airmen, protecting them from the Germans and making arrangements to evacuate them. The British policy is to give full support to the Partisans and in supplying them to fight the enemy they are also giving them arms for the domination of the whole of Yugoslavia as a result of winning the civil war. If American underwriting of Tito and the British policy in Yugoslavia may be considered as the result of giving the British American arms with which they can supply the Partisans, we are most definitely doing that very thing.[2]

. . .

Around September 10, 1944, the Partisans, coming up from southwestern Serbia, penetrated across the Drina River and the Maljen Mountains and began to attack the Pranjane airfield of Mihailović, near his headquarters at Ravna Gora, with ammunition that had been dropped to the Partisans from incoming C-47s, according to Colonel Robert McDowell (the University of Michigan Balkan scholar turned Special Intelligence [SI] officer assigned to Mihailović territory). (These transport planes, as described earlier, normally circled Partisan territory first and dropped nearly all matériel in those areas before heading over to pick up the Allied airmen in Chetnik territories.)

The Red Army, meanwhile, had just then reached the Danube, pushing through a thin German front. Several thousand Chetnik units were, up until the point of the Partisan attacks at Pranjane, beating back German forces near the northwest Serbian-Romanian border, as part of a plan agreed upon earlier that month, with McDowell's knowledge, for a fresh mobilization of his forces against the Axis. With the renewed Partisan attacks, however, the Chetniks were beaten back, and Mihailović ordered his units to retreat into the mountains of northeastern Bosnia. Thus began a five-hundred-mile trek by foot to reach safety and a suitable area to continue Halyard evacuations. Over the next few days, Mihailović, Lieutenant Lalich, Captain Mike Rajacich, Colonel McDowell, Arthur Jibilian, Captain John Milodragovich, three rescued airmen, and about 3,000 to 4,000 Chetnik forces crossed the Visegrad-Belgrade railroad. From there they continued to the Subovor Mountains, near the city of Mačva, where a German garrison threatened from the nearby mountains.

The men pushed through the Trebava Mountains, picking up more airmen along the way as OSS radio signals continued to reach Jibilian's radio, reporting where the stranded airmen had gathered. At the city of Koceljvo, Lalich and the Chetniks built another airstrip in two days, measuring some 450 yards and suitable for a DC-3, which would be the next plane sent to them. That day, September 17, another twenty airmen were evacuated, as well as Dr. Jacques Mitrani, the American medical liaison, one Frenchman, and some Italian soldiers. Then the men crossed the Drina into eastern Bosnia and continued west, parallel to the Sava and to the Bosna, which divides eastern and western Bosnia. They moved gradually into the major town of Doboj, once a significant Partisan stronghold in northeastern Bosnia, and then to Boljanić, about fifty miles from Sarajevo.

Arriving around October 22, 1944, the men built another airstrip there, and on November 1 the three airmen were evacuated in DC-3 transport planes with Colonel McDowell and some of the other American officers, such as Rajacich and Colonel Milodragovich. At that point the OSS instructed Lalich to pick up sixteen half-starved and ill airmen in the vicinity of Višegrad, but these men in turn were being escorted by another American officer at the time to Okrgliče, another village near Sarajevo. The OSS at Bari instructed Lalich to move the airmen to Partisan territory for rescue, which Lalich refused to do. He insisted that he, his mission, and the sixteen men with him would return to Boljanić, their last functioning airstrip, where the OSS planes could get them. He wanted nothing to do with the Partisans. He got his way.

This bad faith toward the Partisans among the men of the Halyard mission (and of Colonel McDowell) underscores one of the more problematic aspects of trying to ascertain exactly how many Allied soldiers were rescued by Partisans and how many by Chetniks. One does not wish to discount the Partisans' efforts to help evacuate Allied soldiers. But exact numbers are difficult to determine for the following reasons: The writer David Martin, described earlier as a postwar activist in defense of Mihailović's reputation, made several critical points worth considering within the context of evaluating Partisan-versus-Chetnik rescues.[3] Martin wrote that in attempting to minimize the Chetnik contribution to the Allied cause, the postwar Yugoslav government put out the number of some 2,000 American airmen rescued by the Partisans as compared with the 500 or so American airmen rescued by General Mihailović. The claim, in circulation for many years, took on the status of gospel truth until a Yugoslav government document that surfaced on August 3, 1977, revealed a more toned-down claim of several hundred Allied airmen—the majority American—as having been rescued by the Partisans. The veteran Operation Halyard commander George Vuchinovich maintained in an interview that there weren't 2,800 American airmen sent to the region in the first place.

Furthermore, many of these rescues came at a time when the Partisans were receiving massive Allied aid and were theoretically in a better position than the Chetniks to take on such operations. There was also the ideological aspect. The Partisans who were not Communist tended to treat the rescued American airmen in a friendly manner, while the Communist leadership dominant in most Partisan units looked upon the Americans with "intense political hatred."[4] According to the testimonies of the rescued airmen, the Chetniks frequently went hungry to feed "their" airmen, while the Partisans in many cases showed no such concern—indeed numerous bitter messages were sent out by American officers attached to the Partisan forces complaining of the maltreatment of rescued airmen.[5]

Airmen continued to be recovered through the end of the war, and the impressions of the airmen with regard to the Partisan versus Chetnik treatment remained consistent. In May 1945, a group of fifteen American airmen was rescued by the Chetniks of Mihailović and of Djurisić, in Montenegro. By Allied order then in full force, the Chetniks had to turn the men over to the Partisans for evacuation to Italy. These airmen remained anonymous in a May 24, 1945, OSS memo, which summarized their experiences in a report. "Their accounts of their treatment by Chetniks and Partisans followed same general pattern," read the memo. "Their impressions of the former ranged from enthusiasm to mild skepticism. Of the latter [the Partisans] they had little to say that was complimentary."[6] As one airman, downed in Podgorica, Montenegro, summed up: "I don't hand either of them much, but I believe that Mihailović got a worse deal than he deserved."[7]

The Partisans also tried to suggest that the Chetniks often killed airmen or surrendered them to the Germans. A total of about 435 American and another 80 Allied personnel were rescued with Chetnik cooperation, extending through the late autumn of 1944, with most of the soldiers extremely malnourished and diseased, yet none had been abused or beaten. An officer on duty at the headquarters of the Fifteenth U.S. Air Force in Italy testified that there had been no known case in which Allied personnel had been given over to the Axis by the Chetniks, despite heavy Partisan propaganda to the contrary, nor any known cases of abuse or killings.

The Partisans also tried to take credit for the rescue of airmen who had actually been rescued by the Chetniks. By October 1944 Mihailović was no longer recognized by the State Department, and all of his messages to the United States were ignored. All recognition and supplies had been cut off. (And many of the American soldiers rescued in Serbia who were trying to get through to their families in the States could not do so. Those families were sent "Missing in Action" notices on their sons in error.) After September–October 1944, with the Red Army pushing into Serbia from the east and the heavily armed Partisan forces driving in from the west, it became increasingly difficult to take on major evacuations—and even minor evacuations became impossible as it became difficult to make contact with the base in Bari, Italy. Both before and after December 27, when the Halyard mission left Yugoslav territory for good, Chetnik forces that rescued American airmen had to guide them to the nearest Partisan units, which then claimed formal credit for the rescue. When the Germans moved their forces out of Yugoslavia after the fall of Belgrade, American airmen who had been taken prisoner and then fell into the hands of the Partisans were left behind, and no special effort was made to repatriate them.

• • •

Colonel Robert McDowell was a University of Michigan professor who taught modern Balkan history there. He was multilingual and had lived some twenty-five years in the Near East, and after 1942 worked in army intelligence. He arrived in August 1944 in Serbia with a small team on an independent SI mission to Mihailović, known as Ranger. He described himself as a liberal, "often called pink," but his observations gave no indication of preexisting sympathies for the nationalist-monarchists around him. Rather, his views were shaped by what he saw as deliberate distortions of information. As an intelligence officer in Cairo during the first half of 1944, he was involved in an Allied committee to evaluate the state of Axis lines of communication in the Balkans, working with all sources of information coming from the Balkans. The Communist communiqués, McDowell saw, describing operations against German communications proved so untrustworthy that he finally had to deem their information as worthless.

Once in Serbia and eastern Bosnia, McDowell reported that he had complete freedom of movement in the Chetnik areas, whereas in the Partisan-controlled territories he was carefully, if not constantly, observed and escorted. American radio was also broadcasting Partisan communiqués describing the Communist "liberation" of certain territories, such as northeast Bosnia and western Serbia, which in fact were openly royalist and pro-Chetnik. Over the course of his travels and observations around Chetnik and Partisan territories, McDowell concluded that the "rank and file of the movement" led by Tito sought to resist the Axis just as did the Mihailović Chetniks, but that resistance was strictly limited by the "priority imposed by the Communist leaders to civil war and the effort to destroy the influence of Mihailovich."[8] "Under the circumstances," concluded McDowell, "no group of Yugoslav resistance was able to make a substantial contribution [to the Allied cause] during 1944 and 1945."[9]

When McDowell arrived in August 1944, he was shown plans for a general Chetnik mobilization against the Axis. Mihailović was hoping to make one last attempt to persuade the Americans of his loyalty, and in early September a series of attacks around Lazarevac took place on German-Bulgarian garrisons and communication lines, resulting in 250 enemy prisoners and around 75 enemy deaths. By then Mihailović's fear of German reprisals was not nearly so pronounced as earlier, and his units began to attack and seize German arms and munitions depots, and disarming unresisting German and Bulgarian units around the area of the "Iron Gates" of the Danube (the border with Romania).

The residual fighting lasted through October and "made a very substantial contribution to the defeat of German forces, including joint operations with the Soviet forces, until Communist intrigue and attacks led to their dispersal," wrote McDowell.[10] The Chetnik offensive was, nonetheless, attributed by the BBC to the Partisans.[11] Sergeant Rajacich, who was, like George Musulin, born of Serbian parents, was liaised to the Ranger mission (following his work for Halyard) and had witnessed the early September Chetnik offensive against the Germans. "My findings were that there was absolutely no Partisan activity against the Germans in this entire area up to and during this period. The Nationalists, that is, the Yugoslav Army in the Fatherland, under Gen. D. Mihailovich, carried out the attacks on their own initiative."[12]

Tito was incensed on hearing of McDowell's relationship with Mihailović. Reports came from Partisan Serbian headquarters that Mihailović was claiming in circulars that McDowell was on a "mission" to him and that assistance could be anticipated from America, thus putting McDowell in the somewhat uncomfortable position, while rescues were ongoing, of having to explain that no such aid could be promised and that he was there only as an observer. Tito, nonetheless, then formally requested the withdrawal of the McDowell unit. Having made it all the way to the Boljanic airstrip in Bosnia on October 22, where he assisted with the last evacuations, McDowell was called back to Bari on November 1, 1944.

• • •

As will be discussed further in a later chapter, just prior to McDowell's departure from Serbia there emerged the strange case of a surrender offer by Hermann Neubacher, the German diplomatic plenipotentiary responsible for southeastern Europe, to Mihailović via McDowell. It was September 1944, and Mihailović would make some visits that autumn to see Rudolf Stärker and the representative of the Reich diplomat for southeastern Europe, Hermann Neubacher, with McDowell's permission, who himself attended.

Up until that time, Mihailović himself had had no private meetings with any German official, having sent representatives in his stead on the three or so occasions in 1941 when such contact was made. Germany was by that time desperate for some relief in one of its war theaters. On September 8, 1944, Bulgaria declared war on Germany, and Sofia was occupied by Soviet troops on the sixteenth of that month. With their eastern flank completely exposed, the Germans hastily began their evacuation of the Mediterranean islands and the Peloponnesus. German officials had made contact with McDowell for the purpose of the surrender of German forces, as the Germans were sending out such feelers on several fronts during the last months of the war.

For the Allies, these offers were considered meaningless unless the Germans agreed to unconditional surrender. McDowell questioned why Mihailović had been chosen by the Germans. "During the period covered by these meetings," McDowell later reported, "the Yugoslav Communist efforts to capture Mihailović were so constant and severe that it must have been evident to the Germans that the General was in no position to aid them or to accept aid from them."[13] For Neubacher, who had previously tried to bring the Chetniks more closely into the Axis sphere, the nationalist-monarchists were, to his mind, the more accessible contact. Furthermore, the Germans saw in McDowell's presence a direct line, in their view, to American intelligence. McDowell then transmitted the surrender proposals to General Harold S. Alexander, the British Supreme Allied Commander (at Allied Headquarters in Caserta, Italy). Over the course of a lunch one day several years later, in the spring of 1952, the former American ambassador to the Soviet Union, Joseph Davies, informed the renowned *Washington Post* columnist Drew Pearson that General Alexander had personally hindered the surrender offer. Nothing was ever heard of the matter again.

• • •

Back in the mountains of Bosnia, what was not known to Mihailović at that point in December 1944 was that his allies were now in every sense about to leave him altogether, and for good. Nick Lalich was in Okruglice, Bosnia, on December 11, 1944, with Arthur Jibilian and the last sixteen American airmen waiting evacuation, when the Halyard mission was formally recalled from Yugoslavia. After a celebration in honor of the Americans deep in the December snows where Mihailović and some two thousand of his men bade farewell to the Americans, the mission prepared to be escorted back to the makeshift airfield at Boljanic, to which they would be led, somewhat festively, by an Olympic skier named Šane who would lead them across the merciless Zivjezda Mountains in that region of Bosnia.

Before leaving, Lalich had asked George Vujnovich at the OSS base at Bari if he could bring Mihailović with him. The OSS approved the request once the State Department approved it, and Lalich excitedly asked Mihailović to come with his men to Allied territory. Mihailović refused. He told the young captain, "I was born on this soil, I will stay with my people on this soil, and I will be buried in this soil."[14] After Lalich, Jibilian, and the sixteen airmen took off in the direction of Boljanic in the early dawn hours, guided by the skier and forty Chetnik escorts, the two thousand Chetniks of Mihailović then present fired rifle salutes in their honor long into the morning.

10

The Unknown Soldier

How are we to be victorious? Our strength is small—and
heroism has its limits. In war guns are stronger than wisdom.
And wicked men are more skilled in cunning. Well then, how?
By faith? But death is more persistent than faith. And what do
ideals mean without the power to put them into practice? Just
self-deception, illusions. . . . They'll only die with a struggle—
each man, alone unknown.

—Dobrica Ćosić, *Far Away Is the Sun*

Draža Mihailović spent the winter of 1944–1945 on Mount Vučjak,
near the city of Prnjavor, in northwestern Bosnia, after the
Americans had left. Typhus was decimating his troops, and recriminations were tearing them apart. Mihailović and his forces had been joined
by Pavle Djurisić, commander of the Montenegrin Chetniks, and several
thousand of his troops. Knowing that Partisan forces in northern Bosnia
would begin to close in on them, Djurisić and Mihailović began to discuss, and then argue, over where their forces should head next. Djurisić
was for moving northwest, possibly as far as Slovenia, while Mihailović
wanted to return to Serbia. But in their search for a passage to safety, both
men were about to be betrayed—one of them by his own men.

Mihailović had no more energy to argue with Djurisić, so the
Montenegrin commander set off on his own, forging a bloody path hundreds of miles north and west as he and his troops were continuously
attacked by remnants of the Ustaše army, which, like the Partisans, were

concentrated in that northern Bosnia-Croatian border area. Djurisić attempted in vain to figure out a course around the Ustaše troops and ultimately decided to seek out the Montenegrin pro-Axis leader Sekula Drljević, whose influence with the Ustaše Djurisić thought might help him to negotiate passage through to Slovenia. Through Drljević, the Ustaše induced the Chetnik officers to surrender—among them the writer Dragiša Vasić—and then proceeded to disarm and slaughter them.

Meanwhile, Mihailović and his now several thousand Chetnik forces headed out in the direction of Serbia, having received information through one of Mihailović's commanders there via radio that the conditions in that country were favorable. Or so Mihailović was led to believe. Milovan Djilas, in his powerful memoirs *Wartime* and *Rise and Fall*, recounts how Nikola Kalabić, at one point one of Mihailović's most loyal commanders, had months earlier been lured to Belgrade by the Partisans, where he was arrested and recruited into their ranks. Kalabić, along with a group of agents from OZNA (Organ Zaštite Narodna Armije, Tito's secret security apparatus), discovered Mihailović's hiding place in Bosnia and drew him into a trap by getting their hands on one of Mihailović's radio operators, who gave away Mihailović's code. The operator then agreed to send spurious messages, which enticed Mihailović into Serbia. Milovan Djilas himself helped to compose the counterfeit messages describing the situation in Serbia as favorable to Mihailović's return.[1]

The winter march across the mountains alone sent hundreds of those troops to their graves. Apart from the brutal weather and the poor condition of many of Mihailović's typhus-ravaged men, their prospects were bleak as the Partisans controlled the bulk of the territory through which they were passing. Yet they fought their way through with bitterness and anger, pushing on, encouraged by the bogus messages coming from the OZNA agents. Just as Mihailović's troops reached the area in southeastern Bosnia around the Sutjeska, the river where the Partisans had fought a decisive battle against the Germans in May 1943, Partisan forces began to close in on the men. Yet, as if in one final burst of rage, the Chetniks wiped out one of the Partisan brigades. Still, they were caught in an impenetrable ring, as Djilas recounts. No prisoners were taken, and "some seven thousand" of the Chetniks, according to Djilas, were killed.[2] Four hundred escaped, among them Mihailović, only to be caught later and taken prisoner by the Partisans. The scale of the

killings shocked even the Partisans who committed them. "Tales of horror reached Montenegro along with tiny groups of crushed Chetniks,"
wrote Djilas in his memoir *Wartime.* "No one liked to speak of this
particular experience—not even those who made a show of their revolutionary spirit—as if it were only a horrible dream."[3]

• • •

On March 24, 1946, the Communist government in Belgrade announced
that it would put Mihailović on trial on charges of collaborating with the
enemy and other war crimes. David Martin, who in 1945 had authored
a book on the Tito-Mihailović rivalry, was with the Royal Canadian Air
Force in England at the time news of the impending trial was announced.
Certain of what the outcome of such a trial would be without, at the very
least, a coordinated international protest, Martin started to organize his
media contacts. These included Sol Levitas, the anti-Communist editor of the *New Leader,* a left-wing but antitotalitarian monthly; Eugene
Lyons, who was known for his criticism of Soviet socialism in his book
Assignment in Utopia; the columnist Dorothy Thompson; and the socialist leader Norman Thomas. The four quickly took to the idea. They then
brought on board Christopher Emmett, a wealthy, well-connected activist from a patrician family of Irish rebels and playwrights, who helped to
found the Committee to Win the War by Aiding the Allies (the William
Allen White Committee) and who was, in Martin's words, "one of the
very rare American liberals who had never closed their eyes to the tyranny
of the Soviet regime."[4]

The modest beginnings of the committee set up shop at Emmett's
apartment in Manhattan, where they started working sixteen hours a
day on average, seven days a week. George Creel, formerly head of the
World War I Committee on Public Information under Woodrow Wilson,
became chairman, and before too long something of a star-studded
cast began to assemble around the cause, including Clare Boothe Luce,
the congresswoman and ambassador who was married to *Time* magazine founder Henry Luce; Sumner Welles, the assistant secretary of state;
the actor John Wayne; the philosopher and reformer John Dewey; former presidential candidate Alfred Landon; Roger Baldwin, the head of
the American Civil Liberties Union;, Oswald Garrison Villard, editor

emeritus of the *Nation*; Lionel Trilling, the literary critic; Ray Brock of the *New York Times*; and the writer John Dos Passos.

Around the time that that group was taking shape, another organization emerged, begun by American airmen who had been downed over Yugoslavia: The National Committee of American Airmen to Aid General Mihailovich and the Serbian People.[5] When news of Mihailović's capture and trial was announced, several of these airmen wrote to their congressmen and to President Truman himself, asking them to intercede in the trial. Among them was Staff Sergeant Mike McKool of Dallas, of the Fifteenth Air Force in Italy, who bailed out with his crew over "Yugo" near the town of Gorni Milanovac on July 4, 1944. Walking five hundred miles for thirty-eight days with Mihailović's Chetniks, McKool and his crew were saved from German attack at one point while ten peasants from the area were taken hostage and shot to death in reprisal. McKool wrote to President Harry Truman: "I feel that I possibly owe my life to General Mihailovich and his Chetniks and I want to do everything I can to help him in his approaching trial. In this I am sure I am expressing the feelings of hundreds of other American airmen who were aided by the Chetniks."[6]

As McKool and other concerned airmen became aware of one another's existence, they agreed to meet on April 10 at the Stevens Hotel in Chicago and form their committee. By April 18 they had received seventy-five telegrams from rescued airmen in fifty-five cities, all offering to "testify anytime, anywhere" on behalf of Mihailović. Using the motto "He Saved Our Lives—We'll Save His!" the airmen collected limited funds and chartered a C-47, the same type of plane that had flown them out of Mihailović's handmade airfields, with the words "Mission to Mihailović" boldly displayed under the fuselage of the plane. The initial group left on April 28, stopping in Detroit, Cleveland, and Pittsburgh along the way, picking up a total of twenty-one American airmen by the time the plane landed in Washington. The aggregate experience of the men covered the time period from January 10 to December 27, 1944. In the nation's capital, they would make their cause known to the State Department, to Congress, and to the president.[7]

If the airmen's mission to Washington took off with a touch of fanfare, their touchdown at Washington National Airport on a Sunday afternoon was just as dramatic. Waiting for them were a hundred or so prominent Washingtonians, such as Senator Robert Taft and Alice Roosevelt Longworth, while a fleet of cabs and a police motorcade waited for them outside the terminal, soon to be decorated by the airmen with "Mission for Mihailovich" placards. By the time of their entry into Washington, the airmen's committee met and joined forces with the "Fair Trial" committee of David Martin, Christopher Emmett, and others. Ray Brock, a *New York Times* correspondent who had spent the first two years of the war in the Balkans and had tried, unsuccessfully, to obtain permission from the British to be a war correspondent with the Mihailović forces, was a powerful, new, press-savvy member on board.

The U.S. government and the press weren't the only places where the Mihailović cause was getting attention. Five British liaison officers, including Brigadier C. D. Armstrong, Colonel S. W. Bailey, Jasper Rootham, Eric Greenwood, and Kenneth Greenlees, submitted a joint deposition in defense of Mihailović through the British Foreign Office.[8] This deposition described Chetnik offensive actions against Axis forces between June 1943 and February 1944, such as their engaging Axis forces around the Pranjane area (near the main town of Čačak) in mid-July 1943 thus enabling urgently needed communications and equipment for the British mission; the attack and capture of the town of Visegrad from a "strong garrison" of German and Croatian Ustaše troops "on whom heavy casualties were inflicted"; and the escorting of British and American troops at Valjevo to the area of Dubrovnik, where they were covered for embarkation to Italy. Two of those officers, Jasper Rootham and Kenneth Greenlees, in a letter to the *Times of London* on April 3, 1946, asked, "Herman Goring is being given a public trial with counsel for his defense. In these circumstances is it too much to hope that General Mihailovitch will be afforded the same facilities?"[9] Closest to Mihailović was most likely Major Kenneth Greenlees, who spent eighteen months in Yugoslavia first as an aide to Bailey and then as an aide to Brigadier Armstrong. He was the one to whom Mihailović "spoke the most freely." In an article in the London *Tablet* of July 16, 1946, Greenlees wrote:

> It seems extraordinary that a man who threw in his lot with the British when they were at their lowest ebb and his own country had been overrun by the enemy should now be accused of collaborating with the same enemy at a time when,

beaten, they were preparing to withdraw from his country and the Allies were heading for a certain victory. To one who watched the building up of the Mihailović movement from the beginning, who served with Mihailović for eighteen months, who continued to follow his gallant struggle from afar to the bitter end, the apparent attitude of indifference on the moral issues involved is painful and shocking.[10]

Then a group of exiled Serbians in London who supported King Peter petitioned UN Secretary General Trygve Lie to set up an international commission of inquiry (none was formed). The petition was led by Milan Gavrilović, the exiled head of the Serbian Peasant Party, and Slobodan Jovanović, the former prime minister. (Jovanović had unsuccessfully sought to establish a commission of inquiry himself in London.) Prime Minister Churchill did publish a letter in the *Reynolds News* on May 19, 1946, saying that he had "no sympathy for the Communists and crypto-Communists in this country who are endeavoring to deny General Mihailovich a fair trial. He it was who took the lead in making revolution in Yugoslavia which played a part delaying the German attack on Russia by several weeks."[11]

Just prior to the two teams meeting up, the "Fair Trial" committee of David Martin wrote to the State Department with the signatures of the founding members asking that Mihailović be turned over to an inter-Allied tribunal or to urge the Yugoslav government to permit the American officers who had served with Mihailović and the American airmen rescued by him to testify on his behalf at his trial. The State Department involved itself immediately "and did so in a language that suggested a deeply troubled conscience."[12] The American Legation in Belgrade delivered a note April 2, 1946, stating:

> As the Yugoslav authorities are no doubt aware, United States Army personnel in an Allied liaison capacity were attached to General Mikhailovitch's headquarters during most of the period of his military activity. They must also be aware of the fact that many United States airmen were rescued and returned to Allied lines through the undaunted efforts of

General Mikhailovitch's forces. A number of these individuals and others in the United States who were closely associated with General Mikhailovitch possess first-hand evidence which cannot but have a bearing upon the charges of enemy collaboration which the Yugoslav authorities have indicated they will bring against General Mikhailovitch.[13]

To which the influential Republican and foreign policy spokesman Senator Arthur H. Vandenberg of Michigan, on the floor of the Congress on April 3, 1946, added:

> I think there is a very deep American interest in this matter because of the numerous American flyers whose lives were saved by General Mihailovich in the course of the war just ended. . . . I do realize that in the latter years of the war he became a highly controversial figure but I cannot close my eyes to the tremendously heroic contribution which he made to the Allied cause in the early years of war.[14]

Nonetheless, the reply from Belgrade was cool, rejecting the State Department's request. The American media response to the rejection was fierce. The *Washington Post* wrote,

> Both the British and American governments have a certain moral responsibility in seeing that "full justice" according to our own understanding of that word, is done. . . . The failure of Great Britain and the United States to insist upon open and impartial justice for General Mihailović would vastly increase existing bitterness and suspicion among Communists and non-Communists every where in the world, and would make all future statements, promises or pledges by either of these powers open to the deepest skepticism. This being so, the case of General Mihailovich contains a serious threat to world amity and peace. As such it may properly be brought before the Security Council of the United Nations.[15]

Yet despite such bold pronouncements—and despite all the mission-
ary zeal, the dramatic entrances, receptions, letters, interviews, congressional floor speeches, editorials, opinions, and personalities—the State
Department and several key senators suddenly seemed to pull back—
somewhat too much. A couple of airmen who secured meetings with
Senator Taft and Senator Robert M. LaFollette Jr., who had welcomed
the airmen at the airport twenty-four hours earlier, "reported a notice-
able cooling" in their attitudes. Instead of reaffirming his support for the
airmen's objectives, "Taft had backed down and was now talking about
the complexity of the international situation, the delicacy of the Trieste
problem [the demarcation of that city in July 1945 into an Allied military
zone and another zone controlled by Tito's Partisans following armed
skirmishes between the two sides], and how this made it questionable
that the United States could intercede strongly as the airmen requested,"
wrote Martin.[16] Then, both the State Department and President Truman
himself declined to meet the airmen. Ray Brock, the *New York Times*
reporter, had requested meetings with the president and the undersecretary of state Dean Acheson, then serving as acting secretary. Yet when
the Fair Trial committee called to confirm appointments on April 29, the
men were told that the president was too busy to see the airmen, and
Acheson's office asked that the airmen meet a desk officer in charge
of southern European affairs. "The reaction of the airmen was one of
stunned disbelief," wrote Martin. "It was impossible for them to believe
that President Truman, their commander-in-chief, did not have the time
to meet with them and receive their petition when he was holding garden
parties and engaging in other lesser activities."[17]

Acheson's failure to meet the airmen was just as upsetting, given the
strong exchanges that had taken place between the State Department
and Tito's government. The airmen imagined the worst possibilities: that
the State Department shied away from Tito's aggressiveness; that elements in the State Department itself wanted a lighter approach with
the Communists; or that the department was divided between political
camps, hence unable to take action. The airmen ended up meeting the
desk officer for Southeastern Europe, Walter Barbour—a second-rung,
completely uninterested, nondescript bureaucrat by all accounts—and
the airmen figured afterward they should not have bothered in the first
place. They reluctantly decided to stay another day in Washington and

on May 1 drafted a terse speech they intended to deliver at a press conference. The "Resolution Adopted by the National Committee of American
Airmen to Aid General Mihailovich and the Serbian People" angrily
described their rebuffs at the top levels of government and reiterated
their independent commitment to pursue a fair trial for Mihailović.

Several sympathetic congressmen who were given a copy of the resolution before the airmen intended to hold a press conference immediately
contacted the State Department, infuriated by the treatment of the airmen. "There in the middle of the Balkans," wrote one congressman from
Nebraska in a February 1945 report on Mihailović and the rescue of the
airmen, "within easy reach of the Mediterranean, stands a forgotten army
of veteran and loyal Allied soldiers who cry for an opportunity to 'shorten
the war' and to liberate their country from terrorists and invaders, and
their cry remains a voice in the wilderness."[18] Such sentiment inspired
Congress to enter the resolution into the *Congressional Record*, and several
hours later Acheson agreed to receive the airmen.

Impressed by their stories, Acheson announced on May 14 that the
United States had once again requested that the American officers who
had been attached to Mihailović (that is, Lieutenant Colonel Albert B.
Seitz, Captain George Musulin, Captain Walter R. Mansfield, Captain
Nick Lalich, and navy radioman Arthur Jibilian) and the airmen who
had been rescued by him be permitted to testify at his trial. (Acheson, for
his part, remained consistently cooperative and supportive for the dura-
tion of the committee's activities.) Tito's foreign minister, Stanoje Simić,
however, labeled such involvement as an "interference" in the internal
affairs of Yugoslavia, and no reply was sent.[19]

• • •

While David Martin and Ray Brock were in Washington, they met up
with Morris Ernst, who at that time was one of the leading trial lawyers in America. He was asked if he would go to Belgrade to defend
Mihailović, along the same lines as Arthur Garfield Hays, a legendary
New York lawyer who had been permitted by Adolf Hitler to participate
in the defense of the Bulgarian Communist leader George Dimitrov,
who had been accused of burning the Reichstag. Brock sent off a letter
in Serbian to Alexander Ranković, Tito's interior minister, asking the

Communists to accept the American counsel, a suggestion that was sum-marily rejected by Ranković. Martin and Brock then decided to set up a kind of "counter-trial" called the Commission of Inquiry in which the testimonies of the airmen would be given. To have the necessary weight, they pulled together a panel of jurists, foremost among whom was Hays. Hays took a lead defense role in several famous trials, including that of John T. Scopes, the Tennessee schoolteacher indicted on the charge of teaching evolution; Sacco and Vanzetti, the two Italians executed in Massachusetts in 1927 for a murder they denied committing right to the tragic end; and the Scottsboro Boys, eight young black men who had been sentenced to death in 1931 for the alleged rape of a white girl. As of 1943, Hays was head of the American Civil Liberties Union.

Hays, then in his mid-sixties, accepted the offer to head up the coun-ter-trial with great enthusiasm. The new commission was made up of Adolf Berle, who had recently served as assistant secretary of state for Latin America; Charles Poletti, the former governor of New York; and Theodore Kiendl, a Wall Street lawyer. The hearings would take place May 13, 1946, at the New York County Lawyers' Association and fea-tured the testimony of seven of the American officers and one enlisted soldier who had been attached to the forces of Tito; and eight American airmen who had been rescued by the Chetniks at various times and places in Yugoslavia. The testimony of the airmen was supplemented by more than 150 statements from other rescued airmen. (Colonel Seitz, in charge of the first military mission to Mihailović, was on active duty overseas during the hearings, and his wife read statements by him; Colonel Robert McDowell, head of the last U.S. mission to Mihailović, was also on active duty but submitted a prepared statement to the Commission of Inquiry.) Following the hearings, copies were delivered to Acheson and to the State Department, and two copies to the U.S. Embassy in Belgrade, with the understanding that one of these would be delivered to Dragic Joksimović, counsel for Mihailović.

As it turned out, Mihailović's state-appointed defense lawyer, Joksimović, took to the case with zeal—too much zeal in the minds of the Partisans, and was attacked in the Yugoslav press for not "helping the court," as Djilas writes in his memoir *Rise and Fall*.[20] On June 14 Joksimović, contacted by the Commission of Inquiry, asked that the air-men be flown to Belgrade to testify, but the judge ruled that such action would not be permitted. On two occasions he tried to introduce the transcript of the Commission of Inquiry into the court record and failed. Another lawyer, Nikola Djonović, urged Mihailović to defend himself as the leader of the other side in a civil war, and not to get involved with the issue of collaboration, saying that the side that loses in a civil war is charged with treason by the other side. But it would all fall on deaf ears.

Mihailović's trial began on July 10, 1946. The Tito government refused to turn him over to an international court or to accept any evidence in Mihailović's defense from nationals of other countries. When the trial began, the Fair Trial committee put together a summary of the American airmen who had been saved by the forces of Mihailović, based on the testimonies of the men before the Commission of Inquiry and an additional 150 other depositions by other rescued airmen. The summary stated, in part:

> Collaboration is a word with a very material meaning. Either the collaborators fight alongside the forces of occupation; or else they place themselves on their command; or else, for services rendered independently, they receive medical supplies, weapons, munitions, or other material; or else they fraternize with them. All of the more than 500 American airmen rescued by the forces of General Mihailovich would testify, if given the opportunity, that at no time during their stay with the Chetniks did they witness anything which suggested collaboration with the Germans; that on the contrary, they witnessed many acts of resistance directed against the German forces of occupation.[21]

The main arguments with which the airmen defended Mihailović were as follows:

- They, the airmen, were frequently rescued "under the very noses of the German searching parties."
- In many cases local Serbs were killed in reprisal shootings after the Germans had failed to find the American crew or because the Chetniks refused to reveal their hiding place.
- American airmen were escorted over long distances to the evacuation airfield at Pranjane while Chetniks "fought rearguard skirmishes with German parties."

- The airmen were often treated in illegal Chetnik hospitals, to which Chetnik doctors traveled forty or fifty miles in order to tend to wounded American airmen.
- The hospitality of pro-Chetnik peasants was overwhelming, giving what they had to eat to the Americans first and eating the leftovers later and letting them sleep in the main bedrooms while they slept in barns or pigsties.
- The airmen witnessed acts of sabotage against the Germans, or witnessed the capture and execution of the Germans "and quisling soldiers."

The American press, outside of any Communist organs, was editorially sympathetic to Mihailović, and not a single member of Congress took the floor to suggest that there might be something to the collaboration charges against Mihailović.

• • •

A bloodstained cradle was brought to the witness stand at the trial that oppressive Belgrade summer afternoon in July 1946. It was evidence, said the Partisan commander then testifying, of a December 1943 killing of a four-month-old baby during the massacre of seventy-two Partisan sympathizers at Vranjić, a Croatian city near Osijek, on the beautiful northwest coast of that country. An old peasant woman was then brought to the courtroom stands, and, speaking through an artificial larynx, showed the scars where her throat was slashed twice by Chetniks, she said, before she was left for dead. Following her testimony, two witnesses began to testify about two United States aviators murdered by the Chetniks in August 1944 when they parachuted from a plane in the Zlatibor district.

The audience in the courtroom, who had been vetted by the Tito government, was allowed to boo and hiss and shout "traitor" at Joksimović, the defense attorney, as such testimony was given. Despite the dramatic atmosphere, the Communists, though sure of their courtroom victory, still did not lack for embarrassing attempts at overkill. On the closing day of the trial, the court took testimony regarding the case of Sergeant David O'Connell of Chicago and three other airmen who parachuted into Serbia on July 6, 1944. One Milenko Jovanović, an "eyewitness," said that after the men had been picked up by the Chetniks, they were never seen again, giving the impression that they had been killed by Chetniks. As it turns out, O'Connell was not only alive and well in Chicago, but he was serving as secretary of the rescued airmen's committee.

It was all part of the Partisan evidence presented in Mihailović's show trial. His onetime trusted lieutenant, Radoslav Djurić, who had switched to the Partisans in 1944 was now testifying against his former commander. Mihailović, said Djurić, was not only ordering such civilian violence but was a collaborator who was endeavoring to form a Balkan anti-Communist bloc instead of fighting the Germans and the Italians. Djurić claimed that he had been ordered to establish contacts with General Damian Veltchev, the minister of war in Bulgaria; General Napoleon Zervas, leader of the rightist *Edes* guerrilla organization in Greece; and an anti-Communist group in Albania, with the object of forming an anti-Communist bloc against the Partisans, all at the expense of fighting against the Germans. After the war, Djurić said to the carefully screened jury, this bloc would become a Balkan federation under the royal Karadjordjević dynasty with a new independent state of Macedonia included in it.

Under the command of Mihailović, Djurić had originally been trusted to negotiate a working agreement between the Partisans and the Chetniks and to persuade both sides to stick to it. But when, on November 7, 1943, Mihailović had ordered a general mobilization for a drive against the Partisans, Djurić had wrestled with his conscience. "He [Mihailović] said the Partisans must be attacked even when fighting the occupier," said Djurić. "I gave the original order to the British mission in the hope that they would intervene, but they never did anything."[22]

The "witnesses" carried on pretty much in this manner, with Mihailović sitting calmly through it all with a serene acceptance of his fate. The trial was covered by London's *Daily Telegraph*, which was not allowed inside the courtroom but received translated summaries of the testimonies, and, presumably, details from Mihailović's sympathetic lawyer, Joksimović. Yet Mihailović barely countered the charges of collaboration, either out of resignation or in tacit complicity with the head of security, Josif Malović, who had urged him to do so as part of a deal to spare his life. Joksimović's defense of Mihailović was an honest defense, and that brave lawyer was sentenced to prison and to labor. He died while incarcerated.[23]

On June 10, 1946, Mihailović delivered his closing speech, which was said to have run for four hours. He said:

> I am a soldier who sought to organize resistance to the Axis for our own country and for the rising of all the Balkan peninsula. . . . I had against me a competitive organization, the Communist Party, which seeks its aims without compromise. I was faced with changes in my own government and accused of secret connections with every possible secret service, enemy and allied. . . . I believed I was on the right road and challenged any foreign journalist or Red Army mission to see everything. But fate was merciless when it threw me into this maelstrom. I strove for much, I worked for much, but the gales of this world took me away and my work.[24]

"His speech," reported the *Daily Telegraph* on June 12, 1946, "which lasted nearly until midnight was delivered with simple dignity. When he finished, the courtroom was silent."[25]

• • •

On July 14 Mihailović was sentenced to death; two days later the Fair Trial committee appealed to President Truman and Prime Minister Clement Attlee to try to save his life. The two were asked to do their utmost to save the life of a man who was "a faithful ally of the democracies and whose only crime was his opposition to a political regime that tolerates no opposition."[26] Nothing was done, and as the final act of the Fair Trial committee, the men put out a statement criticizing the British and American governments for not having intervened in a more forceful manner. While the committee had recognized the active efforts of the State Department prior to the trial, days after the beginning of the trial the Department seemed to hold back. No "energetic plea" on behalf of Mihailović's life by the State Department was entered once the verdict became known. There had been no public response from President Truman to the petitions sent to him on behalf of Mihailović. The *San Francisco Chronicle* of June 13, 1946, contained a somewhat cold editorial, which read in part: " [T]he State Department has done as much as it could to get American officers admitted as witnesses. After suffering two rebuffs, it will try no more, and while the refusals of the Yugoslav government may be deplored, they will have to be accepted."[27]

• • •

Mihailović was executed by firing squad on July 17, 1946, in Lisiciji Potok, a little over six hundred feet from the Serbian royal palace. A day after his execution, an editorial appeared in the *New York Times*. It read:

> The fingers of history, rustling through the pages of the Second World War, may provide an ironic postscript to the scene that took place at dawn yesterday somewhere in the vicinity of Belgrade when General Draza Mihailovic crumpled before the bullets of a Yugoslav firing squad. History may decide that it is not Tito—who was in safety while Mihailovic was fighting in the hills in those early days—but the executed Chetnik leader whose statue should stand in Red Square in Moscow. But Mihailović fell yesterday in Belgrade.

11

The Red Graveyard

Just come into my mind
My thoughts will scratch out your face
Just come into my sight
My eyes will start snarling at you
Just open your mouth
My silence will smash your jaws
Just remind me of you
My remembering will paw up the ground
underneath your feet
That is what it's come to between us

—Vasko Popa, "Give Me Back My Rags"

The airmen did not have time to parachute out of their planes when the first round of gunfire hit their passenger-carrying C-47 transport plane. The American pilot did not expect that there would be any danger in flying over this area of Europe, as this was friendly territory—presumably. But that day it was not the enemy, the Axis powers, shooting at the American plane, but an ally—Yugoslavia. What's more, the war was long over: it was August 19, 1946.

The aircraft, piloted by Captain William Claeys, flew over Bled, Slovenia, en route to Udine, Italy, when the Yugoslav Air Force sent a series of continuous signals to the American pilot to get him to land the plane. For whatever reason, the American pilot did not comply, and two Yugoslav fighters were sent to escort the plane to a landing when suddenly the American aircraft caught fire and crashed to the ground. In a State Department summary of the incident, Washington later concluded that the plane had been shot at by the Yugoslav planes, "instead of being given help, as it would in practically every other part of the world." Two members of the crew were able to bail out, and five other airmen were killed in the incident. The Yugoslav government remained cool, insisting that the U.S. government issue strict orders for no flights over Yugoslav territory without clearance from Belgrade, so that such accidents might be avoided.[1]

It was one of the first events in the slow and profound decline of relations between the United States and Tito. Earlier, on August 9, 1946, the same kind of nonmilitary transport plane had been forced down over Ljubljana. The United States maintained that the plane had inadvertently passed over Yugoslav territory, over a slight jut of Yugoslav land across the Vienna-Rome route, due to bad weather over the Alps. The plane descended to a lower altitude, where it was circling in an effort to stabilize its position, when it was then forced down by Yugoslav planes. Three Yugoslav planes surrounded the C-47, which, still unable to understand the signals being given to it, waggled its wings in reply. The U.S. consul in Zagreb was refused access to the passengers, who were then held incommunicado by the government. The crew remained in custody for twenty days, and the State Department directed its new ambassador, Robert Patterson, to withhold the presentation of his credentials until Tito gave written assurances expressing regret for the earlier loss of American lives; the United States asked the same of the new British ambassador, Charles Brinsley Peake. Later, Tito would accuse the United States of 1,070 airspace violations between February and August 1946.[2]

The United States, in response, mounted the "most exhaustive investigation by our military authorities in Europe," saying that "if any planes in addition to the few noted had flown over Yugoslavia they were not American."[3] When Tito was asked by U.S. ambassador Patterson whether the plane incident was really a demonstration of hostility toward America and its democratic ideals, Tito replied that the elections in his country were "the freest elections in Yugoslav history."[4] Patterson replied, "The majority would have voted against communism. Your personal popularity is something else."[5]

In view of these worsening relations, Secretary of State James F. Byrnes, appointed by President Harry Truman in July 1945, lambasted U.S. contributions to UNRA, the United Nations Relief Agency, through which the

United States had committed close to a half billion dollars in aid by summer 1946. Byrnes wrote to Undersecretary of State Dean Acheson, "I think you will realize the implications of an organization to which the United States contributes 73% continuing to supply a government guilty of such outrageous and unfriendly conduct as Yugoslavia."[6] The total value of UNRA aid scheduled for Yugoslavia up through the end of July 1946 amounted to over $429 million. In the end, the Yugoslav government offered $150,000 for the families of the perished soldiers. The United States then froze $46 million worth of gold held in U.S. banks by the Yugoslav government.[7]

Relations between the two countries had been getting worse for most of 1946, to the point where Tito formally accused American embassy officials of working with a group of Yugoslav "terrorists" to undermine him. The Yugoslav daily *Politika* then weighed in with a story alleging that members of the American Mission to Albania were aiding "Albanian terrorists" to slip into Yugoslavia and presumably also to subvert the country. Tito accused embassy staff of being part of a terrorist cell, having obtained weapons from the American embassy, led by one Eric Pridonoff, a former economic officer there, who later resigned.

The American personnel from the embassy had little freedom of movement, and then practically no freedom of movement at all after the high-profile case of an embassy guard, William Wedge, who on May 1, 1946, while under the influence of alcohol, drove an embassy jeep without authorization and ran into and killed a Partisan officer.[8] He was tried in a Belgrade court and sentenced to eight years' imprisonment and hard labor. The incident inspired Tito's chief of cabinet Vladimir Vlahov and the interior minister Alexander Ranković to write a twenty-two-page memorandum titled "Information on Unfriendly Work of American Military Representatives in Belgrade." The State Department complained about Tito's "neurotic communist control," and Patterson, not believing a word of the accusations, blandly replied that the matter of "terrorist cells" at the embassy would be investigated. He then wrote to Secretary of State Byrnes, who had earlier demanded that Yugoslav accounts be frozen until the incidents regarding the shot-down American planes had been investigated. "[I]n my opinion under present conditions Yugoslav government would not get a dime or a pair of shoes from my Government."[9]

Ambassador Patterson had also criticized Tito for acknowledging only the assistance from Russia and Stalin in his public speeches and never that from the United States and Truman. Tito responded that this was in direct proportion to the amount of aid given to Yugoslavia by Russia and the United States, upon which Patterson reminded him that America contributed close to three-fourths of the aid Yugoslavia received through UNRA. Tito, in turn, countered that that amount was due to him; that "the destruction of Yugoslavia was caused not only by Germans but also by local fighting and allied planes."[10]

The State Department then called for economic sanctions against the country, because, aside from the shooting down of the two planes, the country had maintained since the end of the war a huge army that "was threatening American interests."[11] In response to the sanctions—which included, as mentioned previously, the freezing of $46 million in gold that Yugoslavia had in American banks—the Tito regime closed down the U.S. Embassy's public information service, USIS, in September 1946. "This regime patently considers it vastly more important to keep people out of touch with Western democracies than to cultivate good relations with the US," commented the State Department.[12] Newspapers such as the *New York Times* and the *Baltimore Sun* were now considered "anti-Yugoslav propaganda."[13] The United States was infuriated by the ingratitude of the Yugoslav regime. "The general attitude of [Yugoslav] authorities," commented another State Department communiqué, "as reflected in these difficulties contrasts markedly with the material assistance to the Yugoslav people given by the US freely and without thought of political advantage during and since the cessation of hostilities."[14]

Meanwhile, the powder keg of Venezia Giulia was causing serious damage to Anglo-American and Yugoslav relations. In April 1945 the British Eighth Army opened its final Allied offense in northern Italy and drove up the eastern Po Valley. Field Marshal Sir Harold Alexander believed that unless Stalin exerted pressure on Tito, the latter would refuse to leave the area, and fighting would ensue. What resulted was a tense standoff between the two former allies, which nearly broke out into open conflict during a protracted series of discussions that spring (1945) over how to divide control of Trieste—the port city at the heart of Venezia Giulia, or the "Julian March," an area bordering Italy, Slovenia, and Croatia. Access to the largely undamaged railways to Austria, to the ports, and to other infrastructure was at stake, and Tito saw in those discussions only the encroaching political power of the Allies over Yugoslavia and Yugoslavia's territorial claims in Venezia Giulia, rather than a mere military occupation.

Field Marshal Alexander, for his part, was incredulous when Tito announced that he wanted to maintain control as far west as the Isonzo River, which runs along the border of modern-day northeastern Italy and Slovenia. In June 1945, a tense diplomatic solution was found in the establishment of the seventy-mile-long "Morgan Line," named after British general W. D. Morgan, through the Venezia Giulia and dividing the area between the British—"Zone A," in the western half—and Tito's forces—"Zone B," on the eastern side of the demarcation. The Americans, for their part, were put under the command of the British Eighth Army.

The settlement came just in time, as Tito's forces were carrying out a gruesome series of revenge killings in which suspected anti-Communists and "fascists"—real or imagined—were buried alive in the Foiba, deep natural pits that are a part of Istrian topography. The JNA, the "Yugoslav People's Army" (changed from the "People's Liberation Army of Yugoslavia" in March 1945), was now 650,000 men strong, and Tito thought nothing of sending his patrols to cross into Zone B and attack Allied forces in Zone A. The Anglo-American and the Yugoslav sides then began to argue under which civil law Trieste should be governed. The Allies made the case for a twenty-five-year-old civil law, while the Yugoslavs argued for a twenty-five-day-old law—one of Tito's own—that allowed him control over the Italian ports of the area.

Tito's forces arrested and deported around 3,000 Italian inhabitants and attacked the local population, justifying such actions with the argument that the local Slovene population, in turn, was being terrorized by the Italians. Tito's troops requisitioned or confiscated "everything in sight," according to an American report at the time.[15] The Italian population, meanwhile, began to starve as Yugoslav Partisan forces blocked port distribution of their 700-calorie-a-day Allied-sponsored rations while American and British soldiers were being abducted or taken hostage by Yugoslav troops. "We have been glad to fight for and with the Allies but the Allies could expect to find us equally vigorous opponents," read one OSS memo quoting a Partisan officer in Trieste.[16] Thirty Russian heavy tanks were in Trieste, and the Anglo-Americans, led by complaints from Field Marshal Alexander, accused the Yugoslavs of hindering Allied supply operations into Austria. The Yugoslav troops became openly hostile to the Americans and the British, and the incidents between them, when not openly violent, were bluntly vulgar. The Allies angered the Partisans with slurs on the conduct of female Partisan troops; the Partisans, in turn, commented on the "Trieste whores who are visible on all streets arm in arm with Allied troops."[17]

In contrast to this scene, the conduct of the retreating German armies from the Balkans in May and June 1945 must be briefly given its due. Leaving behind a "trail of heroism," in the words of Milovan Djilas, the German Twenty-first Corps had to withdraw from Greece across Albania and Montenegro, while the German Ninety-first Corps coming out of Kosovo came to its aid, pushing together into the valley of the Lim River. Several Chetnik groups retreated with the Twenty-first Corps. "On the long and only way from Greece to the Drina River the Germans were confronted by a devastated land, demolished bridges, enemy units, and the vengeance of those who were deceived," wrote Djilas.[18] The German soldiers were half-naked and near starving, climbing mountain passages and carving out trails to get to the north. "Allied planes spotted them easily and used them as leisurely target practice on bare mountain slopes, at river fjords."[19] Their fuel had run out. Motorized equipment lay strewn everywhere across the country. The German soldiers seized farm animals and shabby peasant clothing where they could. "No one begrudged them that, because they didn't molest civilians or burn dwellings," according to Djilas. "In the end they got through, leaving a memory of their martial manhood—albeit a fleeting and unrecorded memory."[20]

• • •

But for all the tension between the new Yugoslav regime of Tito and his old wartime Allies, the power of the Yugoslav Communist Party was firmly in place. Nor did the new Yugoslav Politburo make any attempt to couch its elitism in any proletarian sloganeering. As Tito once remarked, unlike the Communist parties of Italy and France, the CPY had no desire to become a "Party of the Masses." It was a party of military groups, a small minority ruling clique, as in Russia. Tito himself had no intention of being a man of the people and displayed an unabashed love of luxury, taking over castles and palaces throughout Slovenia, Croatia, and Serbia as personal residences. Even bourgeois real estate had its appeal. "Soon after the communists entered a small town or village," Djilas recounts,

"Tito took over the best building for himself."[21] He constructed a luxurious house on the island of Brioni entirely constructed by prisoners ("Everything great in history was created by slaves," he told a disapproving Djilas). Hunting lodges where European nobility were entertained and his own private railroad, the "Blue Train," were also part of the lifestyle, as were a series of four wives (two "official" and two "unofficial"), throughout his life. "Tito, with his natural liking for the good things in life", wrote British brigadier Fitzroy Maclean, who accompanied the Partisan ruler through the wine cellars of the White Palace, taken over from the Karadjordjevic royal family, "soon settled in his new surroundings as if he had lived in palaces all his life. His suits and uniforms were made by the best tailor in Belgrade; his shirts came from the most fashionable shirt-maker; he ate the best food and drank the best wine; the horses he rode were the finest in the country."[22]

Behind the scenes of this high life, a less glamorous reality had settled into the foundations of the new Yugoslav state. The regime maintained its power through its secret police, the army, and party sympathizers, and held a firm control over office holders and workers alike. "Many fellow travellers are obliged to go along to hold their jobs," wrote one State Department report.[23] "Since the government is everywhere in business and industry it is virtually impossible for someone who is dissatisfied to give up his job and find one somewhere else. It is difficult and even dangerous to offend the government. As is well known, the authorities keep a secret *karateristika* [personal file] on everyone."[24] The report went on to describe the organization of people's committees, street and house secretaries, commissars in the army, and "all the well known paraphernalia of Communist dictatorship" to keeping this power as widespread and entrenched as possible. Russian "observers" were thought to be working in local ministries of the government, with a high degree of control on the operations of the government.[25]

As one American commentator observed, Tito himself made no secret to the West as to how he viewed his own

> "democratic" status. In the early postwar years he was secretary-general of the party, Prime Minister and Commander-in-Chief of the armed forces. By the 1950s, he held not only these three vital posts—the title of Prime Minister being changed

to President of the Republic—but assumed three more: the presidency of the Socialist Alliance of the Working People, the chairmanship of the Federal Executive Council and of the National Defense Committee. ("He is the only leader in a Communist country who after Stalin's death, can claim '*L'Etat c'est Moi*.'")[26]

Despite all this defiance toward the Americans, however, Tito was no more reassured of his position with Stalin, even as early as postwar 1945. A week after the liberation of Yugoslavia on May 19, 1945, Tito expressed anger in a speech in Ljubljana against the "spheres of influence" meeting between Joseph Stalin and Winston Churchill in Moscow on October 9, 1944. The scene from that meeting is rather well known, when Churchill presented his "naughty document," as he later called it, to Stalin, suggesting the territorial percentages of East European countries and Greece that would be divided between British and Soviet control. Yugoslavia was split "50–50." With one blue-penciled tick by Stalin, the two informally agreed, after which Churchill suggested they take the document and "burn it" and Stalin insisted Churchill keep it.[27] On June 5 Stalin reacted hostilely against Tito's speech, threatening, through Edward Kardelj, the most powerful man in Yugoslavia after Tito and Alexander Ranković, to denounce Tito publicly. The timing was horrible for Tito, who had just then recklessly launched an ambitious "five-year plan" to jump-start the Yugoslav economy in May 1945. Whatever the massive aid given to Tito by the United States, Tito saw his dependency on the Soviet leader as far more important, and such dependency grew to be nearly absolute, in both the economic and the diplomatic spheres.

The ultimate break between Moscow and Belgrade had to do with Greece. Greece was being torn apart by the rebellion of Communist leader General Markos Vafiades. Stalin wanted the rebellion to succeed, and as quickly as possible. On Christmas Eve 1947, Belgrade radio announced the proclamation of a "free, democratic Government of Greece under Markos," which would need immediate recognition; all eyes suddenly turned to Tito.[28] Stalin had wanted to expand influence in Greece and Italy. "Stalin needed the greatest possible upheaval in Greece and Italy for the moment of his quickly-approaching showdown with the Western Powers over Germany," wrote the State Department in one analysis of the situation.[29] In the words of one Yugoslav Communist official speaking some years later, Stalin wanted "a conflict between Yugoslavia and the Western Powers over Greece, Trieste and Italy." In other words, if not General Markos in Greece, then the Italy of Communist leader Palmiro Togliatti, with Trieste as the bait.

The American and British ambassadors, meanwhile, feared Yugoslav recognition of the Greek Communist leader and sought out Tito privately, warning that recognition of Markos would have grave economic consequences, and military ones as well. The undersecretary of state Robert A. Lovett casually reminded Tito that an assault cargo ship carrying 1,000 U.S. marines was sailing, it just so happened, into the Mediterranean at that time. Tito began to back down from defying the United States, while Stalin began to exert more pressure to curb Tito's apparent disloyalty. A Yugoslav trade delegation returned empty-handed from Moscow, despite the fact that Stalin had agreed in July 1947 to supply Tito with the first $100 million for his five-year plan. In order to placate Stalin, Tito delivered on February 9, 1948, in Belgrade what came to be called the most violently anti-American speech of his life.[30] That accomplished, and with pressure then mounting from the Americans and the British over the question of Greece, Tito succumbed to Anglo-American pressure—and bolted. The Soviets' excommunication of Tito took place on June 28, 1948; the break lasted five years. In those intervening years, Tito's Yugoslavia would receive more economic aid from the United States than any other country in Europe.[31]

· · ·

If Stalin had sought, before the excommunication of Tito, to control the state security and secret police structure of Yugoslavia through the presence of so many "Russian observers," it was Tito's own home-grown security apparatus that was standing very well on its own and gaining international renown as the most effective police state apparatus in the world. The Organ Zaštite Narodna Armije, the famous OZNA, was founded on May 14, 1944, by the powerful interior minister Aleksandr Ranković (then still known by his nom de guerre Marko) as an autonomous military entity modeled on Lavrenty Beria's KGB in the Soviet Union, acting as a counterintelligence apparatus against foreign-agent networks. (In 1945 it became known as the Uprava Državne Bezbednosti, or UDBA, but was still commonly referred to as OZNA.) The OZNA became particularly notorious, from the late 1940s through to 1990, for, under peacetime conditions, hunting down Croatian dissidents living in mainly Western jurisdictions.[32]

The first victims were the "obvious" political opponents: the 1945 capture, of course, of Mihailović, and the man who betrayed him, Chetnik leader Nikola Kabalić. Other early victims included Dr. Ivan Protupilac, leader of a Catholic pro-monarchist political party, who was assassinated in Trieste on January 31, 1946. Then followed the imprisonment of Venko Markovski, a Macedonian Partisan turned opera composer and author, and the murders of the poet Ivan Goran Kovačić in 1946 and of the former Croatian Communist military officer turned dissident Zvonko Kučar in March 1949, among others.[33] In one of the more spectacular incidents, Dr. Andrija Hebrang, a former head of the Communist Party who had contacts with high-level Ustaše, was killed by OZNA. The great dissident Archbishop Stepinac, who was both anti-Nazi and anti-Communist (and who had been approved as archbishop by King Alexander Karadjordjević), was imprisoned in September 1946 after being captured by the security apparatus for accusing the Tito regime of killing over 250 Catholic priests and incarcerating another 170 since the onset of the Communist regime in the country. (To the Communists, Stepinac was a collaborator with the Ustaše, a strongly refuted claim, given the dissident priest's outspoken activism against deportation of the Jews in Yugoslavia and his criticism of the Ustaše and the Jasenovac camp in a public speech of May 24, 1942.)

In the 1970s the dissident writer Bruno Busić and Nikola Martović, known in Croatian émigré circles as the caretakers of Croat soldiers and civilians who were killed in the spring 1945 Bleiburg-Maribor Massacre, were both killed.[34] In 1980 Stepjan Dureković, a former high-ranking Communist and head of the state-owned INA, the largest oil refinery in Yugoslavia, was also killed. There were countless kidnappings and failed assassination attempts—the latter including the botched murder attempt of Ante Pavelić, who, according to disputed accounts, fled to Argentina, where he eventually died. At least one hundred OZNA/UDBA assassinations were carried out between 1946 and 1990 (there has never been any official count).[35] The majority of the assassinations targeted

Croat and Slovenian victims; twelve of the known victims were Serbs, and four were Albanian. Twenty such assassinations took place between 1960 and 1969, and from 1970 to 1979 another twenty-eight took place, all carried out in places ranging from Germany to Argentina to Australia to Africa. The success of the Titoist assassinations prompted a highly impressed Colonel Muammar Gadhafi to remark in an interview with *Der Spiegel*: "Tito sends his agents to the Federal Republic of Germany in order to liquidate Croatian opponents. But Tito's prestige does not suffer in Germany. Why should Tito be allowed those things and why am I not allowed to do the same? Moreover I have never given a personal order to have somebody killed in foreign countries."[36]

Nor did the presence of repulsive slave labor camps die out with the end of wartime Yugoslavia. Goli Otok, or "Bare Island," was the infamous concentration-camp arm of the OZNA. Goli Otok was a deserted island of gravel and rock just south of the Croatian town of Senj, on the northern Adriatic coastline of Croatia. With its conversion to a prison camp, the quiet island became a vicious scar across the face of the prized Adriatic Sea—a sea that was for the Yugoslavs like a "violent and beautiful sky rocking beneath our country, making it beautiful, divine and eternally cleansed," in the words of the Serbian writer Miloš Crnjanski.[37] The island, an ugly patch of barren isolation, with strong gales and brutal heat, became one of the most odious symbols of the regime: "the camp for Cominformists"—that is, of followers of Stalin, after the new name for the Comintern, which was dissolved by Stalin in May 1943 and revived in September 1947 under this new name. Its inmates, however, grew to include basically anyone who was considered by the new Yugoslav regime to be an enemy of the state. Founded secretly, without a Yugoslav legal basis, and with no outcry from the foreign media, Goli Otok became, despite its billing as a camp for Stalinist enemies, perhaps the most enduring symbol of the Soviet leader's great influence on Tito and his methods.

It began with "socially useful labor," and no one from the Yugoslav Politburo or the central committee of the Communist Party had a hand in its establishment. It was simply the invention of Tito and Ranković, the interior minister. At the time it made sense to the leadership, as Djilas writes.[38] Though a law limited terms there to two years, prisoners languished for decades. Those who were thought to be proponents of a pro-Soviet line, branching into "illegal" activities, disrupting the one-party state, had to be done away with. But how those arrested and their families were treated went beyond any kind of ideological justification. "Now we treat Stalin's followers the way he treated his enemies!" said Djilas to Ranković as they drove through Serbia one day in 1948. Ranković replied, outraged: "Please don't talk about it now!"[39]

Relatives were fired from their jobs, publicly humiliated, wives (often successfully) encouraged to divorce their husbands. "There is no question that the vast majority of Cominformists would never have been sent to Goli Otok had the proceedings been the least bit legal, reasonable, and undogmatic," wrote Djilas.[40] People were arrested for reading pamphlets or failure to "report" a conversation suspected of being Cominformist. Inmates on the island had to run the gauntlet when they arrived, that is, a double line of inmates who took turns hitting them. "If gouged eyes were a rarity, broken teeth and ribs were not."[41] Torture was routine and applied when anyone failed to be properly "reeducated"—the standard for which was anyone's guess. Visitation and contact with the outside world through letters or packages were forbidden or, at best, closely monitored, while hard labor of Sisyphean absurdity was enforced: the moving of large, brittle marble back and forth from nowhere to nowhere in merciless heat. State economy planners sought to establish export firms or other entrepreneurial ventures with this free labor. The only thing produced, however, was suffering and lunacy.

Tito, maniacal with the fear that once the war was over, his own internal party opposition would overthrow him and the state, became obsessed with arbitrary sentencing of anyone who displeased him. Like the delusional Red Queen from *Through the Looking Glass*, the cry of "Off to Jail with Him!" and "Off to the Camp!" echoed morbidly through those grim years like laughter in the dark. With little interest on the part of the Western press, and with mouthpiece support from such Western left-leaning papers such as *Vidali* in Trieste and *L'Humanité* in Paris, little international attention was focused on the realities of the camp. Goli Otok, still defended as an "anti-Stalinist" prison camp, continued on for years, through the sixties, even after the rapprochement with Nikita Khrushchev. Statistics on Goli Otok are hardly conclusive, but it is estimated that between 17,000 to 206,000 prisoners were killed there between 1945 and 1960. In the words of Djilas,

"Goli Otok was the darkest and most shameful fact in the history of Yugoslav Communism."[42]

• • •

Possibly it was Goli Otok. Or possibly it was the exceptionally depressing chapter of the Bleiburg-Maribor Massacre that was, beyond all else, the most grotesque expression of the Tito regime's power frenzy. On May 15, 1945—the German forces—estimated then at 130,000 in Yugoslavia, had finally recognized the Partisans as a legal Allied army and laid down their arms. Those who had "collaborated"—by Partisan definition—with the Axis, such as the Chetniks, the Ustaše, and the Domobrans (the Croatian or Slovenian "Home Guards"), also laid down their arms. These latter groups, trying to escape the Partisan takeover of Yugoslavia, got through to the British in Austria, who turned them over to the Partisans. Estimates place the number of civilians and soldiers killed from around 80,000 to 120,000, which also included Croatian and Slovenian civilian refugees trapped on the Austria-Slovenian frontier with them, in what became known as the Bleiburg-Maribor Massacre, named after the fields around the Austrian town of Bleiburg, in Carinthia, and in Maribor, just across the border in Slovenia, where the massacre took place.

It is not known how many German soldiers were killed on that retreat, though many were captured and put into makeshift labor camps. The disturbing dimension to this tragedy was the disputed role of the British Eighth Army in the turning over of the retreating soldiers and civilians to the Partisan forces, having declined the victims' surrender.[43] Since then, there have been about 540 mass graves found and registered in Slovenia, with victims totaling about 100,000; those at Lančovo, just outside the capital of Ljubljana, and Tezno, about seventy-five miles northeast of Ljubljana, had about 15,000 corpses found in each one.[44] "These killings were sheer frenzy," wrote Djilas of the massacres. "How many victims were there? I believe that no one knows exactly or will ever know."[45]

What one may also never really know is just how many deaths there were in wartime Yugoslavia, both as a result of Axis violence against the civilian and military populations and from the civil war itself. The number ranges everywhere from around 1,027,000 on the lower end, by Yugoslav political scientists, to 1.7 million or 1.8 million by Milovan

Djilas, quoted throughout these pages; and upward to 1.6 to 2 million estimated, on the higher end, by R. J. Rummel, a University of Hawaii professor noted for his works on twentieth-century "Democide" (and a frequent nominee for the Nobel Peace Prize).[46]

Whether on one or the other side of this scale, the amount of loss was enormous, comprising around 7 percent of the population of Yugoslavia (that is, of what was approximately 15.5 million people, based on the 1939 census for Yugoslavia). In 1945 some official numbers on the war crimes in Yugoslavia were published by Dr. Radomir Zivković, a Serbian member of the United Nations War Crimes Commission, detailing figures of the German and Italian toll on his countrymen. According to that commission, from the first day of Axis aggression to complete liberation in May 1945, 1,685,000 people had died: 25 percent on the battlefield, and the remainder from "war crimes." Three hundred and twenty thousand people were interned and used as slave laborers in Germany. More than 100,000 were interned in Italian concentration camps, 84,512 were taken for forced labor, 131,250 people were disabled, and 41,394 hostages were counted, while 278,122 underwent internment, mock trials, or enforced labor.[47] (Zivković later noted to the United Nations certain gaps: that there were, for instance, no investigating teams operating in Italy, and "Yugoslav traitors" who fled before the liberation were later believed to be in either Austria or Italy.)[48]

In 1954, the U.S. Census Bureau published a report stating that the number of military and civilian deaths for the whole of Yugoslavia was approximately 1,067,000 (calling the figures of Zivković's 1.7 million "overstated," as such numbers were released so soon after the war). Another study, by Vladimir Zerjavić, a Croatian economist, put the figure at a more conservative 1,027,000. Using this "conservative" estimate as a guidepost, Zerjavić's breakdown included military losses of 237,000 for the Yugoslav Partisans; 209,000 Ustaše deaths; an unknown number of Chetnik deaths; and allover civilian deaths of 581,000. Separately, in his estimates, Jewish Holocaust victims amounted to around 67,000. Of the constituent republics, Bosnia was reported to have the most losses at 328,000, followed by Serbia at 322,000, which included 25,000 from typhus alone.[49] However, what makes the Serbia statistic—as well as the allover number for wartime Yugoslavia—so difficult is that the number of Serbian deaths from the Ustaše campaigns has ranged anywhere from

250,000 to 700,000. (Assuming the higher range of Serbian deaths from that extermination campaign, the total Yugoslavia number reverts more closely to Rummel's 1.7 to 2 million mark.) In Croatia proper, the number was 295,000. (As the NDH, or "Independent State of Croatia" which officially incorporated Bosnia-Herzegovina, that number would be over the 600,000 mark.)

Slovenia and Montenegro suffered on average around 30,000 losses, and Macedonia, about 17,000. As described earlier, the statistics on the Jasenovac camp vary wildly, with estimates ranging from 56,000 to 92,000 on the low end by the United States Holocaust Memorial Museum (USHMM) to 600,000 on the high end, according to Yad Vashem, the Holocaust history museum organization in Israel.[50] German prisoners of war and the number of German *volksdeutsche* killed in Yugoslavia are estimated at 80,000 (the breakdown of how many from this number were committed by Partisan or Chetnik forces here is not clear, though it is assumed the Partisans killed most of the Germans); Italian wartime victims were just over 5,000.[51] However, those Italians who, after September 1943, did not join the Partisans, the Germans, the Ustaše, or the Chetniks and ended up lost in the Balkans, numbered an estimated 20,000, and their statistics were never officially known.

As for the military deaths and civilian crimes of the two main antagonists in the civil war, Rummel estimates the number of those killed by the Partisans to be upward of around 150,000 through July 1944. He maintains that from that month, when Tito's Partisans had been essentially acknowledged by the Allied powers as the political leadership of the country, until the close of the war, the number of those killed by the Partisans was 500,000 (again, keeping in mind that Rummel's estimates figure on the higher end of the scale). As for the Chetniks, Rummel maintains that they killed approximately 100,000 in total (military and civilian) for the whole of the war.[52]

• • •

To the rather unsavory end, King Peter still believed that the British would come around to defending him and the Karadjordjević dynasty. He traveled between Cairo, where he had moved from England in order to be closer to events in Yugoslavia, and London, hoping to warn the British of the strengthening Titoist relationship with the Soviets. Increasingly, he saw that his efforts would hardly make a difference, and he began to see himself as the next victim of the machinations of the British government and the Yugoslav Partisan regime.

To begin with, the king started to lose all trust in his government, a chain of events triggered by the revelations of Bernard Yarrow, who was, as mentioned earlier, a Russian émigré who became a lawyer with Sullivan and Cromwell and later an OSS intelligence specialist on Yugoslavia.[53] He met Ivan Šubašić, the former *ban*, or governor, of Croatia, when the latter had been living in exile in the United States since 1941, and who would become the centerpiece of an OSS effort with the British to establish a constitutional monarchy after the war, one that, at first, kept King Peter at its head.

Šubašić promoted himself as a well-connected insider who could penetrate Yugoslavia and obtain information not only on German battle formations but also on the civil war factions in the country. Through Šubašić the Shepherd Project was launched in 1943, earning the former politician the OSS code name "Shepherd." Because of the tangled web of reports about Partisan versus Chetnik effectiveness coming from the various mission officers, however, the Shepherd plan began to broaden to include the rather startling (or naive) idea that the king be reconstituted in the country, with Tito as part of that constitutional monarchy arrangement. Throughout the summer and fall of 1944, Šubašić traveled between Churchill, Stalin, Tito, and Yarrow, putting together what became, in November 1944, the "Tito-Šubašić Agreement," in which Šubašić would become prime minister, a regency government would act on behalf of the king, and Tito agreed to an understanding that the status of the monarchy would be decided "at a future date."[54] As described in earlier chapters, Churchill had then urged King Peter, who rejected the idea of Tito in his government, to accept this arrangement anyway, advising him that it was not safe for him, the king, to return to Yugoslavia. The reestablishment of constitutional monarchy, of course, never materialized, and as we have seen, by the end of the war, Tito had consolidated his power and Communist control of the country.

King Peter was pressured by the British to appoint a regency that was entirely pro-Tito, and only a few months later, on March 7, 1945, a provisional government of the Socijalistička federavtina republika jugoslavija, or SFRY (internationally rendered as the Democratic Federal Republic of Yugoslavia), under the premiership of Tito, was inaugurated, although the Tito-Šubašić Agreement, with its outward acceptance of the king, was still officially the basis for the governmental structure of Yugoslavia.

A disgusted King Peter wrote to Churchill in early May 1945,

> I wish to quote only a few examples of an open non observance of the agreement Tito-Šubašić which was endorsed by the Big Three, as well as the principles laid down in the Yalta decisions. So far that has been no provisional parliament formed in Yugoslavia. The AVNOJ carries on. None of the democratic rights have been re established. There still exists in Yugoslavia only the Press voicing Marshal Tito's opinion. Only one single political movement is admitted. There are only Tito's political manifestations. In communal elections, as much as they take place, there are only candidates of Marshal Tito's National Liberation Movement to be elected. The apprehensions are justified that the free popular will would not come to expression in the election for a Constituent Assembly after the liberation unless there is a radical change in the practice of Government which practice is far from being in conformity to the obligations undertaken by the leaders of the United Government to me and to the Great Allied Nations.[55]

But Churchill was unmoved. His reply, dated May 8 and intercepted and summarized by the OSS, consisted of a very short letter, which simply sidestepped all the points brought up in the king's letter, stating "that there was much happening in Yugoslavia that he [Churchill] regrets but was unable to prevent and that is the sum and substance of his reply."[56]

In one final attempt at exercising authority in his country, King Peter took to the airwaves in August 1945 in a proclamation "to the People of Yugoslavia" in which he made no attempt to hide his anger: "Hitherto I have preserved a strict silence on the present state of affairs within my country in order to adhere to my part of the agreement. . . . But in my country there exists on a full scale the dictatorship of the Tito regime.

Every trace of law has been wiped out from the State organization, thus taking away entirely the free will of the people. There are preparations for a plebiscite by forceful means, and under terror of this special police organization OZNA which replaced the Gestapo. . . . Only one voice is heard, that of Marshal Tito and his totalitarian movement."[57] Of his regents, he announced, albeit somewhat naively: "I hereby proclaim that they can no longer represent me or work in my name. I have therefore decided to withdraw the authority which I gave to them."[58]

Such authority of his own was not to be. Finally, on November 29, 1945, the front-page headline of the *New York Times* read: "Yugoslavs Oust King Peter—Monarch Charges Fraud, Tyranny—Official Britain Silent." The defeated king, in his final radio address, stated simply: "A tyranny unworthy of the great victory of the Allies now reigns in Yugoslavia. A totalitarian regime odious to the moral loftiness and the Christian traditions of the Yugoslav people is introduced. My conscience is shocked when I look at the sufferings of my people, who are subject to merciless violence without freedom or justice."[59] He closed his comments with the dignity the young monarch had displayed throughout the course of the war and in honor of the men who served him:

> My dynasty began its historical life in the struggle for national liberation. The peasant's home out of which the Karadjordje dynasty rose to lead the insurrection against the Ottoman Empire still stands. . . . I am fully conscious of my duties toward my country and despite all steps taken against me by the present regime, shall continue to follow their clear dictates of my conscience in order to liberate Yugoslavia from tyranny—no matter whence it comes.[60]

It wasn't just the Serbian-Royalist side that actively protested the Tito regime. Vladimir Maček, the leader of the Croatian Peasant Party, publicly accused Marshal Tito of seeking to establish a complete Communist dictatorship, predicting that the small farmers of Croatia would never accept it. (Maček, then sixty-six years old, had been interned first in Jasenovac, where he was guarded by one hundred men, then under house arrest at his home in Zagreb. In early May 1945 he had fled with his family from Zagreb to Salzburg.)

"I see things this way," he said to C. L. Sulzberger of the *New York Times* in July 1945. "Tito's government are trying to introduce a complete Communist dictatorship. One thing is certain—it is just contrary to democracy."[61] Calling himself a loyal subject of King Peter's, Maček's ambition, once in Paris, was to go to London to organize a political opposition with Juraj Krnjević, the general secretary of the Croatian Peasant Party. "I saw how the Partisans were lowering an iron curtain over Yugoslavia so that nobody could know what went on behind it."[62] Even the cunning Ivan Šubašić himself would eventually fall victim to that power. After seven months of "coalition," the new prime minister resigned, accusing Tito of forming a dictatorship.

Not that it seemed to matter much to governments in America or Western Europe what was going on behind that curtain. The total gifts and loans received by Yugoslavia from the West from 1949 until around 1955 were estimated at $1.4 billion. Measured against Yugoslavia's productivity and per capita income, American assistance alone to Yugoslavia "was an intervention in the national economy more massive than in the economy of any other nation."[63]

• • •

Of course, the thicket of intrigues that conspired to bring down King Peter at the war's end might have been best avoided had, early on, Churchill simply uttered to the king the one statement that summarized the future of the monarchy in the eyes of the king's allies. The statement came at the end of a conversation they had at the end of one of their last meetings in late 1944.[64] Churchill had begun by saying to the young monarch, "You know I do not trust Tito. . . . He is nothing but a Communist thug but he is in power and we must reckon with that fact. President Roosevelt, Stalin, and I have agreed that there will be a plebiscite by which the people of Yugoslavia will decide on the question of the Monarchy and your return, therefore will have to be postponed until the plebiscite takes place."

King Peter held firm. "What chance do I have in a plebiscite when Tito is in Yugoslavia? It will be nothing but a farce and I will have no chance whatsoever," he replied.

"I shall see to it there will be impartial umpires supervising the plebiscite," Churchill assured him, "in which the British, Americans and
Russians will act as the umpires."

"I have followed your advice, Mr. Prime Minister, since I escaped from
Yugoslavia, and look where I am today," said King Peter.

To which Churchill coolly answered: "Would you have been better off
if you had followed Mr. Mihailovic?"[65]

12

The Politics of Surrender

Now home returning, wild with song,
They come, the colors flying free.
But as within the door they throng,
Why does the army suddenly
Hush the fierce din, and silence keep?—
Why, little brother is asleep.

—JOVAN JOVANOVIC ZMAJ,
"WHY THE ARMY BECAME QUIET"

On the afternoon of January 31, 1952, Drew Pearson, author of the "Merry Go Round" column in the the *Washington Post*, a popular muckraking feature on prominent figures in public life, met with Joseph Edward Davies, the former U.S. ambassador to the Soviet Union, at the latter's "Russian castle," as Pearson called it. That residence was Hillwood, the Washington, D.C., Georgian-Colonial estate of Davies's heiress wife and avid Russian art collector, Marjorie Merriweather Post. The Illinois-born Pearson was one of the most prominent and controversial newsmen of his day; his acerbic political commentaries managed to irritate everyone from Franklin Roosevelt to Harry Truman to Joseph McCarthy.[1] Yet Davies, a millionaire lawyer from Wisconsin who, after his tour as ambassador, had become intellectually obsessed with the question of the "stymied peace" between Russia and the United States, admired Pearson's foreign policy analyses. Davies agreed, among other things, with the journalist's view that British prime minister Winston

252

Churchill "had disrupted the postwar peace."[2] Still, Pearson had been expecting a conversation of a more personal nature that afternoon of their meeting. Davies was emotionally distraught over the likelihood of a breakup with the thrice-divorced Marjorie, and he was en route solo to India to think things through. As it would turn out, the ambassador's reflective mood that day revealed far more than Pearson would ever have imagined.

As recounted in Pearson's *Diaries*, published in 1974, Davies casually told Pearson an extraordinary anecdote about an autumn 1944 German offer of wartime surrender in Yugoslavia and, as Davies explained it, the successful British attempt to block it. The ambassador was already controversial in his own right for being too enamored of the Soviet "experiment" and too uncritically pro-Soviet in his writings.[3] Pearson himself was later criticized by Joseph McCarthy for being soft on Communism. And yet the *Diaries'* account of Davies's anecdote evoked nothing of the ambassador's image as a wild card in matters concerning foreign affairs. Rather, it revealed a sense of detachment on the part of the ambassador that rendered the mysterious episode he described more believable. Nor was Pearson, the receiving end of Davies's confidences, some easily swayed dupe, especially on matters regarding Yugoslavia. He had personal knowledge of the land he frequently wrote about, having spent the last two years of the war directing relief work in Yugoslavia (a town in southern Serbia, Pearsonovatz, was named after him). His columns were critical of Tito, whom he called "Stalin's puppet-in-disguise" and "Dictator Tito."

In describing his meeting with Davies, Pearson began by recounting the well-known story of Roosevelt's October 1944 refusal to make a deal with Churchill for "spheres of influence" in Eastern Europe in the postwar era. It was soon thereafter that Churchill and Anthony Eden, the British foreign secretary, flew to Moscow to work out their famous "unofficial" deal for distinct areas of respective dominance in southeastern Europe: Greece and the Mediterranean coast of Yugoslavia would go to the British; to Stalin, the majority control of Bulgaria, Romania, and the rest of Yugoslavia; Hungary and Austria would be left up in the air. "Shortly thereafter," Pearson wrote, "Joe [Ambassador Davies] said, the twenty-nine German divisions fighting in Yugoslavia had offered to surrender."[4] As alluded to at the end of chapter 9, a rather unusual series of events seemed poised to drastically alter the fate of Mihailović and the Allies in Yugoslavia. Pearson continued:

> The surrender offer was made through [Draža] Mihailović and was relayed to Allied Headquarters in Caeserta [in southwestern Italy, then the headquarters of the Supreme Commander, Allied Forces], where General Sir Harold Alexander stymied it. Alexander wanted the British army to fight up through the Italian peninsula and get into Austria ahead of the Russians; therefore the last thing he wanted was the surrender of twenty-nine German divisions in Yugoslavia. Later Mihailović was captured by the Tito forces and flown to Moscow where he told the Kremlin about the surrender offer [a claim nowhere substantiated by mainstream scholarship]. After that the Russians were so sore and so savage that at times it was nip and tuck whether the Allies would break up. Stalin began a series of brutal notes to Roosevelt which ended only a few days before his death. [Roosevelt died on April 22, 1945.] Finally Roosevelt wrote a letter to Stalin in his own handwriting shortly before he died, which Joe [Ambassador Davies] thought put the situation back on even keel. Joe is optimistic that if Roosevelt had lived it could have continued on an even keel and the postwar peace of the world might have been saved. The fighting in Yugoslavia against the twenty-nine [German] divisions which did not surrender cost the Russians 200,000 men and delayed the final VE day by three or four months.[5]

The ambassador, at least, seemed to believe such an incredible anecdote. As Pearson recounts, Ambassador Davies later told President Truman over a game of poker at Hillwood, located in northwest Washington, D.C., along Rock Creek Park, a nearly three-thousand-acre natural area that bisects the capital city, that "Churchill has only one ambition: to preserve the British Empire and to drive a wedge between the United States and Russia."[6] It was a sentiment typical of many

American officers and diplomats at the time, pro-Soviet or not, and one that revealed the profound, though not then public, wartime mistrust between the British and the Americans with regard to Yugoslavia. But how, if such a story were true, had Mihailović, who by that point had been more or less discarded by the Allies, found himself at the center of such a significant moment in the war? Why had General Alexander so rashly rejected the offer? Would his reaction have been the same had the purported offer gone to the archrival of Mihailović and Allied favorite, Tito? And what of the unsubstantiated claim that Mihailović was sent to Moscow?

Among Davies's papers, two unpublished diary entries of his own from August 1944 relate that the onetime Yugoslav ambassador to Washington, D.C., a very strong Royalist and Mihailović supporter, had told him the same: "Constantine Fotich, former Ambassador of Yugoslavia to the United States, tells me of a development in connection with a German proffer of surrender during this period that was as extraordinary as it was startling."[7] Davies adds:

> He said that a [Lieutentant] Colonel McDowell, an American G-2 officer, assigned to the US Air Rescue Mission in Yugoslavia was attached to Mikhailovitch's headquarters from August to November 1944. His mission was to facilitate the rescue of American flyers who had been "downed" in Serbia. At that time General Newbacher [Neubacher]—the German High Command of German divisions retreating from Greece—sent an emissary, a Colonel Staerker, representing the German Foreign Office, with a proposal for surrender to the Allies of hard-pressed German divisions in Yugoslavia. Mikhailovitch, alleging that he was not in authority, turned him over to Colonel McDowell who received Staerker and a formal offer of capitulation. McDowell transmitted the proposals to General Alexander–the British Supreme Allied Commander [at Allied Headquarters in Caserta, Italy].
>
> . . . Fotich said that the Russians learned this months later from Mikhailovitch. Mikhailovitch was taken prisoner by the Soviets on the 15th of March [1945]. It was not publicly announced by the Russians until the 24th. . . . Their military

and political intelligence were undoubtedly greatly interested in getting this information, disclosing failure by their allies to accept the surrender of these German divisions. It would breed suspicion and Russian distrust [were the other Allies to accept that surrender] . . . and look to them [the Russians] as a treachery by an ally.[8]

Robert H. McDowell, it will be remembered, was a former University of Michigan professor and army intelligence officer assigned to an independent Special Intelligence (SI) mission to Mihailović. McDowell had arrived at a particularly dramatic time. The Red Army was nearing the Yugoslav-Romanian border, reaching it on September 6, 1944, and entering Yugoslavia on the twenty-second of that month. While Chetnik units were present to make contact with the Soviet forces, the Partisans, however, then commanding about 600,000 men, were on the verge of expelling practically all Chetniks from Serbia, who numbered around 20,000. Mihailović insisted to the American rescue officers present with him in Serbia that he could rally several hundred thousand Serbs together were he to be properly supplied. No arms or any other Allied aid had reached him for almost a year.

In a series of memos regarding the Neubacher surrender offer, written between September and October 1944 by the OSS, there was no mention of any "interference"—from British generals or otherwise. On the morning of October 5, 1944, one such cable came into Washington addressed to William Donovan from the OSS offices in Caserta. "We have nothing to report," wrote two unnamed agents.[9] "Neubacher wants a complete surrender" [of German forces cut off in Yugoslavia]. The cable continued:

We have nothing new on Neubacher's envoy [Stärker] to McDowell. However, as a matter of information in regard to AFHQ's [American Forces Headquarters] policy re: surrendering in Yugoslavia and other Balkan areas, the following is of interest: "No Allied officer will be introduced to negotiate. In case of Yugoslavia, SACMED [Supreme Allied Command Mediterranean] policy is pending further conversation *to permit Tito to accept all surrenders within territorial limits of Yugoslavia.* As for other areas such as Albania, Greece etc, in case of approaches of German Commanders as outlined above, the officer approached will not negotiate but will advise German Commander to send a recognized emissary to AFHQ prepared to accept upon arrival here the terms as presented in each case.[10]

The Soviets, for their part, presumably learned all this during Mihailović's alleged visit in March 1945—a visit unsubstantiated, as previously stated, by most mainstream scholarship on the Chetnik leader—but which Davies and, according to Davies, Fotić, the Yugoslav government-in-exile ambassador to Washington and Mihailović-defender, claim was in fact a Tito-mandated compulsory trip to the Soviet capital.[11] Mihailović, a fervent monarchist and anti-Communist, was himself of little interest to Moscow, and whatever Tito ultimately did with him was not their concern. But Moscow was furious with the United States and Britain for conspiring via this botched German surrender offer in Yugoslavia to not only prolong the war with Russian blood but also to prevent the extension of Soviet influence in the Balkans. By the time of this surrender offer and thereafter—between the autumn of 1944 and early 1945—the Soviet Army was fighting its way into Germany, in accordance with Allied war plans. What the Soviets were mainly seeking was the confirmation of their worst suspicions: the attempt by the Americans, through McDowell, to aid the British in their Balkan political offensive at the expense of the Red Army.

• • •

The character at the center of this strange offer of surrender, which so clearly highlighted the desperate state of affairs in Allied policy with regard to Yugoslavia, was the German diplomat Hermann Neubacher. Who was Neubacher? As Nazi officials go, he was something of a "good German." This Viennese special envoy to the Balkans was the top Reich diplomat in the Balkans, one who, working as an economist prior to the war, had a rather nostalgic desire to re-create a Habsburg economic zone in Central and Eastern Europe.[12] That Neubacher's imperial preferences were of a nature more sympathetic to the romantic grandeur of old Austria than to the violence of Adolf Hitler's New World Order may be seen in the diplomat's strong reluctance to participate in the harsher responsibilities demanded by his post in Belgrade. In October 1943, August Meissner, the Gestapo chief in Serbia, ordered the execution of 850 Serbian political prisoners and the destruction of three villages to avenge the murder of 17 Serbian policemen of the Nedić puppet regime. Neubacher's intervention with Generals Hans Felber and Maximilian von Weichs secured cancellation of Meissner's order. Neubacher was not, of course, motivated by altruism so much as by sheer pragmatism: such executions, he maintained, would not only prove pointless, but from a political standpoint they would render his mission to Serbia impossible.

Later that autumn, six more Serbian policemen were killed by guerrillas, and Meissner called for the execution of three hundred hostages. Once again Neubacher secured an order from General Felber to halt the reprisal, and after this second defeat Meissner did not order any more shootings of hostages. Neubacher also tried to stop the persecution of Orthodox Serbs in neighboring Croatia but failed, as he had no official jurisdiction in Zagreb, and the Reich minister to the Ante Pavelić government, Siegfried Kasche, was a supporter of the Ustaše—described by Neubacher as "a terrorist club—the worst the war produced."[13]

In May 1944 three Reuters correspondents who had been assigned to Tito's headquarters were taken prisoner with the intent that they would later be executed on charges of espionage. Neubacher actively objected to the proposed execution, defending them as journalists, and they were set free. "Neubacher was a mitigating influence in the treatment of enemy prisoners as well as in the question of reprisals," wrote one biographer of Neubacher.[14] The German diplomat also initiated a campaign against corruption among the occupation authorities in Serbia, focusing on the "notoriously corrupt" Franz Neuhausen, the Reich's Plenipotentiary General for National Economy and a close friend of Hermann Göring. Neubacher appealed directly to Hitler for Neuhausen's recall in late August 1943, and with the support of Heinrich Himmler and Ulrich von Ribbentrop, the diplomat was able to secure Neuhausen's arrest and confinement to prison. Although Göring later secured Neuhausen's release, he was never restored to his old position in Serbia.

It just happened to be Neubacher's idea to improve relations with the Chetniks as part of a step-by-step plan to gradually improve relations with "nationalist" forces in hopes of creating a united front against "bolshevization." He immediately took steps to reverse the anti-Chetnik policy after the Chetniks suffered serious losses during one of the major German offenses against the Partisans and the Chetniks the summer of 1943. Neubacher's bosses, however, cautioned him to go slowly. In mid-January 1944 he received the revealing instructions from Ribbentrop:

> In your political decisions, please always consider the fact that sooner or later Tito whose importance has in any case been somewhat overrated, must and will be destroyed by our armed forces. This point of view also determines our relationship with Draža Mihailović and the Chetniks. Out of pure expediency temporary agreements with him can be allowed by subordinate military agencies in the struggle against the common enemy, Tito. He [Mihailović] and his followers, however, remain in the last analysis our enemies. Therefore now as before utmost caution is advised with reference to Mihailović and the Chetniks; in particular, the possibility must never be forgotten that any strengthening of Mihailović which we now directly or indirectly give him in the struggle against Tito, may later be turned to us.[15]

Despite this wariness, Neubacher sent feelers to Milan Nedić, the installed puppet leader of the German occupation of Serbia, to build an army with the Chetniks of Mihailović—an idea that incensed Hitler. Hitler had agreed with the idea of exploiting local bands of Chetniks here and there but declared the establishment of a Serbian national army "out of the question."[16] After a while, Neubacher's desire to have cooperative military relations with the Serbs inspired questions about his very mental state. Remarking on Neubacher's defense of the national army idea, in a conversation of September 17, 1944, Hitler observed, "the fellow flutters here and there, it is really astonishing. . . . He was always completely sensible before. Six or eight years ago Neubacher was completely normal."[17]

Plans for such a nationalist army—normal or not—were soon scuttled by the worsening situation of the Germans in the Balkans. By late August 1944 the German position in that region was threatened by the Soviet advance from the East. The Red Armies of Marshal Rodion Yakovlevich Malinovsky and General Tolbukhin, whose ultimate objectives were Budapest and Vienna, were moving rapidly across Romania. By August 30 the Russians were in Ploesti—the Romanian oil fields, which had been lost to the Reich. Bulgaria had already withdrawn from the war in late August and then on September 8 declared war on Germany. Sofia was immediately occupied by Soviet troops on the sixteenth of that month. With their eastern flank completely exposed, the Germans hastily began their evacuation of the Mediterranean islands and the Peloponnesus. On October 1, Soviet troops reached the Iron Gates approximately one hundred miles east of the Serbian capital, and they made contact with Tito's Partisans. Nineteen days later the Germans were finally forced from Belgrade by General Tolbukhin, who had entered the city from the south, via the Morava Valley. If Neubacher had hoped to make some sort of deal with Mihailović for the cause of war, he was now to seek out the Chetnik leader for the sake of peace.

• • •

By late 1944 Germany's military situation was becoming more and more desperate. German diplomatic and military leaders initiated a series of private peace feelers and made contact with Anglo-American leaders on the Northern Italian front, the first of a number of would-be sur-render rumors. Field Marshal Erwin Rommel, having twice tried with Field Marshal Karl Gerd von Rundstedt to convince Hitler after the Normandy landings that the ultimate outcome in the war would favor the Allies, secretly conceived of a plan to approach General Eisenhower or General Bernard Montgomery, the hero of El Alamein, on his own to seek a separate armistice in the West.

"Unconditional surrender" was, however, a problem: President Roosevelt had coined that phrase at the Casablanca Conference in 1942, and it became a policy that was unanimously adopted by the Allies. As Dulles stated, "It was a policy which the Soviet Union accepted with alac-rity, probably because a completely destroyed Germany would facilitate

Russia's post-war expansion program."[18] Still, it was also a policy that may have inadvertently derailed an earlier close to the war. Dulles had learned from American contacts with the military conspirators against Hitler that the policy of unconditional surrender constituted a deterrent to German generals who might otherwise have been wiling to act against Hitler. Unconditional surrender, as they understood it, meant that Germany would be treated with the same harshness by the Allies whether the surrender came early by action of the Germans who dared to defy Hitler or at a later date by one of Hitler's henchmen.

In April 1944—some three months before the assassination attempt against Hitler of July 20, 1944—the conspirators had sent a special emissary to Dulles in Switzerland to see whether there was any hope of getting better terms than unconditional surrender from the West. The answer given was an emphatic no; the Allied position on unconditional surrender could not be changed. The emissary returned with the answer, to the despair of some of the conspirators, many of whom then began to feel that the Soviets, however totalitarian their system, offered some sort of economic plan and political system as an alternative to a thoroughly demoralized German nation, and thus would become the main "ally" of the conspirators against Hitler.[19]

The momentum building toward the possibility of full German surrender began to accelerate around March 1945, when Donovan's OSS representatives in Switzerland had reported to Field Marshal Alexander that "certain key German staff officers were to come to Lugano, Switzerland, in order to discuss the surrender of German forces in Italy."[20] General Alexander was put in charge of conducting the surrender talks. The Allies, through General Dwight D. Eisenhower, had scrupulously adhered to the engagement of no separate truce with the Germans on the Western front and to the involvement of the Soviets on all German approaches of surrender. Several such approaches were made to Eisenhower, and he kept the Soviet High Command informed of all of them. On April 22, 1945, the Germans informed Eisenhower that the Wehrmacht in Denmark would lay down its arms; in late April there was also a proposed truce with the German forces in Holland to prevent the starvation of the civilian population. On April 26 the Soviet Foreign Office was informed that Himmler had approached the Swedish government with an offer to surrender all German forces on the Western front, including those in Norway, Denmark, and Holland.

Still, President Truman (sworn in on April 12, 1945) replied that the only acceptable surrender by Germany was unconditional surrender to the Soviet government, Great Britain, and the United States on all fronts. These German approaches were but preliminary feelers to the ultimate surrender that would take place within a few days.

The Combined Chiefs of Staff directed that all matters concerning surrender would be handled at headquarters in Caserta and that Alexander was to make the necessary arrangements for the presence of Soviet representatives at any discussions that might take place at his headquarters. They also informed the Red Army General Staff that, given that the Germans' proposal was for the surrender of a military force on a British-American front, Alexander, as Supreme Commander in the Theater, would alone be responsible for conducting negotiations and reaching decisions. Stalin, Molotov, and the General Staff were incensed, and the breakdown of negotiations took place as the Soviets began to show a more aggressive attitude. By late April 1945 tensions with the Russians had become all but explosive, nearing a crisis just barely averted by the intervention of U.S. ambassador to the Soviet Union, Averell Harriman. The ambassador sent a complete text of Field Marshal Alexander's message to Soviet foreign minister Molotov, who in turn asked that three Red Army general officers who were at the time in France be able to participate in the discussions—a request that struck General John R. Deane, who headed up Washington's "Lend-Lease" military aid program in Russia, as odd, as there was no "requirement, either of military necessity or courtesy, which dictated that Russia should participate in a surrender of German forces in the Italian theater," as Deane later recounted.[21]

In fact, smaller German surrenders had been taking place on the Russian front without Anglo-American participation in those surrender terms. Nonetheless, whatever the internal political turmoil on the Allied side, the capitulation of all German forces in Italy took place on May 2, 1945. On May 4 the forces in northwest Germany and Denmark had surrendered to Field Marshal Montgomery; on the afternoon of May 5 a representative of German Admiral Karl Dönitz, Admiral Hans Georg Friedeburg, deputy commander of the German U-boat fleet, arrived at General Eisenhower's headquarters offering surrender on the Western front only, which Eisenhower rejected, saying that the Germans would have to surrender simultaneously to the Soviet High Command or there would be no cessation of hostilities. On the following day, a document was drawn up, the "Act of Military Surrender," which provided for the simultaneous surrender on both the Eastern and Western fronts. It was the morning of May 7, at 1:41 A.M., Central European Time, that General Alfred Jodl, representing the German High Command, signed the unconditional surrender of all German land, sea, and air forces to the Allied Expeditionary Forces and to the Soviet High Command.

• • •

If the capitulation of German forces to the Allies in the spring of 1945 demonstrated the unified outlook among the Allies (despite moments of Soviet protest), the strange story of the thwarted surrender offer by the Germans in Yugoslavia highlights just how seriously various competing policies with regard to the civil war in that country had pitted the Americans, the British, and the Soviets against one another. The unfolding of this complex set of events began on September 5, 1944, when Neubacher sent his emissary, Rudolf Stärker, to have a talk with McDowell. As related to William Donovan in a memo of October 20, the Nazi government saw their situation as follows: first, the discussion of total German surrender was possible only as long as a competent group of liberals within Germany could be found to discuss the matter with the Allies, and, again, that negotiations on unconditional surrender be allowed to take place; second, that all Allied troops be in readiness for occupation immediately upon surrender so as to put off the rapid advancement of Soviet troops; third, Hungary was in danger of exploding into complete political anarchy that would further threaten Germany's weakened state; fourth, that northern Yugoslavia was being held by German forces only to postpone this explosion which would start trouble within Germany; fifth, in an effort to hold the Sava River line from East to the West and the Hungarian lines formed by rivers running south to the Danube, the Germans would bring troops from Greece by highway at night through the northern Serbian cities of Smederovo and Niš. General Deane reasoned at the time that "[i]f the Allies would allow the Germans to retreat to the line of the Danube and Sava rivers, Germany would use her troops to fight the Soviets."[22]

The idea of pushing back the Soviets while pushing back the Germans made for a surrender prospect that greatly intrigued OSS chief Donovan. "It is the belief of our representative [McDowell]," wrote Donovan on September 21, 1944, to the State Department and to the U.S. Joint Chiefs of Staff, "that if non-Soviet troops held Trieste or Fiume to the Belgrade line, the Germans would allow Allied entry, and that the only impediment to total surrender is that fear of the Germans that the Allies will permit a state of chaos to exist in Germany over an extended period of time."[23] Meanwhile, in contrast to this ambitious prospect, the cautious McDowell, for his part, was back in the woods of western Serbia telling Stärker that he would not enter into "any conversation founded on deceit and Allied discord, but that he would be glad to discuss with a German representative the conclusion of German resistance in the Balkans and the disposal of German forces."[24]

Prior to the report to Donovan, on September 13 General Deane in Moscow had been sent a report of the conversations between McDowell and Stärker. Deane had been in Russia since September 1943 as head of the military mission for all army, navy, air, and Lend-Lease activities in Moscow under Ambassador Harriman. Deane had become a well-connected member of a colorful wartime American-Soviet elite that reveled in the A-list gatherings of Spasso House, Moscow's monolithic prerevolutionary palace turned legendary U.S. embassy, through which passed everyone from Eisenhower to Lillian Hellman; and in evenings at the luxurious Aragvi, the only restaurant and nightclub that remained open in Moscow throughout the war. Deane's cultivated circle of contacts in Moscow was enough for "Cheston"—Charles S. Cheston, then head of OSS intelligence at Caserta—to tell Deane to go ahead and inform the Soviet government about the prospective German surrender in Yugoslavia. This nod to Moscow had been in the somewhat reluctant spirit of the OSS, which sought military cooperation with the Soviets in the event of the German surrender—and to keep a close eye on Soviet maneuvers thereafter. Deane told an NKVD official, Lieutenant General Pavel Fitin, head of the Soviet External Intelligence Service, of the Neubacher-Stärker-McDowell discussions. A subsequent cable by an unidentified OSS agent to President Roosevelt on September 21, 1944, stated: "Our representative [McDowell] has been instructed not to proceed to Belgrade or to take the initiative in negotiations for peace. It is his belief, however, that Neubacher sincerely desires an immediate and unconditional surrender. He [McDowell] thinks that a State Department representative should be sent to Belgrade for conference with Neubacher." General Fitin was very keen on the idea of an early German surrender in Yugoslavia.

The Americans, however, were still quite wary. In another cable to President Roosevelt, dated October 20, 1944, the same agent forecast that should such a surrender take place it was likely that "a number" of Germans would go on fighting as guerrillas; that America "would have the responsibility for plunging Germany and the entire continent into Communism" as by that time a large percentage of the German population, "being nihilist already," was ripe for Communism. The situation in Germany the winter of 1944–1945 was desperate. Most of the Waffen SS divisions—six in total—were positioned behind the heavily fortified "Siegfried Line" while elderly reservists and soldiers from POW camps were at the mercy of the Red Army. Neubacher was also pessimistic. He expressed the resigned views of many when he wrote after the war that many believed that the country's salvation ultimately lied to the East. While the Soviets were cruel, so the thinking went, they still offered an industrial future of some sort that would protect the Germans against starvation and poverty.

The Stärker/Neubacher episode was not the first of the questionable surrender offers. The leader of the OSS detachment at Tito's headquarters near Istria, the twenty-nine-year-old guerrilla specialist Frank Lindsay, had received a cryptic radio message in September 1944 to go to Zagreb and make contact with an unknown. An agent in contact with Edmund Glaise von Horstenau, the German minister plenipotentiary for Croatia, indicated to Lindsay that he sought to discuss the question of surrender with the British or the Americans but did not want to surrender to the Partisans or the Russians. Lindsay turned down the requested meeting, while von Horstenau was arrested a month later. "It was a game with blinds on every level," wrote Burton Hersh, the CIA historian. "[William] Höttl, von Horstenau's sponsor, kept agents in Tito's camp and read the Partisan ciphers. Höttl made sure Allen Dulles got everything he needed to prod him into making it easy for Horstenau to link up with sympathetic Western representatives. Freshly declassified message records out of the Bari-Caeserta-Bern loop fully document this scheme to detach Yugoslavia."

The Germans had already cleared the Croatian coast and were under orders to evacuate Trieste and Monfalcone in the event of an Allied landing, and the Germans were "ready to cooperate" with the Americans, even ready to turn over the command of Croatia and the whole area between the Danube and the Adriatic. Still, the British were anxious to take control of such developments. Harold Macmillan, then the political adviser to General Maitland Wilson, the predecessor of Sir Harold Alexander as Supreme Allied Commander of the Mediterranean, advised the general to issue a directive on conditions of surrender to the OSS and specifically through the Combined Chiefs of Staff to the independent-minded McDowell, who was still formally attached to Mihailović. The directive spelled out that any offer to capitulate made by the commanding German officer in the Balkans must be forwarded to the Supreme Allied Commander of the Mediterranean for his consideration.

That commander was the larger-than-life British earl and later governor of Canada, Field Marshal Sir Harold Alexander, Earl Alexander of Tunis. If Alexander was at the center of a costly, secretive, "stymied" offer of surrender by the Germans to the Americans supposedly in honor of a British-authored condition that all such offers in Yugoslavia must go through Tito/the British, one must nonetheless give credit to this personality of remarkable personal and military achievement.

Brought up in one of Ireland's great historic families, the legendary "Alexander of Tunis" had been, at twenty-two, the youngest lieutenant colonel in the British army during World War I. Rudyard Kipling had said of him, "his subordinates loved him, even when he fell upon them blisteringly for their shortcomings; and his men were all his own."[25] He led the Baltic German Landeswehr from 1919 to 1920 to drive the Bolsheviks from Latgale, a region of modern-day Latvia, and was later promoted to major-general and joined the British Expeditionary Force. In August 1942 Winston Churchill sent him, as commander in chief Middle East, along with General Bernard Montgomery as commander of the Eighth Army, to North Africa. He presided over Montgomery's victory at the Second Battle of El Alamein. After the Anglo-American forces from Torch and the Eighth Army met in Tunisia in January 1943, Alexander became deputy to Eisenhower and Supreme Allied Commander of the Allied armies in Italy. It is Alexander to whom Churchill gave credit in his Victory Broadcast of May 13, 1945, for having struck with his army of "so many nations the largest part of which was British or British Empire the final blow and compelled more than a million enemy troops to surrender." Harold Macmillan, who, in addition to advising General Wilson also served as Eisenhower's political adviser during the Tunisian campaign, wrote in his memoirs: "If Montgomery was the Wellington, Alexander was certainly the Marlborough of this war."[26] His success as commander in chief of the British Forces in the Middle East in the El Alamein campaign and the subsequent advance to Tripoli made him the obvious and eminently suitable choice as Eisenhower's deputy, both as army group commander for the Battle of Tunis and for the first half of the Italian campaign.

Not everyone thought so highly of Alexander. He was criticized by British Field Marshal Bernard Montgomery for not being a strong commander. ("The higher art of war is quite beyond him," said Montgomery, who told his U.S. counterparts, Mark Clark and George S. Patton, to ignore any orders from Alexander with which they did not agree.) Alexander's forces captured Rome in June 1944 (although U.S. Fifth Army forces at Anzio, under Clark's orders, failed to follow their original breakout plan that would have trapped the German forces escaping northward). Alexander received the German surrender in Italy on April 29, 1945. Yet he was highly trusted: "Anyhow you had a great feeling of trust in him as you knew that he would back you whatever happened, and that if things went wrong, he would accept full responsibility for far more than his own share of the blame."[27]

What is most peculiar in the German decision to try to go through McDowell and Mihailović is that Mihailović was by then almost persona non grata on the American side and completely so for the British. As recounted earlier, the proposal was not accepted. As a result, German army divisions in the Balkans kept on fighting bitterly against the Allies, principally the Red Army, which entered Yugoslavia in September 1944 and which was meeting some of the most bitter resistance in their attack through Bulgaria and Romania. The loss of life to the Red Army was very high, and Moscow saw Washington-London treachery behind the deaths sustained by the Russians. Davies wrote:

> Fotić said that the Russians, of course, learned this from Mihailovic in March 1945 and could see in it an intrigue between the United States and Britain and treachery to their Ally aimed solely for the political reason of preventing the extension of Soviet influence in the Balkans. They, of course, knew that Churchill had been opposing the cross-Channel invasion and advocating attack through the Balkans from 1941 on and never quite gave up the battle until Teheran and even long thereafter.[28]

As for Neubacher, he was later sent to an Allied prison, first in Kufstein, Austria, and later was imprisoned in Belgrade under Tito, during which time he unsuccessfully offered to argue in defense of Mihailović at the latter's postwar trial. McDowell and several airmen had been evacuated from Serbia on November 1, 1944; the two last American officers, Nick Lalich and Arthur Jibilian, as well as sixteen downed airmen would be evacuated a month later. Mihailović, as we learned earlier, was invited to leave with the Americans. He chose to stay behind, and then he disappeared.

EPILOGUE

The Mountain at Twilight

I know that we have long been transformed, that we no longer
remember even what we once were, but we do remember that
we were different. We have been long on the move and our
journey has been hard and we have fallen grievously and come
to rest in this place and on that account we are no longer even
a shadow of what we were. Like the bloom on a fruit which
goes from hand to hand, what leaves a man first is what is
finest in him.

—Ivo Andrić, *Bosnia Story*

A hero's life," wrote the great nineteenth-century Montenegrin poet
and prince bishop Peter II Petrovich Njegos, "is always haunted by a
tragic ending. It was destiny that your head had to pay for the price of its
wreath."[1] On the fiftieth anniversary of V-E Day in 1995, a seventy-four-
year-old retired American air force major, visiting the mountains of Ravna
Gora, watched stunned as around fifty thousand Serbians came out to greet
him with a thunderous ovation. The son of Jewish immigrants from Poland,
he was twenty-one when he enlisted in the U.S. Army Air Corps in July
1942 and quickly became one of its ace navigators. Two years into his service, the young pilot was a second lieutenant flying B-24s as part of the
415th Bombardment Squadron, 15th Air Force, stationed in Lecca, Italy.
Then, in June 1944, the then twenty-three-year-old's B-24 bomber,
somewhat aptly named *Never a Dull Moment,* crashed into the

Ravna Gora Mountains, en route from Bari, Italy, with 250 bombers on their way to bomb the German-controlled Ploesti oil fields in Romania.

The young man was Richard L. Felman, introduced in chapter 6, who would be among the five hundred American airmen rescued by the Serbian troops and loyalist followers of Chetnik leader Draža Mihailović. "When we landed all of us had the same fear," he would later say in a newspaper interview. "We had been warned to stay away from Mihailovich's Chetniks. This came from our Intelligence. It was unfortunate their information came from Tito's Communists. . . . The men with me revered Mihailović. They spoke of him with a deep feeling and told me many times he was the real wartime leader of Yugoslavia. Their faithfulness to his orders was touching."

As recounted earlier, Felman was taken to a cabin, given fruit and *slivovitz*, and there met the Chetnik commander and writer Dragiša Vasić, Mihailović's right-hand man. Once the scope of the rescue mission of Allied airmen that had been going on in the mountains and woods of Serbia was explained to him, the young aviator never left Serbia—not, that is, in a spiritual sense. With a deep sense of loyalty to the people who saved him, Felman undertook to save the name and memory of Mihailović, becoming something of an American hero to the Serbs. The story of the young aviator and his postwar lobbying of the U.S. government is by now a well-known chapter of the Mihailović saga, but one that bears repeating. Personally decorated twice by King Peter of Yugoslavia, Felman received the Royal Order of Ravna Gora in 1946, one of Royal Yugoslavia's highest military decorations, for his activism against the puppet trial of Mihailović in Belgrade that year. Felman was among the twenty-one airmen who, it will be recalled, had petitioned Harry S. Truman and the U.S. government to be allowed to go, at their own expense, to present their testimonies to the jury on trial. They were prohibited from doing so by the State Department. As the rationale at the time maintained, the United States had befriended the Communist-led Partisans in the latter stages of the war and did not want to disrupt its relations with the postwar Yugoslav government.

Despite Felman's resolve, he was not able to reach Belgrade. And so for the rest of his life he petitioned Congress, and eventually, because of his efforts, Mihailović, on the recommendation of General Dwight D. Eisenhower, was posthumously awarded the highest award the United

States can bestow upon a foreign national, on March 29, 1948, by President Truman for "contributions to the Allied victory and the rescue of American airmen from behind enemy lines." However, once again, the award was not publicized for fear of offending the Tito regime. Felman continued on, pushing for congressional recognition of Mihailović.

Meanwhile, the ambivalence that had marked the State Department's attitude toward the trial of Mihailović resurfaced when, for the first time in U.S. history, such an award and its accompanying citation was classified on State Department initiative, presumably, again, to avoid offending relations with the new Tito government. The intervention of Congressman Edward Derwinski of Illinois finally succeeded in 1967 in having the award and citation declassified.

In 1970, Felman went on the *Congressional Record* urging the passage of legislation to erect a statue on Capitol grounds honoring General Mihailović; this was denied, despite a bill introduced in the Senate by Barry Goldwater in favor of such a monument. Here again, the legislation died in the House because of a weak-willed U.S. policy toward Yugoslavia. It was reintroduced several times over the next decades, but failed each time. Nonetheless, the truth of the Halyard Mission, about Mihailović, and about his Chetniks would emerge—not through media attention, public squares, or government honors but through the slow and silent declassification of information about the mission, first in the late 1970s, and then successively through the mid-1990s, around the time when Felman returned to Yugoslavia and to his huge reception there. About a decade later, in 2005, the Legion of Merit award was presented—fifty-seven years after Eisenhower first bestowed it—to Mihailović's then seventy-eight-year-old daughter, Gordana, a retired medical doctor. The American airmen and their Chetniks had triumphed. Almost. During Felman's 1994 visit to Serbia, his first touchdown in the country after fifty years, he sought out the unmarked grave in Belgrade where Mihailović was rumored to have been buried, his heart cut out of him. Neither Mihailović, nor his heart, was ever found.

"The earth groans, but the heavens are silent."[2]

Notes

Prologue: The Blue Graveyard

The chapter epigraph is from Fortier Jones, *With Serbia into Exile: An American's Adventures with the Army That Cannot Die* (London: Melrose, 1921), p. 221. No exact date was given for the 1915 article.

1. The orderliness of the retreat had even won the praise of the Austrian and German press. The correspondent of the *Neue Freie Presse* paid tribute to the spirit of the Serbian army and the magnificent way in which its leaders were carefully drawing it out of the invaders' nest. The unsigned article read, "The Serbian prisoners say with the greatest emphasis that their troops will not hear a word of capitulation and are still full of confidence in the Allies' faith, although for a time they were very bitter. . . . The Serbian artillery are withdrawn at the beginning of our attacks. Up to now the retreat of the Serbians has been made with extraordinary orderliness." Quoted in the *New York Times*, November, 14, 1915, p. 2.
2. The writer, Stoyan Pribičević, was a *Time* magazine correspondent in Yugoslavia during World War II. His father, Svetozvar Pribičević, was the minister of the interior of the first modern united South Slav state, the kingdom of the Serbs, Croats, and Slovenes, of 1917. This quote is from Ann Kindersley, *The Mountains of Serbia: Travels through Inland Yugoslavia* (London: John Murray & Sons, 1976), p. 61.
3. Potiorek's unfortunate mission in Serbia is thought to have been the largely guilt-induced aftermath of the assassination of Archduke Franz Ferdinand in Sarajevo on June 28, 1914. Potiorek, then governor of Bosnia-Herzegovina, had downplayed the security concerns of the Habsburg diplomatic corps following an earlier failed attempt that day to bomb the carriage car of the archduke. Potiorek was in the

273

carriage when Gavrilo Princip later killed the Habsburg heir to the throne and his consort, Princess Hohenberg. Potiorek later volunteered to lead the Balkanstreitekräfte, the Austrian Balkan Army Group, made up of the Austrian Fifth and Sixth armies. The Austro-Croatian general Stefan Sarkotić later succeeded Potiorek as governor of Bosnia-Herzegovina.

4. The term *Entente* was taken from the formal Entente Cordiale of April 1904, when France and Great Britain improved relations in order to thwart the rising power of Germany. The idea was the initiative of French foreign minister Theophile Declassé. Declassé, very pro-Russian, convinced the Entente in 1907 to include Russia. The terms *Triple Entente* or simply the *Allies* were and are used interchangeably to denote the prewar and wartime diplomatic alliance of these three countries. It is important to keep in mind that with inclusion of the British in this alliance, wartime troops from Australia, Canada, India, New Zealand, and the Union of South Africa fought under the Union Jack. The United States was never part of the Entente when it declared war against Germany on April 6, 1917, but was an "Associate Partner."

   The "Central Powers" came to comprise Germany, Austro-Hungary, and Bulgaria. Ottoman Turkey had sided with the Central Powers as of August 1914 but was not formally a member. Originally, Germany and Austro-Hungary became formal allies in the Dual Alliance of October 1879. This expanded to include Italy in May 1882, hence the expression the "Triple Alliance." However, Italy saw this only as a defensive alliance and in 1916 switched sides to the Entente powers.

5. The Second Bosnian Regiment was honored with some forty-two gold medals for bravery (Goldene Tapferkeitsmedaille) in battle. Good sources on this legendary regiment and other exploits of the Austro-Hungarian army include Gunther Rothenberg, *The Army of Francis Joseph* (West Lafayette, IN: Purdue University Press, 1995). For an informative article, see John Schindler, "Defeating Balkan Insurgency: The Austro-Hungarian Army in Bosnia-Herzegovina 1878–82," *Journal of Strategic Studies* 27, no. 3 (September 2004).

6. The Austro-Hungarian Balkan Army Group consisted largely of Austrian, Hungarian, Croatian, and some Czech troops, and, as mentioned previously, a Bosnian Regiment—the First, Fourth, and the famous Second regiments. There had been mass desertions in the First Serbian Campaign in the autumn of 1914, particularly from the Croats. Over 10,000 Croatian and Bosnian Christian soldiers taken prisoner in Russia had asked to be sent to Serbia to fight with Serbs against Austria. On the whole, however, they constituted a formidable fighting force against the Serbs. In the 1914 battles, the Austrian Balkan Army Group lost around 227,000 men, out of a total 450,000 troops then engaged there. See Gordon Gordon-Smith, *Through the Serbian Campaign: The Great Retreat of the Serbian Army* (London: Hutchinson, 1916), pp. 31–33, for these details and mention of the desertions.

7. These *vilayets* included Skadar (modern-day Shköder); Kosovo, Monastir (modern-day Bitola), and Salonika, among others. The Turkish presence in the Balkans was officially ended with the signing of the Treaty of London between Turkey and the Balkan League of Serbia, Greece, Bulgaria, and Montenegro on March 30, 1913.

8. Some battalions of Montenegrins also served in the Austro-Hungarian army, stationed at the Russian front rather than being set against their own countrymen. Albania was first made "autonomous under Turkish suzerainty" at the London Conference of Ambassadors on December 17, 1912. Independence was granted on July 29, 1913.

9. Even the Central Powers admitted to being impressed by the tenacity of the Serbs during the Retreat. The Austrian press sent a correspondent, Eugene Lennhoff, along on the Retreat. He wrote in the *Innsbrucker Nachrichten,* one of the most literary of Austro-Hungarian dailies, and followed with detailed coverage of the events in Serbia that winter of 1915–1916. He wrote, "Here began uniquely the tragedy of these now homeless soldiers. . . . Until Gorni Milanovac [a mountain region in central Serbia where the Serbs had been defeated in the autumn of 1915] did hope still live on in these troops." Eugene Lendorff, "Durch AltSerbien und den Sanschat zur Montenegrischen Front," *Innsbrucker Nachrichten* [the Innsbruck news], December 11, 1915, p. 1.

10. "On the side of the Allies no nation possesses a leader who enjoys the confidence and veneration of the entire people to a greater extent than does General Putnik, the chief of staff of the Serbian forces." From Gordon-Smith, *Through the Serbian Campaign,* p. 40. Field Marshal Putnik had also been the mastermind behind Serbian strategy in the First Balkan War (1912–1913), which pitted Serbia, Bulgaria, Greece, and Montenegro—the "Little Entente"—successfully against Turkey; and the Second Balkan War (1913), in which Serbia, Greece, Montenegro, and Romania fought and triumphed over their old ally Bulgaria.

11. Count Carlo Sforza, *Fifty Years of Diplomacy in the Balkans: Pashich and the Union of the Yugoslavs,* translated by J. G. Clemenceau Le Clerq (New York: Columbia University Press, 1940), p. 130.

12. Ibid., p. 133.

13. Alice Askew and Claude Askew, *The Stricken Land: Serbia as We Saw It* (London: Nash, 1916), p. 50. Alice and Claude Askew were a British couple with the First British Field Hospital for Serbia, attached to the Serbian Second Army as a field hospital.

14. The number of 750,000 is cited in Gordon-Smith, *Through the Serbian Campaign,* p. 36. The number of 12,000 is cited in a letter to the editor in the *Times* (London). See: A. F. London, Herbert Samuel, et al., "Serbian Needs: The Flight into Exile, Difficulties of Relief," *Times* (London), December 23, 1915, p. 3.

15. Askew and Askew, *The Stricken Land,* p. 54.

16. Ibid, p. 55.

17. Report by Serbian premier Nikola Pašić to Minister of War Božidar Terzić, cited in Sforza, *Fifty Years of War and Diplomacy,* p. 150. For the whole of World War I, Serbia had 1,264,000 casualties; about 28 percent of its total population and 58 percent of its male population.

18. Jones, *With Serbia into Exile,* pp. 329–340.

19. C. E. J. Fryer, *The Destruction of Serbia, 1915* (New York: Columbia University Press, East European Monographs, 1997), p. 11. This work received lukewarm reviews at the time of its publication but is valuable for its account of the British

Naval Mission to Serbia in 1915 and the role of Admiral Ernest Troubridge in the Retreat. See also the informative review of this book by historian Alex Popović, "An English Perspective on World War I in Serbia," *Habsburg, H-Net Reviews* (September 1999), www.h-net.org/reviews/showrev.php?id=3382.

20. The exact number of assembled troops of the Central Powers at that time in Serbia varies from source to source. These numbers are taken from Gordon-Smith, *Through the Serbian Campaign*, p. 67.

21. See: Annika Mombauer, *Helmuth von Moltke and the Origins of the First World War* (Cambridge, UK: Cambridge University Press, 2001), p. 166.

22. For the German perspective on the Serbian campaign, see Erich von Falkenhayn, *General Headquarters 1914–1916 and Its Critical Decisions at General Headquarters* (East Sussex, UK: Naval & Military Press, 2004). A work written by a German journalist on the campaign that gives poignant testimony to the courage of the Serbian troops is Rudolph Dammert, *Der Serbische Feldzug* (Leipzig: Jauchintz, 1916).

23. Gordon-Smith, *Through the Serbian Campaign*, p. 67.

24. A squad is the smallest element in army structure, with 9 to 10 soldiers. A platoon consists of 2 to 4 squads, or 16 to 44 soldiers. A company is formed from 3 to 5 platoons, or 62 to 190 soldiers. A battalion is 4 to 6 companies, or 300 to 1,000 soldiers. A brigade is 3,000 to 5,000 soldiers, and a division is 10,000 to 15,000 soldiers, or three brigades. A corps is 20,000 to 45,000 soldiers, or 2 to 5 divisions. From Militarydial.com, www.militarydial.com/army-force-structure.htm.

25. The 1878 Treaty of Berlin introduced the "alliance system," à la Bismarck, into European politics. In this particular treaty, Balkan states were enlarged or reduced in size. Bulgaria had been enlarged by the addition of former Turkish provinces in a previous treaty, the Treaty of San Stefano, with Russian support, following the Russo-Turkish war of 1877–1878. The Berlin treaty reduced Bulgaria's size, at Serbia's insistence, based on an earlier Serbian-Bulgarian treaty in which territorial changes had to have mutual agreement. More significantly, it was the treaty that gave Austria-Hungary the right to occupy Bosnia-Herzegovina.

Nor was interest in Bosnia-Herzegovina limited to the Adriatic dimension. Bosnia itself was coveted for its agricultural wealth (Herzegovina, on the other hand, being a "limestone desert," as it was called). "The country is traversed from south to north by four main rivers—the Una, the Vrbas, the Bosna, and the Drina, all tributaries of the Sava. These long winding waterways here and there expand into alluvial basins that yield good crops of maize, while on the declivities are cultivated, often to a great height, wheat, barley, rye, oats, millet, and other cereals. . . . [H]owever long or short the course of a stream may be, it invariably gives rise to a most luxuriant vegetation." See Robert Munro, *Rambles and Studies in Bosnia and Herzegovina and Dalmatia: With an Account of the Proceedings of the Congress of Archaeologists and Anthropologists Held in Sarajevo August 1894* (London: William Blackwood and Sons, 1895), p. 24.

The Treaty of Bucharest, marking the end of the Second Balkan War (1913), gave to Serbia central Macedonia, including the key cities of Ohrid and Bitola, and the eastern half of the Sandzak of Novi Pazar. Further east, Serbia obtained the territories of the Vardar Valley leading to the border of Greece. Greece obtained Epirus, southern Macedonia—including Salonika—and the Aegean coastline up to the mouth of the Nestos River. Bulgaria received so-called Pirin Macedonia in the east of that territory, up to the Strumica River. Romania intervened late in the Second Balkan War against Bulgaria and won back territories in the Danube-Dobruja region, which had been given to Bulgaria in earlier treaties. Much of the then northern part of Bulgaria was transferred to Romania. Bulgaria evacuated the city of Adrianople (Erdine) in eastern Thrace, and Turkey took repossession of it. Montenegro doubled its size, and Albania became independent by this treaty as well.

The Treaty of London (1914) was an enormous geopolitical cash cow for Italy. According to the terms of the treaty, Italy was promised the Austrian-held Trentino; the southern Tyrol; Trieste; the counties of Gorizia-Gradisca; and the Istrian peninsula as far as the Quarnero, including Volosca and the islands of Cherso and Lussin. Fiume (Rijeka) was conspicuously excluded. Italy would receive the strategic port of Valona and a protectorate over the rest of Albania. Italy was also promised the Dodecanese archipelago; part of the Anatolian littoral, if the Turkish empire were partitioned; possibly territories in Libya, Eritrea, and Somaliland; a share of the war indemnity and an immediate loan of fifty million sterling; British and French naval assistance against the Austrian fleet; Russian military assistance through intensified pressure on the eastern Austrian front; the exclusion of the Vatican from the peace conference; and a pledge that the terms of the London treaty would not be revealed to nonsignatory powers, including Italy's new ally Serbia. See Charles Vellay, *La Guerre Européenne et La Question de L'Adriatique 1914–1918* (Paris: Chapelot, 1938), and Bernadotte Everly Schmitt, *The Annexation of Bosnia-Hercegovina 1908–1909* (Cambridge, UK: Cambridge University Press, 1937).

The Ottoman-German Alliance of August 1914 was the extent of Turkey's "joining" the Central Powers. Sultan Mehmed V, the commander in chief of the army, wanted to stay neutral. Because of Russia's entry into the war on the side of the Entente, however, the Ottoman grand vizier Said Haim Pasha and the minister of war Ismail Enver Pasha urged the German-proposed alliance. Although Sultan Mehmed V never did sign the pact, the Ottomans entered the war on October 28, 1914. The Dardanelles, hitherto open to international shipping, were closed to Entente traffic after Turkey's entry into the war on the Central Powers' side in October 1914.

For the British, maintaining a stable relationship with the Ottomans was a centerpiece of foreign policy. As Sir Arthur Nicolson, British ambassador to St. Petersburg, once remarked, "I need not say that we have always kept most carefully in view the necessity of us doing as little as possible to arouse Moslem feelings, as we know very well the effect which would be produced among our Mussulmans in India." Quoted in Ernst Christian Helmreich, *The Diplomacy of the Balkan Wars, 1912–1913* (Cambridge, MA: Harvard University Press, 1938), p. 150.

26. Alan Palmer, *The Gardeners of Salonika* (London: Deutsch, 1965), p. 44.
27. Wire report, "Population Joins Retreat," *New York Times*, November 3, 1915.
28. Gordon-Smith, *Through the Serbian Campaign*, p. 48.

29. Palmer, *Gardeners of Salonika*, p. 46.
30. Gordon-Smith, *Through the Serbian Campaign*, pp. 49–50.
31. Admiral Troubridge, the descendant of a long line of distinguished seamen, including a great-grandfather who had been one of Lord Nelson's "Band of Brothers" and a grandfather who was Lord of the Admiralty, was very critical of Serbia and Serbian military strategy throughout the war. While some historians attribute his views to cynicism once he was assigned to Serbia following his unsuccessful leadership in the 1915 Dardanelles Campaign against the powerful German-Ottoman warship *Goeben*, his comments on Serbia's own strategic errors during the war are of considerable interest. See his "Serbian Diary," excerpted in Fryer, *The Destruction of Serbia, 1915*. Despite his criticisms of the Serbs, he assisted in the evacuation of the Serbian army at San Giovanni di Medua, in northern Albania on the Adriatic coast, and later became an adviser to Prince Regent Alexander Karadjordjević in 1916.
32. E. Hilton Young, *By Sea and Land* (London: Methuen, 1924), p. 16.
33. Palmer, *Gardeners of Salonika*, p. 44.
34. An account of the French participation in the retreat to the Adriatic was chronicled in the dispatch of Captain Vitrat, head of the French Military Aviation Mission in Serbia from March to December 1915. See ibid., p. 45.
35. "Echoes of the Serbian Retreat: All Guns Destroyed," *Times* (London), December 18, 1915. Quoted in Palmer, *Gardeners of Salonika*, p. 45.
36. Riveting memoirs about World War I Serbia were written, elegant eulogies to a broken country. See also (the aforementioned) Gordon-Smith, *Through the Serbian Campaign*; Monica Stanley, *My Diary in Serbia* (London: Simkin, 1915); James Berry, *The Story of a Red Cross Unit* (London: Churchill, 1916); Ingeborg Steen-Hansen, *Under Three Flags: With the Red Cross* (London: Macmillan & Co, 1916); Cora-Josephine Gordon, *The Luck of Thirteen: Wanderings in Serbia* (London: Smith, Elder, 1916); Olive Aldridge, *The Retreat from Serbia: Through Montenegro and Albania* (London: Minerva, 1916); Askew and Askew, *The Stricken Land*; and Nicolas Petrovitch, *Agonie et Ressurection* (Paris: Courbevoie, 1920). One of these exceptional works, John Clinton Adams's *Flight in Winter: The Heroic Account of the Serbian Retreat* (Princeton, NJ: Princeton University Press, 1942) was the only book by a man once voted by *Esquire* magazine as one of the ten best professors in the United States, in 1966. Many poems and essays were also dedicated to Serbia. One of the most beautiful is *Les Quatre Boeufs du Roi Pierre* by Edmond Rostand, the creator of *Cyrano de Bergerac*. Rostand's poem may be found in French novelist Jean Richepin's *Prose de Guerre, 1915*. Pierre Loti, the "Turcophile" French essayist, penned a moving tribute to Serbia after the Balkan Wars: "Pour La Serbie," in *Le Figaro*, August 14, 1914.
37. Jones, *With Serbia into Exile*, p. 220.
38. More on Albania follows in the narrative, but suffice it to say the following: Serbian and Montenegrin forces had attacked Albania during the First Balkan War against Turkey, when most of Albania was a *vilayet*. With the goal of controlling an outlet to the Adriatic, the Serbs fought to retain the port of Durazzo (Durrës);

the Montenegrins tried to hold Scutari (Shköder), gallantly defended by Pasha, a member of the powerful Toptani clan and himself once on good terms with the Serbs. The Albanian uprising against the Turks took place just after the First Balkan War in October 1913. Under pressure from both the Entente and the Central Powers, neither Serbia nor Montenegro gained possession of these cities. For a good account of Toptani and the Serbs, see Edith Durham, *High Albania* (London: Edward Arnold, 1919), pp. 10–24.

39. Among such aid workers, the British were perhaps the most actively involved. Their hospitals included several British Field Hospitals, or "British Farmers Hospitals" as they were often called, located around the country. These were in addition to military hospitals and Red Cross units. The United States also maintained a substantial presence. Lady Arthur Paget, the Boston-born socialite wife of Sir Ralph Paget, the British ambassador to Belgrade, founded a famous hospital in Skopje, Macedonia, during the war. Lady Paget contracted typhus and overcame it and stayed in Skopje for the course of the war tending to typhus victims. Dr. Edward W. Ryan of New Jersey and Dr. Ethan Flagg Butler of Washington, D.C., ran the American hospital at Belgrade and had five hospitals under their care. The French and the Russians also responded nobly to the appeal of the Serbian government for aid, sending hundreds of their own Red Cross units. For fascinating descriptions of both the British and American aid workers, see Edwin W. Morse, *America in the War: The Vanguard of American Volunteers in the Fighting* (New York: Charles Scribner & Sons, 1918).

40. Askew and Askew, *The Stricken Land*, p. 198.

41. Gordon-Smith, *Through the Serbian Campaign*, p. 9.

42. See also: George M. Trevelyan, "The Frightful Condition of Serbia," letter to the editor, *New York Times*, April 23, 1915, p. 12; and Cecil Howard, "Serbia Battles with Typhus: Young American Sculptor Working with Red Cross Writes of Conditions," *New York Times*, May 9, 1915.

43. Jones, *With Serbia into Exile*, pp. 217–218.

44. I have not been able to obtain the numbers of those soldiers who went to Vido as opposed to Corfu. The source for the numbers used here is the report of Serbian prime minister Nikola Pašić to his defense minister, Colonel Boris Terzić, quoted in Sforza, *Fifty Years of War and Diplomacy*, p. 150.

45. It should be noted that no German or Austrian airplanes bombed Corfu itself at this time and that the inhabitants of the island, though known to be pro-German, "behaved with exquisite courtesy towards the Entente ministers and with a touching compassion towards the Serbs." Ibid., p. 145.

46. Jones, *With Serbia into Exile*, pp. 220–223.

47. Askew and Askew, *The Stricken Land*, p. 362.

48. See: Andre Visson, "Guerrilla Leader: First General on the Third Front," *Washington Post*, January 3, 1942; "The Eagle of Yugoslavia," *Time*, May 25, 1942, www.time.com/time/magazine/article/0,9171,766569–4,00.html.

49. For a short but excellent account of prewar literary Serbia, see *Serbian Poetry and Milutin Bojić*, translated and edited by Mihailo Dordević (New York: Columbia University Press, 1977), pp. 11–14.

50. Ibid., p. 89.
51. Ibid., pp. 88–89. "The Sea Grave" is a poem from Bojić's collection *Pesme Bola I Ponosa* (Poems of Suffering and Pride), first published in Salonika in 1917, just before the poet's death from tuberculosis. "About no land is it more difficult to get the truth," Bojić wrote of Serbia in another poem, "Untold Thoughts," cited by Dordević on page 89 of *Serbian Poetry*.
52. Lena Yovitchich, *Pages from Here and There in Serbia* (Belgrade: S. B. Cvijanović, 1926), p. 73.
53. To name a few: Bogdan Popović, Jovan Skerlić, Milan Čurčin, Milan Rakić, Jovan Dučić—these last two being the great poets of the early twentieth century. Of literary reviews and magazines there were seemingly not enough. The founding of a new literary review, *Srpski Knijezveni Glasnik*, in 1901 was the dividing line between the Serbian literatures of the nineteenth and twentieth centuries; another, *Glasnik*, achieved high artistic and cultural standards, and it played the same role in Serbian literature that the *Revue des Deux Mondes* played in nineteenth-century French literature. Among the papers in which Serbian literature survived there was *Novine Srpske*, *La Patrie Serbe* (in French), *Le Bulletin Yugoslave* (in French), *Srpski Glasnik*, and *Velika Srbija Napred* (with an edition published in French titled *En Avant*).
54. The 1878 Treaty of Berlin reduced Bulgaria's size, at Serbia's insistence.
55. As tensions grew between Austria-Hungary and Serbia at the turn of the century, Vienna closed the Hungarian border to trade with Serbia; the famous so-called Pig War had begun. This refers to the large amount of trade in Serbian black pigs— sought after for the quality of their meat—which Serbia then exported, along with cattle, to Austria-Hungary. The trade in pigs accounted for about 20 percent of Serbia's income then. The closed market seemed to affect Austro-Hungary more severely, however: it deprived the inhabitants of their regular supply of cattle and meat and exposed them to the extortions of the Agrarian parties in Hungary. See Henry Wickham Steed, *The Hapsburg Monarchy* (London: Constable and Company, 1913), pp. 242–243. Also, the Serbian decision to buy armaments from the French firm Creusot rather than from Bohemia's Skoda is mentioned in Steed, *The Hapsburg Monarchy*, p. 110.
56. Sforza, *Fifty Years of War and Diplomacy*, p. 50.
57. Garašanin wanted Russian as well as Austrian influence out of Serbia altogether. He maneuvered Serbia out of war with Russia against Ottoman Turkey in 1853. He maintained Serbian neutrality during the Crimean War, and he obtained the evacuation of the Turks from Serbian fortresses in the 1860s without battle. The Garašanin Constitution also drafted a moral code of civil law, the first such act of jurisprudence since Czar Stefan Dušan's Code of 1349.
58. Jovanović's son, Slobodan Jovanović, was considered by some literary critics to be the best Serbian writer of the twentieth century and became prime minister of the exiled Yugoslav government in London from 1941 to 1944.
59. The Obrenović dynasty ruled Serbia during two periods: first, between 1815 and 1842, and then again from 1858 to 1903. Under the leadership of the dynasty's founder, Milos Obrenović I and his dynastic rival, Kara-djordje ("Black George"), Serbia fought back Ottoman rule.

60. The longtime family-dynasty rival to the Karadjordjević, the Obrenović, was no less captivating a family, with intrigues, assassination, and rather surprisingly good relations with Vienna. For an excellent treatment of this issue and of Serbia's Karadjordjević-Obrenović rivalries in general, see Alexander Dragnić, *Serbia, Nikola Paši and Yugoslavia* (New Brunswick, NJ: Rutgers University Press, 1974), pp. 38–58.

61. The first major wave of local Serbian rebellion against Ottoman rule lasted from 1804 until 1817, when the Sublime Porte de facto recognized the autonomous Principality of Serbia. The de jure recognition of that principality was not until 1830. The international recognition of the Principality of Serbia took place with the Congress (and Treaty) of Berlin in 1878. Serbia was elevated to a kingdom in 1882.

62. Gordon-Smith, *Through the Serbian Campaign*, p. 72.

63. Sforza, *Fifty Years of War and Diplomacy*, p. 35.

64. Palmer, *Gardeners of Salonika*, p. 45.

65. See ibid., pp. 40–55. For more detail on Austrian aspirations with regard to Salonika, see A. J. May, *The Habsburg Monarchy 1867–1914* (Cambridge, MA: Harvard University Press, 1960), pp. 22–40; Ernst Christian Helmreich, *The Diplomacy of the Balkan Wars, 1912–1913* (Cambridge, MA: Harvard University Press, 1938), pp. 449–452; Herbert Feis, *Europe: The World's Banker 1870–1914: An Account of Europe's Foreign Investment and the Connection of World Finance with Diplomacy before the War* (New Haven, CT: Yale University Press, 1930), pp. 120–135.

66. Palmer, *Gardeners of Salonika*, p. 228.

67. Ibid., p. 26.

68. Ibid., p. 45.

69. The Vojvodina, which became part of Serbia in the sixteenth century, had quite a different status at this time. Consisting of four regions—Syrmia, Bačka, Baranja, and the Banat—it moved from Ottoman control in the seventeenth century to becoming an autonomous Habsburg military frontier in the eighteenth century (officially the Voivodship of Serbia and Tamiš Banat). This frontier was abolished in 1860, and the region was incorporated into Hungary in 1867.

70. Palmer, *Gardeners of Salonika*, p. 215.

71. To raise money for the Serbian cause, Flora Sandes wrote a captivating memoir of her time in Serbia and Macedonia titled *An English Woman Sergeant in the Serbian Army* (London: Hodder & Stoughton, 1916). She was promoted to the rank of sergeant-major in the Serbian army and then to captain, receiving the Star of Karadjordjević, the highest military honor. Later she married the White Russian army chief Yuri Yudenić, who commanded the anti-Bolshevik forces in the 1927 Russian civil war.

72. Palmer, *Gardeners of Salonika*, pp. 204–206.

73. Ibid., p. 200.

74. How close the Black Hand was to individual members of the Serbian government remains in dispute to this day. It is known that the Pašić government was fairly well informed of Black Hand activities. Prince Regent Alexander is said to have been

an early supporter but that such friendly relations had cooled by 1914. The group was displeased with Prime Minister Nikola Pašić, whom they thought did not act aggressively enough toward a more nationalist, "pan-Serb" cause. They engaged in a bitter power struggle over several issues, such as who would control territories Serbia annexed in the Balkan wars. It is also said that "Apis" (Dmitrijević) at the last minute called the assassins back from Sarajevo as word began to spread of the plot. However, this apparently happened two weeks before the visit of Archduke Franz Ferdinand, and either nothing was done to stop them in the intervening days or the three men simply took it upon themselves to work as independent zealots. For two compelling accounts of the Black Hand assassination of Archduke Franz Ferdinand, see Edith Durham, *The Sarajevo Crime* (London: George Allen, 1925); and Henry Gilfond, *The Black Hand at Sarajevo* (Indianapolis: Bobbs-Merrill, 1975).

75. For more on the Corfu Declaration, see Ivo Lederer, *Yugoslavia at the Paris Peace Conference* (New Haven, CT: Yale University Press, 1963). The name of the country changed to the Kingdom of Yugoslavia after the imposition of centralized rule on January 6, 1929. With the abolition of the monarchy on November 29, 1945, the country became the Federal People's Republic of Yugoslavia.

76. Palmer, *Gardeners of Salonika*, p. 180.

77. For a good account of the history of the concept and usage of the word *Chetnik*, see Matteo J. Milazzo, *The Chetnik Movement and the Yugoslav Resistance* (Baltimore: Johns Hopkins University Press, 1975).

78. Vazov's late-nineteenth-century work, *Pod Igoto* (Under the yoke), is a famous account of life in Bulgaria under Ottoman rule.

79. Palmer, *Gardeners of Salonika*, p. 186.

80. Ibid., p. 230.

81. Ibid., p. 240.

82. Ibid.

1. Lawrence of Yugoslavia: An Allied Awakening inside a Civil War

The chapter epigraph is from Owen Meredith (Bulwer, Edward Robert Earl of Lytton), *Serbski Pesmes; or National Songs of Servia* (London: Chapman and Hall, 1861). Stefan Lazarevic (1374–1427) was the son of Prince Lazar, who died at the Battle of Kosovo against the Turks in 1389. Lazarević became prince in 1389 and then despot of Belgrade in 1402, proclaiming that city the capital of Serbia the following year. A poet, Lazarević wrote this beautiful work for his brother.

1. OSS Memo, Edward J. Green, lieutenant commander, USNR, CO. B, 2677th Reg., OSS (Prov) to Commanding Officer, 2677th Regt. OSS (Prov.), October 11, 1944, Record Group 226. Box 40, Entry 154, #NND867144.

2. Ibid.

3. Fitzroy Maclean, *Eastern Approaches* (London: Jonathan Cape, 1950), p. 251.

4. Report of Lieutenant Colonel L. M. Farish, AUS, Senior American Officer, AAMM, "Official Relations between Partisans and U.S. Government," March 3, 1944. OSS Record Group 226, #NN853154.

5. OSS Memo, 2677th Regiment, APO 534, U.S. Army, "Recommendation for Award," October 8, 1944. OSS Record Group 226, NND#867144.

6. Dobrica Ćosić, *Far Away Is the Sun* [*Daleho je Sunce*], translated by Mureil Heppel and Milica Mihajlović (Belgrade: Jugoslavija Publishing House, 1963), p. 171.

7. OSS Memo, 2677th Regiment, APO 534, U.S. Army, "Recommendation for Award," October 8, 1944. OSS Record Group 226, NND#867144.

8. OSS Cable 5159 (7) from Donovan to SSO, August 4, 1944. 2677th Reg. APO 534 U.S. Army, OSS (Prov), August 26, 1944. OSS Record Group 226, #NND 843099.

9. OSS Memo, 2677th Regiment OSS (Pro), APO 534, U.S. Army, "Recommendation for Award: Arthur Jibilian," October 9, 1944. OSS Record Group 226, #NND877190; p. 1.

10. Ibid., p. 2.

11. OSS Cable 5159 (7) from Donovan to SSO, August 4, 1944. 2677th Reg. APO 534 U.S. Army, OSS (Prov), August 26, 1944. OSS Record Group 226, #NND 843099.

12. Ibid.

13. Joseph Morton, "Allies Fly Scores of Babies from Yugoslavia," *Los Angeles Times*, July 8, 1944.

14. OSS Report of Lieutenant Nels J. L. Benson, "Almark Mission Activities in Croatia with Fourth Corp Partisans, 10 June 1944 to 10 October 1944," OSS Record Group 226, #NND867144.

15. OSS Memo, Linn M. Farish, AUS, Senior American Officer, AAMM, "Official Relations between Partisans and U.S. Government," March 3, 1944. OSS Record Group 226, #NN853154.

16. Ibid.

17. Ibid.

18. Ibid.

19. Stephen Clissold, *Yugoslavia and the Soviet Union 1939–1973: A Documentary Survey*, published for the Royal Institute of International Affairs (London: Oxford University Press, 1975), p. 33.

20. Report of Lieutenant Colonel L. M. Farish, AUS, Senior American Officer, AAMM, "Official Relations between Partisans and U.S. Government," March 3, 1944. OSS Record Group 226, #NN853154.

21. Ibid.

22. B. N. Deranian, Chief Special Operations, OSS Bari, OSS Memo, 2677th Regiment, OSS (Prov), "Proposed Citation for the Award of the Distinguished Service Cross to Major Linn M. Farish," October 11, 1944. OSS Record Group 226, NND #867144.

23. Lieutenant Colonel Linn M. Farish, AUS, Senior American Officer, AAMM, OSS Memo, "Partisan Position," March 9, 1944. OSS Record Group 226, NND #853154.

24. See the testimony of Staff Sergeant Gus T. Brown in David Martin, ed., *Patriot or Traitor: Proceedings and Report of the Commission of Inquiry of the Committee for a Fair Trial for Draza Mihailovic* (Stanford, CA: Hoover Institution Press, 1979), pp. 10–20.

25. OSS Report, "SO Progress Report 15–31 August 1944," Co. B, 2977th Reg. OSS, p. 2. OSS Record Group 226, #NND843099.
26. OSS, Record Group 226, Farish Report.
27. From the testimony of Staff Sergeant Gus T. Brown to the Commission of Inquiry of a Fair Trial for Draža Mihailović. Brown said, "And he [Mihailović] told me that all he wanted out of the war was a bit of America in Yugoslavia; he said he wanted no personal gain whatsoever. He said he was a soldier and he would remain a soldier. He said what he wanted was 'a scrap of the Atlantic Charter and a bit of America.'" Martin, *Patriot or Traitor*, p. 15.

2. The Mountain at Dawn

The chapter epigraph is from Milovan Djilas, *Land Without Justice* (New York: Harcourt Brace Jovanovich, 1958), p.107.

1. The descriptions of Serbia's mountain landscape in this section are from a beautiful work of travel literature in a class of its own: Anne Kindersley, *The Mountains of Serbia* (London: John Murray, 1976), p. 63.
2. Ibid., p. 66.
3. Owen Meredith, *Serbske Pesme; or National Songs of Servia* (London: Chapman and Hall, 1861), pp. 40–44. Owen Meredith was the nom de plume of Edward Robert, Earl of Bulwer-Lytton.
4. The major battles of Kosovo took place on June 28, 1389, and October 20–22, 1448, against the Ottoman Turks. There were frequent battles in Kosovo during World Wars I and II. Most recently, the 1998–1999 Kosovo war was a two-tiered conflict: first, a local civil war between ethnic Albanians and Serbs in that province; then, an international war involving NATO action against Serbia. A Kosovo state was created in 2008 under international auspices, inspiring vehement Serbian protests.
5. Rade Mihaljcic, *The Battle of Kosovo in History and Popular Tradition*, trans. Milica Hrgovic, Vesna Bjelogrlic-Goldsworthy, Ruzica White, and John White (Belgrade: Beogradski Izdavacko-Graficki Zavod, 1989), p. 5.
6. The Stara Planina—"Old Mountain"—is the name used in Serbia and Bulgaria to denote the Balkan mountain range. Note also that the words *Planina* and *Gora* are used interchangeably to mean "mountain." *Gora* is more a specific peak or hill within a mountain range.
7. Kindersley, *The Mountians of Serbia*, p. 61.
8. Mihailović's father, Mihailovico, had been a kind of county clerk, and his mother, Smilja, was the daughter of Dragoljub-Draza Petrović, a prominent peasant. He had one sister, Jelica, who was two years younger. They were orphaned quite young and raised by their father's brother, Vladimir Mihailović. The blood ties of Serbia maintain that the oldest uncle becomes the adoptive father should one's own father die or be killed in war.
9. Scholars still vigorously debate whether it was the Chetniks who were the first to stand up to the Germans or the Tito-led Partisans. Jozo Tomasevich, the late, prominent Yale historian of Yugoslavia and Eastern Europe, maintained that the

Partisans formed the first real resistance force in terms of organizational value. Even German generals were of differing opinions as to whether the Chetniks or the Partisans were doing the fighting first. See Petar Broucek's first volume of his three-volume work on Generaloberst Edmund Glaises von Horstenau, the Austrian-born Wehrmacht general plenipotentiary for Croatia, *Ein General im Zweilicht: Die Errinnerungen Edmund Glaises von Horstenau* (Vienna: Böhlau, 2005), vol. 1, pp. 21–23; and the memoir of the Austrian Generaloberst Lothar Rendulic, commander of the Second Panzer Army in Yugoslavia during World War II and later strategist behind Operation Rösselsprung in May 1944, intended to capture Tito. See Lothar Rendulic, *Gekämpt, Gesiegt, Geschlagen* (Wels: Verlag Elsermühl, 1952), p. 164. In both cases the Germans recognized Tito's Partisans as a superior force, yet the Chetniks, too, were every inch the enemy. Perhaps what is the most comprehensive book on the Yugoslav civil war, Klaus Schmider's *Partisanenkrieg in Jugoslawien 1941–1944* (Hamburg: Berlin, 2002), maintains that the Chetniks had organized the first resistance around May 1941, versus the Partisans' official July 4, 1941, date as the beginning of their resistance. See pp. 55–57.

10. On April 13, 1941, Churchill sent a telegram to Sir Ronald Ian Campbell, the British minister in Belgrade: "We do not see why the King or Government should leave the country, which is vast, mountainous, and full of armed men." See Walter Roberts, *Tito, Mihailovic, and the Allies* (New Brunswick, NJ: Rutgers University Press, 1975), p. 17. A former Royal Army officer turned Partisan commander, Arso Jovanovic, exclaimed, "The government forced the surrender of the army, which didn't have to surrender, and then they fled the country!" Quoted in Milovan Djilas, *Wartime* (New York: Harcourt Brace Jovanovich, 1977), p. 70.

11. Wireless report, "Australia Sees New Ally; Yugoslav Coup Hailed as Giving Britain a Balkan Partner," *New York Times*, March 28, 1941. Quoted in R. L. Knejevitch, "Prince Paul, Hitler and Salonika," *International Affairs* (January 1951): 40.

12. Schmider, *Partisanenkrieg in Jugoslawien 1941–1944*, pp. 55–56.

13. Jasper Rootham, *Missfire, The Chronicle of a British Mission to Mihailovich 1943–1944* (London: Chatto & Windus, 1946), p. 212.

14. F. W. D. Deakin, *Embattled Mountain* (London: Oxford University Press, 1971), p. 126.

15. Matteo J. Milazzo, *The Chetnik Movement and the Yugoslav Resistance* (Baltimore: Johns Hopkins University Press, 1957), p. 65.

16. Walter Hagen, *Die Geheime Front: Organisation, Personen und Aktionen des Deutsches Geheimdienstes* (Linz and Vienna: Nibelungen Verlag, 1947), p. 247ff.

17. Ibid.

18. Tomasevich's two-volume English-language history of World War II Yugoslavia, of which *The Chetniks* is the first, is considered an indispensable secondary source. Some critics have found him decidedly pro-Partisan in outlook, and his treatment of Communist political views and political figures lacks strong critical analysis. Nonetheless, as a deeply researched, very well written chronicle of the period, it cannot be dismissed. The "standard" English-language sources include Matteo Milazzo's *The Chetnik Movement*, cited above. Milazzo is one of the very few English-language scholars to provide unpublished source material from the Italian archives of the

Comando Supremo, including summaries of Italian high-level talks with Germans on Yugoslav affairs and analyses of the Mihailović movement. Walter Roberts's *Tito, Mihailovic, and the Allies*, cited elsewhere, is clearly written, and particularly of interest in its chronological account of the beginnings of the Allied relationship with the Chetniks and the Partisans. Kirk Ford's *OSS and the Yugoslav Resistance 1943–1945* and Lucien Karchmar's *Draza Mihailovic and the Rise of the Chetnik Movement, 1941–1942*, vols. 1 and 2 (New York: Garland, 1987), are also standard works. David Martin's *Patriot or Traitor: The Case of General Mihailovich* (Stanford, CA: Hoover Institution Press, 1979) is unapologetically sympathetic to Mihailović yet remains a well-researched, engrossing account of behind-the-scenes Allied attitudes regarding the Chetniks and the Partisans. Of non-English works outside of Yugoslavia, Klaus Schmider's *Partisanenkrieg 1941–1945* is the most outstanding. Of the main Yugoslav sources cited throughout this work Marjanović's *Ustanak i Narodnooslobodila ki* and *Knežovi Knigi o Draži* are considered by Yugoslav and non-Yugoslav scholars fluent in the language to be among the most objective works on this period.

19. Milazzo, *The Chetnik Movement* (Baltimore: Johns Hopkins University Press, 1975), p. 30.

20. Zvonimir Vukovitch, *A Balkan Tragedy, Yugoslavia 1941–1946: Memoirs of a Guerrilla Fighter* (New York: East European Monographs, 2004).

21. According to Yale scholar Jozo Tomasevich, the political ideals of Mihailović's Ravna Gora Movement were borrowed mainly from the program of the Organization of Yugoslav Nationalists (ORJUNA), "an organization that relied on force to spread the ideas of integral Yugoslavism." See Jozo Tomasevich, *War and Revolution in Yugoslavia 1941–1945: The Chetniks* (Stanford, CA: Stanford University Press, 1975), p. 120. Tomasevich continues: "It also worked with the Serbian National Youth (SRNAO), a creation of the Radical Party presenting itself as the protector of the heritage of the Serbian nation in the new Yugoslav state against both foreign and domestic enemies."

22. The Italian Second Army sought to bring order to their areas of control after the August 1941 Chetnik-led Dvar Uprising against the Ustaše and the Partisans, which took place throughout the western border of Bosnia and into the Croatian province of Dalmatia, where an estimated 100,000 Serbs lived. By late October of that year, the Italians had extended their occupation zone into the NDH, the "Independent State of Croatia," and sent a delegation to Djujic's Dinaric Division in November to conclude a peace agreement. If the Chetniks left them alone, the Italians would not assist the Ustaše against the Chetniks. The Germans required that the Chetniks of the Dinaric Division turn over their arms, however, and the men refused to do so. Several of Djujic's men, taken to a POW camp near the Croatian border with Slovenia, chose to committ suicide rather than hand over their guns. As for Djurisić, by February 1942 he had established ties to the Italian Taro Division and signed an agreement with General Alessandro Pirzio Biroli, commander of the Italian Ninth Army, for mutual cooperation against the Partisans. Pirzio Biroli, it should be noted, fought with the Serbs in World War I and had been decorated with the White Eagle military order of the Kingdom of Serbia.

23. Roberts, *Tito, Mihailovich and the Allies*, p. 35.

24. See Schmider, *Partisanenkrieg in Jugoslawien* 1941–1944, pp. 264–266.
25. See the following informative site on the life of Crnjanski, www.serbiatravelers .org/en/index.php/literature/497-milos-crnjanski.
26. Miloš Crnjanski, born on October 26, 1893, was one of the great Serbian writers of the twentieth century. As part of the retribution by Austria following the assassination of Archduke Franz Ferdinand, Crnjanski was drafted into the Austro-Hungarian army and sent to fight the Russians at the Galician front during World War I. He spent most of his time in a war hospital recovering from wounds, and was then sent to fight on the Italian front just prior to the close of the war. He later served as cultural attaché to the embassies of the Kingdom of Yugoslavia to Berlin, Lisbon, and Rome. He died on November 30, 1977. This quotation is from the poem "Lyrics of Ithaca" (1918).
27. The Axis had 2,236 aircraft available for the operation in total, consisting of 1,062 bombers, 885 fighters, and 289 reconnaissance aircraft. Yugoslavia had a total of 420 aircraft before the war, consisting of 60 Dornier Do-17 bombers, 47 Bristol Blenheim bombers, and 40 CM-79 bombers; 61 ME-109E fighters; 35 Hawker Hurricanes; 30 Hawker Fury fighters; and 6 Yugoslav-made Ikarus Ik-3. The Axis assembled 880 planes, including 280 bombers, Dornier Do-17, Junkers Ju-88, Heinkel He-111, and Juka 87 Stuka diver bombers; 280 ME-109F fighters; and 80 Me-110 fighters. The Axis used air bases in Wiener Neustadt (Austria), Sofia (Bulgaria), Arad, Deva, Turnu-Severin, and Timisoara (Romania), and Kaposvar (Hungary). Several of these bases had been built up by Hitler for the preparation of Operation Barbarossa, the invasion of the Soviet Union in June 1941. See Hal Buell, ed., *World War II: A Complete Photographic History* (New York: Black Dog & Leventhal Publishers, 2002), pp. 83–93.
28. Several of the organizers of the bombing were executed for war crimes. German Wehrmacht field marshal Ewald von Kleist was commander of the First Panzergruppe, comprising the Eighteenth and Fifteenth Panzer Corps, which spearheaded the assault on Yugoslavia in 1941. He was extradited to Yugoslavia in 1946 to face war crimes charges. He testified there: "The air raid on Belgrade in 1941 had a primarily political-terrorist character and had nothing to do with the war. That air bombing was a matter of Hitler's vanity, and his personal revenge." One of the key charges was that there had been no declaration of war against Serbia when the bombing was ordered. Alexander Löhr, commander of the Luftwaffe for the bombing of Belgrade, was tried and executed in Belgrade in 1946. (Information from www.Serbianna.com.)
29. Secretary of State Cordell Hull to U.S. minister in Belgrade (Lane), Cable 80, April 6, 1941. *Foreign Relations of the United States*, vol. 2, Europe (Washington, DC: United States Government Printing Office).
30. Roberts, *Tito, Mihailovich, and the Allies*, p. 126.
31. Stephen Clissold, *Whirlwind: An Account of Marshal Tito's Rise to Power* (Oxford: UK: Oxford University Press, 1975), p. 25.
32. George Lepre, *Himmler's Bosnian Division: The Waffes-SS Handschar Division, 1943–1945* (Atglen, PA: Schiffer's Military History, 1997), pp. 12–20.

33. Eugen Kvaternik (1825–1871) was the leader of the Croatian Party of the Right and was the brainpower behind the first attempt at a "Yugoslavia"—the "Triune Kingdom" of Croatia, Slavonia, and Dalmatia, for which he sought Serb support in exchange for the protection of their rights. With Serbian help, Kvaternik led an uprising against the Habsburgs known as the Rakovica Revolt, during which he was killed. The Slovenes were also active in the search for south Slav unity. In 1872, the Slovenes, in agreement with the Serbs and Croats, formulated a so-called Yugoslav Programme, which gained ground during the Balkan Wars of 1912–1914. The Programme tried to petition Vienna, where Slovenians and Croatians had parliamentary representation, for the autonomy of a Yugoslav kingdom.

34. Djilas, *Wartime*, p. 139.

35. See Chris Hedges, "War Crimes Horrors Revive as Croat Faces a Possible Trial," *New York Times*, May 2, 1998.

36. Djilas, *Wartime*, p. 207.

37. Ivo Rudin, "Jasenovac Martyrdom of the Serbian People," Testimony to the Embassy of the Kingdom of Yugoslavia, Washington, DC, May 8, 1944.

38. Gabriel Partos, "Dinko Sakic, Commander at Jasenovac" (Obituaries), *Independent on Sunday*, July 21, 2008. See "Dinko Sakic: Concentration Camp Commander," *Independent* online, www.independent.co.uk/news/obituaries/dinko-sakic-concentration-camp-commander-875730.html. See also "Vjekoslav 'Maks' Luburic," *Pavelic Papers*, www.pavelic-papers.com/documents/luburic/index.html.

39. The actual quote reads: "The movement of the Ustase is based on religion. For the minorities we have three million bullets. We shall kill one part of the Serbs, expel the second part, and convert to Catholicism the third part of them." See Stella Alexander, *Triple Myth: A Life of Archbishop Alojize Stepinac* (New York: Columbia University Press, 1987), p. 21.

40. For the estimates of Ivo Banać and of Generaloberst Alexander Löhr, see Schmider, *Partisanenkrieg in Jugoslawien 1941–1944*, 167, ff. 306. For the other numbers cited by German generals, see Lothar Rendulic, *Gekämpt, Gesiegt, Geschlagen* (Wels: Verlag Elsermühl, 1952), p. 161; and Hermann Neubacher, *Sonderauftag Südost: 1940–1945. Bericht eines fliegenden Diplomaten* (Göttingen: Musterschmidt, 1956), p. 31. He writes, "Auf Grund der mir zugekommenen Berichte schätze Ich die Zahl der wehrlos Abgeschlachteten auf drei viertel million" ("Based on the reports I received, I estimate the number of unarmed casualties at three-quarters of a million").

41. Aron Rodrigue, "Sephardim and the Holocaust," Ina Levine Annual Lecture, United States Holocaust Museum, Center for Advanced Holocaust Studies, Washington, D.C., February 19, 2004. See the report at www.ushmm.org/research/center/publications/occasional/2005-07-01/paper.pdf.

42. The United States Holocaust Museum, *Holocaust Encyclopedia: Jasenovac*, www.ushmm.org/wlc/article.php?ModuleId=10005449.

43. Rootham, *Missfire*, p. 57.

44. Djilas, Milovan, *Land without Justice* (New York: Harcourt Brace Jovanovich, 1958), p. 107.

45. Jozo Tomasevich, *War and Revolution in Yugoslavia 1941–1945: Occupation and Collaboration* (Stanford, CA: Stanford University Press, 1975), p. 558.
46. Ibid.
47. See Alexander, *The Triple Myth*, pp. 26–30. In 1998 Pope John Paul II declared Archbishop Stepinac a martyr and beatified him.
48. Quoted in Stella Alexander, *Church and State in Yugoslavia Since 1945* (Cambridge, UK: Cambridge University Press, 1979), p. 23. The source of the original citation is as follows: *Akten zur Deutschen Auswärtigen Politik*, Ser. E, vol. 1 (December 12, 1940–February 28, 1942), Document 277, Security Police Report of 17.ii.42, "Causes of Guerrilla Activities," Göttingen, 1969.
49. Richard West, *Tito and the Rise and Fall of Yugoslavia* (London: Carroll and Oraf, 1996), p. 74.
50. Ibid., p. 102. See also Daniel Carpi, "The Rescue of the Jews in the Italian Zone of Occupied Croatia," Shoah Research Center, Yad Vashem, Jerusalem, 1977.
51. While General Biroli undertook severe reprisals against civilian peasants in October 1941 near Kamenik, in Montenegro, following a Partisan attack there on an Italian column, they were nowhere near the scale of the average German reprisals against the Serbs. The case of General Roatta, the successor to General Vittorio Ambrosio as commander of the Italian Second Army, is more difficult. By most accounts a man who was both hero and monster, he circulated a pamphlet titled "3C" among his commanders in March 1942; it listed severe measures to intimidate the Slavic populations into silence, including "summary executions, hostage taking, reprisals, internments and the burning of houses and villages." Nonetheless, Roatta refused to round up Serbs, Partisans/Communists, or Jews and was credited with having saved both Serbs and Jews from persecution by Germans and the Ustaše. See Carpi, "The Rescue of the Jews in the Italian Zone of Occupied Croatia."
52. Michele Sarfatti, *The Jews in Mussolini's Italy: From Equality to Persecution*, trans. John Tedeschi and Anne C. Tedeschi (Milwaukee: University of Wisconsin Press, 2006), pp. 159–160.
53. Tomasevich, *War and Revolution in Yugoslavia*, p. 117.
54. Martin, *Patriot or Traitor*, p. 83.
55. The command structure of the Chetniks included about six divisions and around thirty-five "Korpus," or mountain, staffs.
56. Djilas, *Wartime*, p. 28.
57. Among his top commanders were the former Orthodox priest Momcilo Djujic, the *vojvode* Pavle Djurisic, Dragutin Keserovic, and the commander Cvijetin Todic. Djujic, from the Montenegrin village of Topolje, grew to be one of the fiercest leaders under the authority of Mihailović, commanding the famous Dinaric Chetnik Division around the Dalmatian hinterlands of Krajina. The division was formed in October 1941 and included some of the deadliest regiments of the Chetniks: the Gavrilo Princip regiment, and the Petar Mrkonjic Karadjordjević regiments, out of a total of six regiments.
58. There were local, mainly Serbian, women who worked as spies and couriers, but rarely as fighters, which was frowned upon by Chetnik leadership.
59. For more on the fascinating Ms. Mitchell, see her memoir: Ruth Mitchell, *The Serbs Choose War* (New York: Doubleday, 1943).

60. Ivan Avakumović, "The Communist Party of Yugoslavia," *Occident, Anno* 12, no. 3 (Rome 1956): p. 201.
61. Ibid., p. 203.
62. Ibid., p. 207.
63. Ibid., p. 210.
64. Barbara Joncar-Webster, *Women and Revolution in Yugoslavia, 1941–1945* (Denver: Arden Press, 1990), p. 30.
65. Fitzroy Maclean, *Eastern Approaches* (London: Jonathan Cape, 1950), p. 406.
66. Joncar-Webster, *Women and Revolution*, p. 31.
67. Ibid., p. 48.
68. Ibid., p. 43.
69. Ibid., p. 29.
70. Clissold, *Whirlwind*, p. 28.

3. Lawrence of Yugoslavia II: Into the Partisan-Chetnik Quagmire

The chapter epigraph is from F. W. D. Deakin, *The Embattled Mountain* (London: Oxford University Press, 1971), p. i. Ivan Goran-Kovacic (1913–1943) is considered one of the great Croatian poets of the twentieth century. He joined the Partisans in 1942 and was killed by Chetnik forces in eastern Bosnia on July 13, 1943. This citation is the first line in his wrenching poem *Jama* ("The Pit"), a lament for the victims of Ustaše violence.

1. Jasper Rootham, *Missfire, The Chronicle of a British Mission to Mihailovich 1943–1944* (London: Chatto & Windus, 1946), p. 20.
2. Fitzroy Maclean, *Eastern Approaches* (London: Jonathan Cape, 1950), p. 433.
3. Deakin, *The Embattled Mountain*, p. 185.
4. Ivan Goran-Kovacic, *Jama* ("The Pit"). See en.wikipedia.org/wiki/Ivan_Goran_Kovačić.
5. Walter R. Roberts, *Tito, Mihailovic, and the Allies, 1941–1945* (New Brunswick, NJ: Rutgers University Press, 1973), p. 27.
6. Ibid.
7. Ibid., p. 31.
8. Deakin, *The Embattled Moutain*, p. 126.
9. Milovan Djilas, *Wartime* (New York: Harcourt Brace Jovanovich, 1977), p. 69.
10. Ibid., p. 72.
11. Roberts, *Tito, Mihailovic, and the Allies*, p. 29.
12. Ibid., p. 35.
13. Ibid., p. 37.
14. Ibid.
15. Deakin, *The Embattled Mountain*, p.173.
16. Ibid., p. 170.
17. Ibid., pp. 170–171.
18. Ibid., p. 172.
19. Ibid., p. 173.
20. Ibid., p. 174.
21. Ibid., p. 179.

22. Ibid., p. 180.
23. OSS Memo, "Mihailovic Criticisms of Tito," March 8, 1943. OSS Record Group 226, OSS Microfilm Collection 1939–1946, series M1642, roll 125, frames 67–80 ("Mihailovic Cables"). National Archives and Records Administration, Washington DC, College Park, MD.
24. Roberts, *Tito, Mihailovic, and the Allies*, p. 116.
25. Michael Howard, "Sir William Deakin: Historian and Founding Warden of St. Antony's College, Oxford" (Obituary), *Independent*, January 27, 2005, www.independent.co.uk/news/obituaries/sir-william-deakin-488334.html.
26. F. W. D. Deakin, *The Brutal Friendship: Mussolini, Hitler, and the Fall of Italian Fascism* (New York: Harper & Row, 1962).
27. Deakin, *The Embattled Mountain*, p. 25.
28. William M. Leary, "The U.S. Army Air Forces in World War II: Fueling the Fires of Resistance: Army Air Forces Special Operations in the Balkans During World War II," Air Force History and Museums Program, Washington, DC, 1995: pp. 8–9. This report is available at www.airforcehistory.hq.af.mil/Publications/fulltext/Fueling_the_Fires_of_Resistance.pdf.
29. Maclean, *Eastern Approaches*, p. 410.
30. Ibid., p. 406.
31. Ibid., p. 407.
32. Ibid., p. 431.
33. Report of Fitzroy MacLean, November 6, 1943, "The Partisan Movement in Yugoslavia." Quoted in *Foreign Relations of the United States—1944*, vol. IV: Europe (Washington DC: Government Printing Office, 1966), p. 1336ff.
34. Ibid.
35. David Martin, *Patriot or Traitor: The Case of General Mihailovich* (Stanford, CA: Hoover Institution Press, 1979), pp. 70–71.
36. Ibid., pp. 76–79.
37. Ibid., p. 84.
38. Ibid.

4. The Balkan Prize

Marko Kralyevich was a fourteenth-century Serbian hero who led a nationwide rebellion in Serbia after he was prevented from inheriting the his father's title and thus becoming the ruler of the Serbs. Goethe regarded Kralyevich, a legendary figure who is esteemed as the personification of the Serbian people, as a counterpart to Hercules.

1. Andrew Browne Cunningham, *A Sailor's Odyssey: Early Days to Matapan, 28th March 1941*, vol. 1 (London: Dutton, 1951), p. 161.
2. OSS Memorandum #14667, Record Group 226, October 28, 1943, the National Records and Archives Administration, Washington DC, College Park, MD.
3. See Telegram: The Minister in Yugoslavia [Lane] to the Secretary of State [Cordell Hull], March 21, 1941, *Foreign Relations of the United States—1941*, vol. 2: Europe (Washington, DC: Government Printing Office, 1959), p. 962.

4. "Appreciation Regarding the Military Situation in Serbia so as to Determine What in the Future Should Be Our Policy," November 19, 1943. From OSS Record Group 226, #NMD 853154, National Archives, College Park, MD.

5. Henry R. Ritter, "Hermann Neubacher and the German Occupation of the Balkans, 1940–1945" (PhD diss., University of Virginia, 1969). For more on the strategic interests in the Balkan region during the war, see also "The Defence of Yugoslavia: A Vital Flank, German Threat to Macedonia" *Times* (London*)*, February 18, 1941, p. 4.

6. Count Gian Galeazzo Ciano, *Ciano's Diary 1939–1943*, ed. Malcolm Muggeridge (London: William Heinemann, 1946), p. 124.

7. Cecil Parrott, *The Tightrope* (London: Faber and Faber, 1975), p. 98.

8. Ibid.

9. Ibid., p. 99.

10. David A. T. Stafford, "SOE and British Involvement in the Belgrade Coup d'Etat March 1941," *Slavic Review* 36, no. 3 (1977): 99.

11. Parrott, *The Tightrope*, p. 105.

12. Stafford, "SOE and British Involvement in the Belgrade Coup d'Etat," pp. 399, 408ff.

13. Ibid., p. 410.

14. Ibid., p. 413.

15. Ibid., p. 414.

16. Parrott, *The Tightrope*, pp. 103–104.

17. Cecil Parrott's memoir quotes Maček: "I have a conscience too and a sense of tremendous responsibility towards our people. I cannot lead them to slaughter and that is what we must expect if we precipitate a war with Germany." *The Tightrope*, p. 95.

18. Telegram from the Minister in Yugoslavia (Lane) to the Secretary of State (Cordell Hull), February 23, 1941, *Foreign Relations of the United States* 1941 (Washington, DC: Government Printing Office, 1959), pp. 947–948.

19. Ibid.

20. Ibid., p. 948.

21. Memo of the Minister in Yugoslavia (Lane) to the Secretary of State (Cordell Hull), March 21, 1941, *Foreign Relations of the United States—1941*, vol. 2: Europe (Washington, DC: Government Printing Office, 1959), p. 963.

22. Memo of the Minister in Yugoslavia (Lane) to the Secretary of State (Cordell Hull), March 7, 1941, *Foreign Relations of the United States—1941*, vol. 2: Europe (Washington, DC: Government Printing Office, 1959), p. 950.

23. Telegram from Minister in Yugoslavia (Lane) to Secretary of State (Cordell Hull), March 24, 1941, *Foreign Relations of the United States—1941*, vol. 2: Europe (Washington, DC: Government Printing Office, 1959), p. 967.

24. Stafford, "SOE and British Involvement in the Belgrade Coup d'Etat," p. 403.

25. Parrott, *The Tightrope*, 92.

26. Ibid., p. 106.

27. Ibid.

28. Ibid., p. 95.

29. Robert Murphy, *Diplomat among Warriors* (London: Collins, 1964), p. 272.
30. See Peter Broueck, *Ein General im Zwielicht: Die Erinnerungen Edmund Glaises von Horstenau, Bd.3: Deutscher Bevollmächtigter General in Kroatien* [A general in the shadows: the memoirs of Edmund Glaises von Horstenau], vol. 3: German Plenipotentiary in Croatia (Vienna: Böhlau, 1988).
31. Murphy, *Diplomat among Warriors*, p. 272.
32. Major Richard Weil Jr. was a New York lawyer in civilian life turned OSS agent in Yugoslavia. In April 1944 he wrote that in spite of Tito's affiliation with Russian Communism "most of the population seems to regard him first as a patriot and the liberator of his country and secondarily as a Communist. . . . For whatever it may be worth, my own guess is that if he is convinced that there is a clear cut choice between the two on any issue his country will come first." Quoted in Murphy, *Diplomat among Warriors*, p. 273.
33. Telegram from Minister in Yugoslavia (Lane) to the Secretary of State (Cordell Hull), February 8, 1941, *Foreign Relations of the United States—1941*, vol. 2: Europe (Washington, DC: Government Printing Office, 1959), p. 941.
34. "Ambivalent Soviet Attitude Towards the Coup of March 27: *Dementi* That the Government Sent Congratulations 1 April 1941," in *Yugoslav and Soviet Relations: A Documentary Survey 1939–1973*, ed. Stephen Clissold, p. 121. The excerpt Clissold cites was published originally in the Soviet newspaper *Pravda*, April 1, 1941.
35. Ilija Jukic, *Tito between East and West* (London: Demos, 1961), p. 4.
36. Ibid.
37. Parrott, *The Tightrope*, pp. 113–115.
38. Memo, Minister in Yugoslavia (Lane) to the Secretary of State (Cordell Hull), March 21, 1941, *Foreign Relations of the United States 1941*, vol. 2: Europe (Washington, DC: Government Printing Office, 1959), p. 963.

5. Allied Rivals, Allied Destruction

The chapter epigraph is translated in Francis R. Jones, ed., *Works of Love: Selected Poems of Ivan V. Lalic* (London: Anvil Press, 1981). Jones was Lalic's main English translator. Lalic (1931–1996) was one of the most important Serbian poets of the postwar generation, and was called by London's *Independent* newspaper "one of the finest European poets of his time" (Cecilia Hawkesworth, "Obituary: Ivan Lalic," August 2, 1996). His works were passionately concerned with the power of memory, and with the influence of mixed civilizations—Renaissance, Mediterranean, and Byzantine—on his troubled Balkan homeland. His books have been translated into six languages, and individual poems into more than twenty languages. For the translation of the stanza of *Mnemosyne* featured here, see: Francis R. Jones, (ed. and trans.), *Works of Love: Selected Poems of Ivan V. Lalic* (London: Anvil Press, 1981). Jones was Lalic's main English translator.

1. Walter Roberts, *Tito, Mihailovic, and the Allies, 1941–1945* (New Brunswick, NJ: Rutgers University Press, 1973), pp. 126–127.
2. Cable from Undersecretary of State (Sumner Welles) to Yugoslav Ambassador (Fotich), 31 December 31, 1942, *Foreign Relations of the United States—1942*, vol. 3: Europe (Washington, DC: Government Printing Office, 1961), p. 841.

3. David Martin, *Patriot or Traitor: The Case of General Mihailovich* (Stanford, CA: Hoover Institution Press, 1979), p. 91.
4. Roberts, *Tito, Mihailovic, and the Alllies*, p. 118.
5. Richard Harris Smith, *OSS: The Secret History of America's First Central Intelligence Agency* (Berkeley: University of California Press, 1972), p. 35.
6. Ibid.
7. Ibid., p. 36.
8. Albert Blazier Seitz, *Mihailovich: Hoax or Hero?* (Columbus, OH: Leigh House, 1953), p. 21.
9. Roberts, *Tito, Mihailovic, and the Allies*, p. 180. See also Martin, *Patriot or Traitor*, pp. 120–124.
10. OSS Report, Linn M. Farish, "The Farish Report," April 6, 1943. OSS Record Group 226, OSS Microfilm Collection, series M1642, roll 124, frame 860. National Archives and Records Administration, Washington DC, College Park, MD.
11. OSS Memo, Lt. Col. Richard Weil criticisms of Brigadier Fitzroy Maclean, May 19, 1944. OSS Record Group 226, Microfilm Collection 1939–1946, series M1642, roll 8, frames 1129–1134. National Archives and Records Administration, Washington DC, College Park, MD.
12. Memorandum of Cavendish W. Cannon, Division of European Affairs, May 17, 1943, *Foreign Relations of the United States—1943*, vol. 2: Europe (Washington, DC: Government Printing Office, 1964), pp. 1009–1010.
13. Memorandum of Conversation, by the undersecretary of state (Welles), June 28, 1941, *Foreign Relations of the United States—1943*, vol. 2: Europe (Washington, DC: Government Printing Office, 1964), pp. 1041–1042. See also the subsequent communications on the organization of a Yugoslav air force unit under OSS auspices and under the command of the U.S. Army Air Force (as it was then called), and how members of that detachment were later commissioned or enlisted in the U.S. Army, pp. 1042–1048.
14. OSS Memo, OSS agent Bernard Yarrow to OSS Director William J. Donovan, February 6, 1945. OSS Record Group 226, Microfilm Collection 1939–1946, series M1642, roll 86, frames 783–786. National Archives and Records Administration, Washington DC, College Park, MD.
15. Ibid.
16. OSS Memo, Record Group 226, Entry 134, Box 160.
17. OSS Report, Lt. Col. Alfred Seitz report on Yugoslavia October 25, 1943. OSS Record Group 226, Microfilm Collection 1939–1946, series M1642, roll 132, frames 1-106. National Archives and Records Administration, Washington DC, College Park, MD.
18. Ibid.
19. OSS Memo, Lt. Col. Paul West, Chief Operations Officer, OSS-ME, to Joseph M. Scribner, Esq., "Political Situaion in the Balkans," December 20, 1943. OSS Record Group 226, NND #853154.
20. Roberts, *Tito, Mihailovic, and the Allies*, p. 101. See pages 100–106 for Roberts's clear analysis of collaboration and Operation Weiss.
21. Martin, *Patriot or Traitor*, p. 84.

22. Ibid.
23. Ibid., p. 85.
24. Ibid., p. 86.
25. Cable #25824, "From 109 and 154 to Toumlin," February 29, 1994. OSS memo, Record Group 226 (no page numbers given).
26. Ibid.
27. OSS Memo, Director of Strategic Services, "British Request for Concurrent Withdrawal of British and American Officers with Mihailovich." OSS Record Group 226," #NND877190, Microfilm Collection 1939–1946, series M1642, roll 84, frame 9–19. National Archives and Records Administration, Washington DC, College Park, MD.
28. Richard Crossman, *New Statesman*, December 15, 1956. Crossman, though a prominent Socialist, was strongly anti-Communist and edited the famous collection of essays by disillusioned Communist intellectuals, *The God That Failed* (1949).
29. OSS Memorandum, Major Louis Huot, Chief Operations Officer, OSS Middle East, to Lieutenant Colonel Atherton Richards, August 16, 1943, OSS Record Group 226, #NND 853154.
30. Ibid. The dispute also concerned OSS intelligence operations in Bulgaria and Romania.
31. Murphy to Chapin, Algiers, OSS cable #33271, May 27, 1944. OSS Record Group 226, #NND 750140.
32. Telegram of Richard C. Patterson Jr. (ambassador to Yugoslavia government-in-exile as of September 21, 1944) to Secretary of State (Cordell Hull), November 21, 1944. *Foreign Relations of the United States—1944*, vol. 4: Europe (Washington DC: Government Printing Office, 1966), p. 1423.
33. Ibid.
34. Ibid.
35. Ibid.
36. Ibid.
37. Roberts, *Tito, Mihailovic, and the Allies*, p. 119.
38. William M. Leary, "The U.S. Army Air Forces in World War II: Fueling the Fires of Resistance: Army Air Forces Special Operations in the Balkans During World War II," Air Force History and Museums Program, Washington, DC, 1995, p. 16. This report is available at www.airforcehistory.hq.af.mil/Publications/full-text/Fueling_the_Fires_of_Resistance.pdf.
39. Martin, *Patriot or Traitor*, p. 121.
40. Fitzroy Maclean, *Eastern Approaches* (London: Jonathan Cape, 1950), pp. 461ff.
41. Telegram: The Charge to the Yugoslav Government in Exile (Schoenfield) to the Secretary of State, 4 July, 1944, *Foreign Relations of the United States—1944*, vol. 4: Europe (Washington, DC: Government Printing Office, 1969), pp. 1385–1386.
42. Milovan Djilas, *Wartime* (New York: Harcourt Brace Jovanovich, 1977), p. 349.
43. Memo from Chief SO to Commanding Officer, Co. B 2677, Reg. OSS "Lieutenant George S. Musulin's Report on Observations and Activities While on Mission to

Mihailovitch, Part 2," July 10, 1944; OSS Record Group 226, National Archives, Washington, DC (no page number given).

44. Ibid.
45. Ibid.
46. Telegram from the Ambassador to the Yugoslav Government in Exile (MacVeagh) to the Secretary of State, February 5, 1944. *Foreign Relations of the United States—1944* vol. 4: Europe (Washington, DC: Government Printing Office, 1966), pp. 1344ff.
47. OSS Memo, Record Group 226, Entry 99, Box 50.
48. Ibid.
49. Ibid.
50. OSS Memo, Record Group 226, Entry 134, Box 177.
51. Ibid.; see also OSS Memo, July 4, 1944. OSS Record Group 226, Microfilm Collection 1939–1946, Microfilm Series M1642, roll 125, frames 594–597. National Archives and Records Administration, Washington, DC, College Park, MD.
52. Ambassador Joseph P. Davies, "Yugoslavia, Fotich and the King," (Journal) May 3, 1944. Papers of Ambassador Joseph P. Davies, Box 14, May 1944, Library of Congress, Washington, DC.

6. A Mission (Nearly) Impossible

The chapter epigraph is taken from Charles Simić's memoir, *A Fly in the Soup: Memoirs* (Ann Arbor: Universtiy of Michigan Press, 2000), p. 1. Simić, Serbian-American, was named poet laureate of the United States in 2007. He was born on May 9, 1938, in Belgrade.

1. The following descriptions of Felman's crash landing in the Ravna Gora Mountains, his meeting with Mihailović, and the chronological events of the rescue are indebted to four main sources: OSS cables and reports from the National Archives and Records Administration in College Park, Maryland (known as National Archives II, as distinguished from the Archive branch in Washington, DC). See Record Group 226, in particular, entries 210, 221–222; other entries contain invaluable political background information, such as 92, 134, 144, 154, 440–442, and 504–507. Also used here are the testimonies and reports by American liaison officers to both the Partisans and the Chetniks (including Lieutenant George Musulin, Captain Ellery Huntington, and Captain Walter R. Mansfield) covering the period from July 1943 to May 1945 also filed in Record Group 226; an overview of Richard Felman from www.Serbianna.com, to be found in several of that informative Web site's articles; Felman's testimony to David Martin's Commission of Inquiry; and Gregory A. Freeman's 2008 book, *The Forgotten 500: The Untold Story of the Men Who Risked It All for the Greatest Rescue Mission in World War II* (New York: NAL, 2008).
2. Carl Savich, "Draza Mihailovich and the Rescue of US Airmen during World War II," www.serbianna.com/columns/savich/038.shtml. See also Sandy Marquette, "Goodbye to a Tireless Warrior: Richard L. Felman (U.S.A.F., ret), May 29, 1932–November 13, 1999," www.serbianunity.net/culture/history/wwii/felman.html.
3. Marquette, "Goodbye to a Tireless Warrior."

4. Freeman, *The Forgotten 500*, pp. 81–86.
5. OSS Memo, September 20, 1944. OSS Archive, Record Group 226; Entry 99, Box 26, Folder 4. National Archives, College Park, MD.
6. Jasper Rootham, *Missfire, The Chronicle of a British Mission to Mihailovich 1943–1944* (London: Chatto & Windus, 1946), p. 29.
7. Ibid., p. 28.
8. OSS Report of Captain Walter Mansfield, "Mihailovic and His Forces," April 24, 1944. This copy was retrieved from the British Public Records Office under: FO 371/44271, R7885/11/92, the National Archives (UK), Kew, London.
9. Ibid.
10. Ibid.
11. Ibid.
12. OSS Memo: Chief SO to Commanding Officer, Co. B 2677, Reg. OSS, Lieutenant George S. Musulin's Report on Observations and Activities While on Mission to Mihailovitch, Part 2," July 10, 1944; OSS Record Group 226, NND 917174, National Archives, College Park, MD.

7. Legends of Blood and Honor: The Sad, Strange End of the British-Mihailović Relationship

The chapter epigraph is from Mauro Orbini, *Il Regno degli Slavi* [The empire of the Slavs] (Pesaro: Girolamo Concordia, 1601), pp. 18–30 (translation by Imma Pia de Simony). Orbini, a sixteenth-century Dalmatian intellectual and writer from the Republic of Ragusa, today's Dubrovnik, was most famous for this work, one of the earliest historical works dealing with the unification of Slavic lands. This passage is from a long chapter on the medieval Kosovo legend.

1. "Either They Die or We Do," *New York Times*, March 1, 1942; "General Draja Mihailovich, Yugoslav Robin Hood," *Washington Post*, March 1, 1942; "The Balkan Eagle Fights On," *Chicago Tribune*, October 11, 1942.
2. "General Mihailovich's Part in Allied Victory in Africa," *Congressional Record Extension of Remarks*, the Honorable Hugh Butler of Nebraska, United States Senate, February 12, 1945, p. 1.
3. Ibid.
4. Ibid.
5. Ibid., p. 4.
6. Ibid., p. 1.
7. Ibid.
8. Ibid., p. 3.
9. Ibid., p. 2.
10. Ibid., p. 4.
11. Ibid.
12. David Martin, *Patriot or Traitor: The Case of General Mihailovich* (Stanford, CA: Hoover Institution Press, 1979), p. 46.
13. Ibid.

14. "General Mihailovich's Part in Allied Victory in Africa," Hugh Butler of Nebraska, United States Senate, p. 2.
15. Ibid.
16. Desanka Maksimović, trans. Dragana Konstantinović, www.geocities.com/draganakonstantinovic/poetry.html.
17. Quoted in Martin, *Patriot or Traitor*, p. 47.
18. Telegram 100 of February 24, 1942. The list of these demotions was part of Mihailović's request to Jovanović for military broadcasts to be made by active officers of the prime minister's military section "on Thursdays and Saturdays" through Radio Karadjordjevic, a Jerusalem-based station with BBC transmission. OSS memo: "Aide Memoire of the Yugoslav Government on the Subject of the Communication Made by Mr. Lozovski to Our Minister in Kuibishev on August 3rd, 1942," #NND877190, pp. 8–9, OSS Archive, the National Archives, College Park, MD.
19. Ibid., p. 10.
20. Ibid.
21. Ibid., p. 9.
22. Ibid., p. 10.
23. William M. Leary, "The U.S: Army Air Forces in World War II: Fueling the Fires of Resistance: Army Air Forces Special Operations in the Balkans During World War II," Air Force History and Museums Program, Washington, DC, 1995, pp. 10–16. This report is available at www.airforcehistory.hq.af.mil/Publications/fulltext/Fueling_the_Fires_of_Resistance.pdf.
24. Martin, *Patriot or Traitor*, p. 135.
25. Jasper Rootham, *Missfire, The Chronicle of a British Mission to Mihailovich 1943–1944* (London: Chatto & Windus, 1946), p. 47.
26. Ibid., p. 48.
27. Ibid.
28. Ibid., p. 49.
29. Martin, *Patriot or Traitor*, p. 126.
30. Walter Roberts, *Tito, Mihailovic, and the Allies,1941–1945* (New Brunswick, NJ: Rutgers University Press, 1973), p. 126.
31. OSS memo: "Aide Memoire of the Yugoslav Government on the Subject of the Communication Made by Mr. Lozovski to Our Minister in Kuibishev on August 3rd, 1942," #NND877190, p. 11.
32. Quoted in a telegram from the Ambassador to the Yugoslav Government in Exile (Biddle) to the Secretary of State, October 7, 1942, *Foreign Relations of the United States—1942*, vol. 3: Europe (Washington, DC: Government Printing Office, 1961), pp. 822–823.
33. "Yugoslav Minister Reports Vyshinsky's Reaction to Request for Recognition of Mihailovic to Government in Exile," November 17, 1941, in *Yugoslavia and the Soviet Union 1939–1973: A Documentary Survey*, ed. Stephen Clissold, published for the Royal Institute of International Affairs (London: Oxford University Press, 1975), p. 133, Documents on German Foreign Policy, Ser. D., vol. 12, p. 485.

34. Telegram from the Ambassador in the Soviet Union (Standley) to the Secretary of State, October 1, 1942, *Foreign Relations of the United States—1942*, vol. 3: Europe (Washington, DC: Government Printing Office, 1961), pp. 819–821.

35. OSS memo, "Aide Memoire of the Yugoslav Government on the Subject of the Communication Made by Mr. Lozovski to Our Minister in Kuibishev on August 3rd, 1942," #NND877190, p. 11.

36. Ibid.

37. Ibid.

38. Ibid., p. 12.

39. Martin, *Patriot or Traitor*, p. 47.

40. "Memorandum for the President, from Mrs. Hemingway, as Dictated to Mrs. Boetigger," March 21, 1944. OSS Record Group 226, #NND 877190.

41. Martin, *Patriot or Traitor*, p. 99.

42. Ibid., p. 100.

43. Ibid.

44. Ibid., p. 102.

45. Ibid, pp. 102–103.

46. Ibid. For this series of correspondence, see: OSS Record Group 226, microfilm series T1642, roll 46, frames 190–208, National Archives, College Park, MD.

47. Ibid.

48. Ibid.

49. Ibid.

50. Ibid.

51. Ibid.

52. Memo to Sir G. Rendel (Foreign Office Dispatch No. 100), "Disunity in the Yugoslav Government," ref. Yu/43/5, vol. 33, folio 375, May 21, 1943. FO 954/33B, the National Archives (UK), Kew, London.

53. Martin, *Patriot or Traitor*, p. 101.

54. "Note from Mr. Churchill to the Yugoslav Government about the Speech of General Mihailovich," March 20, 1943, No. R2538/2/g. WO 202/No. 37 Military Mission. "Telegrams from General Mihailovich to Jugoslav Prime Minister," November 1942–June 1943, the National Archives (UK), Kew, London.

55. Ibid.

56. Ibid.

57. "The Yugoslav Prime Minister's Message to General Mihailovic," Cairo telegram No. 1932, "Secretary of State to Prime Minister Talk with King Peter (Tito and Mihailovich)," Reference Yu/43/18, vol. 33, folio 393, FO 954/33B, the National Archives (UK), Kew, London.

58. "The Proposition of the British Government for an Agreement with General Mihailovich," May 7, 1943, No. R 3995/2/G, the National Archives (UK), Kew, London. [Emphasis added.]

59. "Memorandum of the Conversation Between the Yugoslav Prime Minister and the British Ambassador to Yugoslavia," May 11, 1943. Telegram to Cairo, No. 1282. Yu/43/14, vol. 33, folio 386, August 7, 1943, FO 954/33B, the National Archives (UK), Kew, London.

60. Ibid.
61. "The Proposition of the British Government for an Agreement with General Mihailovich," May 7, 1943, WO 202/No. 37 Military Mission. "Telegrams from General Mihailovich to Jugoslav Prime Minister," November 1942–June 1943.
62. Telegram no. 1598, "The Orders of the British Middle East Command to General Mihailovich, and His Answer," June 1, 1943, WO 202/No. 37 Military Mission. "Telegrams from General Mihailovich to Jugoslav Prime Minister," November 1942–June 1943, the National Archives (UK), Kew, London.
63. Ibid.
64. Telegram no. 1597, "Minister of War, General Mihailovich Accepts the Proposition of the British Government," June 1, 1943, WO 202/No. 37. "Telegrams from General Mihailovich to Jugoslav Prime Minister," November 1942–June 1943, the National Archives (UK), Kew, London.
65. Basil Davidson, *Partisan Picture: Jugoslavia 1943–44* (London: Bedford Books, 1946).
66. Martin, *Patriot or Traitor*, p. 116.
67. OSS Record Group 226, Memo of Walter Mansfield, August 28, 1943.
68. Ibid.
69. OSS Report of Walter Mansfield, "Mihailovic and His Forces," April 24, 1944, FO 371/44271, R7885/11/92, the National Archives (UK), Kew, London.
70. Ibid.
71. Ibid.
72. Ibid.
73. Ibid.
74. Of that 400,000 sent to Germany and later to Soviet Russia, an estimated 11,000 were eventually repatriated to Italy. See Dr. Elena Aga Rossi, "Italian Armed Forces in the Balkans After the Italian Armistice," *Ricerca Italiana* 7 (June 2002), pp. 1–7.
75. Fitzroy Maclean, *Eastern Approaches* (London: Jonathan Cape, 1950), pp. 461ff.
76. Memorandum of Carl F. Norden, Division of European Affairs, to James C. Dunn, Director of the Office of European Affairs, and H. Freeman Matthews, Deputy Director of the Office of European Affairs, January 19, 1944. *Foreign Relations of the United States—1944*, vol. 4: Europe (Washington, DC: Government Printing Office, 1966), pp. 1337ff.
77. "General Mihailovich's Appeal to Be Placed Under the Allied Command," *Congressional Record, Extension of Remarks of Hon. Hugh Butler of Nebraska*, United States Senate, February 12, 1945.
78. Memorandum of Carl Norden, *Foreign Relations of the United States—1944*, vol. 4: Europe, p. 1336.
79. Ibid., p. 1338.
80. Memorandum by Cavendish W. Cannon of the Division of European Affairs, "The Mihajlovic-Partisan Problem in Yugoslavia," May 1, 1943, *Foreign Relations of the United States—1943*, vol. 2: Europe (Washington, DC: Government Printing Office, 1964), pp. 1005–1006 states:

> There is no evidence whatever that Mihajlovic has acted in collusion with the *Germans*. There may have been some minor traffic—which may, however, be

a kind of fifth-column work—with the *puppet regime* (Neditch) in Belgrade. He has not refuted very satisfactorily the charges of his relations with the Italians. He certainly has received some supplies and equipment from them, probably in exchange for prisoners, and has not been fighting against them. That he has actually participated with them in actions against the Partisans appears doubtful. Only small amounts of supplies from the British are getting through to Mihajlovic. The British still control his communications. In periods of tension between the British Foreign Office and the Yugoslav Government the Yugoslavs complain that they are not permitted to communicate directly with Mihajlovic, and suggest that some of their messages, and his in reply, do not get through, and others may be "mutilated" in transmission. This is one of the chief Yugoslav grievances at the present time.

81. Roberts, *Tito, Mihailovic, and the Allies*, p. 117.

8. Their Brother's Keeper: The Downfall of Soviet-Tito Relations

The chapter epigraph is from the Code of Czar Stefan Dušan, the first great legal system of medieval Serbian civilization, promulgated in the twelfth century.

1. Stephen Clissold, *Yugoslavia and the Soviet Union 1939–1973: A Documentary Survey*, published for the Royal Institute of International Affairs (London: Oxford University Press, 1975), p. 10.
2. Ibid.
3. Ibid.
4. Milovan Djilas, *Wartime* (New York: Harcourt Brace Jovanovich, 1977), p. 71.
5. Ilija Jukic, *Tito Between East and West* (London: Demos, 1961), p. 4.
6. Stephen Clissold, *Yugoslavia and the Soviet Union*, p. 130 (original source of document, Vladimir Dedijer, *Prilozi*, pp. 319–320). Tito reported the murder of "one thousand men, women and children" at the Sanski Most, as well as the presence of mass graves. This was one of the earliest reports of Ustaše violence as witnessed by either the Partisan or the Chetnik side.
7. Clissold, *Yugoslavia and the Soviet Union*, p. 13.
8. Ibid., p. 16.
9. Ibid., p. 132.
10. Ibid.
11. Ibid.
12. Ibid.
13. Ibid., p. 135.
14. Ibid., p. 136.
15. Ibid., p. 141.
16. Ibid., p. 142.
17. Ibid.
18. Ibid.
19. Ibid., p. 144.
20. Ibid.

21. Ibid., p. 146.
22. Ibid.
23. Walter Hagen, *Die Geheime Front* (Vienna: Nibelungen Verlag, 1950), p. 263.
24. Ibid., pp. 263–266.
25. Djilas, *Wartime*, p. 244.
26. Walter Roberts, *Tito, Mihailovic, and the Allies, 1941–1945* (New Brunswick, NJ: Rutgers University Press, 1973), p. 109; see also pp. 103–110 for details on German-Partisan meetings.
27. OSS Report, Record Group 226.
28. Telegram, Lincoln MacVeagh, Ambassador to Yugoslav government-in-exile to Secretary of State (Cordell Hull), January 29, 1944. *Foreign Relations of the United States—1944*, vol. 4: Europe (Washington DC: Government Printing Office, 1966), p. 1341.
29. Memorandum, prepared for the Mission to London of the Undersecretary of State (Edward R.) Stettinus, March 3, 1944, *Foreign Relations of the United States—1944*, vol. 4: Europe (Washington DC: Government Printing Office, 1966), p. 1353.
30. Roberts, *Tito, Mihailovic, and the Allies*, p. 203.
31. Ibid., p. 205.
32. OSS Report, "Supply Line to Yugoslav Partisans," May 20, 1944. OSS Record Group 226, Microfilm Collection 1939–1946, Series M1642: roll 125, frames 578–592.
33. Ibid., frames 590–592.
34. Maclean, *Eastern Approaches*, pp. 461ff.
35. OSS Report on allied quarters caeserta evening.
36. F. W. D. Deakin, *The Embattled Mountain* (London: Oxford University Press, 1971), p. 253.
37. Ibid.
38. Djilas, *Wartime*, p. 359.
39. Ibid., p. 363.
40. F. W. D. Deakin, *The Embattled Mountain*, p. 253.

9. Night into Death into Day

1. OSS Memo, August 12, 1943. OSS Record Group 226, Entry 99, Box 50, Folder 5. National Archives and Records Administration, Washington DC, College Park, MD.
2. OSS memo, Chief SO to Commanding Officer, Co. B 2677, Reg. OSS, "Lieutenant George S. Musulin's Report on Observations and Activities While on Mission to Mihailovitch, Part 2," July 10, 1944; OSS Record Group 226, NND #917174, National Archives, College Park, MD.
3. David Martin, *Patriot or Traitor: The Case of General Mihailovich* (Stanford, CA: Hoover Institution Press, 1979), pp. 172–174.
4. Ibid, pp. 170–172.
5. Martin, *Patriot or Traitor*: "From a very careful reading of the press at the time," writes Martin, "I can recall no instance where an American airman went to press moved by a feeling of moral obligation to tell the American people that the Partisans had lost their lives, or risked their lives to save his. Several American liaison officers who spent months with the Partisans have also stated that they could personally

recall no instance where the Partisans risked or lost lives to save American airmen." From the Notes to the Commission of Inquiry Report, pp. 172–173. Also unclear is whether the reports of rescue of American airmen by the Partisans involved any casualties on the part of the Partisans; see p. 173.

6. Cable: "Experiences of Airmen with Chetniks and Partisans," OSS Headquarters, 2677th Regiment, May 24, 1945, p. 1. National Archives and Records Administration, Washington DC, College Park, MD.

7. Ibid.

8. Robert McDowell, "Statement of Colonel Robert H. McDowell to Commission of Inquiry into Case of Draja Mihailovich," in Martin, *Patriot or Traitor*, pp. 489–493. The quote appears on p. 493.

9. Ibid.

10. Ibid., p. 492.

11. OSS Memo, Major Sargeant Michael Rajacich's observations and comments on operations of Halyard Mission in his "Ranger Mission Report" of August 14, 1944, October 17, 1944. OSS Record Group 226, #NND937196.

12. Ibid., p. 4.

13. Martin, *Patriot or Traitor*, p. 493.

14. OSS Report of Lieutenant Nick Lalich on the Halyard Mission, January 10, 1945. OSS Record Group 226, File No. XL-5727. National Archives, College Park, MD.

10. The Unknown Soldier

The chapter epigraph is from *Daleko je Sunce* (Belgrade: Jugoslavija Publishing House, 1963). From the translation by Muriell Heppel and Miclica Mihajlović, *Modern Jugoslav Novels* (London: Lincoln-Prager, 1964). Cosić was born in Serbia in 1921 and joined the Partisan Yugoslav Liberation Movement in 1941. He was among the first to make public the postwar Yugoslav concentration camp Goli Otok ("Bare Island") in the northern Adriatic. The camp was called by writer Milovan Djilas "the darkest and most shameful fact in the history of Yugoslav Communism." See *Rise and Fall* (New York: Harcourt Brace Jovanovich, 1983), p. 245.

1. Milovan Djilas, *Wartime* (New York: Harcourt Brace Jovanovich, 1977), p. 389.

2. Ibid.

3. Ibid.

4. David Martin, *Patriot or Traitor: The Case of General Mihailovich* (Stanford, CA: Hoover Institution Press, 1979), p. 45.

5. The twenty-one airmen who made up the National Committee of American Airmen to Aid General Mihailovich and the Serbian People, Washington, included First Lieutenant William L. Rogers, of Manteno, Illinois; Lieutenant Richard L. Felman, New York, New York; Staff Sergeant Hal D. Souter, Milwaukee, Wisconsin; Lieutenant Oscar Menaker, Forest Hills, New York; Tech Sergeant Gerald E. Wagner, Roanoke, Virginia; Lieutenant Donald F. Rice, Brooklyn, New York; Lieutenant Charles L. Davis, Washington, D.C.; Lieutenant Charles F. Gracz, Chicago, Illinois; Staff Sergeant John F. O. Grady Jr., Clifton, New Jersey; Lieutenant George Salapa Jr.,

Cleveland, Ohio; Tech Sergeant Gus T. Brown Jr., Luling, Texas; Staff Sergeant Mike McKool, Dallas, Texas; Staff Sergeant David J. O'Connell, Chicago, Illinois; Staff Sergeant Neal S. Janosky, Milwaukee, Wisconsin; First Lieutenant John E. Scroggs, Kansas City, Missouri; First Lieutenant John P. Devlin, Pittsburgh, Pennsylvania; First Lieutenant Robert W. Eckman, Chicago, Illinois; Staff Sergeant David E. LaBissoniere, Milwaukee, Wisconsin; and Staff Sergeant Denzil Radabaugh, Masontown, West Virginia. This list is from Martin, *Patriot or Traitor.*

6. Ibid., p. 57.
7. Ibid., p. 60.
8. Ibid., p. 65.
9. Ibid.
10. Ibid., p. 69.
11. Ibid., p. 70.
12. Ibid., p. 71.
13. Ibid., p. 76.
14. Ibid., p. 79.
15. Ibid., p. 81.
16. Ibid., p. 80.
17. Ibid.
18. "General Mihailovich's Appeal to Be Placed under the Allied Command," *Congressional Record Extension of Remarks*, the Honorable Hugh Butler of Nebraska, the United States Senate, February, 12, 1945, p. 19.
19. Ibid., p. 65.
20. Djilas, *Rise and Fall*, p. 77.
21. Martin, *Patriot or Traitor*, p. 89.
22. Stephen Clissold, *Whirlwind: An Account of Marshal Tito's Rise to Power* (Oxford, UK: Oxford University Press, 1975), p. 110.
23. Martin, *Patriot or Traitor*, p. 79.
24. Clissold, *Whirlwind*, p. 112.
25. Ibid.
26. Martin, *Patriot or Traitor*, p. 79.
27. Ibid., p. 80.

11. The Red Graveyard

Vasko Popa (1922–1991) was a famous Serbian poet of Romanian descent, known for his Surrealist and Symbolist works. During World War II he was imprisoned in a German concentration camp in the Vojvodina province of Serbia. Poem translation by Anne Pennington.

1. The C-17 downing incident caused considerable friction between Washington and Belgrade; the United States suspected that the attacks were deliberate. As the pilot of one of the two planes testified:

> The only flights which have taken place over Yugoslavia are those of planes which are lost and through inadequate radio beaming cannot find

out where they are and when they come out of the overcast they are several miles into Yugoslav territory. It is the kind of thing which would happen on the Mexican border or the Canadian border, between many countries. Nobody shoots down planes that are lost between clouds and are trying to get home. That isn't the ordinary aid to navigation with which they are familiar.

Foreign Relations of the United States—1946, vol. 6: Yugoslavia, pp. 923–924.

2. *Foreign Relations of the United States—1946*, vol. 6: Europe, August 31, 1946, pp. 943–944.

3. *Foreign Relations of the United States—1946*, vol. 6: Europe, November 16, 1946, p. 975.

4. *Foreign Relations of the United States—1946*, vol. 6: Yugoslavia, August 31, 1946, p. 939.

5. Ibid., pp. 954ff.

6. Telegram, Secretary of State Byrnes to the Undersecretary of State for Economic Affairs, William Clayton, August 28, 1946, *Foreign Relations of the United States—1946*, vol. 6: Europe (Washington DC: Government Printing Office, 1969), p. 930.

7. Telegram, Acting Undersecretary of State Dean Acheson to William F. Knowland, Senator of California, August 28, 1946, *Foreign Relations of the United States—1946*, vol. 6: Europe (Washington DC: Government Printing Office, 1969), p. 931.

8. Telegram, Ambassador to the Yugoslav Government-in-Exile, Robert Patterson, to Secretary of State Byrnes, September 20, 1946, *Foreign Relations of the United States—1946*, vol. 6: Europe (Washington DC: Government Printing Office, 1969), p. 953.

9. Telegram, Ambassador Patterson to Secretary of State Byrnes, August 3, 1946, *Foreign Relations of the United States—1946*, vol. 6: Europe (Washington DC: Government Printing Office, 1969), pp. 944–945.

10. Ibid.

11. Telegram, Ambassador Patterson to Undersecretary of State for Economic Affairs William Clayton, September 4, 1946, *Foreign Relations of the United States—1946*, vol. 6: Europe (Washington DC: Government Printing Office, 1969), pp. 946–947.

12. Telegram, Ambassador Patterson to Undersecretary Acheson, September 26, 1946, *Foreign Relations of the United States—1946*, vol. 6: Europe (Washington DC: Government Printing Office, 1969), pp. 960–961.

13. Ibid., p.961.

14. Ibid.

15. Telegram, Air Force Headquarters (AFHQ), Caeserta, to Acting Secretary of State William Clayton September 30, 1946, *Foreign Relations of the United States—1946*, vol. 6: Europe (Washington DC, Government Printing Office, 1969), p. 962. See also Telegram, AFHQ Caeserta to Acting Secretary of State Acheson, October 24, 1946, *Foreign Relations of the United States—1946*, vol. 6: Europe (Washington DC: Government Printing Office, 1969); pp. 970–971.

16. Ibid.

17. Ibid.
18. See Milovan Djilas, *Rise and Fall* (New York: Harcourt Brace Jovanovich, 1983), p. 236.
19. Ibid., p. 237.
20. Ibid., p. 240.
21. Ibid., p. 241.
22. Maclean, *Eastern Approaches,* p. 489.
23. Telegram, Ambassador to the Yugoslav Government-in-Exile Lincoln MacVeagh to the Secretary of State, February 9, 1944, *Foreign Relations of the United States— 1944,* vol. 1: Europe (Washington DC: Government Printing Office, 1966), pp. 1344–1345.
24. Telegram, Acting Secretary of State Dean Acheson to Acting Secretary of State to the Charge in Yugoslavia (Shantz), August 14, 1946, *Foreign Relations of the United States—1946,* vol. 6: Europe (Washington DC: Government Printing Office, 1969), pp. 920–921.
25. Ibid.
26. Ibid. The main leaders of the Tito government, which was officially formed on February 1, 1946, included Tito as head of the government, general secretary of the party, and the status of national hero. Edvard Kardelj was first vice president and president of the Control Commission; Aleksander Ranković, minister of the interior; Sreten Zhujović, minister of finance and secretary general of the People's Front of Yugoslavia; Andrea Hebrang, minister of industry and president of the Planning Commission; Milovan Djilas, minister without portfolio; Boris Kidrić, minister of industry and chairman of the Economic Council; and Mosa Piljade, chairman of the Agrarian Council and vice president of the Yugoslav National Assembly.
27. Walter Roberts, *Tito, Mihailovic, and the Allies, 1941–1945* (New Brunswick, NJ: Rutgers University Press, 1973), p. 344.
28. Ilija Jukic, *Tito between East and West* (London, Demos 1961), p. 16.
29. Telegram, Acting Secretary of State William Clayton to the Ambassador in Yugoslavia, September 24, 1946, *Foreign Relations of the United States—1946,* vol. 6: Europe (Washington DC: Government Printing Office, 1969), pp. 956–957.
30. Jukic, *Tito between East and West.*
31. Telegram, Acting Secretary of State Dean Acheson to William Knowland, Senator of California, August 28, 1946, *Foreign Relations of the United States— 1946,* vol. 6: Europe (Washington DC: Government Printing Office, 1969), p. 931.
32. See Nikola Stedul and Tomislav Sunić, "Marshal Tito's Killing Fields: Croatian Victims of the Yugoslav Secret Police outside Yugoslavia, 1945–1990," *Revisionist, Journal for Critical Historical Inquiry* (February 2004), p. 71. Dr. Stedul was himself the target of a failed UDBA (OZNA) assassination attempt in the 1980s.
33. Ibid., p. 72.
34. Count Nicholas Tolstoy, "The Bleiburg Massacres," in *An International Symposium: Southeastern Europe 1918–1995,* ed. Aleksander Ravlic (Zagreb: The Croatian Cultural Center, 1998), available online at www.hic.hr/books/seeurope/ 015e-tolstoy.htm.

35. Stedul and Sunic, "Marshal Tito's Killing Fields," p. 76.
36. Ibid.
37. Ibid.
38. Djilas, *Rise and Fall,* p. 236.
39. Ibid.
40. Ibid.
41. Ibid.
42. Ibid.
43. The story of the massacre set off a highly charged public debate in England between Count Tolstoy, who wrote a book on the incident, and Lord, who subsequently sued the author. Tolstoy was found guilty of violating England's strict libel laws; the Russian noble and scholar still stands by his story. For an overview of Tolstoy's position see his speech, available online.
44. "Slovenian Mass Graves," *International Herald Tribune,* October 20, 2007.
45. Djilas, *Rise and Fall,* p. 381.
46. See "20th Century Democide," www.hawaii.edu/powerkills/20TH.HTM. This well-documented Web site of historian and scholar R. J. Rummel, professor emeritus of the University of Hawaii, first coined the term *democide* to mean "murder by government"—that is, the genocides and mass murders of the twentieth century carried out by governments against their own people.
47. Dr. Radomir Zivković,"Report to the United National War Crimes Commission (1948)" in *Reports of Trials of War Crminals: Selected and Prepared by the United Nations War Crimes Commission,* vol. 5 (London: The United Nations War Crimes Commission by His Majesty's Stationary Office, 1948). See www.loc .gov/rr/frd/Military_Law/pdf/Law-Reports_Vol-5.pdf.
48. "War Crimes Commission Slow, Yugoslav Representative Asserts," *New York Times,* October 5, 1945.
49. Vladimir Zerjavic, *Yugoslavia: Manipulations with the Number of Second World War Victims* (Zagreb: Hrvatska Tiskara, 1998). For the online translation of this book see www.hic.hr/books/manipulations.
50. See the Yad Vashem Web site at www.yadvashem.org.
51. Ibid.
52. Rummel.
53. OSS Memo, OSS agent Bernard Yarrow to "Chesterton," December 21, 1944. Record Group 226, Microfilm Collection 1939–1946, Series M1642, roll 24, frames 999–1006.
54. Telegram, President Franklin Roosevelt to King Peter II of Yugoslavia, May 12, 1945, *Foreign Relations of the United States—1946,* vol. 6: Europe (Washington DC: Government Printing Office, 1966), pp. 1366–1367.
55. Telegram, King Peter to Prime Minister Winston Churchill, November 21, 1944.
56. OSS Memo, King Peter to Churchill, May 25, 1945. Record Group 226, Microfilm Collection 1939–1946, Series M1642, roll 25, frame 20.
57. OSS Memo, King Peter to Churchill, April 25, 1945. Record Group 226, Microfilm Collection 1939–1946, Series M1642, roll 25, frames 108–109.
58. Ibid.

59. OSS Memo, King Peter to Churchill, January 22, 1945. Record Group 226, Microfilm Collection 1939-1946, Series M1642, roll 25, frame 79.
60. Ibid.
61. C. L. Sulzberger, "Matchek Predicts Tito Dictatorship," *New York Times*, July 23, 1945.
62. Ibid.
63. Aleksa Djilas, "Tito's Last Secret: How Did He Keep the Yugoslavs Together?" in *Foreign Affairs* (New York: The Council on Foreign Relations, July/August 1995).
64. OSS or Kew records. OR Quoted in OSS cable of January 24, 1945 (NND 867108), #28104, Caeserta-London 13744, Caeserta-Paris #5064.
65. Ibid.

12. The Politics of Surrender

The chapter epigraph is from Nikola Tesla, trans. and ed., "Zmaj, Iovan Iovanovic," *Century*, vol. 48, no. 1 (May 1894). The poem may be found at www.enwikisource .org/wiki/Author.Jovan_Jovanovic_Zmaj Zmaj (1833–1904) was a Serbian poet. Born to a wealthy, aristocratic family near the border of Hungary, Zmaj is best known for a collection of lyrical poetry, *Djulici* (Roses).

1. Pearson had often been accused of Communist leanings but, for the most part, was critical of McCarthy's tactics. Roosevelt was no particular fan either. When McCarthy made his first speech attacking Drew Pearson as a Communist sympathizer, Harry Vaughn then rushed a copy to President Truman. The president is said to have remarked: "Good. I hope they kill each other off." As quoted in Wikipedia, "Drew Pearson."
2. Drew Pearson, *Diaries 1949–1959* (New York: Holt, Rinehart, and Winston, 1974), pp. 196–197.
3. Davies was befriended by Stalin, whom he met for the first time during the last year of his ambassadorial post in Moscow (1936–1938). Through Stalin's personal intervention Davies was able to collect, through a curator of the Imperial art gallery, Tretyakov, twenty-three valuable Russian icons and countless other works of art that had been confiscated from Russian estates and families. Far more ethically questionable, Davies had attended the Soviet purge trials during his tenure as ambassador and was casually, if naively, sympathetic with decisions against the defendants, as described in his book *Mission to Moscow*. That book was turned into a popular film in 1947 and was later used by the House Un-American Activities Committee as an example of American pro-Communist propaganda. Later U.S. ambassador to Moscow Charles "Chip" Bohlen wrote, "Ambassador Davies was not noted for an acute understanding of the Soviet system and had an unfortunate tendency to take what was presented at the trial as the honest and gospel truth"; and "He ardently desired to make a success of a pro-Soviet line and was probably reflecting the views of some of Roosevelt's advisors to enhance his standing at home." See Charles E. Bohlen, *Witness to History* (New York: Random House, 1970).
4. Pearson, *Diaries.*
5. Ibid. Those twenty-nine divisions kept on fighting ferociously against the Allies—in this case the Russians, whose armies were meeting strong resistance in their attack through Bulgaria and Romania and on to Hungary and ultimately Vienna.

6. Ibid., p. 197.
7. Papers of Ambassador Joseph Davies, Diary Entry 1–15, August 1944, Box 48, Library of Congress, Washington, DC.
8. Ibid.
9. OSS.
10. OSS Tito surrender [emphasis added].
11. Papers of Joseph P. Davies.
12. Henry R. Ritter, "Hermann Neubacher and the German Occupation of the Balkans, 1940–1945" (PhD diss., University of Virginia).
13. Ibid.
14. Ibid.
15. Ibid.
16. Ibid.
17. Ibid.
18. Quoted in Ann Armstrong, *Unconditional Surrender: The Impact of the Casablanca Conference upon World War II* (New Brunswick, NJ: Rutgers University Press, 1961), p. 63.
19. Allen Dulles, *The Secret Surrender* (New York: Harper & Row, 1966), p. 30.
20. W. G. F. Jackson, *Alexander of Tunis as Military Commander* (London: B. T. Batsford, 1971), p. 35.
21. John R. Deane, *The Strange Alliance: The Story of America's Efforts at Wartime Cooperation with Russia* (New York: Viking Press, 1947), p. 163.
22. Ibid., p. 162.
23. Henry R. Ritter, *Hermann Neubacher and the German Occupation of the Balkans, 1940–1945*, PhD dissertation (Charlottesville: University of Virginia, 1969), p. 147.
24. Ibid., p. 151.
25. Joseph Rudyard Kipling, *History of the Irish Guards in the Great War: The Second Battalion* (New York: Da Capo, 1977), p. 186.
26. Harold Macmillan, *Memoirs: The Blast of War, 1939–1945* (New York: Harper & Row, 1968), p. 310.
27. Ibid. p. 312.
28. Papers of Ambassador Joseph Davies, Diary Entry 1–15, August 1944, Box 48, Library of Congress, Manuscripts Division, Washington, DC.

Epilogue: The Mountain at Twilight

The chapter epigraph is from Ivo Andric, *Bosnia Story*, trans. Kenneth Johnstone (London: Lincoln-Prager, 1961), p. iv. Andric was born in Bosnia-Herzegovina, the son of Serbian and Croatian parents, in 1892. He won the Nobel Prize for Literature in 1961.

1. Peter II Petrovich Njegos, *The Mountain Wreath*, trans. Vasa D. Mihailovich (Chapel Hill: University of North Carolina Press, 1986). One of the most beautiful epic poems in the literature of the Balkans, *The Mountain Wreath* was composed in 1847 by Njegos, the ruling prince bishop of Montenegro from 1832 until his death in 1851.
2. Ibid.

Index

Page numbers in *italics* refer to illustrations.